Prelude to Civil War

PRELUDE TO CIVIL WAR

THE NULLIFICATION CONTROVERSY
IN SOUTH CAROLINA
1816–1836

William W. Freehling

HARPER TORCHBOOKS
Harper & Row, Publishers
New York, Hagerstown, San Francisco, London

First HARPER TORCHBOOK edition published in 1968 by Harper & Row, Publishers, Incorporated, New York, N.Y. 10022.

Library of Congress Catalog Card Number: 66-10629.

80   20 19 18 17 16 15 14 13

For my mother and father

Contents

Abbreviations

Abbreviations used in the footnotes and in the bibliographical essay are as follows:

   AHR = *American Historical Review*
    DU = Duke University Library
    LC = Library of Congress
    NC = Southern Historical Collection, University of
         North Carolina Library, Chapel Hill
   S Ag = The Southern Agriculturist
    SC = South Caroliniana Library
  SCHS = South Carolina Historical Society
   SR = *The Southern Review*

Preface

The feuds of historians are often contested as sharply as the elections or wars about which they write. For example, the American Civil War, our most vicious, bitter war, has provoked some of our most angry, partisan historical writing. The issues that war raised are still alive a century later, and will be relevant for centuries hence unless democracy itself becomes a past illusion.

The interpretation of the Nullification Crisis remains a center of calm within this welter of controversy. Any textbook on American history repeats the familiar—and uninspiring—story. South Carolina cotton planters, according to the standard interpretation, faced with declining prices and exhausted soil, could no longer compete with planters on fresh southwestern lands. Meanwhile Charleston, the state's commercial capital, could compete with neither the powerful trade center of New York nor the rising cotton ports of other southern states. Since most Carolinians blamed this profound economic depression on the post-1815 protective tariffs, South Carolina nullified the tariffs of 1828 and 1832, defied President Andrew Jackson to collect them, and brought the nation to the verge of civil war.

Revisionist history is often plagued by a tendency to tear down the legitimate as well as the fallacious aspects of an old interpretation. In this case I believe it would be a serious mistake to underestimate the economic causes of the Nullification Controversy. Indeed, part of my purpose is to clarify the nature and extent of the acute pecuniary embarrassments which afflicted South Carolinians by the thousands in the 1820's and 1830's.

Yet the most cursory glance at South Carolina's social structure and political alignments reveals that the Nullification Controversy must have been caused by something more than the declining income of cotton planters and the stagnant trade of Charleston. The coastal districts of Beaufort, Colleton, Charleston, and Georgetown, for example, constituted the most radical area in South Carolina and contributed a disproportionate amount of leaders, voters, and funds to the nullifiers' crusade. Yet the main crop of this lowcountry region was *rice*, not cotton, and the wealthy rice aristocracy was faced with neither severely declining prices nor extensive soil depletion. A majority of Charlestonians involved in the urban economy—as opposed to the town-dwelling planters—voted *against* nullification; in fact most unionist leaders lived in Charleston, and the Charleston merchants formed one of the strongest pressure groups in the unionist party.

Experts on nullification have always realized that the crusade of 1832, although ostensibly aimed at lowering the tariff, was also an attempt to check the abolitionists.[1] Charles M. Wiltse has reemphasized the point in an excellent recent essay.[2] But previous writers have not successfully documented or adequately explained the central importance of the slavery issue, and their findings have been ignored. In the following study I hope to show that the nullification impulse was to a crucial extent a revealing expression of South Carolina's morbid sensitivity to the beginnings of the antislavery campaign.

My reasons for presenting a re-examination of the Nullification Controversy go beyond a desire to clarify its causes. The crisis of 1832–3 is one of the more dramatic events in United States history, and has, I think, never been chronicled fully or accurately. Further

---

[1] David F. Houston, *A Critical Study of Nullification in South Carolina* (Cambridge, Mass., 1896), pp. 48–52; Frederic Bancroft, *Calhoun and the South Carolina Nullification Movement* (Baltimore, 1928), pp. 19–20, 115; Granville T. Prior, "History of the *Charleston Mercury*, 1822–1852" (unpubl. diss., Harvard, 1946), pp. 134–5; Gerald M. Capers, *John C. Calhoun, Opportunist* . . . (Gainesville, Fla., 1960), pp. 101–2, 119–20.

[2] *The New Nation, 1800–1845* (New York, 1961), ch. 6, esp. pp. 115–17, 121.

more, the Nullification Crisis has usually been presented as an isolated event. Viewed in proper perspective, the confrontation between Andrew Jackson and the Carolina nullifiers was the central occurrence in the broader transition of South Carolina from the enthusiastic nationalism of 1816 to the extreme sectionalism of 1836. And I hope the following analysis of the acute anxieties surrounding the mere discussion of slavery during these years of transition will help to explain why South Carolina led the South in a suicidal assault on the federal Union a generation later.

The present volume could not have been undertaken or completed without the help of numerous individuals and institutions. The research and preliminary writing were financed by two Woodrow Wilson fellowships, awarded by the Graduate Division of the University of California at Berkeley. A grant from the Horace Rackham School of Graduate Studies at the University of Michigan aided in the final stages of revision.

The research libraries cited in the bibliographical essay all provided numerous courtesies. I am particularly indebted to E. L. Inabinett, Clara Mae Jacobs, Charles Lee, and W. Edwin Hemphill for their hospitality, aid, and encouragement during a wonderful year of research at Columbia. Charles G. Sellers, Jr., first suggested that I undertake a re-examination of the Nullification Controversy and has given helpful advice ever since; I am very grateful to him. My manuscript benefited from the discerning criticisms of Richard H. Sewell and Louis Hartz. The maps were drawn by Karl M. Kriesel; the typing was expertly managed by Mrs. Henry D. Lynn, Jr., and Mrs. Robert J. Foster. Unfortunately I do not know how to acknowledge the two most important debts of all. I can only hope that Kenneth M. Stampp and Natalie Paperno Freehling realize the full measure of my gratitude. The above individuals are hereby absolved from blame for any errors which remain in this volume. But all of them have helped make it a labor of love from the beginning.

WILLIAM W. FREEHLING

Ann Arbor, Michigan
January 1966

Prologue: February 1833

February was the gay month in ante bellum Charleston. From all over the lowcountry planters came, from the golden rice fields in Georgetown, from the lush sea-island cotton lands on St. Helena Island, from the sickly swamps of the Savannah. The wealthiest of the Carolina chivalry, as they loved to call themselves, came in carriages with coats of arms, drawn by high-stepping horses, driven by Negroes dressed in livery. They came to watch the Jockey Club Races on the Washington Course, to dance at exclusive balls, to inspect the new fashions, and to indulge in idle chatter. It was a decaying aristocracy, but it still displayed enormous wealth and exquisite cultivation, and made Charleston the most English city in America.

The gaiety in February 1833 was noticeably muffled. The races were run, the balls continued, the wine flowed, but the gentry played less than half-heartedly. A grim tension hung over the state. South Carolina had become an armed camp. In Charleston the South Carolina and federal armies eyed each other nervously across the waters of the harbor, ready for an attack which might lead to civil war. The Nullification Crisis had reached its final stage.

In November 1832 a convention of the people of South Carolina had declared the tariffs of 1828 and 1832 unconstitutional and null and void within the state limits after February 1, 1833. More ominously, the Nullification Convention had proclaimed that if any attempt were made to collect the duties by force, South Carolina would secede from the Union.

In Washington an angry Andrew Jackson, victorious over the British at New Orleans and, more recently, triumphantly re-elected President after a successful skirmish with the United States Bank, met his newest foe with his usual resolution. The scarred, white-haired old hero loved nothing better than a fight and hated no man as cordially as Senator John C. Calhoun, the most famous nullifier of them all. Privately the President threatened to hang Calhoun and to lead the federal army into South Carolina himself. Publicly he announced his determination to enforce the laws against nullifiers or seceders. To back up his threats, Jackson sent reinforcements to Fort Moultrie and Castle Pinckney, two federal forts in Charleston harbor, and several revenue cutters to patrol the area. To direct military preparations, the President dispatched his leading general, Winfield Scott, also a hero in the War of 1812 and as determined a fighter as the old man in the White House. Many South Carolina unionists, led by Joel Poinsett, stood ready to desert their state and to help Scott enforce the tariff.

In January the nullifiers had retreated a bit, virtually suspending the Ordinance until after Congress had finished its deliberations on a compromise tariff. The delay was a strategic maneuver, not a final surrender. At the very meeting where suspension was adopted, James Hamilton, Jr., former governor of the state, president of the Nullification Convention, and the most astute political manager among the Carolina radicals, had announced his determination to reconvene the Convention and propose secession if Congress gave Jackson authority to coerce the nullifiers.

All over the state, nullifiers prepared for an imminent encounter. In Charleston Governor Robert Y. Hayne, the former United States senator whose debates with Daniel Webster in 1830 had given national publicity to the Carolina doctrines, tried to form an army which could hope to challenge the forces of "Old Hickory." Hayne recruited a brigade of mounted minutemen, 2,000 strong, which could swoop down on Charleston the moment fighting broke out, and a volunteer army of 25,000 men which could march on foot to save the beleaguered city. In the North Governor Hayne's agents bought over $100,000 worth of arms; in Charleston Hamilton readied his volunteers for an assault on the federal forts. True to the chivalric spirit which demanded courageous battling for violated honor, Carolina nullifiers stood ready to take on the nation. As Congressman George McDuffie solemnly proclaimed at the Nullification Convention, "We would infinitely prefer that the territory of the State should be the cemetery of freemen than the habitation of slaves."[1]

The only hope of averting hostilities lay in the halls of Congress. President Jackson himself had urged tariff reform, and Senator Henry Clay, a leading protectionist, was working hard for a tariff compromise. But in Washington, as in Charleston, nullifiers expected the worst. In late January Calhoun had almost given up hope for a compromise and was desperately trying to convince his cohorts to renounce secession. By mid-February Governor Hayne saw "not the slightest chance" of Clay's compromise succeeding. McDuffie noted that "all hope of adjusting the tariff . . . has now vanished." He made it clear that the nullifiers would repudiate Calhoun's counsel of moderation. "It is now the duty of every citizen of So. Carolina," he wrote, ". . . to defend the rights and liberties of the State." "Dreadful as this alternative is," added James Hammond, "I am for it rather than become a slave myself and meanly throw upon posterity the duty of resistance."[2]

[1] *State Papers on Nullification* . . . (Boston, 1834), p. 71.
[2] Calhoun to William Campbell Preston, n.d. [late Jan. 1833], Virginia Carrington Scrapbook, Preston Family Papers, LC; I. W. Hayne to James Hammond, Feb. 20, 1833, Hammond to [Preston], Jan. 27, 1833, Hammond Papers, LC; George McDuffie to Armistead Burt, Feb. 19, 1833, McDuffie Papers, DU. See Abbreviations, p. ix.

PART ONE

Background for Crisis

Dangers are around and above and below and within our poor little State. . . . *We* are (I am quite sure) the *last* of the *race* of South-Carolina; I see nothing before us but decay and downfall.
                    —Hugh S. Legaré to I. E. Holmes, April 8, 1833

I

The Land and the People

In the 1820's and 1830's South Carolina contained, paradoxically, both great differences and a remarkable degree of unity. The deadly swamps of the lowcountry were the antithesis of the healthful mountains of the upcountry;[1] the huge plantations of the tidewater contrasted with the predominantly smaller plantations of the piedmont; the absentee aristocrats of the coast differed from the hard-working agriculturists of the hills. But although these differences in climate and economy caused divergences in social values which still persist, by 1830 the lowcountry style of life had greatly influenced that of the upcountry.

2

In its natural state, the mainland of the lowcountry is a dense swamp cut in sections by numerous rivers which flow from the upcountry down to the sea. It is a deep, dark swamp, filled with a luxuriant forest of cypress and gum, cotton and oak. Long festoons of gray Spanish moss, hanging from the thick, gnarled branches, and a rich variety of flowers, blooming at the roots of the trees, help give the swamp a haunting loveliness. But the dominant color is the melancholy purple of the iris; the dominant tone, the somberness of the moss. The beauty of the swamp never quite conceals

---

[1] By "lowcountry" I mean the coastal districts of Beaufort, Colleton, Charleston, and Georgetown; by "upcountry," the rest of the state. I use the term "lowcountry" more in a socioeconomic than in a geographical sense, to denote the swampy coastal area of the large rice and sea-island cotton plantations.

7

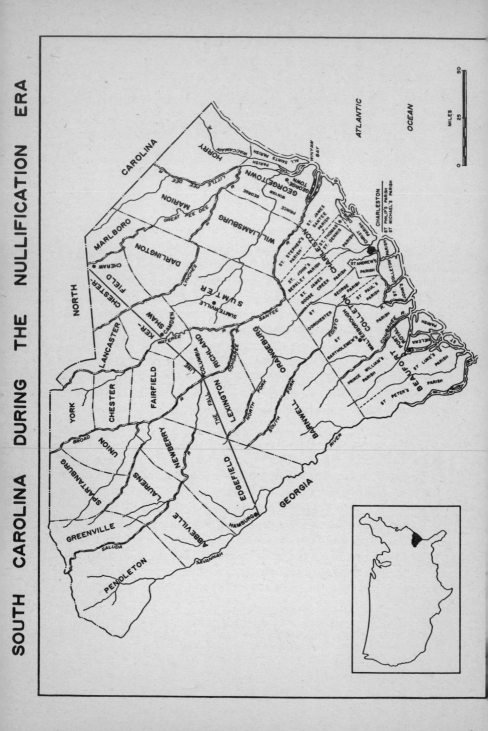

SOUTH CAROLINA DURING THE NULLIFICATION ERA

its dankness. At its heart lie secluded lagoons and secret marshes, and in ante bellum times these often stagnant waters were a breeding place for the malaria-bearing mosquito, which made man pay a heavy price for exploiting the riches of the land. James Hammond captured the mood of the swamp perfectly:

There is something in the solemn gloom of these swamps which strikes me more than any other kind of landscape. Even the still dead black water seems to concert with the sluggishness of my spirit.[2]

In the eighteenth century South Carolinians planted rice in inland swamps and indigo throughout the lowcountry, from the sea islands along the coast to the sand hills of Orangeburg. In the 1790's lowcountry planters moved toward the sea. They abandoned the exhausted inland swamps and cultivated rice in the almost inexhaustible coastal tide swamps. Inland indigo plantations were deserted, too, and sea-island, long-staple, luxury cotton was grown on the old coastal and sea-island indigo fields. Some indigo planting persisted in Orangeburg; some inland swamps were cultivated in Christ Church. But in the main, lowcountry planters had settled down to grow luxury cotton near the sea and rice on the rivers, a pattern which persisted until the surrender at Appomattox.[3]

The development of the South Carolina coastal plantation constitutes one of the great epics in American economic history. The large gangs of black slaves, following their white overseer, stepped into the jungle. Slowed down by the steaming tropical heat and ravaging swamp diseases, they hacked down the trees and brush, laying the land bare beneath the burning sun.

On luxury cotton plantations, land could be plowed almost as soon as it was cleared. But on rice plantations the slaves' initial tasks had just begun. The bondsmen dug away at the slimy swamp muck, carving deep parallel ditches from the river through the fields and forming shallower parallel drains between the new canals. The rice field became a giant checkerboard, cut in squares

---

[2] Hammond Diary, entry for May 21, 1841, Hammond Papers, LC.
[3] For an excellent discussion of the shift, see Marjorie S. Mendenhall, "A History of Agriculture in South Carolina, 1790 to 1860" (unpubl. diss., Univ. of N.C., 1940), pp. 133-4.

by the redirected water flow. Along the river bed, across the new canals, black laborers constructed intricate dams and sluices. The planter could then harness the tidal flow, flooding his fields to help the rice to sprout, draining water off to kill the rampant weeds. Finally, the slaves erected a gleaming plantation mansion on the highest ground and built their own rude shacks near the fields of grain. Many months, sometimes several years, had to elapse before rice could sprout and cotton bloom on the lush marsh mud of the lowlands.[4]

The slaves had pushed back the jungle, but the swamp diseases remained. Carolinians failed to connect the mosquito's bite with malarial chills; they blamed the debilitating fevers on some mystic miasma in the air of the swamp. No systematic precautions were taken against the pesky insects, and, inadvertently, planters helped to make the swamp deadlier than ever. As abandoned plantations lapsed back toward their natural state, the stagnant pools and half-cleared growth formed an ideal spawning ground for the insect hordes. As a result, malaria became increasingly prevalent, forcing more and more white families to flee the area during the summer months. A few leading planters even deserted their new plantation mansions.[5]

Yet if some mansions were abandoned, the plantations remained. Planters were loath to give up the rich marsh mud; moreover, white overseers could be paid and Negro slaves forced to risk their health for the planters' profits. Although middle-class slaveholders lived in the coastal parishes, everything conspired against them. The richness of the land and the cost of clearing it caused the price of improved land to spiral. Furthermore, rice and sea-island cotton plantations were worked most efficiently by large gangs of slaves. Even if a small entrepreneur could scrape together enough cash and credit, the gamble for profits seldom seemed worth the risk of malaria. Rice and sea-island cotton were not the poor man's crops.

---

[4] The best discussions of rice planting are in David Doar, *Rice and Rice Planting in the South Carolina Lowcountry* (Charleston, 1936), and Duncan Clinch Heyward, *Seed from Madagascar* (Chapel Hill, 1937). For a graphic description of the area, see Samuel G. Stoney, *Plantations of the Carolina Lowcountry* (Charleston, 1938).

[5] James Edward Calhoun Diary, entry for Jan. 22, 1826, microfilm in SC; *SR*, IV (Aug. 1829), 124–5.

Thus a relatively large number of lowcountry plantations were owned by absentee planters, managed by white overseers, and worked by many Negro slaves. Even in the winter, when most planters lived on their estates, the ratio of Negroes to whites reached unsettling proportions. In 1830, in the district of Charleston, Negroes outnumbered whites three to one; in Colleton the ratio was four to one; in Beaufort, five to one; in Georgetown, eight to one.[6] But in the summer, when the bulk of the white population fled from malaria, the proportion of Negroes must have been enormous. No other area in the Old South contained such a massive, concentrated Negro population.

The characteristics of lowcountry slaves added the final touch to the ominous mood of the coastal black belt. From 1803 to 1807 South Carolina, alone among the southern states, legalized the reopening of the African slave trade. Almost 40,000 Africans poured into Charleston, as Yankee ship captains and southern slave-traders joined hands to reap the lucrative profits. Many of the black imports were sold into the rice swamps, where they formed a significant percentage of the tidewater labor force. The African natives, with their bizarre customs and their eerie glances, sometimes seemed the epitome of the untamed savage. Even slave families who had lived at tidewater for generations retained disturbing remnants of their African heritage. Barred from extensive contact with white men during the long season of sickness, coastal slaves conversed in a Gullah dialect which few masters completely comprehended. The dense concentration of these quasi-assimilated slaves, along with the increasingly virulent malaria, gave the small society of rice and sea-island aristocrats, squeezed among the dank swamps near the open sea, a sense of ever-present danger.

3

The lowcountry aristocracy was a leisure class dedicated to achieving the exclusiveness and refinement displayed by English country gentlemen. They drank expensive Madeira wine and smoked choice Spanish cigars, quaffed glasses of brandy and sipped bowls of turtle soup. The gentry hunted with hound and horn, attended horse races and cockfights, gave formal tea parties, and

[6] U.S. Census Bureau, *Ninth Census* (Washington, D.C., 1861), I, 60–1.

danced at balls. The wives of these aristocrats cultivated an air of
dignity and refinement, playing chess, performing on the piano,
lounging in the richly furnished library. It was a life of taste, of
polish, of elegance.[7]

The books which lined a planter's library were more often
displayed than read. But few lowcountry aristocrats failed to
glory in the medieval tales of Sir Walter Scott. Scott's chivalric
knights, with their exalted principles, their princely deportment,
and their unswerving courage seemed exemplars of well-bred
country gentlemen. Like the heroes in the Waverly Novels, tidewater planters took enormous pride in their wealth, their families,
and their class. And like Scott's dashing knights, properly chivalric
Carolinians stood ready to defend their honor against the least
imagined insult.[8]

Even in the midst of polite conversation, gentlemen were on
guard to protect their integrity. The Carolina social code also
called for relaxed cordiality in the drawing room. Combining these
two notions required a delicate touch; and the affable talk at tea
parties never hid the possibility of a duel.[9] The great social art was
to slip, without ostentation, into an easy familiarity with all companions. The besetting social sin was to permit one's companion to
take advantage of the relaxed cordiality. The balance often broke
down. A jest which went a bit too far could be taken as an insult,
a clever argument could be interpreted as an affront. Then came
the inevitable challenge and often the tragic duel. No wonder
that in the less refined air of political controversy, lowcountry
aristocrats often took offense and frequently challenged the nation
to another duel.

It was, of necessity, an idle aristocracy. From the beginning
of May to the first frost in November, the river barons deserted
their country seats in order to escape the fever. Some retired to the
pineland above the swamp—to summer villages like Walter-

[7] For an excellent discussion, see Rosser H. Taylor, *Antebellum South Carolina: A Social and Cultural History* (Chapel Hill, 1942), pp. 1–23.
[8] Jack Kenny Williams, "The Code of Honor in Antebellum South Carolina," *South Carolina Historical Magazine,* LIV (July 1953), 113–28; H. L. Greenleaf to Joel Eastman, Sept. 10, 1825, Greenleaf Papers, SC.
[9] William J. Grayson Autobiography, typecopy in SC, pp. 113–15, 167.

borough in Colleton, McPhersonville in Beaufort, Pineville in St. John's. From these healthful towns they could visit their plantation by day and return before the malaria struck at night. Most planters traveled farther—to the upcountry, to Charleston, to the springs in Virginia, to the North, to Europe. For these aristocrats, direct supervision of the plantation was usually impossible.[10]

Barred by fear of disease from summer work, imbued with a social code which required cultivated gentility, the lowcountry gentry despised manual labor, detested moneygrubbers, and hated penny-pinching. In the years before the American Revolution, great planters had often been great merchants. But in the early nineteenth century foreigners from the North and from Europe captured control of the Charleston countinghouses. After that even wealthy new merchants usually failed to attain the top rank in the social hierarchy. A financier could rarely hope to overcome the refined contempt of planters who shared Hugh Legaré's attitudes: "The *town bourgeoisie* is *so* odious! . . . Alfred Huger's remark always occurs to me, that the greatest absurdity in the world is a 'Liverpool Gentleman.' "[11]

Planters only looked down on merchants; they reserved their most cordial contempt for white "mechanics"—the early-nineteenth-century term for a skilled laborer. Merchants were sometimes wealthy and cultivated; mechanics were usually poor and coarse. More important, white mechanics competed with Negroes for the right to make a living with their hands! The only sort of mechanic that planters could stomach was a well-groomed, dressed-up master mechanic who, with gloves carefully pulled over his hands, directed a gang of slaves.[12]

For some gentlemen planters, contempt for work extended to agricultural endeavor. A southern plantation was as much a capitalistic enterprise as a northern factory; and a planter-manager, to be successful, needed the qualities of calculating shrewdness, hard

[10] Lawrence F. Brewster, *Summer Migrations and Resorts of South Carolina Lowcountry Planters* (Durham, 1947).

[11] Legaré to his sister, Aug. 4, 1833, Legaré Papers, SC; Taylor, *Antebellum South Carolina*, p. 44; *Charleston Mercury*, June 15, 1827; "Answer to Query 33," in William Ogilby Papers, SC; Benjamin F. Perry Diary, entry for Aug. 12, 1837, NC.

[12] [Charleston] *City Gazette*, Apr. 14, 1832; *Camden Journal*, July 2, 1831.

work, and Yankee practicality which chivalric aristocrats affected to despise. As one astute observer noted:

We are somehow strangely given to regard all labours which employ time, and compel exertion as inconsistent with a proper gentility. Noble blood will not trade in merchandise—can it be expected that noble blood will sow and reap, and devise modes and means by which the arts of sowing and reaping shall be . . . improved? . . . you will never see the plough drawn upon the panel of a planter's coach.[13]

An idle aristocracy which sometimes found its own profession distasteful, lowcountry planters had time to engage in politics, to study, to write. The gentry produced famous politicians, such as James Hamilton, Jr., and William Lowndes, and fine scholars, such as Stephen Elliott, the botanist, and Hugh Legaré, the classicist. If there was time for creative leisurely pursuits, there was also time to brood. Some spent their days haunted by prospects of disease:

For several days I had labored under a thousand apprehensions of evils which my disordered imagination conceived; and, amongst others, felt much agitated with the alarms of yellow fever, which at this season of the year, never fails to haunt the minds of hundreds like myself, who have nothing else to do but listen to idle reports and help to give them currency.[14]

Others brooded about their idleness and their distaste for managing plantation slaves:

. . . dissipation—or to speak more correctly—Idleness is the order of the day here. . . . There is William Heyward, with a fine disposition, and an excellent capacity—lounging away his mornings . . . drinking away his afternoons. . . . I am sure that he is not satisfied himself with his mode of existence— He is going to Silkhope in a few days to see how things are going on there & he confessed to me that he hated to have anything to do with Negroes, but he thinks it will please his Father.[15]

Still others were absorbed with the sense of imminent disaster which hung over the lowcountry:

---

[13] S Ag, IX (July 1836), 355ff.
[14] Charleston Mercury, Aug. 10, 1822.
[15] M. I. Manigault to [Gabriel] Henry Manigault, Dec. 6, 1808, Louis Manigault Papers, DU.

Ah, why should such a happy state of things—a society so charming and so accomplished—be doomed to end so soon, and perhaps, so terribly! . . . My heart sinks within me often when I think of what may too soon be.[16]

At best it was a cultivated, dignified life—a round of books, of music, of rich conversation. At worst it was a dissipated one, filled only with the chase, the duel, and the table. The lowcountry barons were often idle, brooding aristocrats, often tending toward decadence, but sometimes capable of producing a disinterested scholarship, above material concerns, which was so rare in America, and which they prided themselves on so haughtily.

4

Charleston, unofficial capital of the lowcountry, was in every sense a planter's city. The great planters came in February for the races and balls, and returned in the summer, despite the oppressive humidity and heat and the risk of yellow fever. Charlestonians who were not planters—the mechanics, merchants, lawyers, and doctors —served the agricultural community. Urban Charleston re-emphasized the agrarian nature of South Carolina.

Like all great American colonial cities, Charleston was built where rivers from the interior flow into the sea. It is located on a fingerlike peninsula which juts out from the mainland and separates the Ashley and Cooper rivers before they converge to join the ocean. The advantage of the location was its ample harbor facilities. The disadvantage was that neither the Ashley nor the Cooper was a big river, extending to the upcountry. As the nineteenth century progressed the disadvantage became increasingly obvious.

The tip of the peninsula, along the Cooper River side, became the dock area; it was called the East Bay, and the great import-export merchants were known as East Bay merchants. King Street, the road from the mainland proper down to the tip of the peninsula, became a great retail area, the shopping center of Charleston. The land between the city proper and the mainland was called,

---

[16] Legaré to I. E. Holmes, Oct. 2, 1832. Legaré to Holmes, Apr. 8, 1833, Legaré, *Writings* . . . , Mary S. Legaré, ed. (2 vols.; Charleston, 1846), I, 203, 215.

appropriately, Charleston neck, and wagoners coming from the upcountry traveled along King Street and passed through the neck on their way to Charleston.

Charlestonians hoped to make their metropolis the most European of American cities, and, for once, the weather conspired in their favor. The crucial factor in making Charleston look like an Old World city was not the narrow cobblestone streets or the quaint old markets, not the graceful Episcopalian churches or the venerable live oak, not the Spanish balconies or the European book stores, but the incredible humidity and the excessive dew. The heavy air and smoky vapors gave the walls of the houses a gloomy stain, which made them seem truly ancient and produced the European look the gentry tried so hard to cultivate.[17]

Few foreigners came to South Carolina, but those who did usually remained in Charleston and contributed to the city's cosmopolitan tone. Approximately one-eighth of the population was from Ireland; they made St. Patrick's Day one of Charleston's favorite holidays. Several hundred Frenchmen from San Domingo had fled to Charleston in the 1790's to escape the wrath of the rebellious Negroes; these *émigrés* supported themselves by teaching the sons and daughters of the river barons the social graces and served as constant reminders that servile insurrection *could* succeed. A small number of Germans, many East Bay merchants, and ships and crews from all over the world added to Charleston's Old World charm.[18]

The city looked aristocratic as well as old, primarily because of the planters' town mansions. These grounds were beautifully landscaped, with lovely formal gardens and carefully spaced orange and oak trees. One side of each house faced the street; its front door faced the walled-in garden, and was entered through the piazza, or screened-in porch. What looked like a street door to the house was actually a side door to the piazza, and hence a

---

[17] For a good description of Charleston, see Samuel Gaillard Stoney and Bayard Wootten, *Charleston: Azaleas and Old Bricks* (Cambridge, Mass., 1939).

[18] *The Irishman, and Charleston Weekly Register*, Sept. 11, 1830; Chapman Milling, "The Arcadian and San Domingan French," *Transactions of the Huguenot Society of South Carolina*, LXII (1957), 5–36; Robert Mills, *Statistics of South Carolina . . .* (Charleston, 1826), p. 176.

Charleston drawing room was two full doors from the curious gaze of plebeians. The piazzas, built on all three stories as a refuge from the heat, were blocked off from the pedestrians' view, and the windows in the house had venetian blinds and wooden shutters, both customarily snapped shut. The town-dwelling gentry would brook no "vulgar familiarity."[19]

But the lovely formal gardens, the cultivated talk at exclusive tea parties, the elegantly furnished drawing rooms, were only one part of the urban scene. Charleston was also a town of sordid poverty and unpaved streets, of filthy hovels and crumbling walls. The ugly slums were packed with slaves and free Negroes, white mechanics and transient seamen. Furthermore, Charlestonians knew firsthand the anxiety of slave conspiracy and incessantly guarded against it. Every night curfew bells in St. Michael's Church warned Negroes without passes to get off the streets. Every night the town guard marched into position. Planters could escape malaria by going to Charleston. But even in the carefully secluded drawing rooms in their discolored town mansions, they could not quite escape the danger and decadence of the low-country.

5

Traveling away from the coast, one comes to a middle district of sand hills and pine above the swamps, then to a region of rolling hills and red clays which extends almost to the North Carolina line. The hills and clay, as characteristic of the piedmont as the swamps are of the tidewater, offered neither the great advantages nor the severe obstacles of the lowcountry pestilential muck. The red clay, though often containing a rich soil, was never so lush as the swampy marsh mud. The problem of erosion on upcountry hills, a serious difficulty, was not so destructive as the swarms of malaria-bearing mosquitos in the lowcountry. Thus an acre of upcountry land was neither as expensive to buy nor as dangerous to cultivate, which helped make the piedmont far kinder to the interests of a middling slaveholder.

[19] The phrase is Legaré's. Legaré to his mother, Sept. 9, 1834, Legaré Papers.

Before 1790 the upcountry was a land of yeoman farmers, with few slaves and only an occasional large plantation. Farmers grew their own provisions and raised tobacco to earn a little cash. But in the 1790's, and particularly in the first three decades of the nineteenth century, the upcountry plunged enthusiastically into the cotton bonanza which Eli Whitney's cotton gin had started all over the Deep South. Slaves poured into the upcountry and cotton poured out; for a time piedmont South Carolina was the greatest American cotton producer. Along the great upcountry rivers a new class of Carolina gentry emerged, composed of frontier entrepreneurs, who borrowed heavily and gambled boldly for a fortune in cotton profits.

Yet even where plantations were densest, the concentration of Negroes remained well below the levels of those of the low-country. Most piedmont slaveholders owned few slaves, and the majority of farmers owned none at all. Upland short-staple, green-seed, ordinary cotton—unlike lowcountry long-staple, black-seed, luxury cotton, and unlike lowcountry rice—was a crop with which poor men often made their fortune. One could grow upcountry cotton on cheap land, without slaves or, as an alternative, with several slaves. Profits could buy another hand, especially since a bank might lend the bulk of the price in exchange for a mortgage. The upcountry was filled with small slaveholders, always striving for one more Negro and always dreaming of matching the estates of the comparatively few large slaveholders.

The shift from the arcadian simplicity of yeoman farmers to the aggressive capitalism of cotton entrepreneurs went faster and further in some regions than in others. The cotton-slave complex tended to flow south and west from the South Carolina central plains, toward the Savannah River and Georgia. In the North, particularly toward the North Carolina boundary, yeoman farmers retained their hegemony. In 1830, for example, in Greenville, Spartanburg, and York, three northern counties, whites outnumbered Negroes in a three-to-one ratio. On the other hand, in Richland, Lexington, and Edgefield, three counties running west from the center of the state, Negroes outnumbered whites almost one and one-half to one.[20] The self-sufficient farmer was not entirely

[20] *Ninth Census,* I, 60–1.

swept away by the rush of slaves and cotton into the clay hills of the upcountry.

6

If by 1810 a new gentry had emerged in the upcountry, it differed in almost every respect from the older aristocracy on the coast. A large piedmont slaveholder in the early nineteenth century was a frontier entrepreneur—an unpolished, hard-fisted, crude businessman, immersed in his planting enterprise and dedicated to seizing the main chance. He would have been absurdly out of place at a Charleston tea party, just as an elegant lowcountry gentleman would have been absurdly out of place directing a frontier cotton plantation.

By 1830 many upcountry planters had shed their coarse habits and had attained some of the polish of a mature aristocracy. The Wade Hamptons provide a superb example. The first Wade Hampton was one of the earliest great upcountry entrepreneurs. A hard-driving, unscrupulous capitalist, he built a great cotton fortune near the new town of Columbia and then parlayed it into a colossal sugar fortune in Louisiana. His son, the second Wade Hampton, was a notoriously poor businessman but a thoroughly cultivated aristocrat. Married to a Charleston heiress, he designed and erected an elegant plantation mansion on his Millwood estate, bred great race horses, built a splendid library, and served the best Madeira and the finest turtle soup. As Charles Cauthen put it, "Colonel Hampton personified the gentler virtues of a matured aristocracy rather than the rugged qualities of a society on-the-make."[21]

The second Wade Hampton's brother-in-law, James Hammond, was a poverty-stricken upcountry lad in the 1820's until, by a fortunate marriage to a wealthy Charlestonian, he acquired a fine plantation on the Savannah River. The *nouveau riche* Hammond immediately posed as a lowcountry aristocrat. He bought famous race horses, built a luxurious town mansion, hung expensive paintings, and looked down his not-very-well-bred nose at the "poor bred country gentlemen" who could only talk about

[21] Charles E. Cauthen (ed.), *Family Letters of the Three Wade Hamptons, 1782–1901* (Columbia, 1953), esp. p. xiv.

politics and agriculture.[22] A generation earlier a frontier entrepreneur would have shunned Hammond's airs.

The increasing refinement of the piedmont gentry was most
apparent in Columbia, unofficial capital of the upcountry and
official capital of the state. Strategically located where the Broad
and Saluda rivers unite to form the Congaree, built on a high, level
plain, Columbia, with wide, regular, tree-lined streets, many taste-
ful houses and lovely formal gardens, rarely failed to charm its
most sophisticated critics. The social graces of the town were
equally impressive. A leading upcountryman, Benjamin F. Perry,
noted that "the citizens are inclined to be proud and aristocratic";
a discriminating lowcountryman, William Elliott, was impressed
by the "fine houses—fine equipages—fine dresses—and some polish
of manners."[23] The nightly balls and daily tea parties during the
legislative session in December were only a bit less genteel than
Charleston's. In intellectual cultivation, because of Thomas Cooper
and his excellent South Carolina College, Columbia achieved a
cultural level Charleston might well have envied. Henry W. De
Saussure, a native of the tidewater and a resident of the piedmont,
accurately summed up Columbia's, and the upcountry's, increasing
sophistication:

Dr. Cooper is a man of great learning and skill in communicating
his knowledge; & he is devoted to his duties—so are the other profes-
sors, two of whom are eminent. Our upper country, formerly so un-
lettered, is gradually filling with young men of pretty good education,
& becoming more enlightened & liberal. And the young women, not
to be far behind, are generally obtaining a very good education.[24]

To some extent the new refinement De Saussure described was
the natural product of time and of the growth of a second upcountry planting generation, no longer *nouveau riche* and now
anxious to assume a more cultivated stance. But the shift from
coarse frontiersmen to sophisticated gentlemen came too fast and

[22] Hammond Papers, SC, *passim.*
[23] Perry Diary, p. 20, NC; William Elliott to Mrs. William Elliott, Dec. 5, 1829,
Elliott-Gonzales Papers, NC; Taylor, *Antebellum South Carolina,* p. 31; G. W.
Featherstonhaugh, *Excursion Through the Slave States* . . . (New York, 1844), p. 155.
[24] Henry W. De Saussure to Charles Cotesworth Pinckney, May 17, 1824, Pinckney
Family Papers, LC.

extended too far to be explained wholly in such terms. The more important reason for the quick maturing of the upland gentry was its intimate social contact with the older aristocracy on the coast.

The social ties between the two sections took a variety of forms. By the 1830's, for example, members of the most illustrious lowcountry families often resided in the uplands. Thomas Pinckney, Jr., and Francis K. Huger in Pendleton, the De Saussures and the Prestons in Columbia, William A. Bull in Abbeville, were all leaders in their respective upcountry districts. The historian of Sumter County estimates that one-third of its inhabitants originally migrated from the lowcountry.[25] Several tidewater leaders were emigrants from the piedmont—James Petigru, Ker Boyce, and Langdon Cheves of Charleston, John L. Wilson of Georgetown, and Frank Elmore of Colleton.

Marriage ties also united the two sections. Some important upcountry politicians, such as the second Wade Hampton, Benjamin F. Perry, James Hammond, George McDuffie, and John C. Calhoun, married lowcountry heiresses. The Petigru family, originally of Abbeville, illustrates the possibilities of intersectional marriage. James Petigru, the great lawyer, married the daughter of a Beaufort planter and lived in Charleston; three of his sisters married prominent lowlanders and resided at tidewater; another sister married a lowcountryman who migrated to Abbeville; and the fifth sister remained in Abbeville.[26]

Common social experiences added to the effect of marriage and migration. The poorest uplander and the wealthiest lowlander often attended South Carolina College together and formed intimate, lifelong friendships. Most important of all, many tidewater aristocrats spent their summers in the upcountry, at Pendleton, or Greenville, or Statesburg. Here leading lowcountry planters entertained, and were entertained by, an upcountry frontier gentry whose values and ideals they were profoundly influencing.

[25] Anne King Gregorie, *History of Sumter County, South Carolina* (Sumter, 1954), p. 15.
[26] J. H. Easterby (ed.), *The South Carolina Rice Plantation as Revealed in the Papers of Robert F. W. Allston* (Chicago, 1945), pp. 17–18.

7

This increasing social intimacy had important political effects. Close personal friendships led to unified political parties. More important, intimate social conversation resulted in an understanding of separate political problems. By the 1830's this mutual sensitivity had progressed so far that the mood of one aristocracy profoundly influenced the political reaction of the other.

The intimate political relationship between many tidewater and piedmont planters paralleled the close political ties between the piedmont gentry and its poorer neighbors. The relationship between grimy red-necks and cultivated gentlemen had its tense moments. Small slaveholders and slaveless farmers often coveted the rich estates of nearby planters. When economic depression undermined hopes of a quick vault into the planter class, the red-neck's envy was often tinged with hatred. At other times and in other lands, similar status tension has led to bitter political controversy.

But the rich and poor in a slaveholding district had too much in common to risk a quarrel. All types of slaveholders, and yeoman farmers who hoped to become slaveholders, wanted to protect slavery, raise cotton prices, decrease the cost of living, and ease debtor-creditor relations. A measure which helped the aristocrats would also help the plebeians, and the dangerous northern attack prevented excessive southern division.

Impoverished red-necks gained great satisfaction from joining hands with the planters in a South Carolina crusade. By supporting the gentry, poorer southerners could claim membership in the "chivalry" and feel they were part of a great planter community. Leading politicians fully understood how well the mystique of the chivalry eased the red-neck's frustrations. This is why the nullifiers' propagandists always appeared to assume that all readers were planters although they knew that most readers only hoped to become planters. This is why orators continually called on everyone to join the campaign of the Carolina chivalry.

When they enlisted in the ranks of the South Carolina nullifiers, poorer uplanders never hoped to lead the campaign. The aristo-

cratic gentry would brook no red-neck revolt; plebeians were expected to defer to their betters. Petty slaveholders rarely expressed
displeasure with their deferential role. They considered it a privilege to participate in the crusade.

Because the gentry's political control depended largely on personal influence and on psychological stresses which its personal
presence created, the aristocrats' political power rarely extended
to areas which the plantation economy had not greatly penetrated.
Yeoman farmers in the mountain districts, for example, had little
contact with large plantations and wasted a minimum of energy
striving for more slaves. They usually regarded the invitation to
join the chivalry as inexplicable nonsense. Elsewhere, the East
Bay merchants of Charleston viewed the chivalry's antics with
ill-disguised contempt.

The Charleston merchants and the mountain yeomanry remained the only major pressure groups outside the tightly knit
community of white men which stretched across South Carolina
in the ante bellum years. Lowcountry planters, upcountry nabobs,
and even nonslaveholders in the piedmont planting districts had
the sort of close political relationship which only common interests and social contact can produce. No other state in the Deep
South had achieved such complete unification by the years of the
Nullification Controversy.

The growth of statewide channels of communication, however, never completely obliterated the substantial differences between upcountry and lowcountry South Carolina. The tidewater
plantations, with their huge slave population and their intense
cultivation of rice and luxury cotton, continued to bear the unmistakable stamp of the malarial swamps. Upcountry districts continued to possess proportionately fewer plantations and slaves.
And on the red clays of the piedmont hills, uplanders continued
to stake their fortunes on short-staple cotton.

Both these surviving sectional differences and the emergence of
a statewide planter community were of the greatest importance
in the Nullification Controversy. Because of the divergent nature
of the areas they cultivated, the crops they grew, and the plantation systems they developed, the planters of the swamps and the

planters of the hills reacted differently to the political issues of the 1820's and 1830's. The upcountry, more affected by economic depression, expressed greater excitement over the tariff as an economic issue. The lowcountry, where slavery was a more tense affair, was angrier at the first stirring of the abolitionist crusade. In another state, with less intimate connections between sections, each region might have entered the same crusade for somewhat different reasons. Such a campaign would never have been so violent. In South Carolina, the tidewater and the piedmont, sharing their somewhat separate problems, lashed each other into an increasingly frenzied campaign.

On the other hand, groups outside the slaveholding nexus had little in common with one another. The yeoman farmers of the mountains and the East Bay merchants of Charleston had divergent economic interests, wholly different values, and no opportunity to meet and converse. Any opposition to a slaveholding political crusade was doomed by the state's social structure to have, initially, neither the political cohesion nor the emotional unity which helped sweep the Carolina chivalry on toward revolution.

2

A Spotty Economy

There was nothing more commonplace in pre-Civil War America than a southern crusade against high protective tariffs. What remains unique about the South Carolina nullifiers is the extreme to which they carried the traditional antitariff protest. Southern politicians usually warred against protection in Congress and in the courts. The South Carolina nullifiers, on the other hand, were willing to take their cause to the battlefields. As Carolina radicals eventually discovered to their dismay, no other southern state approved of such techniques. Why, then, was antitariff excitement so intense in South Carolina?

One obvious hypothesis is that a severe economic depression afflicted the groups who supported the nullifiers' crusade. One might also expect that South Carolinians who opposed nullification were relatively untouched by the hard times of the period. A close examination of the South Carolina economy in the 1820's and 1830's reveals that this explanation is partially correct. The upcountry cotton producers, Charleston mechanics, and Charleston retailers were all victims of depression and proponents of nullification. The Charleston merchants and the mountain yeomanry escaped pecuniary distress and opposed the radicals. Only one anomaly upsets the picture. Lowcountry rice and luxury cotton planters, although overwhelmingly in favor of nullification, remained somewhat prosperous in the twenties and thirties. Their extreme radicalism cannot be explained solely in terms of the economic history of South Carolina in the era of nullification.

2

In 1816 the American people, with the years of deprivation caused by embargo and war securely behind them, plunged enthusiastically into a jubilee of spiraling prosperity. The boom seemed endless, and entrepreneurs, seduced by the charms of low interest rates and a grossly inflated currency, incurred too many debts and overextended their investments. With South Carolina's staples selling for twice their normal prices, many planters mortgaged their estates to the limit and acquired extravagant tastes for luxuries. Upcountry textile factories were closed in order to concentrate capital in the cotton bonanza, and investments were shifted from Charleston countinghouses to flourishing plantations. By 1819 the South Carolina economy was almost entirely dependent on agricultural enterprise.[1]

Depression came as suddenly as prosperity and, unfortunately, lasted far longer. Hard times actually came in two distinct stages. The first stage, commencing with the Panic of 1819 in America and ending with the English resumption of specie payments in 1822, had little to do with the special problems of South Carolinians. It affected producers all over the country, and was primarily characterized by a sharp contraction of the nation's currency. The heady prosperity of the 1815–18 period was often based on no more than a sea of paper money. In 1819 the bubble burst, and banks throughout the land fell victim to the panic. As customers by the droves demanded gold or silver coin in exchange for paper money, the nation's bankers called in their loans and curtailed paper-money issues. The English resumption of specie payments put the finishing touch on the deflationary spiral. With circulating currency cut approximately in half between 1819 and 1822, the American people plunged into their worst depression since the founding of the Republic.

During the 1819–22 currency contraction, South Carolina's cost-of-living index, reflecting the nationwide deflation, declined over 35 percent.[2] The decreased cost of living offset declining

---

[1] *Charleston Courier*, June 11, 1831; Mills, *Statistics*, pp. 515–16; [Charleston] *Southern Patriot*. Oct. 18, 1823.

[2] See below, Appendix A, Table 2, Part 1.

income, and therefore the curtailed currency was not necessarily destructive to the interests of all producers. But the decreased money supply was necessarily injurious to all debtors. Since money appreciated in value and became harder to procure, a debt contracted in 1817 was almost twice as difficult to pay back in 1822.[3]

The second stage of the South Carolina depression, 1822–9, was marked by a price decline of certain products because of over-production. The second stage of the depression affected the price of fewer commodities than had the first, and the overall price index fell less—only 21 percent in South Carolina from 1822 to 1829.[4] With consumer prices remaining relatively steady, a sharply falling income was far more harmful than it would have been during the 1819–22 currency contraction. For debtors, already in trouble because of appreciated currency, a plunging income in the late 1820's was a disaster.

The first stage of the depression affected planters throughout South Carolina. But the second stage affected only the piedmont slaveholders. Whereas debtors in both sections were hurt by the currency contraction, the upcountry alone had to shoulder the crushing added burden of overproduction and lower prices in the late 1820's.[5]

3

If cotton was king of the entire ante bellum South, rice reigned supreme at the South Carolina tidewater. Genteel Charleston could talk of little else when rice, over six cents a pound in 1818, plunged to under three cents in 1822. Gangs of slaves and prime swamp tracts went on the auction block as onerous mortgages crushed some aristocrats. After 1822 the pressure eased. Rice climbed over three cents again despite the general price decline; during the entire 1818–29 depression, rice prices fell only a bit more than the cost of living.[6]

[3] For a superb contemporary analysis, see A Democratic Republican [pseud.], *The Calhoun Doctrine, or Nullification Discussed* . . . (Charleston, 1831).
[4] See below, Appendix A, Table 2, Part 2.
[5] See below, Appendix A, Table 2, entire.
[6] See below, Appendix A, tables 1 and 2; Charlotte Ann Allston to Robert F. W. Allston, March 17, 1820, Charles Kershaw to Charlotte Ann Allston, May 11, 1823, Easterby (ed.), *South Carolina Rice Plantation*, pp. 54, 374.

Of course it is easier in retrospect than it was at the time to see that lower consumer prices offset lower rice prices. Producers with plummeting annual incomes often think they are afflicted regardless of the consumer price index; and man's conception of his economic condition, rather than what is objectively true, causes political controversy. Yet in the 1820's rice planters could see that their product was yielding good incomes. Viewed in proper perspective, rice sold for around three cents a pound in the 1820's, just as it had in most years since 1800 and would in most years until 1854. From 1816 to 1819 rice prices were abnormally high. In the decade preceding the Nullification Crisis, rice planters received close to average prices for their product.

Yields were also steady, primarily because of the almost inexhaustible swamp muck. Every year rich silt deposited by flooding rivers replenished the thick marsh mud, and if the soil showed signs of wear, some careful fertilizing usually restored it.[7] Robert Barnwell Rhett, the great rice planter and leading southern fire-eater, summed up well the steady profitability of planting the golden grain: "The lands I own," he wrote, "I have planted eleven years and have lost but one crop. Our tide swamp lands in the production of rice are the most certain in the world and the price of the commodity the least fluctuating."[8]

Thus the specter of imminent bankruptcy, so distressing in 1822, proved in the main to be a false alarm. As Robert F. W. Allston, the noted rice planter, pointed out, "the profits of a rice plantation of good size and locality, are about eight per cent per

[7] Calvin Emmons to S. Fleet, Sept. 10, 1839, Carolina Planter, Feb. 26, 1840; S Ag, VII (Feb. 1834), 67–9; Southern Patriot, Nov. 16, 1824; Easterby (ed.), South Carolina Rice Plantation, p. 36; Mendenhall, "South Carolina Agriculture," p. 338.

Albert V. House has argued that Carolina rice fields were "thin and powdered" by the 1830's. But the evidence House cites proves the reverse, according to his own indirect admission. House claims that the new method of "claying" the rice seed was the crucial way in which planters compensated for worn soil. But he admits that "strong, rich" fields could alone prosper with "claying"! In fact, the increased use of "claying" is a good indication of the continued strength of the rice fields. House, Planter Management and Capitalism in Ante-Bellum Georgia: The Journal of Hugh Frazer Grant, Ricegrower (New York, 1954), esp. pp. 20–1, 34; House (ed.), "Charles Manigault's Essay on the Open Planting of Rice," Agricultural History, XVI (October 1942), 184–93. For an example of the consistently good yields of rice fields see Account Book, Sparkman Family Papers, NC.

[8] Rhett to John Stapleton, Jan. 16, 1841, Rhett Papers, NC.

annum, independent of the privileges and perquisites of the plantation residence."[9] The "privileges and perquisites"—the mansion,
the many servants, the stables, and the food—were worth a tidy
sum in addition. Aided by these substantial profits, the bulk
of the rice gentry, although sometimes short of funds, was infrequently dragged under by the heavy debts contracted in the
days of jubilee.[10]

4

The belt of sea-island cotton, the lowcountry's secondary
money crop, ran from the Savannah to the Santee and from
the ocean to within twenty miles of the Orangeburg–Barnwell
line. Few fields of short-staple upland cotton could be found in
this coastal black belt; the long, delicate, silky fibers of sea-island
brands predominated wherever tidewater gentlemen directed their
cotton to be planted.[11] The quality of luxury cotton, however,
varied considerably within the region. Superfine cotton was
grown by a few island planters; regular sea-island cotton, slightly
less fine, was also raised on the islands; finally, planters cultivated
the far less silky mains and santee varieties on the mainland and
in the Santee River basin.

Planting even a low grade of luxury cotton gave tidewater
aristocrats one supreme advantage. The product had an independent market of its own and was relatively unaffected by overproduction of short-staple cotton. In the early nineteenth century
consumers throughout the world eagerly purchased the laces,

[9] R. F. W. Allston, *Essay on Sea Coast Crops* . . . (Charleston, 1854), p. 37.
Allston wrote this in the early 1850's, but rice prices had been the same in the
1820's. See Appendix A, Table 1. Sometimes profits ran higher. For example, Charles
Manigault averaged 12½ percent a year on his "Gowrie Plantation" in the 1830's
despite average yields. Statement of Sales, Gowrie Plantation, Manigault Plantation
Records, NC.

[10] For example, Elias Horry, one of the great rice planters, had an estate worth
$417,101 and debts of $204,896 in 1829. Horry noted that property could be sold
to pay the debts without significantly diminishing income. Horry Estate Papers in
Edward Frost Papers, LC. John Berkeley Grimball had debts of $10,000 and an
estate worth $75,000 in 1832. Grimball Diary, entry for May 23, 1832, NC. For a
superb example of the seemingly inexhaustible wealth of the rice aristocracy, see the
John Ball Papers, DU, *passim.*

[11] Whitemarsh B. Seabrook, "Memoir on the Cotton Plant," *The Proceedings of
the Agricultural Convention and of the State Agricultural Society of South Carolina* . . .
(Columbia, 1846), p. 128.

muslins, and scarves made from the sea-island staple. As a result, sea-island crops yielded rich returns, and many planters ceased taking pains with their product. The delicate fibers were ginned with stained products enclosed and tossed into a bag with potato skins, crushed seeds, and rusty jack knives. On the eve of the Panic of 1819, the worst bags of luxury cotton were only slightly higher in quality than short-staple upland cotton.

During the hard times of the 1820's, disgusted manufacturers were no longer disposed to pay high prices for a defective product. The best bags of superfine cotton commanded fancy prices throughout the depression. But the regular sea-island, mains, and santee varieties plunged over 45 percent in price from 1819 to 1822, compared to a mere 35 percent drop in the cost of living. In addition, the ravages of caterpillars destroyed several promising crops in the mid-1820's. For a time the slovenly techniques on sea-island plantations and the increasing quality of textile factories threatened to obliterate all differences between luxury and short-staple cotton.[12]

Faced with the prospect of being dragged under by the plunging price of upland cotton, coastal planters drastically changed their picking, sorting, and packing techniques to avoid staining, tangling, and bruising the delicate fibers. Furthermore, extensive fertilization salvaged much worn-out soil; some exhausted plantations, particularly on Edisto Island, were transformed into choice cotton tracts. Thin, powdery soil remained a serious problem on many plantations, and some coastal planters abandoned their land. Still, both the quality and quantity of luxury cotton production *increased* in the 1820's; hence soil exhaustion was probably not a serious problem for tidewater cotton planters. Lowcountry orators occasionally wailed about deserted lowcountry tracts. Yet most of the deserted tidewater plantations were in the inland swamp area and had been left behind when rice production on the rivers became more profitable.[13]

[12] For proof of the continued high prices of superfine cotton, see Seabrook, *A Report . . . on the Production of Fine Sea Island Cotton . . .* (Charleston, 1827). For the prices of the other two grades of sea-island cotton, see Appendix A, tables 1 and 2.

[13] The sea-island agricultural renaissance can best be followed in Seabrook's essays, cited above; Mendenhall, "South Carolina Agriculture," pp. 140ff.; and the 1828–

As a result of the extensive agricultural renaissance of the mid-1820's, the different kinds of sea-island cotton remained quality products which were not in competition with southwestern short-staple cotton. The finest long-staple cottons went into exquisite laces and muslins; the inferior mains and santees were used for the warp and the short-staple upland fiber for the weft of ordinary cotton cloth.[14] The sea-island varieties, protected by the independent uses to which they were put, declined in price an average of only 15 percent from 1822 to 1829, compared to the 36-percent drop of upland cotton, and compared to a cost-of-living decrease of 22 percent. In the overall 1818–29 period, luxury cotton prices, like rice prices, declined only slightly more than the cost of living.[15]

Still, sea-island planters were more disturbed about their financial conditions than were rice producers. The income of sea-island planters, unlike that of rice planters, was probably lower in the 1820's than it had been in the years before the 1816–19 inflation. Furthermore, luxury cotton producers, but not rice producers, suffered from the cost of fertilization and the destruction wrought by caterpillars. Luxury cotton planters continued to seek ways to meet high mortgage payments, and this search brought, in the late 1820's, the sea-island agricultural renaissance to full flower. While most sea-islanders struggled to keep the quality of their cotton above that of the coarse cottons, a few experimenters, led by Kinsey Burden, achieved the silkiest fiber the lowcountry had yet produced. In 1826 Burden sold 18,000

1832 issues of the *S Ag*. Production figures on sea-island cotton can be found in *Proceedings of the Agricultural Convention*, p. 159. Except for the 1824–6 period, when the crops were extensively injured by caterpillars, sea-island production reached all-time highs throughout the 1820's. Since these depression-streaked years were hardly the time to clear more swampland, acreage cultivated probably remained constant. Thus yields probably increased.

[14] Seabrook, "Memoir on Sea Island Cotton," *Supplement to the Proceedings of the State Agricultural Society of South Carolina* (Columbia, 1847), pp. 3–5.

[15] See below, Appendix A, Table 2, Part 3. In 1828 William Elliott claimed that sea-island planters were depressed because good prices came only in years of poor yields. But a comparison of the production figures given in *Proceedings of the Agricultural Convention*, p. 159, and the price figures given below in Appendix A, Table 1, do not bear him out. The prime cause of hard times for luxury cotton growers, as Elliott also pointed out, was the earlier inflated valuation of property and the resulting high mortgages. *S Ag*, I (Apr. 1828), 157.

pounds at $1.10 a pound. In 1827 he received $1.25 a pound. Burden's secret became the subject of a great lowcountry guessing game; at one point he almost sold it to the state legislature for $200,000. By 1830 speculation had given way to certainty. Burden's secret, everyone believed, lay in the tufted seed.

By 1832 most sea-islanders and numerous mainlanders were growing superfine cotton. The great experiment was by no means an unqualified success. Burden's technique, it turned out, required lush soil as well as proper seeds. Many planters received high prices and still failed because of poor yields. For the purposes of understanding the causes of the Nullification Controversy, their failure, which became clear well after the 1832 elections, is unimportant. Indeed, those who quickly succeeded with the new techniques were as fully in favor of nullification as those who ultimately failed; Kinsey Burden himself was a conspicuous nullifier.[16] The crucial point is that sea-island nullifiers, on the eve of nullification, were not hopelessly impoverished, but were aggressively experimenting, hopeful that the last stages of an agricultural renaissance would yield a fabulous new prosperity.[17]

5

The central economic problem of the lowcountry planters remained the old mortgages. Depleted income was almost offset by lower consumer prices; rice soil was rich and luxury cotton land was on the road to restoration; and lowcountry products were not competing with the Southwest's short-staple cotton. For these

[16] [Charleston] *Evening Post*, Oct. 9, 1832. The nullifiers had the enthusiastic support of almost all those who secured huge profits with superfine cotton, including Thomas Fripp, John R. Mathews, William Pope, Joseph Pope, Elias Vanderhorst, and Hugh Wilson, Sr. See *Proceedings of the States Rights and Free Trade Convention . . . February, 1832* (Charleston, 1832), pp. 3–4; *Charleston Mercury*, Aug. 15, 24, 1831, Sept. 12, 1832. In addition, Edisto Island, the center of the sea-island renaissance and the most successful agricultural region in the state, was a hotbed of nullification sentiment. See *S Ag*, X (Apr. 1838), 151–63. In this perspective, it is significant that Edisto Island was one of the first lowcountry areas to explode over antislavery schemes. See Brutus [Robert J. Turnbull], *The Crisis . . .* (Charleston, 1827), p. 128.

[17] The great guessing game can be followed in the *S Ag*, 1828–30. The universal experiment with superfine cotton was first pronounced a failure by Seabrook in late 1833. *S Ag*, VII (Jan. 1834), 9ff. Seabrook summed up and evaluated the Burden affair in *Supplement to the Proceedings of the State Agricultural Society*, pp. 3–5.

reasons, income from lowcountry plantations, particularly from rice plantations, was usually sufficient to meet mortgage payments. Some coastal plantations, however, did not yield enough to compensate for the folly of the boom years. One important reason was that the conditions of lowcountry agriculture limited the amount of prosperity which could be achieved.

The problems all revolved around the pesky—and fatal—mosquito. Although Negroes were apparently immune to the most deadly forms of malaria, they often were stricken with, and sometimes died of, less virulent strains.[18] The disease was particularly severe on the Savannah River. As James Hamilton, Jr., confessed, "the mortality on the River . . . is a drawback to the otherwise certain profit of our fine and fertile land." Samuel Patterson, an important Charleston rice factor, was much more explicit: "It was never expected," he noted, "that the number of their people should increase— If they could keep up the force—which in many cases they could not do—it was all they hoped."[19]

The slaves' susceptibility to malaria had devastating economic consequences. On many plantations in the Old South, the natural increase of slaves gave slaveholders a lucrative source of profits. But in the South Carolina swampland, slave births rarely exceeded slave deaths. More often the onslaught of fever led to a decrease of bondsmen, and planters had to spend thousands of dollars to buy additional slaves. The swamp diseases also led to large medical bills and often deprived slaveholders of labor at crucial times of the year.[20]

The white man's susceptibility to the deadlier forms of malaria caused equally severe economic problems. The disease-ridden

18 Dr. S. H. Dickson, "Essay on Malaria," *Proceedings of the Agricultural Convention*, p. 169. Dr. Dickson, sometimes professor at South Carolina Medical College and one of the lowcountry's leading doctors, leaves no doubt that Negroes did contract malaria. For an excellent discussion, see Kenneth M. Stampp, *The Peculiar Institution: Slavery in the Ante-Bellum South* (New York, 1956), pp. 300–2.

19 James Hamilton, Jr., to Langdon Cheves, Apr. 14, 1830, Cheves Papers, SCHS; Grimball Diary, entry for June 6, 1832.

20 David Gavin Diary, entry for Nov. 20, 1857, NC; [William Drayton], *The South Vindicated from the Treason and Fanaticism of the Northern Abolitionists* (Philadelphia, 1836), p. 121. The profitability of a natural increase of slaves is ably discussed in Alfred Conrad and John R. Meyer, "The Economics of Slavery in the Ante-Bellum South," *Journal of Political Economy*, LXVI (Apr. 1958), 95–130.

swamps forced tidewater aristocrats to depend on overseers and caused potentially good overseers to shun lowcountry employment. White overseers, particularly on rice plantations, invariably contracted malarial fever and not infrequently died of it. If an able man was willing to encounter the diseases of the swamp, he was rarely willing to endure the stigma of belonging to an inferior, degraded caste. Some skilled overseers, such as Jordan Myrick and James Kirk, climbed into the planter class. But given the conditions of lowcountry agriculture, they were exceptions. The poor lot of "needy wanderers" who became overseers were ill-equipped to handle the intricate, technical, delicate nature of rice and sea-island planting. Gross inefficiencies and expensive accidents often resulted.[21]

The prevalence of incompetent overseers made the gentry's commitment to absentee ownership a foolhardy economic gamble. When a skillful planter supervised his overseer, accidents could be minimized and yields raised. The planter's supervision, according to one contemporary observer, boosted gross income at least 10 percent. Though more owners than ever supervised their plantations from pineland villages in the 1820's, most aristocrats still left the area. The supervising planters, despite excellent intentions, could effect only limited improvements; hampered by many years of absence, they knew little about planting. Even sea-islanders often left the details of their agricultural renaissance to the overseers to work out.[22]

The crux of the matter was that lowcountry planters were very large capitalists who often despised the painstaking care and economy which a capitalistic enterprise requires.[23] The more disdainful patricians never escaped the suspicion that enthusiastic plantation management smacked of Yankee practicality. Instead of eliminating inefficiencies from their mortgage-ridden planta-

[21] The overseer problem is analyzed throughout the *S Ag*. See esp. II (Nov. 1829), 520–1, VII (Dec. 1834), 636–8, IX (Apr. 1836), 189–91, XII (Aug. 1839), 414. The economic importance of good overseers is evident in Statement of Sales, Gowrie Plantation, Savannah River, 1857–64, Manigault Plantation Records.
[22] *Charleston Mercury*, Oct. 4, 1831; *S Ag*, II (June 1829), 248–9, VII (Apr. 1834), 177ff.; "Visit to the Carse of Gowrie," Gowrie Plantation Book, Manigault Plantation Records.
[23] See the intriguing editorial by J. D. Legaré, *S Ag*, I (Aug. 1828), 357–9.

tions and economizing drastically, the gentry continued to grace
its table with choice wine and to squander time and fortune at
exclusive summer resorts. The deeper the planter fell into debt,
the more strenuously he kept up the grand style, as if trying
to conceal his embarrassments by a showy display.[24]

Capitalists who disliked capitalism, the lowcountry gentlemen
impeded the success of their own plantations. The malaria and
the currency contraction set limits to lowcountry prosperity. But
they seldom caused the bankruptcies which did occur. No economic necessity forced planters to contract ruinous debts in the
first place, to play while the plantation degenerated, to make
overseeing a despised profession, or to continue their conspicuous
display of wealth. For these reasons, lowcountry aristocrats sometimes did not prosper well enough to meet mortgage payments.

The most intriguing—and tragic—result of the gentry's economic folly was the plight of the younger generation, which
drank and idled away its time in Charleston. The older planters,
beset by mortgages and bent on extravagance, often lacked the
funds to give their children a planting interest. The "honorable"
professions—the clergy, law, medicine—were overcrowded. The
well-bred sons of the Carolina chivalry refused to enter the
"despised" professions—to become merchants or overseers or
mechanics. Unable to find "genteel" work, the cadet class of
Charleston spent more and more of their fathers' limited money,
yielding "to the baleful influence of inactivity and *ennui*," leading
the threadbare life of an aristocracy gone to seed.[25]

Yet the decadent younger gentry, the malaria-infested plantations, and the occasional mortgage foreclosures throw off a false
image of economic disaster at the South Carolina tidewater. The
cultivation of rice remained the leading lowcountry occupation;
and both rice yields and rice prices stayed at profitable levels
throughout the prenullification decade. As Whitemarsh Seabrook
summed up the more agreeable lesson of the 1820's, rice was "a
much more certain crop than Cotton, liable to few diseases, less

[24] Taylor, *Antebellum South Carolina*, pp. 17–18; *S Ag*, I (June 1828), 255, VII
(June 1834), 288; *Charleston Observer*, Oct. 3, 1827.
[25] *Southern Patriot*, Sept. 28, 1829; *City Gazette*, Dec. 23, 1831; *Charleston
Courier*, Feb. 16, 1833; *S Ag*, II (Jan., Nov., 1829), 1–7, 520.

likely to be seriously affected by physical causes, and but seldom subject to ruinous fluctuations in price."[26] Meanwhile sea-island cotton planters, although more affected by the economic depression, continued to hope that Kinsey Burden's methods would point the way to fabulous new profits in the 1830's. The boom days were over. But despite mortgages and extravagances, inefficiencies and sickness, the lowcountry gentry, in the days of nullification, remained one of the wealthiest groups in the United States.

6

If some lowcountry aristocrats were short of funds, most upcountry planters were impoverished in the 1820's. The combination of the currency contraction and the overproduction of short-staple cotton sent upland-cotton prices plunging 72 percent from 1818 to 1829, compared to a 49-percent drop in the cost of living.[27] The protective tariff, which propped up consumer prices but not the price of raw cotton, contributed to the discrepancy.

Low prices were made the more intolerable by poor yields, which in turn were caused by the piedmont's sadly depleted soil. The upcountry land was not worn out but rather washed away, stripped of its fertile clay by the effects of torrential rain on hilly land. The top soil—even the subsoil—had begun rolling down toward the sea long before the cotton era. The superficial plowing of the cotton entrepreneur speeded up the erosive process. By 1832 the piedmont was full of deserted fields choked with broom sedge and briar, and the soil which continued to be cultivated often yielded a sparse crop of thin pods.[28]

Some upcountry planters abandoned their lands and set off for the storied virgin lands of Alabama, Mississippi, and Louisiana. They could hope that on fresh southwestern land superior yields and lower costs would offset declining prices. Those who remained in South Carolina were often crushed by the old mort-

---

[26] *Southern Patriot*, Jan. 23, 1828.
[27] See below, Appendix A, Table 2, Part 3.
[28] Mendenhall, "South Carolina Agriculture," p. 184; Mills, *Statistics*, pp. 491, 637; Whitfield Brooks to Richard Singleton, Nov. 1, 1825, Singleton Family Papers, DU.

gages. One issue of the *Edgefield Hive* contained nine columns of sheriff's sales. As J. E. Colhoun described it:

> The times are so dreadful that there is no possibility of selling any kind of property . . . there is not property enough in the Dist. of Abbeville to purchase what is under execution. . . . [Ezekiel Noble's family] has had everything sold, even the beds from under them, and they are now left with only a fine house, which is . . . mortgaged . . . and nothing in it.[29]

There were many like Ezekiel Noble all over the upcountry in the 1820's.

The fresh lands of the Southwest were a devastating force against which to contend in a time of declining prices. Still, piedmont slaveholders, like tidewater aristocrats, were not merely victims of an overpowering fate. The uplanders had one supreme advantage over their lowland allies: their plantations, except on the Savannah, were healthy, and they could count on the profitable natural increase of slaves. Expanding slave families could offset declining cotton prices; masters could sell occasional bondsmen to meet mortgage payments. Added slaves could also be used to set up the gentry's children in a plantation enterprise. One leading upcountry slaveholder claimed that the cash value of the increase of slaves constituted over 10 percent of the planter's average income. In a decade of plunging cotton prices, like the 1820's, the percentage sometimes ran considerably higher. Benjamin F. Perry exaggerated only a little when he noted that in the years before the Nullification Controversy, "the greater part" of the profit from slaves came "from their increase, which is very considerable. At this time they sell well, and always bring their value at sheriff's sale, whilst everything else is sacrificed."[30]

The long-term profits from an increase of slaves allowed careful upcountry planters to prosper despite fluctuating cotton prices. The secret of the permanently successful piedmont planter,

[29] J. E. Colhoun to James Edward Calhoun, May 4, 1827, James Edward Calhoun Papers, SC; *Charleston Courier,* Oct. 3, 1828; *S Ag,* X (May 1837), 237; John Carter to Drayton, Dec. 25, 1832, Poinsett to Drayton, June 5, 1834, Drayton Papers, Historical Soc. of Pennsylvania.

[30] Perry Diary, entry entitled "Sketch of My Life," NC; J. H. Furman Plantation Journal, p. 112, DU.

as George McDuffie pointed out incessantly to visitors at his prosperous upcountry tract, was to limit the risks inherent in the operation of a nineteenth-century cotton plantation. A temporary decline of cotton prices was never disastrous if yields were kept up, if mortgages were kept down, and if the plantation grew its own supplies. When soil erosion was minimized by horizontal plowing and proper drainage, and soil exhaustion was controlled by fertilizing and then letting the land lie fallow, the amount of cotton produced could be kept relatively steady. When excessive debts were avoided, the planter was no longer at the mercy of currency fluctuations. When the plantation lived off its own produce, the planter could not be seriously injured by spiraling consumer prices. Using precisely these methods, McDuffie, starting in 1821 with 300 acres and only a few slaves, had by 1845, despite many years of extremely low cotton prices, developed a 5,000-acre plantation manned by 175 slaves.[31]

McDuffie's conservative methods aimed at steady, long-term profits; they represented the antithesis of the cotton-boom psychology. During the flush times of the post-1815 inflation, most enterprising uplanders had no use for such precautions. With cotton selling at thirty cents a pound, raising corn seemed a waste of time. Since virgin land apparently abounded, conserving soil seemed overly prudent. With profits leaping ever higher, avoiding debts seemed the sheerest folly. Like all reckless gamblers in any speculative boom, the upcountry entrepreneur gloried in his chance to seize an instant fortune.

When depression struck, the uplander paid dearly for his spree. By incurring too many debts, the planter left himself vulnerable to the worst consequences of the currency contraction. By importing his food, his clothing, and his supplies, he fell victim to the differential between the cotton and consumer price indexes. By careless plowing and by exhausting the land, he allowed his soil to flow away and his yields to drop at the very moment of low cotton prices. External economic forces crushed the upcountry planter because he left himself completely exposed to them. Not a few planters, using McDuffie's precautions and rely-

[31] *Carolina Planter*, Dec. 9, 1840; Furman Plantation Journal, p. 112.

ing on the natural increase of slaves to bolster sagging cotton income, prospered even in the depression-streaked 1820's.[32]

For many of the same reasons, the yeoman farmers in the mountain districts usually escaped the depression. Often unencumbered by debt, characteristically raising their own supplies, yeoman farmers retained their simple mode of life throughout the booms and the busts which altered the fortunes of upcountry entrepreneurs.

7

In the days of jubilee, when there seemed no limit to South Carolina's prosperity, the state embarked on a $1 million internal-improvement campaign designed to make the major river systems navigable to the North Carolina line. This grand scheme, which cost $2 million before it was finished, turned out to be a dismal failure. Above the fall line of the rivers, wagoners continued to bring goods to inland towns, avoiding the splendid but impractical canals. Below the fall line, however, where comparatively little money was spent, the river improvements and the invention of the steamboat revolutionized the system of trade in South Carolina and profoundly altered the economy of Charleston.[33]

Before 1819 and the advent of the steamboat, thousands of wagoners traveled down from the upcountry every harvest season, bringing their staples to Charleston and buying their supplies for the year. The center of Charleston's economy was upper King Street, along the neck, where hundreds of petty retailers met the men from the hills before they reached the metropolis. Here wagoners bartered cotton for goods before driving on to the city and procuring needed repairs from Charleston mechanics.

From 1819 to 1823, the wagon trade, which was both more expensive and less convenient than the steamboat traffic, dramatically shrank to one-fourth its former size. By 1828 upcountry

[32] *Ibid.;* James Edward Calhoun Diary, 1830–4, James Edward Calhoun Papers, NC; Proceeds of crop entry for 1832, Silver Bluff Plantation Stock and Crop Book, 1832–41, Hammond Papers, LC; *S Ag,* IV (Jan. 1831), 24; *City Gazette,* Sep. 22, 1831.

[33] David Kohn (ed.), *Internal Improvements in South Carolina, 1817–1828* (Washington, D.C., 1938).

wagoners rarely came to Charleston. At the fall line of the major rivers, a string of towns became economically important for the first time: Hamburg, across the Savannah from Augusta, Georgia; Columbia on the Congaree; Camden on the Wateree; Cheraw on the Pee Dee. Cotton was usually brought by land to fall-line towns, where some of it was sold to fall-line buyers and the rest consigned to Charleston merchants. The old retail center on the neck was almost deserted, its houses left tenantless, the value of its land cut in half, and grass left to grow in its streets.[34]

Some former King Street retailers successfully transferred operations to Hamburg or Columbia; others prospered on the East Bay. But the Charleston economic revolution concentrated commerce in fewer hands, squeezing out the bulk of the old King Street retailers. The days of petty barter were over. Transferring a load of goods to Columbia or setting up shop on the East Bay required a line of cash and credit which few King Streeters could raise. As the number of purchasers coming to Charleston declined, many Charleston retailers entered a prolonged season of financial misfortune.[35]

The steamboat revolution was equally unkind to the interests of Charleston mechanics. But for white laborers, the depression caused by the decreasing number of uplanders coming to the metropolis was made infinitely worse by a sudden increase of black competitors. From 1810 to 1820 the free Negro population of Charleston almost doubled; at the moment jobs declined, the number of men competing for them rose sharply. In addition, white mechanics were at a disadvantage in this competition. In a community which looked down on manual labor and detested free blacks, white mechanics, to retain self-respect, had to charge almost double the rates of the Negroes. Worse still, white laborers could not submissively obey orders or "obtrude" to solicit business without obliterating the thin line which separated them from complete degradation. By the late 1820's free Negroes and slave

<hr />

[34] *Ibid.*, p. 233; *Charleston Courier*, Oct. 8, 1824, March 13, 1828; *Southern Patriot*, May 20, 1834.

[35] Mills, *Statistics*, p. 699; *Cheraw Intelligencer*, Oct. 2, 1823; *Charleston Courier*, Dec. 3, 1824; *City Gazette*, Oct. 27, 1824; account of the Adger family in South Carolina, James Adger Papers, SCHS; circular letter of a committee appointed by a Charleston public meeting, Oct. 30, 1822, William and Benjamin Hammett Papers, DU.

artisans were driving white mechanics out of Charleston and were gaining a foothold in white-collar clerkships. By 1837 white mechanics who did not own slaves had been almost squeezed out. Hopelessly impoverished, rabid racists, often degraded in their own eyes, the Charleston mechanics were even more ripe for revolution than the retailers of King Street.[36]

The steamboat revolution, which devastated the economic prospects of Charleston's retailers and mechanics, enhanced the profits of East Bay merchants. As much cotton as ever flowed onto the Cooper River wharves; and the decline of the petty King Street cotton buyer gave import-export merchants greater control over the original purchasers of cotton. Columbia merchants, for example, often depended on East Bay financiers for a line of credit. The central tendency of the changed trade routes of the 1820's was to concentrate economic power on the East Bay as it never had been before.[37]

The solid prosperity of East Bay merchants was securely based on Charleston's stable amount of trade. Charleston's decline as a mercantile center in the 1820's was relative, not absolute. The commerce of the Carolina metropolis did not decrease; rather, it failed to rise as fast as the trade of other ports. The river systems of South Carolina did not tap so large an area as the rivers which flowed into New Orleans or Mobile or New York. These ports sped past Charleston, but the South Carolina metropolis was exporting more bales than ever in 1832. If the direct import trade from Europe declined, the indirect import trade through New York rose proportionately, and since not a few East Bay merchants had been merely agents of European firms before 1820, it mattered little that some became agents of northerners thereafter.[38] Too much must not be made of Charleston's demise. The crucial point

---

[36] U. B. Phillips (ed.), *Plantation and Frontier* . . . (2 vols.; Cleveland, 1909), II, 107; *Charleston Courier*, Nov. 22, 1822, Sept. 22, 1832; *Charleston Mercury*, May 17, 1828; *Southern Patriot*, Feb. 13, 1826; *Camden Journal*, July 2, 1831; Edward Laurens, *A Letter to . . . Whitemarsh B. Seabrook* . . . (Charleston, 1835), pp. 9–10; James O'Neale to Poinsett, March 3, 1837, Poinsett Papers, Historical Soc. of Pennsylvania.

[37] [Columbia] *Southern Times*, Dec. 1, 1830.

[38] "Answer to Query 38," Ogilby Papers. Some merchants undoubtedly made *more* money when Charleston traded directly with Europe. But since the great merchants were almost all unionists, their decline in income had nothing to do with bringing on the nullification crusade.

is that while the changed trade routes inside the state undermined the prosperity of Charleston's mechanics and retailers, the commerce flowing through the port stayed relatively constant, and the great East Bay merchants remained as affluent as ever.

8

The import-export merchants prospered, but South Carolina benefited very little from their good fortune. In the early 1830's East Bay magnates did finance a railroad to Hamburg, designed to protect their share of the Savannah River trade. This important exception aside, Charleston financiers did not extensively reinvest in the Carolina economy. On the contrary, successful Charleston merchants, who were characteristically emigrants from the North or from Europe, usually returned home with their newly won fortunes in order to escape the ravages of Charleston's yellow fever. The "stranger's fever," as yellow fever was appropriately called in Charleston, vied with malarial fever in the damage it inflicted on the Carolina economy.[39]

Outsiders controlled not only East Bay countinghouses but also most aspects of South Carolina's commerce. Northerners owned the greater part of Charleston's shipping, controlled the bulk of the insurance policies, and dominated the upcountry peddler trade. Profits from all these enterprises were customarily spent outside the state. The resulting specie drain was one of the heaviest prices planters paid for concentrating capital in agriculture in the days of jubilee.[40]

The gentry made the problem worse by its migratory habits. Each summer vacationing aristocrats spent over $500,000 outside South Carolina. Every year hordes of emigrants from the upcountry carried away their life savings on their trek to the Southwest.[41]

The protective tariff administered the final blow. Customs offi-

---

[39] Samuel Derrick, *Centennial History of the South Carolina Railroad* (Columbia, 1930), chs. 1–9; *Charleston Mercury*, Sept. 17, 1831; *Southern Patriot*, Feb. 18, 1826; "Answer to Query 33," Ogilby Papers.

[40] *City Gazette*, May 29, 1832; *Charleston Courier*, March 24, 1825; *Georgetown Gazette*, Sept. 15, 1826.

[41] *Southern Patriot*, Aug. 5, 1826.

cers at the port of Charleston annually collected over $500,000 more in duties than the federal government spent in South Carolina, thereby adding impressively to the flow of capital to wealthier sections of the country. Carolinians exaggerated the tariff's pernicious effect on their economy. Still, by bolstering consumer prices and draining away specie, the tariff contributed to the hard times in South Carolina in the early 1830's.[42]

The specie drain from South Carolina was rendered more destructive by the upcountry's lack of adequate banking facilities. The rise of a moneyed economy in the fall-line towns demanded a greater number of upcountry banks. Yet in the years before the Nullification Controversy, the expansion of piedmont banking lagged far behind the expansion of piedmont trade.

In the 1820's South Carolina's four private banks were all concentrated in Charleston and controlled by East Bay merchants. Charleston private banks issued few long-term mortgages; they helped finance Charleston's far-flung trade by granting short-term loans to the mercantile community. Since Charleston entrepreneurs were convinced that continued favors from New York merchants depended on reliable South Carolina bank notes, they kept a close rein on paper-money issues. A branch of the United States bank, also located in Charleston and soberly managed by East Bay magnates, employed its resources in providing bills of exchange on other cities.[43]

The final Carolina bank, the Bank of the State of South Carolina, was owned and operated by the state government, with branch offices in Charleston, Georgetown, Camden, and Columbia in the 1820's. Despite its two upcountry branches, however, several factors restrained the Bank of the State from pouring many paper dollars into the piedmont's economy. The bank's charter

[42] Mills, *Statistics*, pp. 163–4; *Southern Patriot*, July 1, 1823; *City Gazette*, Dec. 21, 1824.

[43] *Southern Patriot*, July 3, 1823; Report of the state House of Representatives' Committee on Banks, Dec. 15, 1826, Banking Papers, South Carolina Archives; George Trenholm to Robert F. W. Allston, Apr. 18, 1837, Easterby (ed.), *South Carolina Rice Plantation*, pp. 69–73. For proof that East Bay merchants controlled Charleston banking, compare the annual lists of boards of directors with the ship-arrival columns in the Charleston newspapers. The surviving Charleston City Directories, collected in the SC, also list the bank directors.

limited its loans to no more than double its capital. Furthermore, the bank was required to bestow roughly equal favors on up-country and lowcountry borrowers. Most important of all, the bank's funds were largely tied up in long-term agricultural mort-gages. The Bank of the State was essentially a restricted agricul-tural loan office; it could offer few new loans to upcountry entrepreneurs.

Stephen Elliott, a leading rice planter and botanist, was presi-dent of the Bank of the State throughout the 1820's. The bank's inherently limited loans were restricted even more by his exces-sively conservative policies. Elliott's bank management provides a classic example of the tidewater aristocracy's ambivalence to-ward capitalistic enterprise. The bank president, a radical inno-vator in banking theory, advocated divorcing paper money from specie and issuing an expanded rag currency based on landed values. Conservative bankers considered Elliott's essays a danger-ous bit of wild-eyed "agrarianism."

However, in practice, Elliott headed one of the most soberly run banks in the United States. With loans legally limited to twice the bank's capital, he could dole out new paper dollars only by calling in stagnant old debts. Yet most of the debtors were Elliott's fellow planters, and the gracious bank president preferred renew-ing their loans to foreclosing their mortgages. The bank dealt in gentlemanly fashion with its customers, but had little capital with which to revitalize the economy. In the end, Stephen Elliott's bank reflected his genteel codes rather than his entrepreneurial theory.[44]

With the bank supplying an insufficient quantity of bank notes, the South Carolina upcountry had to look elsewhere for its cir-culating medium. Usually planters used the depreciated paper dol-lars of North Carolina and Georgia. This unstable rag money subjected uplanders to damaging currency fluctuations. Moreover, other states' dollars were useless when South Carolina tax col-lectors paid their annual visit. South Carolina taxes were payable

[44] Report of the Committee on Ways and Means, Dec. 7, 1830, House Journal, 1830, pp. 119–21, South Carolina Arch. Elliott's essays on banking and most of the documents on the Bank of the State are available in *A Compilation of . . . Documents in Relation to the Bank of the State . . .* (Columbia, 1848). The Bank of the State's original charter is in Thomas Cooper and D. J. McCord (eds.), *Statutes at Large of South Carolina* (10 vols.; Columbia, 1836–41), VIII, 24–31.

in South Carolina bank notes, and South Carolina dollars commanded a fancy premium when they were traded for Georgia or
North Carolina notes. The scarcer the South Carolina notes, the
more they were hoarded, and currency contracted and tax problems multiplied. The vicious circle of conservative banking could
be as destructive as the booms and busts of wildcat financiers.[45]

The lack of adequate upcountry banking facilities caused particularly serious problems in the fall-line towns. New trading
centers could not flourish when merchants had little access to
short-term loans. With only the meager funds of the Columbia
branch of the Bank of the State at their disposal, Columbia merchants were forced to borrow funds from Charleston banks, which
were controlled by East Bay financiers who required the signature
of a Charleston merchant on all notes. Charleston merchants
charged 2½ percent interest for their services, and Columbia
merchants took a lower profit or passed the charge on to planters;
the piedmont suffered either way. With no banks of their own,
Hamburg merchants had to borrow funds from Augusta banks,
which were controlled by rival Augusta financiers; this gave
Augusta a decisive advantage in the competition for control of the
upper Savannah River trade. Cheraw's merchants, also forced to
operate without a bank, suffered in similar fashion.[46]

The state legislature sporadically tried to redress the banking
imbalance. In the early 1820's Hamburg and Cheraw won private
bank charters. Irresponsible entrepreneurs quickly captured the
Cheraw bank, and it failed a few months after opening its doors.
Meanwhile Henry Schultz, the eccentric founder of Hamburg,
preferred to open his own bank rather than accept the specie-
paying requirement of the state bank charter. Schultz issued paper
money based on cotton rather than gold, and was crushed by his
Augusta rivals.[47]

[45] *Pendleton Messenger*, Oct. 24, 1821; *Charleston Courier*, July 19, 1823; *Southern Patriot*, Dec. 18, 1823; *Compilation of Documents of the Bank of the State*, pp.
619ff.

[46] *Southern Times*, July 29, 1830; *Charleston Courier*, Sept. 18, 1828; *Pendleton
Messenger*, Sept. 22, 1830; *Cheraw Intelligencer*, Nov. 12, 1824; Petition of the Town
of Hamburg, 1826, Banking Papers, South Carolina Arch.

[47] Petition of the Town of Cheraw, Oct. 8, 1827, Banking Papers, South Carolina
Arch.; Charles G. Cordle, "The Bank of Hamburg, South Carolina," *Georgia Historical Quarterly*, XXIII (July 1939), 148–53.

In the mid-1820's several upcountry towns entered bids for bank charters. But private banks would compete with the state's bank, and whereas private banking profits enriched individuals, the Bank of the State contributed close to $100,000 each year to the public treasury. The legislators were torn between their loyalty to the Bank of the State and their recognition of the need for expanded upcountry banking facilities.

In 1826, and again in 1827, the legislators attempted a compromise. The state offered capitalists the chance to buy several million dollars' worth of stock in the Bank of the State provided that $1 million were subscribed. The state would retain its previous investment and its previous profits. Private subscribers would augment the bank's capital and receive only a proportionate share of increased profits. Meanwhile the increased banking capital could expand piedmont loans.[48]

The compromise, while perfectly fulfilling the public interest, failed to take into account the desires of private capitalists. Charleston merchants had no wish to invest in an agricultural loan office and every reason to oppose piedmont mercantile banking. Upcountry merchants wanted a bank of their own, not the chance to divide loans with upcountry planters. South Carolina planters were more interested in paying off mortgages than in buying bank stock. Private individuals never subscribed close to the requisite $1 million, and the state legislature withdrew the offer. South Carolina entered the decade of the 1830's with the same unbalanced banking structure.[49]

Thus the combination of a heavy specie drain and an inadequate upcountry banking system limited the circulating currency in South Carolina and intensified the piedmont's economic depression. The shortage of hard money was in large part a reflection of the colonial nature of the South Carolina economy. Yet there was no *economic* reason why more upcountry banks could not be chartered, why aristocrats had to spend so freely on summer jaunts, why Charlestonians could not recapture control of their own countinghouses. The *exaggerated* scarcity of circulating cur-

[48] *Statutes at Large,* VIII, 53–6.
[49] *Ibid.,* VIII, 57.

rency was another way in which South Carolinians helped to weaken themselves by questionable economic practices.

9

By 1832 the Carolinians had begun a hesitant campaign to revive their economy. In the upcountry a few planters experimented with horizontal plowing and proper drainage in order to reduce the destructive effects of erosion. At tidewater summer villages slowly multiplied as aristocrats wandered home to supervise their plantations. In Charleston native Carolinians began their reconquest of the East Bay countinghouses. By 1832 Columbia had finally received a private bank charter, and Hamburg had at last been given an agency of the Bank of the State. Despite these hopeful signs, however, slovenly planting techniques, absenteeism, idle younger sons, and inadequate upcountry banking continued to persist.

In one sense, the campaign against the tariff was the most articulate expression of South Carolina's slowly awakening desire to end the avoidable aspects of the depression of the 1820's. The nullification crusade came at a moment of transition in South Carolina's economic history, and the fury of the campaign was in part an intriguing manifestation of the nullifiers' doubts about whether they could achieve an aggressive, efficient capitalist system. Nullifiers often declared the tariff doubly pernicious because it gave bounties to contemptible northern materialists. This angry rhetoric scarcely concealed their gnawing fear that genteel southerners could never again flourish in a nation Yankee entrepreneurs dominated.

But the deeper economic cause of the nullifiers' crusade was the indigence which afflicted Carolinians by the thousands. Throughout the state, citizens in danger of losing land, shops, and slaves focused their frustration and anger on the protective tariff. The white mechanics, engaged in a degrading and unsuccessful competition with Negro laborers; the Charleston retailers, impoverished by the cessation of the upcountry wagon trade; the piedmont cotton planters, overwhelmed by lower prices and declining yields—all prayed that tariff reform would stave off financial disaster.

At the South Carolina tidewater, rice and luxury cotton planters, like most southern agriculturalists, spent many evenings cursing the tariff. Yet it must be stressed that Carolina nullifiers pushed the South's antitariff crusade to a revolutionary extreme which most southerners repudiated. The question is not whether the lowcountry gentry opposed the tariff but rather why its opposition took so violent a form. A minority of tidewater gentlemen, upset by their own imminent bankruptcy or alarmed by the plight of their penniless offspring, had sufficient economic reasons for risking a war to obtain tariff reform.

But most rice and luxury cotton planters prospered in the 1820's, and many sea-islanders anticipated better profits in the 1830's. Seen from a narrowly economic viewpoint, fabulously wealthy planters like the Burdens and the Heywards, the Seabrooks and the Manigaults, were hardly the men one would expect to embrace a revolution. Theirs was not a crusade which fed on the despair of deprivation.

3

A Disturbing Institution

A society reveals its deepest anxieties when it responds hysterically
to a harmless attack. The South Carolina lowcountry's morbid
sensitivity to the relatively undeveloped abolitionist crusade in the
1820's is a case in point. The northern antislavery campaign, although slowly gaining strength in the years before the Nullification Controversy, remained a distant threat in 1832. Yet during
the prenullification decade, the Carolina tidewater was periodically
in an uproar over the slavery issue. In the 1820's lowcountry congressmen delivered fire-eating harangues at any mention of the
subject. And in the early 1830's the lowcountry gentry embraced
the nullifiers' cause partly to win constitutional protection against
a nascent abolitionist crusade. Throughout the period, the discrepancy between the abolitionists' innocuous attack and the slaveholders' frenzied response was a measure of the guilt and fear
which made Negro slavery a profoundly disturbing institution in
ante bellum South Carolina.

2

During the years from 1820 to 1832, only the most prescient
Americans realized they were witnessing the first signs of a growing crusade against slavery. In the benevolent reform empire which
stretched along the eastern seaboard, idealists were more concerned with temperance and Sunday schools than with the plight
of American Negroes. Those reformers who were distressed by
racial problems usually soothed their consciences by joining the

American Colonization Society. The society, dedicated to removing free Negroes from the United States, had at best only a tangential interest in freeing southern slaves.

However, as the twenties progressed a handful of antislavery crusaders initiated the campaign which would convulse the nation's politics in the years ahead. In 1821 Benjamin Lundy began his influential newspaper, *The Genius of Universal Emancipation*. In 1828 young William Lloyd Garrison assumed control of the Bennington (Vermont) *Journal of the Times*, wrote his first antislavery editorial, and collected over 2,000 signatures on his first antislavery petition. In 1829 David Walker, a militant free Negro, published his *Appeal*, urging slaves to revolt against their masters. Finally, on January 1, 1831, Garrison founded his bellicose newspaper, the *Liberator*. By the eve of the Nullification Controversy, the Nat Turner Revolt and its alleged connection with Garrison's writings had made the *Liberator* notorious in the nation's households.

Yet by 1832 Garrison had gained little support for his crusade. When Garrison organized the New England Anti-Slavery Society at the end of 1831, he managed to persuade only eleven disciples to sign the constitution. The founding fathers could contribute little more than their zeal; not one of them could have scraped together over $100. In the ensuing year, the Garrisonian onslaught continued to lack both funds and followers.

A more significant development of the prenullification years was the mounting evidence that the slavery issue could not be kept out of national politics. The 1820's commenced with a long congressional debate over slavery during the Missouri Controversy. Frightened by the savage emotions which the debates revealed, leading American statesmen attempted to bury the issue. But in 1824 the Ohio state legislature raised the subject again by proposing a national program of gradual emancipation. In 1826 a presidential proposal for a delegation to the Panama Congress of Spanish-American nations touched off a stormy discussion. The delegates would have to hobnob with the successful slave conspirators of San Domingo, and the United States might appear to sanction servile insurrection. In 1827 the American Colonization Society's request for congressional aid inspired another ominous dispute over slavery. It was fitting that the famed Hayne-Webster debate of 1830, with its far-ranging discussion of public issues, should focus at last on the vexing problem which the nation could not avoid.[1]

It must be emphasized again that most Americans—including most southerners—paid little heed to these nagging controversies. The slavery issue would not become a major national political problem until the gag-rule disputes of the mid-1830's. The point is that the South Carolina lowcountry was too uneasy about slavery to tolerate the slightest signs of a growing abolitionist attack. One leading Charlestonian wrote, as early as 1823, "all the engines and all the means and machines, which talent, fanaticism, false charity, fashionable humanity, or jealousy or folly can invent, are in dreadful operation and array."[2]

South Carolinians raged at the first indications of an antislavery crusade partly because they viewed emancipation with dread. Abolition conjured up grotesque specters of plunder, rape, and murder. The slave, too barbaric and degraded to adjust peaceably to freedom, seemed certain to declare race war the moment he threw off his chains. Moreover, in South Carolina alone, $80 million worth of slave property would be wiped out. Upcountry planters, like most slaveholders, could at least hope to salvage landed property from the wreck of emancipation. But tidewater gentlemen feared they would lose their huge investment in improved land as well as a fortune in slave property. Negroes would never work efficiently without bondage and the fatal swamps could never be cultivated without Negroes. "The richest, most productive land in the State, must be forever left waste," wrote Frederick Dalcho, a conservative Charlestonian. ". . . Can we reasonably be expected to submit to this state of things? Certainly not by reasonable men."[3] Abolition posed a greater *economic* threat than the abominations of the highest protective tariff.

The possibility of an abolitionist triumph was enough to make

[1] The best survey of the abolitionist movement is in Louis Filler, *The Crusade Against Slavery, 1830–1860* (New York, 1960). See also Dwight L. Dumond, *Anti-Slavery: The Crusade for Freedom in America* (Ann Arbor, 1961).

[2] Caroliniensis [Robert J. Turnbull and Isaac E. Holmes], *Caroliniensis on the Appeal of a British Seaman* . . . (Charleston, 1823), p. 24.

[3] *Practical Considerations Founded on the Scriptures, Relative to the Slave Population of South Carolina* (Charleston, 1823), pp. 7–8.

Negro slavery the most explosive issue an American Congress has ever faced. The fear of ultimate emancipation, however, pervaded the South throughout the ante bellum period, and became more intense as the abolitionist crusade grew stronger. The Carolina lowcountry's intransigence in the 1820's was more explicitly a reaction to the first stages of the conflict over slavery. The real issue in the period of transition was not so much whether slavery should be abolished but rather whether slavery could be discussed. If emancipation could unleash a race war, antislavery agitation could inspire a servile insurrection. An abolitionist attack would also force planters to defend slavery, and many of them regarded slavery as an abomination which should never be defended. The tidewater gentry had every reason to tremble at a full-scale discussion of the slavery issue; and its acute anxiety over facing the issue made the era of nullification a time of great crisis along the South Carolina coast.

3

In the late eighteenth century, such southerners as Thomas Jefferson and James Madison had helped to forge an American liberal philosophy which was still dogma in South Carolina during the years of the Nullification Controversy. Before the 1830's southerners often admitted that slavery had no place in a land which assumed that men had a natural right to life, liberty, and the pursuit of happiness. Moreover, they could never forget that insurrection was legitimate if men were deprived of their natural rights. The sight of a slave listening to a Fourth of July oration chilled the bravest southerner. "The celebration of the *Fourth of July*, belongs *exclusively* to the white population," wrote a leading Charlestonian. ". . . In our speeches and orations, much, and sometimes more than is politically necessary, is said about personal liberty, which Negro auditors know not how to apply, except by running the parallel with their own condition."[4]

Of course abolitionists insisted that the theory which the Fourth celebrates belongs to Negroes as well as whites. That assertion, no matter how dispassionately presented, made slaveholders con-

[4] *Ibid.*, p. 33n.

sider any abolitionist tract "incendiary" if it reached the eyes of a slave. Thomas Jefferson's felicitous Declaration of Independence seemed almost as dangerous as David Walker's fiery *Appeal*.

The South Carolina tidewater, with its high proportion of slaves and its considerable number of African imports, was always more apprehensive about slave revolts than any other region in the Old South. Thus the lowcountry gentry watched the Missouri debates with considerable concern. Governor John Geddes of Charleston warned the state legislature of 1820 that "the Missouri question . . . has given rise to the expression of opinions and doctrines respecting this specie of property, which tend not only to diminish its value, but also to threaten our safety." He called for measures which would "oppose at the threshold, everything likely in its consequences to disturb our domestic tranquility." The lawmakers responded by enacting laws designed to halt the increase of free Negroes. South Carolina masters were no longer permitted to free their slaves, and colored freemen were denied the right to enter the state. The legislature also provided heavy penalties for distributing "incendiary" papers. But as South Carolinians soon discovered, these laws were in no way sufficient to keep at least some slaves from taking in deadly earnest the cardinal tenets of the white man's political dogma.[5]

4

The nullification crusade had many heroes. Still, the man most responsible for bringing South Carolina to the boiling point was not a great planter-politician, such as John C. Calhoun or James Hamilton, Jr., but a lowly Charleston mulatto named Denmark Vesey. The tragic slave conspiracy which Vesey inspired, although completely crushed in 1822, remained in 1832 and long thereafter a searing reminder that all was not well with slavery in South Carolina.[6]

[5] Message of Nov. 27, 1820, Governors Papers, South Carolina Arch.; *Statutes at Large*, VII, 459–60.
[6] Unless otherwise noted, the following account of the Vesey Conspiracy is based on the standard published sources: Lionel H. Kennedy and Thomas Parker, *An Official Report of the Trials of Sundry Negroes Charged with an Attempt to Raise an Insurrection . . .* (Charleston, 1822); [James Hamilton, Jr.], *Negro Plot. An Account of the Late Intended Insurrection Among a Portion of the Blacks in the City of Charles-*

Early in the nineteenth century Denmark Vesey purchased his freedom with a lottery jackpot and prospered as a Charleston carpenter. But freedom and prosperity were not enough. The aging mulatto seethed at the enslavement of his numerous wives and many children, and fumed at the stigma of inferiority under which his race labored. A brilliant man, well traveled and well read, Vesey found abundant evidence in the Bible, in American political theory, and in the congressional debates on slavery during the Missouri Controversy to prove the immorality of slavery and the legitimacy of revolt. As a free Negro he could travel as he pleased, up and down the coastal black belt, and through the byways and into the dark corners of Charleston's slums. An eternal gadfly, he relentlessly attacked Negroes who endured racial insults. If a slave stepped into the street to allow a white man to pass, Vesey "would rebuke him, and observe that all men were born equal, and that he was surprised that anyone would degrade himself by such conduct; that he would never cringe to the whites, nor ought anyone who had the feelings of a man. When answered, We are slaves, he would sarcastically and indignantly reply, 'You deserve to remain slaves.' "[7]

---

ton, South Carolina (Boston, 1822); *Niles Weekly Register*, XXIII (Sept. 7, 1822), 10.

For the purposes of understanding the Nullification Controversy, the most important aspect of the Vesey Conspiracy was its impact on the political behavior of the low-country gentry. I have chosen to describe the conspiracy as the South Carolinians themselves viewed it. The planters' beliefs about the affair, rather than what was objectively true, produced their intransigence in the face of abolitionists.

There remains, however, substantial doubts about whether the conspiracy was as widespread as Charlestonians believed, doubts that were expressed at the time by Governor Thomas Bennett and have been recently re-emphasized by Professor Richard Wade. Bennett believed that a serious conspiracy was afoot, but he doubted that it involved more than eighty Negroes and questioned whether it ever came close to being consummated. Wade, going a step further, seems to disbelieve in any conspiracy; the Vesey affair, he writes, "was probably never more than loose talk by aggrieved and embittered men." In my judgment, Bennett's position, but not Wade's, is consistent with all the evidence. While the terrorized community exaggerated the extent of the danger, there was, in fact, a conspiracy worth getting excited about. Since the evidence is complex and technical, I will deal with it in a separate essay, to be published shortly. For now, the important point is that Bennett's contemporaries almost universally condemned his position and repudiated his leadership. For Bennett's opinion, see his Message #2 to the state legislature, Nov. 28, 1822, Governors Papers, South Carolina Arch. For Wade's verdict, see his "The Vesey Plot: A Reconsideration," *Journal of Southern History*, XXX (May 1964), 143–61. South Carolina's reaction to Bennett is evident in the Cheves-Potter correspondence, 1822, Cheves Papers, and *City Gazette*, Dec. 4, 5, 10, 1822.

[7] Kennedy and Parker, *Official Report*, p. 19.

When Vesey grew tired of discussing the Declaration of Independence on the streets, he discoursed on the Bible at the
Negroes' African Church. Many of the city's slaves had erected
the church in Charleston's suburbs in December 1821. The
Charleston congregation was connected with Philadelphia's
African Methodist Society; the tie with Philadelphia Negroes
ranked with Vesey's reading of the Missouri debates as a rich
source of abolitionist ideas.[8] At the church and in his home, Vesey
preached on the Bible, likening the Negroes to the Children of
Israel, and quoting passages which authorized slaves to massacre
their masters. Joshua, chapter 4, verse 21, was a favorite citation:
"And they utterly destroyed all that was in the city, both man
and woman, young and old, and ox, and sheep, and ass, with the
edge of the sword."

When preaching and logic failed, the rebel chief employed lies
and threats. Sometimes he maintained that Congress had freed
the slaves during the Missouri Controversy; sometimes he claimed
that San Domingo had promised to send reinforcements to help
Carolina Negroes win another race war; sometimes he threatened
to murder any Negro who did not join the crusade. Powerful and
unscrupulous, given to fits of rage and violence, Vesey seemed,
even to Negroes he could not convince, a bloody dictator whose
command they could not question. Conspirators claimed to fear
him more than they did their masters—sometimes more than their
God.

The secret of Vesey's charismatic power was his skillful fusion
of the high ideals of the Age of Reason with the ruthless savagery
of a barbaric chief. His most important lieutenant, Gullah Jack,
made the amalgam more weird and potent by supplying a pipe-
line to the African gods. Possessed of tiny limbs, which looked
grotesque despite his small frame, Gullah Jack had enormous
whiskers, which would have seemed monstrous on the hulking
Denmark Vesey. No witch doctor ever looked more the part.
Born in Angola, inheriting the tribal role of conjurer and physi-

---

[8] Richard Furman to Thomas Bennett, n.d. [early fall 1822], Furman Papers, SC;
Charles C. Pinckney, *An Address Delivered in Charleston . . . the 18th August, 1829*
(Charleston, 1829), p. 20.

cian, Gullah Jack came to America along with the nearly 40,000 slaves which South Carolina imported in the early nineteenth century. In Charleston Gullah Jack remained a sorcerer whose bizarre appearance, wild gestures, and malevolent glances could terrorize the bravest slave. Recruited by Vesey early in the campaign, Gullah Jack gave each convert a portion of parched corn and ground nuts to eat on the morning of the rebellion and a crab claw to carry at the moment of revolution. These tokens, the revered witch doctor promised, would invoke the aid of the African gods and protect rebels against capture or death.

Vesey's conspiracy proved easier to organize in the compact city than on scattered plantations. Although country Negroes learned about the impending revolution, communication between plantation insurgents and their Charleston allies broke down a week before the fateful evening. Vesey lessened the difficulty by scheduling the revolution for a Sunday, the evening when some country Negroes arrived in canoes to sell goods in the town market. But in the end, the conspiracy was almost entirely confined to Charleston.

The inability to organize country slaves little dampened the conspiratorial efforts in Charleston. The deeper problem was that city slaves belonging to harsh, strict masters were rarely receptive to Vesey's overtures. Slaves who, by the indulgence of kindly owners, lived in a twilight zone between bondage and freedom responded most readily to the vision of emancipation. The conspirators were almost all either trusted house servants or slave mechanics who hired their time and controlled their own workshops. Yet depending on indulged servants was dangerous, for these slaves had the most to lose if they were caught and sometimes felt the fondest attachment to their masters. As a result, Vesey's lieutenants warned recruiters not to approach "the waiting men who receive presents of old coats, etc. from their masters," although most rebels were trusted servants. An indulged slave was both the most likely to revolt and the most likely to betray the revolution; this was the flaw in the most carefully planned ante bellum Negro conspiracy.

Vesey's hopes depended on Charleston's carelessness. Every

night the city patrol straggled through the streets, carrying only bludgeons and sheathed bayonets. The apathetic guard, composed mainly of shopkeepers, depended on the Negro liquor trade for their prosperity; these men allowed slave customers to stroll around Charleston after the curfew.[9] Conspirators patronized the right dram shops and did not worry excessively about the guard.

Equally irresponsibly, Charlestonians left their stables and arsenals unguarded. Slave draymen and kitchen boys had access to many horses, and some conspirators had quarters in livery stables; William Garner, Vesey's cavalry commander, would have no trouble finding mounts for his men. The main door of the public arsenal opposite St. Michael's Church could be reached easily from the street and readily forced open. A conspirator had a key to Mr. Duquercron's store on the neck; his establishment alone had hundreds of muskets and a large supply of powder.[10] The neck arsenal, upper guardhouse, and powder magazine were equally accessible.

The conspiracy was designed to take instantaneous advantage of Charleston's vulnerability. The rebels' elite were enrolled in six battle units responsible for the surprise attack. Rendezvousing separately yet striking simultaneously, each unit was assigned a key position to capture. Denmark Vesey and Peter Poyas would converge on the main guardhouse from opposite directions. Each leader would masquerade as a white man (Vesey had had the foresight to order a pair of excellent white wigs), and they hoped to stride into the guardhouse unchallenged. If they were questioned, their armies would not be far behind. After they captured the guardhouse, Poyas and Vesey would seize the nearby arsenal and pass out guns to the conspirators. Meanwhile Gullah Jack's band would take Duquercron's store, Ned Bennett's company would capture the neck arsenal, and other groups would control major roads.

As attackers rushed out, William Garner's slave cavalry would supply a defensive cover, galloping through the Charleston streets and scattering the white counterattack. In the yards of great town

---

[9] Phillips (ed.), *Plantation and Frontier*, II, 113.
[10] John Potter to Cheves, July 20, 1822, Cheves Papers.

mansions, slaves, hiding with axes and knives, would be ready to
leap out and slay masters who tried to reach the streets. The
aristocracy would pay for building its houses so well shielded
from "vulgar familiarity" with the "poor white trash." Attack,
defense, and ambush would all start at the stroke of midnight,
when the sentinel's voice in St. Michael's echoed through the city,
reassuring the slumbering gentry that all was well.

Ultimate success depended on a complete initial victory. If the
six attacking bands captured the arsenal and roads, the impoverished, poorly armed insurgents would control almost all the
weapons in Charleston and could hope to hold their own against
the tidewater aristocracy. Plans were geared for winning the battle
of Charleston; ultimate intentions were vague. Peter Poyas hoped
to hold Charleston against white counterattack. Denmark Vesey
expected the victorious rebels to sail to San Domingo.

Plans for the conspiracy had begun in 1817 when many Negroes
decided to secede from white Methodist churches and form their
own African Congregation. The rebels' hopes were temporarily
dashed when the whites broke up one Negro church in 1820. But
at the end of 1821 the new African Church in the Charleston
suburbs provided an ideal meeting ground for restless slaves. In the
late spring of 1822 Vesey formulated tentative plans. He set the
rebellion for July 14 and assigned the conspirators to the six battle
units on the basis, significantly, of their original African tribes.
Spears were readied, rendezvous stations assigned, and plans
perfected.

Then, on May 30, the first betrayal occurred. A loyal house
servant informed the authorities that William Paul had urged him
to join a servile insurrection. Paul, a distinctly secondary figure
in the conspiracy, was arrested immediately, and confessed the
next morning. His statement implicated both Mingo Harth and
Peter Poyas, two of Vesey's leading lieutenants. The two archconspirators, however, "treated the charge . . . with so much
levity . . . that the wardens . . . were completely deceived."[11]
Poyas and Harth were released, and William Paul was thrust into
solitary confinement.

[11] Confession of Bacchus Hammett, Benjamin and William Hammett Papers.

On June 8 the prisoner divulged more details. This time Ned Bennett, one of Governor Thomas Bennett's most trusted house servants, voluntarily submitted himself for questioning and coolly denied all charges. Within a matter of hours, authorities were again convinced that William Paul was lying. For the second time in ten days the rebels had deluded the authorities and barely escaped detection.

But the conspirators were alarmed by the possibility of more disclosures. Vesey moved back the date of the revolution from July 14 to June 16. Rebel leaders traveled throughout the city, warning their recruits of the imminent rebellion. Meanwhile the town guard continued to wander out aimlessly every night, and Charleston authorities continued to ignore William Paul. On June 13, with only seventy-two hours remaining until the fatal stroke of midnight, Charleston slept peacefully, blissfully unaware that a revolution was at hand.

Then, on June 14, a second house servant confessed, throwing Intendent Hamilton and Governor Bennett into frenzied activities. They ordered out five military companies on the sixteenth, commanded by Colonel Robert Y. Hayne. In the slums of Charleston, Vesey and his cohorts, frightened by the display of military power, suspended the revolution. But in the great town mansions, Charleston aristocrats spent an unforgettable night, conjuring the slightest sound into a specter of murder, rape, and plunder. By a slim margin Charleston had escaped the reality of slave revolution. The lowcountry gentry would never again forget the possibility. As Edwin C. Holland put it:

Let it never be forgotten, that "our NEGROES are truly the *Jacobins* of the country; that they are the *anarchists* and the *domestic enemy;* the *common enemy of civilized society,* and the barbarians who would, IF THEY COULD, become the DESTROYERS *of our race.*"[12]

In the next two months, thirty-five Negroes were hanged and thirty-seven others banished from the state. The doomed rebels usually wept only over their cause; Peter Poyas, when asked if

---

[12] *A Refutation of the Calumnies Circulated Against the . . . Southern States . . .* (Charleston, 1822), p. 86; Hazel Wilson MS in Theodore D. Jervey, *Robert Y. Hayne . . .* (New York, 1909), p. 132.

he wished to murder his master, only smiled. The leading conspirators usually refused to give the names of their followers.
Poyas, for example, died without betraying one member of his
supposedly large and important band. Charleston had to live with
the distressing conviction that most rebels remained at large.

This was the least important reason for the persistent uneasiness
engendered by Denmark Vesey's scheme. No Charlestonian could
forget the chilling cogency of the rebels' plan. "You cannot think
how cunningly devised the scheme was," wrote one conservative
banker. "Had the execution been as well supported, many of us
this day would not have been left to tell the tale." Plantation
owners who believed African immigrants were savages, and had a
large number of them, trembled when they remembered Gullah
Jack's witchery and the potency of old tribal loyalties. Charlestonians shuddered at the influence of the example of San Domingo
and the possibility of communication between Vesey's lieutenants
and San Domingan rebels. The treachery of some of the most
famous personal servants in the state made Carolinians wonder
whether any slave could be trusted. Governor Thomas Bennett
left his wife and children in the charge of his beloved slave Rolla
when public business called him away. Rolla turned out to be
an archconspirator. "When we have done with the fellows," said
Rolla Bennett to a fellow rebel, "we know what to do with the
wenches."[13]

But the most pervading legacy of the trauma Denmark Vesey
wrought was a compulsion to check abolitionist propaganda and
to stop congressional slavery debates. "By the Missouri question,
our slaves thought, there was a charter of liberties granted them
by Congress," wrote Robert J. Turnbull in 1827. ". . . the events
of the summer of 1822 . . . will long be remembered, as amongst
the choicest fruits of the agitation of that question in Congress."
Thomas Napier added, in 1835, "The year 1822 . . . I shall never
forget. I then had an opportunity of seeing something of the fruits
of Abolitionists. After such a sight, anyone that would advocate

[13] Kennedy and Parker, *Official Report*, p. 63; Potter to Cheves, July 16, 20, 1822,
Cheves Papers.

their principles is, in my opinion, the worst enemy of man and destitute of every Christian principle."[14]

5

The Vesey Conspiracy touched off only the most serious of the insurrection panics which rocked lowcountry South Carolina in the decade preceding nullification. On Christmas Eve, 1825, an $80,000 fire raged on King Street. Thereafter, night after night for over six months, arsonists put the torch to Charleston's wooden buildings, sometimes starting five fires in one evening. In late January the city council offered a $1000 reward for the capture of the incendiaries; in mid-February angry mobs almost lynched suspected arsonists. Slaves were universally blamed, and at least three Negroes were convicted. Before the nightly terror ended, a $100,000 blaze in mid-June burned away more of King Street.[15]

The Charleston Fire Scare of 1826 was in some ways as disquieting as the Vesey affair. The 1822 conspiracy, despite the evidence of careful planning, had an air of grotesque fantasy. Yet if some Carolinians could not believe that their slaves would start a race war, every slaveholder, no matter how skilled and humane, was occasionally bothered by passive resistance and petty sabotage. An unorganized campaign in which vengeful individual Negroes set nightly fires seemed entirely plausible. The Charleston Fire Scare also renewed all the distressing emotions of the Vesey Conspiracy. As one observer put it, "it is vain to conceal, what every trifling incident brings to our notice, that there are many who dread the scenes of 1822."[16]

Charlestonians, while alarmed by the events of 1822 and 1826, were reassured when the contagion did not spread extensively to the country. Although a slave conspiracy was easier to organize in

[14] [Turnbull], *The Crisis*, p. 133; *Charleston Mercury*, Sept. 17, 1835.

[15] The Charleston Fire Scare can be followed most conveniently in the *Southern Patriot*, esp. Dec. 24, 1825, Jan. 27, Feb. 4, 8, 28, March 6, Oct. 3, 1826. See also Williams-Chestnut-Manning Papers for 1826, *passim.*, SC; James Edward Calhoun Diary, entry for Jan. 16, 1826, SC; William A. McDowell to A. Alexander, Jan. 23, 1826, Presbyterian Moderators Coll., Historical Soc. of Pennsylvania; *City Gazette*, Jan. 27, 1826.

[16] *Southern Patriot*, Oct. 16, 1826.

the city, it was also easier to repel; in the summer Negroes barely outnumbered whites in Charleston, but numerically overwhelmed them on lowcountry plantations. The fancied freedom from plantation conspiracy was rudely shattered in 1829 when "an insurrectionary spirit" in Georgetown was "accidentally discovered . . . barely in time to obviate the terrible consequences of contemplated insurrection." For a time, Georgetown jails were packed with suspects. ". . . you must take care and save Negroes enough for the rice crop,'" remarked one Charlestonian, only a little facetiously. At least six rebels, and perhaps many more, were convicted and hanged.[17]

After the conspiracy was discovered, the town council of Georgetown petitioned the state legislature for a $5000 town guard. The appropriation was granted in 1829 despite heavy upcountry opposition. A year later Georgetown planters begged the legislature for further protection. Their appeal amounted to a confession that their slaves seemed almost out of control. The Senate's Committee on Finance reported that "the spirit of Rebellion has been smothered not quelled," and warned that if the guard were removed, "all the elements which formerly contributed to the unfortunate state of things in 1829 will react with greater violence." The committee listed the incendiary elements: "The existence of insubordination among the slaves, the immense number of that class of population in the surrounding county, the sparseness of the White population, the extreme sickliness of the climate in the summer season and consequently the almost total desertion of the Town during that period." But in 1830 the upcountry blocked the appropriation, leaving Georgetown with only its sketchy patrols to protect the nervous gentry.[18]

The Georgetown Conspiracy, like the Vesey plot, was blamed

[17] James Petigru to Joseph W. Allston, misdated as Apr. 17, 1829, James Petigru Carson (ed.), *Life, Letters and Speeches of James Louis Petigru, The Union Man of South Carolina* (Washington, D.C., 1920), p. 66. Information on the Georgetown conspiracy was kept out of the newspapers. One can follow the developments only in the legislative petitions, messages, and journals in the South Carolina Arch. See esp. Petition of Town Council of Georgetown, 1829, in Slavery Insurrection Papers; Miller's Message #2 to State Legislature, Dec. 3, 1830, Governors Papers; Senate Journal, 1830, pp. 118–19.

[18] Senate Journal, 1829, p. 60; *ibid.*, 1830, pp. 118–19; House Journal, 1830, pp. 222–6; *Statutes at Large*, VII, 451–60.

on northern abolitionists. The chief mischief makers, claimed rice planters, were Yankee peddlers who met slaves at night, traded them liquor for stolen plantation supplies, and filled their ears with talk of civil rights during wild, drunken sessions. Charles C. Pinckney, one of the great rice planters, estimated after fifty years of experience that 25 percent of his rice was annually pilfered. A group of leading Carolinians unanimously agreed in 1829 that many slaves were drunkards and that liquor was often paid for with stolen goods. A drunken slave cavorting with Yankee traders was hardly a sight fit to make slaveholders sleep easily at night.[19]

The disturbances of 1822, 1826, and 1829 concerned the low-country, but the Nat Turner Revolt of 1831 affected slaveholders all over South Carolina. In Virginia, Nat Turner, with more than seventy slaves, murdered almost sixty whites in the most successful slave rebellion of the ante bellum years. Although it never spread to South Carolina, the possibility of contagion created a serious panic over insurrection. In Columbia a vigilance association offered a $1,500 reward for the capture of anyone distributing incendiary pamphlets; in Camden the patrol was ordered to maneuver with added vigor; in Laurens two slaves were convicted for allegedly announcing what they would do if Turner came their way; in Union "a great many negroes" were imprisoned and the women and children gathered in one place to be better guarded; in Charleston wild rumors of bloody Cheraw and Georgetown uprisings forced Robert Y. Hayne and Henry L. Pinckney to issue soothing statements. In the wake of the panic over Turner, the legislature approved a one-hundred-man cavalry unit, called the Charleston Horse Guard, to protect the nervous city. At least one upcountry county set up its own cavalry force.[20]

To Carolinians, the causes of Turner's revolt were almost as

[19] Senate Journal, 1830, pp. 118–19; Charleston Mercury, Oct. 6, 1829; S Ag, II (Nov. 1829), 525; Proceedings of the Temperance Society of Columbia, S.C. . . . (Columbia, 1829); Seabrook, An Essay on the Management of Slaves . . . (Charleston, 1834), p. 8.

[20] Charleston Mercury, Oct. 4, Dec. 9, 1831; T. J. Withers to Miller, Sept. 29, 1831, Chestnut-Manning-Miller Papers, SCHS; Rosannah P. Rodgers to David S. Rodgers, Oct. 29, 1831, William W. Renwick Papers, DU; Samuel Townes to George Townes, Oct. 8, 1831, Townes Family Papers, SC; Statutes at Large, VIII, 560; Camden Journal, Feb. 25, 1832.

frightening as the possibility that it might spread. In a widely circulated letter to Governor Hamilton of South Carolina, Governor John Floyd of Virginia claimed that the "spirit of insubordination" originated among "Yankee peddlers and traders" who told Negro drinking companions "that all men were born free and equal." The insurrectionary impulse matured, continued Floyd, in Negro churches, where black preachers discoursed on the Bible and distributed antislavery tracts. Black savages turned madmen by evangelical Christianity and abolitionist "fanatics"—this seemed to Carolinians the crucial cause of Turner's uprising as well as of all the others.[21]

Uneasy, even in decades of calm, because of the heavy concentration of Negroes, lowcountry South Carolina faced four serious slave disturbances in the ten years preceding the Nullification Crisis. These recurrent conspiracies seemed particularly alarming because they followed on the heels of the first signs of an antislavery attack. The Denmark Vesey Conspiracy occurred two years after the Missouri congressional debates; the Nat Turner Revolt occurred less than a year after the appearance of Garrison's notorious *Liberator*. By 1832 the lowcountry gentry understandably believed that a slight growth of antislavery "fanaticism" immediately led to mounting cases of servile insurrection.

In the longer perspective of ante bellum history, the decade which began with Denmark Vesey and ended with Nat Turner emerges as the great period of slave conspiracies in South Carolina. Never before and never again did the slaves conspire so shrewdly, so widely, so often. Perhaps the rising abolitionist crusade influenced bondsmen, and perhaps they sensed their masters' uneasiness and irresolution in the face of external attack. After 1835, when slaveholders defended slavery as a "positive good" and tightened controls, slaves seldom dared to seek freedom by revolution. By 1860 South Carolinians were probably less apprehensive about servile insurrection. The famous slave conspiracies of the prenullification decade, like the exaggerated fear they helped to create, were products of the period of transition in southern history, when the beleaguered Carolinian tried to find the nerve

21 Floyd to Hamilton, Nov. 19, 1831, Floyd Papers, LC.

to defend a system which he regarded as an abomination against outsiders who believed abominations should be abolished.

6

The grim chronicle of sabotage and conspiracy, however necessary for an understanding of slavery in South Carolina, distorts the peculiar institution. A small minority of slaves were involved in overt rebellions. Moreover, if planters sometimes regarded slaves with fear and trembling, they often viewed "their people" with kindly affection and an abiding sense of parental duty. The gay barbecues, the Christmas holidays, the homecoming celebrations, however exaggerated in the Old South's myth of plantation life, fulfilled a real need to treat one's slaves with warmth and affection. Indeed, the myth of the mellow old plantation and the dutiful, carefree Sambos who worked on it, like all utopian myths, has an important reality of its own. A society's vision of perfection reveals its most acutely frustrated desires. In the myth, southerners expressed their craving for a kindly, paternalistic slave system, without tension or punishment or violence, where master and slave lived together in rich comradeship and intuitive understanding.[22]

Even if plantation life could have approximated the utopian myth, southerners would not have rested easily. The philosophy which planters so enthusiastically celebrated on the Fourth of July would have remained a nagging moral burden. Moreover, the Carolina social code limited the value of an idyllic master-slave relationship. The drawing-room code, which insisted upon conversation between honorable equals, condemned the fawning slave, while accepting his inferiority with a smile, as a hopelessly degraded human being. Judged by the southerner's own values,

[22] The following view of South Carolina slavery is based on the plantation journals listed in the bibliographical essay. The most important sources are the Manigault Plantation Records, NC, and the James Hammond Plantation Records, 1831–55, SC. An edition of the Hammond Records, edited by the author, will be published shortly. My interpretation of slavery has been heavily influenced by Wilbur J. Cash, *The Mind of the South* (New York, 1941); Charles Grier Sellers, Jr., "The Travail of Slavery" in Sellers (ed.), *The Southerner as American* (Chapel Hill, 1960); the penetrating analysis of the dilemmas of conscientious slaveholders in Stampp, *The Peculiar Institution;* and the methodological insights of Henry Nash Smith, *Virgin Land: The American West as Symbol and Myth* (Cambridge, Mass., 1950).

a utopian plantation remained an illegitimate form of human exploitation.

Unfortunately plantation reality was rarely so sublime as the flawed utopia of the myth. Of course many southern slaves resembled the Sambo stereotype. Indulgent masters and their dutiful house servants often enjoyed a lifetime of friendship. But every plantation manager had to cope with a significant percentage of troublesome bondsmen. And the attempt to impose discipline on recalcitrant slaves frequently made managing the southern plantation a grim, ugly way of life. As one South Carolinian lamented, slaveholding subjected "the man of care and feeling to more dilemmas than perhaps any other vocation he could follow."[23]

The dilemmas of the scrupulous planter centered around the problems of discipline. As the Denmark Vesey Conspiracy demonstrated, indulged slaves could become archconspirators. And though few slaves emulated the notorious Rolla Bennett, many resisted their chains with devious sabotage and destructive laziness. When masters stopped painting their slaves as banjo-strumming Sambos or bloodthirsty savages, they presented another, equally revealing, stock portrait: the seemingly innocent but cunning laborer who could misunderstand adroitly, loiter diligently, or destroy guilefully. Indulgence and kindness, *by themselves*, could neither avoid rebellions nor produce an efficient labor force. Whipping, deprivation of privileges, and other punishments were accepted everywhere as a necessary part of plantation government. "Were *fidelity* the only security we enjoyed," exclaimed one slaveholder, ". . . deplorable indeed would be our situation. The fear of punishment is the principle to which we must and do appeal, to keep them in awe and order."[24]

Occasionally planters tried to escape from this unpleasant conclusion. In the halcyon days before the Vesey affair, many slaveholders "exulted in what they termed the progress of liberal ideas upon the subject of slavery." Planters experimented with a regime which, like the plantation of the myth, eschewed the lash and other forms of punishment, and relied on incentives, praise, and

[23] *S Ag,* III (July 1830), 238.
[24] *Southern Patriot,* Feb. 10, 1826.

kindness to keep the slaves in order. Charleston's slaves were permitted "to assemble without the presence of a white person
for . . . social intercourse or religious worship." Many bondsmen
were given "the facilities of acquiring most of the comforts and
many of the luxuries of improved society." Slaves were allowed
"means of enlarging their minds and extending their information."
But the events of 1822 proved to everyone that the peculiar institution could not endure if only humane treatment was employed. We must proceed "to govern them," Charlestonians concluded sadly, "on the only principle that can maintain slavery, the
principle of fear."[25]

Still, employing the lash was distasteful to owners who liked to
regard their slaves as personal friends. "We think it a misfortune,"
wrote William Harper, "that we should be compelled to subject
to a jealous police, and to view with distrust and severity, those
whom we are disposed to regard with confidence and kindness."
The "misfortune," one suspects, seemed most upsetting with indulged house servants, who often had a close personal relationship
with their masters, but still needed an occasional whipping. The
unpleasant problems of discipline could be most clearly seen in
Charleston, where personal servants formed a high percentage of
the slave population and masters were forced to inflict stripes
personally rather than pass the task on to plantation overseers. Few
ante bellum events are more revealing than the obscure decision
of the Charleston city council, in 1825, to erect a treadmill in the
city workhouse, thereby relieving sensitive masters of the necessity of whipping their own people. "Such a mode of correction
has long been a desideratum with many of our citizens," reported
Robert Mills in 1826. Many slaveholders had "been often induced
to pass over faults in their slaves demeriting correction, rather than
resort to coercive measures with them, who now will, without
doing violence to their feelings, be able to break their idle
habits."[26]

The large slaveholder, closer to his house servants, probably
found disciplining his field hands a less disturbing business. Still,

[25] Phillips (ed.), *Plantation and Frontier*, pp. 103ff.
[26] *SR*, I (Feb. 1828), 230; Mills, *Statistics*, pp. 420–1.

field hands were "his people" as well as his property, and planta-tion management was fraught with dilemmas. The most successful disciplinarians were so rigid and strict that they rarely had to punish. But even such planters went through a distressing period of frequent punishment when they "broke in" their slaves, and they never escaped the necessity of proving to bondsmen that the system was screwed tight. "When I first began to plant I found my people in very bad subjection," James Hammond ex-plained to a new overseer. ". . . It required of me a year of severity which cost me infinite pain and gained a name which I detest of all others to subdue them. They are now entirely broken in, & . . . it will be seldom necessary to use the lash." But overseers on his plantation could never forgo the lash for long.[27]

Many planters could not emulate Hammond's agonized persist-ence; rigorous discipline was simply too severe a strain on uneasy consciences. This—not the weather—was the crucial cause of the lazy pace and inefficient practices on many declining plantations. Yet those who could not bear to impose strict plantation rules and punish all transgressions in the end whipped all the more. Spotty discipline encouraged passive resistance, devious sabotage, and—with the more willful slaves—overt violence. James Edward Calhoun, traveling through the lowcountry in 1826, encountered one unforgettable example of the tension which pervaded the plantation of an inconsistent disciplinarian. James Kirk, a leading Beaufort planter, told Calhoun that "if he lives 10 or 15 yrs. longer" his slaves would "gain ascendency over him . . . is sensible they are gaining on him: confesses whips in a passion & half the time unjustly. . . . Confesses scruples of conscience about slavery."[28]

In the 1820's leading South Carolinians admitted that inconsist-ent disciplinarians abounded in their state. "The relaxed, senti-mental, *covert abolitionist*," lamented the editor of the *Southern Agriculturist*, "first begins by spoiling his slave, next becomes severe, which is followed by running away, this again by enormous depredations . . . a large proportion of our ablest and most in-

[27] Hammond to [John] Walker, Dec. 27, 1836, Hammond Papers, LC.
[28] James Edward Calhoun Diary, entries for Jan. 25 through Feb. 1, 1826, SC.

telligent slaves are annually sent out of the State for misconduct arising from the most erroneous notions of discipline." The editor of the *Southern Review* added: "One great evil of the system is its tendency to produce in process of time, laxity of discipline, and consequently, disorders and poverty . . . by the excessive indulgence of careless or too scrupulous masters . . . some of the worst symptoms of the time are owing to this ill-judged, but we fear, inevitable facility and indulgence."[29]

The slaveholder's guilt was thus more than a reaction to the discrepancy between Jefferson's Declaration and southern slavery. It was also a response to the gulf between the plantation myth and the realities of bondage—a gulf evident day after day in the painful dilemmas of discipline. Planters who eschewed fear entirely and relied only on kindness invited economic bankruptcy and servile insurrection. Slaveholders who employed punishment erratically lived with periodic flareups and sometimes faced the unpleasant necessity of having to sell rebellious bondsmen. Planters who imposed discipline consistently had the least trouble in the long run, but endured the anxiety of inflicting perpetual punishment during the breaking-in period.

Of course many planters rarely worried about the morality of slavery or the dilemmas of discipline. At the other extreme, a few slaveholders, convinced that profits could be kept up only by a distasteful driving of slaves, sold out their plantations. Many others found solace in treating slaves as kindly as possible within the limits set by proper discipline. Plantations fell apart when control was based entirely on indulgence and incentives. But when punishment and fear were employed, kindness and courtesy effectively produced a more contented, efficient labor force. This, in turn, reduced the necessity to punish. As one astute observer noted, humane planters were "saved from many painful feelings at home and cared less about being traduced abroad." For many planters, however, the acts of kindness and the familial relationships were never quite enough. "I have a just partiality for all our servants

[29] *S Ag*, II (Dec. 1829), 575–6: *SR*, IV (Nov. 1829), 358. For some superb examples of the psychic stress inconsistent discipline caused, see James Holmes' compulsive attempts to convince Lucy Ruggles that he believes in slavery in Lucy Ruggles Diary, DU, and the M. L. Dorsey incident, 1824, in Pinckney Family Papers, LC.

from many touching recollections, & expect my residence at home made very comfortable by having them about me," remarked Hugh S. Legaré. "This circumstance is after all sometimes a great compensation for the unquestionable evils attendant upon the institution of slavery."[30]

7

Just as the unusually heavy concentration of slaves in tidewater Carolina intensified the lowcountry's fear of slave uprisings, so the special problems of the coastal plantation may have increased the gentry's guilt. As always, the problems centered around the malaria. Paternalistic masters felt compelled to protect their people's health. Yet planters knew that a slave thrust into the swamp was likely to become debilitated with illness and would sometimes prematurely die. Many owners must have pushed the ugly problem out of their minds. Some salved their conscience by employing fine plantation physicians. But for others, providing excellent medical care could not compensate for subjecting the slaves to malarial fever in the first place. The planters betrayed their qualms by incessantly claiming what they knew to be false —that Negroes were immune from the diseases of the swamp. One leading slaveholder even exposed his uneasy conscience in his plantation journal. On James Hammond's Savannah River plantation, slaves were required to cut fodder in river swamps every September:

September 23, 1833: At plantation all day nursing the sick. Some very low—High grade of bilious fever—Twenty-two on the sick list . . . September 26, 1833: Sick all better and the list reduced to 15—Pulling Fodder today in the Lower Bluff. *Fearful that it will produce more sickness.* . . . September 26, 1834: Saw Dr. Galphin who anticipates cholera here. Ordered all hands to be removed from the river . . . September 29—The cholera has driven almost everybody from the swamp. September 30—hands pulling fodder. Another case of cholera —Eleanor—very severe—It happened in my presence—Left her better —Ordered them to pull no more fodder. . . . October 3—Mr. Dawkins

[30] W. J. Myddleton to Cheves, Sept. 8, 1821, Cheves Papers; Seabrook, *Essay on the Management of Slaves,* pp. 1–10; P. M. Butler to John M. Walker, March 18, 1837, Hammond Papers, LC; *Carolina Planter,* Apr. 1, 1840; Legaré to his mother, Jan. 26, 1835, Legaré Papers.

[the overseer] came up this evening and stated that there had been no new cases of cholera. He says he has put the hands to pulling fodder in the swamp again—*Feel uneasy about it.*[31] [Italics mine.]

Later Hammond noted that on his plantation slaves died faster than they were born. "One would think from this statement that I was a monster of inhumanity," he added. "Yet this one subject has caused me more anxiety and suffering than any other in my life."[32]

Disease-ridden swamps led planters to rely on unsupervised overseers, which raised special moral problems. Every contract between owners and overseers contained a clause binding the manager to treat Negroes with moderation and humanity. Overseers were frequently dismissed because they whipped slaves passionately or passed out medicine sparingly. Still, overseers were most often judged by their skill at raising yields. Overseers, like slave-traders, were more involved in the economic, exploitative side of slavery than the personal, paternalistic side; this is one reason they were despised. The incompetent young men who served as overseers on many tidewater plantations, and the absence of the owner's restraining word, undoubtedly increased the severity of slavery. As James Hammond summed up the matter in the midst of a famous proslavery polemic, a "leading" cause of cruelty to slaves was "the absenteeism of proprietors. Agents are always more unfeeling than owners, whether placed over West Indian or American slaves, or Irish Tenantry. We feel the evil greatly even here."[33]

Finally, the nature of absentee ownership involved tidewater gentlemen in a curious paradox. On the one hand, they were shielded from observing the unseemly side of plantation slavery during the summer months; in this sense they could ignore the dilemmas of discipline more easily than other planters. On the

[31] Hamilton to Dr. Furth, May 19, 1828, Miscellaneous Manuscripts Coll., New-York Historical Soc.; [Dalcho], *Practical Considerations,* p. 7; Hammond Plantation Records, SC.

[32] Hammond Diary, entry for Sept. 5, 1841, LC. Two qualifications are in order: (1) Hammond was *also,* perhaps *more,* concerned about pecuniary losses from slave decreases and (2) he did not *always* blame the high death rate on the location of the plantation. The Hammond plantation was geographically in the upcountry, but the Savannah River fields gave it all the characteristics of lowcountry tracts.

[33] *Carolina Planter,* Feb. 19, 1840; Sellers (ed.), *Southerner as American,* p. 60; William Harper *et al., The Pro-Slavery Argument* (Philadelphia, 1853), p. 128.

other hand, aristocrats who owned hundreds of slaves and often left their plantations had few memories of warm relationships with field hands to soften the exploitative aspect of slavery. They also had the detachment, time, and cultivated education to agonize over the morality of owning slaves. Elsewhere, relatively uneducated planters, personally involved day after day with building an economic empire, were less likely to stand back and question the means they were employing. One suspects that reasons like these help to explain why the Charleston aristocracy found it necessary to conduct "liberal" experiments with discipline and to build treadmills to punish slaves.

The diseases of the coastal Negro, the character of lowcountry overseers, and the nature and effects of absentee ownership *might* (for this is speculative) have intensified the guilt of the tidewater planter. Although less important than the lowcountry's particularly intense fear of slave revolts, this acute guilt may have helped to make slavery at the South Carolina tidewater so peculiarly disturbing.

8

The anxieties which Carolina slavery engendered are particularly evident in the intriguing debate over the religious education of slaves in the 1820's and 1830's. Nineteenth-century southern theologians maintained that eternal salvation depended on earthly conversion. Genuine conversion, in turn, depended on Biblical education. Thus, paternalistic masters felt obligated to give their slaves proper religious training. But spiritual dogma was a dangerous weapon in the hands of such as Denmark Vesey and Nat Turner. A slave who could read the Bible could also read the *Liberator*, and a slave read his Paul differently after he had read William Lloyd Garrison. Trapped between their obligations to the slaves as persons and their desire to safeguard slave property, South Carolinians writhed over the subject of religion for slaves until well into the 1830's.

Before the encounter with Denmark Vesey, many masters were indifferent rather than hostile to the religious education of slaves. Some slaves learned to read in order to study the Bible; others conducted class meetings in white churches; others formed their own congregations. But the conspiracy of 1822 demonstrated that churches could be centers of intrigue and that slaves could acquire what seemed to Carolinians the most erroneous religious notions. As a result, class meetings and Negro churches were disbanded. A long debate ensued over the matter of reading the Bible. The Reverend Richard Furman argued that the Bible sanctioned slavery and curbed insurrection. "The Scriptures," he wrote, "are given to man without respect of persons, to make him wise unto salvation; and all are required by Divine Authority to read them." Other Carolinians, remembering that Vesey's interpretation differed from Furman's, preferred to risk their salvation rather than their necks. Teaching slaves to read, although not legally barred for over a decade, had largely ended by 1822. Even oral religious training was frowned on. Some slaves attended services with their masters, but in the lowcountry no missionaries sought out the vast majority of bondsmen who lived miles from a white church. Slave preachers supplied coastal Negroes with the only available religious instruction. Soon these meetings were discouraged. Most lowcountry gentlemen believed that "their slaves who professed to be followers of Christ, were generally the most negligent in their duty and the most difficult to manage." Most tidewater slaves were "left almost without any religious instruction."[34]

The suppression of the late 1820's was at best an uncomfortable business. In 1829 Charles C. Pinckney created a minor sensation by requesting Methodist missionaries for his slaves. He argued that the repression of Negro preachers had "been attended with the usual effects of religious persecution, secrecy and nocturnal meetings." He believed that ignorant black exhorters could be combated best by trained white preachers.[35]

The excitement over Pinckney's essay was a sideshow compared to the furor caused by a group of conscience-stricken Beaufort planters two years later. Swept up by the religious revival that was

[34] Furman to Thomas Bennett, n.d. [early fall 1822], Furman Papers; *Charleston Mercury*, Nov. 21, 1831; J. L. Clark to Hammond, Dec. 19, 1831, Hammond Papers, LC.

[35] *Address, August 18, 1829*, pp. 21-4.

turning thousands of Carolinians into religious zealots, a number of wealthy St. Luke's planters formed an association to support the preaching of itinerant missionaries. Since slaves are "dependent on us for everything they have," urged the association, planters are "imperatively bound to consult, not only their bodily, but their spiritual good." Noting that many slaves had no "more knowledge of a holy and merciful God, than if they had lived and died among the Heathen," the planters called for a South Carolina crusade to "do something for the thousands of immortal souls who are perishing for lack of knowledge." Henry L. Pinckney, editor of the *Charleston Mercury*, toned down the association's plea before publishing it, and even then trembled to print such a document. The plan, widely condemned in Charleston when first presented, was still the object of vigorous attack three years later. The St. Luke's example did not inspire other lowcountry planters to form associations in the early 1830's. Pinckney's *Mercury* never dared to broach the subject again.[36]

Occasionally a crusader responded to the community's uneasy conscience by beginning a sabbath school for Negroes. But the slaveholders' qualms were usually too much of an obstacle. In 1833, for example, Francis Goulding, a young slaveholder, founded a sabbath school in Columbia. Slaves needed the written permission of their owners to attend, and classes were always open to the surveillance of suspicious whites. At first Goulding used pictures to illustrate key Biblical phrases. But the community, realizing that illustrated texts were used in teaching infants to read, soon demanded that other means be employed. Goulding then passed out slips of paper engraved with scriptural quotations, which he ordered slaves to give to their masters. The owner read the text aloud until the slave memorized it. "The negro," however, "easily learnt to recognize each particular word, and inevitably ended by learning to read." Compelled by slaveholders to abandon this method too, Goulding was reduced to the inadequate technique of oral instruction in class with no home lessons. Even then the harried teacher was frequently called before the city council.

[36] *Charleston Mercury*, Nov. 21, 1831, Jan. 28, 1832; Seabrook, *Essay on the Management of Slaves*, pp. 23–4.

Late in 1833 Goulding was forced to suspend operations entirely when the community discovered that he favored colonizing free Negroes in Africa! And so slaves who sought religion could again find it only in the white man's often incomprehensible sermons.[37]

The problem with Goulding's school, as with many other attempts to bring religion to the slaves, was that planters distrusted the clergy and teachers who volunteered their efforts. Slaveholders had a point. No other group in South Carolina—or in the nation —criticized slavery so severely. A synod of leading South Carolina and Georgia ministers, meeting in Columbia in December 1833, demanded that the South "extend the privileges of the Gospel to this neglected, dying people," and added this description of the peculiar institution:

We are chained to a putrid carcass; it sickens and destroys us. We have a millstone hanging about the neck of our society, to sink us deep in the sea of vice. Our children are corrupting [sic] from their infancy; nor can we prevent it. . . . If that were all, it would be tremendous. But it follows us into youth, into manhood, and into old age. And when we come directly in contact with their depravity in the *management* of them; then comes temptations and provocations and trials that unsearchable grace only can enable us to endure.

Planters were understandably reluctant to allow such men loose among their slaves, no matter how enthusiastically the clergy maintained that the Bible sanctioned slavery and outlawed insurrection.[38]

In the early 1830's Thomas Clay of Georgia argued that the shortage of trustworthy clergymen compelled conscientious planters to conduct nightly services for their slaves. Although Clay's plan won wide acceptance in the later ante bellum period, it aroused angry opposition in South Carolina in the 1830's. The proposal inspired one leading lowcountry slaveholder to wonder

---

[37] *Columbia Telescope*, Sept. 10, 1833.

[38] *Report of the Committee . . . [on] Religious Instruction . . . of the Synod of South Carolina and Georgia* (Charleston, 1834), esp. p. 20. For some intriguing examples of South Carolina's distrust of clergymen see Seabrook, *Essay on the Management of Slaves*, pp. 16–19, and the uproar caused by the Columbia Theological Seminary's request for northern contributions in *Columbia Telescope*, July 10 through Aug. 6, 1833.

if Clay was really a planter. Nineteenth-century evangelical preaching depended on inspiration and persuasion; planters relied on discipline and commands. Moreover, a nineteenth-century Baptist or Methodist preacher was more an exhorter than the commander of his congregation; efficient slave management required the complete supremacy of the plantation supervisor. By becoming a preacher, owners or overseers risked making fatally ambiguous a role which required complete clarity. The "wild and fantastic" Clay plan, proclaimed Whitemarsh Seabrook, proposes "to rule our slaves by perpetual prayer and exhortation, instead of the practical exercise of the master's authority. . . . I cannot imagine a contrivance better calculated in time to separate us from our property."[39]

Thus the dilemma of discipline sometimes prevented planters from solving the problem of teaching religion by acting as lay preachers to their slaves. Most slaveholders advocated special religious education for their people if preachers were orthodox on slavery and if they employed oral methods alone. The clergy was too suspect for much progress to be made until the late 1830's. By the end of 1833 only twelve white men in the whole South devoted themselves exclusively to ministering to the slaves. Only one slave in twenty was a communicant in white churches, and these bondsmen, unable to comprehend the erudite sermons addressed to educated citizens, were noted only for "their stupid looks, their indifferent staring, their profound sleeps, and their thin attendance." As evangelical Christianity swept over the Old South, another burden was added to the uneasy consciences of many slaveholders.[40]

9

After 1836 few planters admitted publicly that slave-owning posed serious moral problems. But in the 1820's, as earlier, southerners vied with northerners in their condemnation of the peculiar institution. William Drayton, defending the South against northern attack in Congress in 1828, did not defend Negro slavery:

[39] Thomas S. Clay, *Details of a Plan for the Moral Improvement of Negroes* . . . (n.p., 1833) ; Seabrook, *Essay on the Management of Slaves*, pp. 22–5.
[40] *Ibid.*, pp. 25–6; S *Ag*, V (Nov. 1832), 564–5; *Report of the Committee* [*on*] *Religious Instruction*, p. 7.

Slavery, in the abstract, I condemn and abhor. . . . However ameliorated by compassion—however corrected by religion—still slavery is a bitter draught, and the chalice which contains the nauseous potion, is, perhaps, more frequently pressed by the lips of the master than of the slave.[41]

Although slavery was a curse, admitted most South Carolinians in the 1820's, it was a "necessary evil" which the South had no responsibility for originating and could do nothing to end. The villains of the piece were the northern slave-traders who had forced slaves on resisting southerners in colonial days. "An African slave ship," argued William Drayton, "is a spectacle from which all men would recoil with horror, unless the vilest lust of lucre had steeled their hearts against every feeling of humanity." The victims were not the Negroes, who were a degraded, inferior race, incapable of prospering as freemen, but the slaveholders, who, to avoid the bloody race war which would follow abolition, were forced to maintain their inherited curse. Northerners treated free Negroes worse than southerners treated their slaves. Even slavery had its compensations. The slaves, better fed and better clothed than free laborers, were protected from the burdens of sickness, old age, and unemployment, which made freedom a curse for the lower class.

South Carolinians not only admitted slavery was an evil in the 1820's but also permitted several idealists to publish emancipation schemes. The lesson of the Vesey Conspiracy, Nicholas Herbemont put forth in an intriguing 1822 pamphlet, was that "indulgent masters were the first sacrificed" and that "great severity is the surest means of keeping slaves in due subjection. But God forbid that such a plan be adopted! Humanity forbids it." A way out of the dilemma, suggested Herbemont, was to convert the useless sand hills and pine barrens into wineries, thereby building up the white population and making emancipation, and relaxed discipline, possible. Robert Mills, later the architect of the Washington Monument, proposed a massive campaign of swamp drainage. The lowcountry, Mills asserted, would then be healthy for white laborers, and their profits could be used to emancipate and colonize the slaves. Frederick Dalcho, a Charleston minister, claimed a

[41] *Register of Debates,* 20 Cong., 1 sess., I, 974–5.

trifle optimistically in 1823 that "if the non-slave-holding States will purchase our plantations and slaves, and send the latter to Africa . . . there would [not] be many Planters in South-Carolina, who would hesitate one moment, to get rid of both, even at something below their value."[42]

Most Carolinians rejected these "utopian" schemes. A special committee of the state House of Representatives, answering a petition for emancipation in 1823, argued that governments could not confiscate property without fair compensation. Emancipation would cost almost $80 million in South Carolina alone, to say nothing of the exorbitant expense of colonization. Abolition, if right theoretically, was impossible practically; hence antislavery talk did "more harm than good." The committee concluded: "Almost all the commotions and disturbances that have taken place in this state for several years past . . . may be traced . . . to writings of various descriptions on the subject of emancipation." Never again would the possibility of abolition engage the attention of a Carolina legislative committee. The evil was indeed necessary.[43]

The "necessary evil" argument, however, lacked the philosophical foundation which might have made it persuasive; the South Carolina mind was divided against itself. The "necessary evil" argument rested on the premise that utility was the appropriate standard for political decision and expediency the proper criterion for government action. But Carolinians, as Christians and Americans, upheld the wholly different assumption that a political action, to be right, must accord with a priori universal postulates. No matter how much Carolinians wanted to believe that slavery should be supported because it was necessary, they could never escape the suspicion that bondage should be abolished because it violated natural rights. Even if a sensitive slaveholder rested easily with the conviction that the South should preserve the evil, he could not evade responsibility for his personal involvement in the

[42] [Nicholas Herbemont], *Observations Suggested by the Late Occurrences in Charleston* . . . (Columbia, 1822), esp. p. 5; Robert Mills, *Internal Improvement* . . . *Particularly Adapted to the Low Country*, reprinted in Kohn (ed.), *Internal Improvements*, pp. 199–226; [Dalcho], *Practical Considerations*, p. 6.
[43] House Journal, 1823, pp. 51ff., South Carolina Arch.

moral dilemmas of slavery. "They say," noted one Carolinian, "the necessity of procuring labor of this kind, compels them to hold their fellow man in bondage. But does necessity compel them to reside where there is no service but that of slaves to be found?" The "necessary evil" argument afforded little protection against this sort of condemnation.[44]

Thus planters who came in contact with northerners often found themselves outargued and—to the alarm of leading southerners—often became covert abolitionists themselves. The *"oily tongues"* of Yankee peddlers, claimed one disturbed upcountry man, ". . . lead astray the minds of our too credulous neighbors. . . . The influence which one of those Northern emissaries has, in giving tone to the feelings and sentiments of a community, far exceeds our expectations." William Harper lamented: "What is most surprising of all [is that] some individuals among ourselves, instead of attending to what passes before their own eyes . . . are content to take up their opinions, ready made, from the haphazard speculations and vehement invectives of these . . . distant instructors." John Townsend, a leading tidewater *moderate*, added: "The chances are as ten to one" that abolitionists can "exhort" from vulnerable planters "some admissions which are neither true in principle or in fact. . . . witness the effects of the too easy acquiescence of Planters in the doctrines and schemes of these wily plotters. . . . What means the womanish qualms of conscience which we so often witness among many of our own citizens, as to the justice and morality of keeping men in bondage?" Townsend urged "every planter" to "brace up his mind by every possible information on this subject." The peculiar institution could never be defended unless planters believed in their cause.[45]

In order to "brace up" the community against the coming storm, several South Carolinians published proslavery polemics in the 1820's. These early versions of the "positive good" argument, like the antiabolitionist impulse behind the nullifiers' crusade, indicate South Carolina's sensitivity to the relatively undeveloped

---

[44] *Southern Times*, Apr. 8, 1830.
[45] *Camden and Lancaster Beacon*, Apr. 12, 1831; *Southern Review*, I (Feb. 1828), 219; *Charleston Mercury*, Nov. 27, 1828.

antislavery campaign in the pre-1832 period. Moreover, the relatively few proslavery theorists and their extremely qualified arguments provide a superb illustration of the uneasy consciences which helped make South Carolinians apprehensive about the issue. The most advanced proslavery crusaders in the state were reluctant to call their curse a blessing in the 1820's.

The early proslavery theorists were often ministers, disturbed by the abolitionists' effect on all members of their congregations. Because of the Vesey affair and the antislavery attack, Richard Furman argued in 1823, slaveholders were "embarrassed" by moral scruples and slaves were denied permission to read the Scriptures. Both problems could be solved if the community realized that according to the Bible, slavery is "lawful and right." This view of the subject "affords relief," Furman claimed, from the "inadmissible" doctrine that slavery is "indefensible" but "necessary." Slaveholders could safely give Scriptures to their people and listen to abolitionist attacks without being "perverted."[46]

Yet the proslavery ministers were too much creatures of the 1820's to give slavery their unqualified approval. Richard Furman did not think "that liberty . . . is a blessing of little moment," and he hoped that eventually Negroes could be freed and the lot of the oppressed everywhere ameliorated. His colleague, Frederick Dalcho, deprecated "the evil which attends" slavery and prayed that someday the slave could be freed and colonized.[47]

The defense of slavery by the ministers' secular allies was usually an equally qualified polemic. In 1822 Edwin Holland published his *Refutation of the Calumnies Circulated Against . . . Southern . . . Slavery*. In it he argued that slavery was an ancient institution, sanctioned by the Bible and necessary to cultivate the miasmatic lowcountry. Yet he admitted that human bondage was "an evil, the curse of which is felt and acknowledged by every enlightened man in the Slave-holding States."[48]

In 1825 Whitemarsh Seabrook issued an important tract, *A Concise View of the Critical Situation and Future Prospects of the Slaveholding States, in Relation to their Colored Population*. He

[46] *Rev. . . . Furman's Exposition of the Views of the Baptists Relative to the Coloured Population . . .* (Charleston, 1823), esp. p. 13.
[47] *Ibid.*, pp. 14–15; [Dalcho], *Practical Considerations*, p. 6.
[48] Esp. p. 22.

pointed to the signs of a worldwide antislavery attack and urged the slaveholders to prepare for an imminent encounter. The low-country pamphleteer confessed, however, that southerners "detested" slavery. "We feel its fatal effects," he wrote. "We abhor, we deplore it ourselves with all the pity of humanity."[49]

Edward Brown's *Notes on the Origin and Necessity of Slavery*, published in 1826, echoed the opinions of Holland and Seabrook. Brown maintained that "slavery has ever been the step-ladder by which civilized countries have passed from barbarism to civilization." He considered "perfect and universal equality . . . but another name for barbarism." Yet Brown explicitly attacked southerners who painted the slaves' "condition as one so easy, so free from care or want, as to border on a perfectly happy state." He admitted that slavery was "alien to the feelings and principles of the human mind," and he congratulated the few societies which were sufficiently advanced to be "happily released from its burden."[50]

In 1829 Governor Stephen D. Miller, calling upon South Carolinians to fight the tariff in order to check the abolitionists, employed striking language to defend the southern system. "Slavery," he declared, "is not a national evil; on the contrary it is a national benefit." The governor warned, "Upon this subject it does not become us to speak in a whisper, betray fear, or feign philanthropy."[51]

Miller's brief argument offered little foundation for his doctrine. The "national benefit" turned out to be the rice and cotton which the slave produced. From "a philosophical point of view," Miller claimed that involuntary servitude was no worse than voluntary free labor. The superiority of bondage could be seen only "from a political point of view." When laborers were slaves, the poorer classes had no vote and therefore could not be bribed to disturb property relations. This was more an argument for restricted suffrage than for involuntary servitude. Moreover, in the same speech, Miller called for extensive bankruptcy legislation to bribe mortgage-ridden farmers to stay in South Carolina at the expense

[49] Charleston, 1825; esp. p. 15.
[50] Charleston, 1826; esp. pp. 6, 9, 31–2, 39.
[51] *Southern Patriot*, Nov. 27, 1829.

of creditor property rights! Even coming from the governor, Miller's proslavery statement was ill-equipped to salve an ailing conscience. The novel doctrine, although usually honored by neglect, was occasionally the butt of caustic criticism. "The deuce take such blessings and a fig for such philosophy," remarked one disgusted slaveholder.[52]

Thus the proslavery argument of the 1820's, although growing in strength, was still a fragmentary and qualified polemic which was not widely accepted. The few proslavery theorists made almost as little headway convincing the community that slavery was a blessing as the few Carolina abolitionists made in persuading the planters that bondage could be abolished. The huge majority of slaveholders, distressed by slavery but seeing no way out, clung stubbornly to the untenable "necessary evil" position. They did not widely discuss or accept the "positive good" thesis until *after* South Carolina adopted nullification.

10

The most revealing public reaction to the tensions slavery generated in the 1820's and early 1830's was neither the "necessary evil" nor the "positive good" argument but rather the attempt to repress open debate. The conviction that slavery was an abomination ran too deep to be overcome in a season, and antislavery opponents easily refuted the argument from necessity. If subjected to a barrage of criticism, conscience-stricken planters might become covert abolitionists who would fight half-heartedly for slavery's perpetuation and relax the discipline which kept their slaves in order. Moreover, public debate might increase the restlessness of Negro slaves and would certainly magnify the apprehensions of the white community.

[52] *Columbia Free Press and Hive*, March 12, 1831. Thomas Cooper and Robert J. Turnbull are often included among the proslavery writers of the 1820's. But Cooper's proslavery argument occupies less than a page and consists of a list of points one could use to defend slavery. On the next page, Cooper listed the necessary-evil argument. Turnbull merely proclaimed that "if there be an evil in slavery, the evil is ours." Senator William Smith's famous diatribe in Congress during the Missouri Controversy appears to be the only *unqualified* proslavery argument developed by a South Carolinian in the 1820's. Cooper, *Two Essays . . .* (Columbia, 1826), esp. pp. 45–6; [Turnbull], *The Crisis*, esp. p. 130; *Annals of Congress*, 16 Cong., 1 sess., I, 259–75.

Thus South Carolina profoundly desired to keep the subject buried. The discovery of a copy of Walker's *Appeal*, or an issue of Garrison's *Liberator*, or a handkerchief stamped with Negroes in a state of defiance was enough to start a panic over insurrection. Charleston's newspapers avoided notice of slave conspiracies, and upcountry sheets gave only cursory details. Lowcountry editors trembled at items that approached the issue and refused to meet the matter head on. Pre-1833 editorials chanted that the evil was necessary and the subject too dangerous to discuss.[53]

In 1832, when the Virginia legislature engaged in a month of searching arguments on the merits of slavery, and Thomas Ritchie's *Richmond Enquirer* doubled the danger by printing the debates, even Carolina unionists were flabbergasted. Benjamin F. Perry, a moderate, refused "to comment on a policy so unwise, and blended with so much madness and fatality"; the sober *Camden Journal* rejected an essay *against* the Virginia experiment with open discussion because "it is a subject that ought not to be agitated at all in this State."[54]

If the unionists fumed, the fire-eaters raged. In Sumter, John Hemphill urged patrols to be on the alert and denounced Ritchie as "the apostate traitor, the recreant and faithless sentinel, the cringing parasite, the hollow-hearted, hypocritical advocate of Southern interests . . . who has scattered the firebrands of destruction everywhere in the South." In Washington, Duff Green proclaimed that Ritchie's heresy was "calculated to unsettle everything—the minds of masters and slaves." The *Charleston Mercury* added: "We cannot too earnestly deprecate the public discussion of such a topic. . . . The very agitation . . . is fraught with evils of the most disastrous kind."[55]

For a moment in early 1832, one Carolina editor dared to broach the forbidden subject. Young Maynard Richardson, son of the Carolina jurist and editor of the Sumterville *Southern Whig*,

[53] Benjamin F. Hunt to Harrison Gray Otis, Oct. 4, 1831, Hayne to Otis, Oct. 14, 1831, Samuel Eliot Morison, *The Life and Times of Harrison Gray Otis* . . . (2 vols.; New York, 1913), II, 277–81; *Pendleton Messenger*, Oct. 5, 1831; *Camden Journal*, Apr. 21, 1832.

[54] *Greenville Mountaineer*, Feb. 4, 1832; *Camden Journal*, Feb. 11, 1832.

[55] *Sumter Gazette*, Apr. 28, 1832; *United States Telegraph*, Jan. 26, 1832; *Charleston Mercury*, Jan. 16, 1832.

opened his columns "for a *liberal* and *guarded* discussion of slavery." Southerners invited northern attack, he argued, by their "own sensitiveness. We receive their objections with bitter revilings, nor do we ever deign any answer save the most unqualified contempt and abhorrence. This course augurs badly for us. It implies consciousness of a weak cause, and an unwillingness to undergo scrutiny."

Richardson printed a communication from "W. E." in the *Southern Whig* "without hesitation" because it merely discussed the "abstract question . . . upon which we . . . are . . . safest." The "W. E." essay was the type of argument which leading southerners wished neither guilty whites nor restless slaves to read. "Is it an argument," asked the correspondent, to assert that slavery is legitimate because northerners abuse their free Negroes? "Is it not rather the retort, 'You do so too'? . . . Is it an argument," inquired "W. E.," to blame slave-traders for the inception of bondage? "Or is it not rather an attempt to cover our own weakness, in yielding to seduction, by throwing the blame on the seducer?" Does the Negro's mental imbecility justify slavery? For

the mental imbecility of the Negro is the result of our own injustice and oppression. Do we not endeavor, by every means in our power, to debase his mind? . . . And why do we act thus towards him? Is knowledge inconsistent with justice and the safety of the majority? . . . Is it an argument when he tells us, that our lands cannot be cultivated without them? Or does it not rather prove that we are resolved, at all hazards, on the gratification of our lust for power?[56]

John Hemphill, editor of the rival *Sumter Gazette*, spoke for a frightened community when he castigated Richardson's policy and called on the patrol for greater vigilance. Still, Hemphill refused to answer "W. E." With "a dense slave population at our own firesides," he wrote, South Carolinians would never allow anyone to "discuss the subject *here*." The value of an essay refuting "W. E." could never justify the danger involved. "Must we free ourselves," asked Hemphill's *Gazette*, "from such misrepresentation at the risk of such appalling mischief?"[57]

Maynard Richardson countered by accusing Hemphill of "the

[56] March 8, 1832.
[57] March 10, 1832.

sickly sensitiveness and ridiculous squeamishness, about touching the subject of slavery which have ever been the subject of our misunderstanding abroad and of which there is not a nervous female who is not thoroughly ashamed." Yet Richardson stopped printing communications on slavery and picked a quarrel with Hemphill to cover his isolation in the community. A vituperative battle royal ensued between the two editors. Newspaper epithets soon gave way to physical violence. On an April day at Sumter Court House, Richardson, armed with a dirk, and Hemphill, equipped with a pistol, scuffled for their honor. Other Sumterites swarmed in the street, wanting to join the brawl, and Judge Richardson plunged into the fray. Before the riot ended, the combatants were marked by bloody heads and torn clothing. And the image of the honorable judge wrestling in the dirt for the pistol comments on the eclipse of Maynard Richardson's rather noble aims and the disturbing nature of slavery in South Carolina.[58]

The Hemphill-Richardson affair was the most dramatic incident in the decade-long Carolina attempt to repress public discussion of slavery. But this policy in South Carolina could hardly be reconciled with the strategy of vigorous defense in Washington. Leading South Carolinians always believed that they must put down the smallest beginnings of a political antislavery campaign. An incessant abolitionist attack was expected to reach menacing proportions in the North and to provoke servile insurrections in the South. Yet a vigorous proslavery campaign in Congress would flounder without the enthusiastic support of southerners at home. A thoroughgoing propaganda campaign was needed to convince slaveholders to crusade for their institutions. And the incessant discussion of slavery in South Carolina seemed almost as dangerous as a growing abolitionist crusade in the North.

This irreconcilable commitment to both a strategy of militant defense in Washington and a policy of complete repression at home was the essence of South Carolina's dilemma in the 1820's. Desperately anxious to keep the distressing subject buried, the South Carolina congressmen lashed out stridently at the mildest

---

[58] Both papers, March and April 1832, esp. *Southern Whig,* March 15, 1832. See also *Pendleton Messenger,* May 16, 1832; *Winyaw Intelligencer,* July 16, 1831; Stephen La Coste to Miller, Apr. 20, 1832, Hemphill to Miller, Apr. 29, 1832, Chestnut-Manning-Miller Papers.

antislavery proposals during the 1820's. And one of the crucial
appeals of crusading for nullification on the tariff issue was that a
weapon could be won to check the abolitionists without discussing
slavery. The event would reveal that South Carolina could not
escape the dilemma so painlessly.

11

Slavery, to recapitulate, was always a more disturbing affair
at tidewater than in the piedmont. The dense slave population,
the Denmark Vesey Conspiracy, the Charleston Fire Scare, the
Georgetown plot, the Nat Turner uprising in Virginia—all made
the lowcountry apprehensive of slave revolt. The slaves' susceptibility to malaria, the nature of absentee ownership, and the reliance on unsupervised, sometimes incompetent overseers may
have burdened the uneasy conscience which plagued sensitive
slaveholders. Finally, the tidewater gentry had by far the greatest economic stake in the peculiar institution. Lowcountry planters were acutely sensitive to any sign of an antislavery crusade, just
as the upcountry gentry and Charleston's mechanics and retailers
were especially sensitive to the economic consequences of protective tariffs.

Yet the tensions of slavery were far from absent away from
the coast. Nat Turner's crusade set off insurrection scares in
many piedmont communities; Francis Goulding's school was
closed in Columbia; the Hemphill-Richardson affair took place in
Sumter. If the lowcountry, although relatively prosperous, was
sufficiently bothered by mortgage problems to understand the
economic plight of the upcountry, the piedmont, although freer
of slavery tensions, was sufficiently disturbed by fear and guilt
to appreciate the anxieties at tidewater. Excellent channels of
communication made this mutual sensitivity the more acute.

But the yeoman farmers of the mountains and the Charleston
merchants on the East Bay were neither greatly disturbed by
the depression nor much bothered by abolitionists. Both groups
prospered in the 1820's; neither used slave labor to secure profits.
They were the natural opponents of the crusade against protectionists and abolitionists which swept up the majority of South
Carolinians in the twenties and thirties.

PART TWO

Crisis: The Tariff and the Indirect Defense of Slavery, 1816–1833

If it is not, it ought to be understood, that the Tariff is only one of the subjects of complaint at the South. The Internal Improvement, or general bribery system, and the interference with our domestic policy—most especially the latter—are things which . . . will, if necessary, be met with something more than words.
—*Winyaw Intelligencer*, May 12, 1830

4

Qualified Nationalism to Qualified Sectionalism, 1816–1827

Throughout the years of transition from nationalism to sectionalism, and indeed throughout the pre-Civil War era, South Carolina's political order reflected the high-toned conservatism of an entrenched landed aristocracy. The planters' political ideal was the House of Lords rather than the halls of Congress, and their political assumptions derived from the elitest cult of the English country gentry. Nowhere else in America did the wealthy class so successfully conspire to keep power away from the common man.

The South Carolina gentleman, in truth, was a democrat with reservations; he had faith only in the right kind of republic. If upper-class patricians had a free hand to govern, the Carolina planter could afford to be a democrat. He conceded that plebeians should choose which aristocrats would rule. As James Hamilton, Jr., put it, "the people expect that their leaders in whose . . . public spirit they have confidence will think for them—and that they will be prepared to *act* as their leaders *think*."[1]

The South Carolina constitution of 1790, as amended in the early nineteenth century, institutionalized this limited faith in democracy. Any adult white male who had resided in South Carolina for two years could vote for state legislators. But the legislators elected almost all other state officials, from the governor to tax collectors, as well as United States senators and presidential

---

[1] Hamilton to Miller, Aug. 9, 1830, Chestnut-Manning-Miller Papers.

electors. Moreover, a high property qualification for the legislature kept the lower class outside the statehouse. Political power in South Carolina was uniquely concentrated in a legislature of large property holders, which set state policy and selected the men to administer it.[2]

The apportionment of legislators made even more sure that those with a stake in society would continue to rule. In the years before plantations came to the piedmont, tidewater planters controlled most seats in the legislature although upcountry farmers overwhelmingly outnumbered them. Men from the hills demanded a reapportionment, and for over two decades controversy raged. In 1808 the issue was finally compromised. Lowcountry planters gave in partly because the pressure grew too great, partly because the development of upcountry plantations reduced the economic differences between the two sections, and partly because they were forced to give up remarkably little. The lowcountry parishes, with their small white populations, remained in control of the Senate and retained a disproportionate influence in the House.

The conflict between tidewater and piedmont still flared up in the 1820's, but had lost much of its urgency. The Compromise of 1808 had soothed tempers, and the continued spread of the plantation system to the uplands made the lowcountry more willing to share its power. The decline of state sectionalism left the gentry free to unite against external foes in South Carolina crusades which lowcountry aristocrats would often dominate.[3]

The special features of South Carolina politics secured the complete control of upper-class planters. Elections to the state legislature—the only control the electorate had over the government—were often uncontested and rarely allowed voters a clear choice between parties or policies. Even in the legislature, statesmen eschewed organized parties. Rigid coalitions, they believed, would interfere with the felicitous debates of disinterested aristocrats. More important, leaders of a well-disciplined legislative party

[2] J. M. Lesesne (ed.), *The Constitution of 1790* (Columbia, 1952).

[3] William A. Schaper, *Sectionalism and Representation in South Carolina,* in *Annual Report of the American Historical Association for the Year 1900* (2 vols.; Washington, D.C., 1901), I, 237–463.

might organize a statewide popular ticket and, by debating issues, encourage plebeians to overreach themselves. Inferior demagogues, rising to power by bribing and deluding the rabble, would seize control from patriotic patricians and reduce government to a scramble for patronage. Political parties would overturn the rule of the rich, the well-born, and the able, and would upset the precariously balanced, limited democracy which alone won the approbation of the South Carolina patricians.[4]

Although loose coalitions of legislators were important in the post-1816 period, many politicians shunned factional attachment. Elections in the legislature as a rule turned on personalities rather than on issues. Popular men who dissented from popular policies frequently won high office. Such obscure politicians as Eldred Simkins, Patrick Noble, and John B. O'Neall were powerful legislators, not because they espoused great programs or wielded extensive patronage, but because they charmed and impressed their compatriots. The narrative of South Carolina politics from 1816 to 1827 properly focuses on the two major factions which developed and the issues they debated. But the centers of legislative organization must never completely overshadow the essentially unorganized political conditions which the patricians of South Carolina perpetuated as a matter of principle.

2

The glory and the shame of the War of 1812 had, by 1816, created a fervent American nationalism which altered the mood of a generation and deflected the direction of its politics. The disgraceful British burning of Washington was as unforgettable as Andrew Jackson's splendid triumph at New Orleans. The surprisingly favorable terms of the Treaty of Ghent did not make Americans forget that inadequate roads and banks, manufactories and armies, had come uncomfortably close to permitting a British victory.

National defects were the more intolerable because the treaty

4 Hammond Diary, entry for Dec. 15, 1850, Hammond Papers, LC; Henry William De Saussure, *An Oration . . . on the Fourth of July . . .* [Columbia, 1826] ; *Edgefield Hive,* Apr. 26, 1830; [Cheves], *Occasional Reviews, I–III* (Charleston, 1832); Clement Eaton, *The Mind of the Old South* (Baton Rouge, 1964), ch. 2.

seemed to suspend rather than end the war. In the perspective of the twentieth century, we can see that the Treaty of Ghent marked the culmination of American involvement in the Napoleonic Wars. But in 1816, after almost a quarter century of European strife, American nationalists suspected that the ordeal by battle would soon begin again.

South Carolina had been an enthusiastic proponent of the War of 1812 and had contributed four leading "war hawks"—John C. Calhoun, William Lowndes, David R. Williams, and Langdon Cheves—to the Congress that had pushed President James Madison toward a declaration of war. Calhoun and Lowndes were still in Congress in 1816, and they became natural leaders of postwar nationalism. In November 1817 Calhoun joined James Monroe's cabinet as secretary of war and was soon using his new position to espouse nationalist dogmas and to climb toward the presidency.

The chronicle of how the nullification crusade altered and finally wrecked Calhoun's national political career forms one of the great themes of the Age of Jackson. Calhoun's early career, however, was marked by a meteoric rise and effective service in the nation's councils. The son of an established, moderately wealthy upcountry family, educated at Yale and the Litchfield Law School, Calhoun made his fortune and entered Congress before he was thirty, and was a presidential candidate before he was forty. His fortune had come with his bride, a young lowcountry rice heiress, Floride Bonneau Colhoun. Early presidential ambitions had accompanied his hard riding of the doctrine of nationalism to the higher offices in the land in the years before, during, and after the War of 1812. Monroe's tardy offer of the secretary of war portfolio was a just reward for services rendered the Union, and Calhoun had accepted it after a period of agonizing indecision. As secretary of war, the young Carolinian could implement one of his central assumptions, that lasting peace depended on an army strong enough to deter potential aggressors. He could also gain the administrative experience necessary for the presidency and could keep a close eye on such potential rivals as John Quincy Adams, secretary of state; and William H. Crawford, secretary of the treasury.

The secretary of war was a tall, gangling man, with high cheekbones, deep-set burning brown eyes, and unruly chestnut hair; his was the appearance of a vigorous, optimistic, bright young man, untouched by defeat or tragedy. His mind was razor sharp, fully able to cut through the most abstruse logical argument and yet sensitively attuned to the pragmatic pressures of everyday politics. His vision of politics was not yet a maze of abstraction; his naïve optimism did not yet camouflage the difficulties ahead. Affable and popular, a superb conversationalist and an incisive debater, he seemed to John Quincy Adams "above all sectional and factious prejudices more than any other statesman of this Union with whom I have ever acted." High nationalism seemed best for the Union, best for South Carolina, and best for his own ambition; never again would the world seem so manageable.[5]

The case for nationalism Calhoun and Lowndes presented in 1816, and South Carolina nationalists defended thereafter, was premised on the exigencies of national defense. Since unstable national currency could complicate war finance, Calhounites favored a national bank. As poor roads could slow down military transportation, the nationalists advocated internal improvements. Because dependence on foreign factories could be dangerous if an enemy controlled the seas, Calhounites accepted a protective tariff. Since a weak local militia invited external attack, they demanded a strong national army.

But the South Carolinians' plea for an active national government was not an unqualified demand for unlimited interference in the economy. Their program was always restricted by the patriotic and disinterested motives which inspired it. South Carolina planters had little financial interest in the nationalist economic program. South Carolina's road and canal projects, for example, were intrastate enterprises which required no federal aid. A system of national roads was not likely to pass through South Carolina; thus federal appropriations would more directly invigorate the economy of other American states.

As long as they were persuaded that road and canal proposals

[5] John Quincy Adams, *Memoirs* . . . , C. F. Adams, ed. (12 vols.; Philadelphia, 1874–7), V, 361; Charles M. Wiltse, *John C. Calhoun: Nationalist, 1782–1828* (Indianapolis, 1944).

were "truly national," the Calhoun-Lowndes nationalists could not have been more ardent champions of federal internal improvements. The American nation, Calhoun told the House of Representatives in 1817, is "rapidly, I was about to say fearfully, growing. This is our pride and danger—our weakness and our strength. . . . Let us, then, bind the Republic together with a perfect system of roads and canals. Let us conquer space." Calhoun's "perfect system," however, envisioned a few great projects and did not include the many "local" schemes which other American nationalists believed should receive bountiful federal aid. As early as 1825, before South Carolina passed her states' rights resolutions, Calhounites vigorously opposed "local," "piecemeal" internal improvement schemes.[6]

The Carolina nationalists' support of protective tariffs was even more qualified, disinterested, and directly tied to the necessities of national defense. South Carolina's economy had always been based on the production of staple crops for export. As a result, Carolina planters had always advocated a free international trade. In colonial times, rice had quickly oversupplied English markets, and the gentry had secured the freedom to trade with other European countries. By 1790 the commitment to free trade was so complete that Pierce Butler could tell an amazed American Congress that a protective tariff would produce "a dissolution of the Union, with regard to his State, as sure as God was in the firmament." As Margaret K. Latimer has pointed out, South Carolina's enthusiasm for the War of 1812 was partially caused by the planters' disgruntlement with Jefferson's restrictive embargo and by their commitment to freedom of the seas. The postwar gentry was not disposed to throw away the fruits of victory by voting for high protective tariffs.[7]

Historians have long assumed that South Carolina planters supported the tariff of 1816 because they planned to develop their own textile factories. But this standard interpretation is based

---

[6] Calhoun, *Papers* . . . , Robert L. Meriwether and W. Edwin Hemphill, eds. (15 vols. planned, 2 publ.; Columbia, 1957–   ), I, 401; *Register of Debates*, 18 Cong., 2 sess., I, 211–12, 223–4, 245–9, 261, 285ff., 553.

[7] Houston, *Critical Study*, p. 4; Latimer, "South Carolina—A Protagonist in the War of 1812," *AHR*, LXI (July 1956), 914–29.

on no more than the historians' faith in economic causation. In the dozens of speeches, letters, and editorials defending the tariff of 1816, South Carolina nationalists never hinted that they expected their state to turn to manufacturing. Congressman William Mayrant, a factory owner, might have hoped to benefit from protective rates. But he was a conspicuous exception. By 1816 South Carolinians were abandoning their handful of textile factories in order to raise more staples for export. The gentry continued to believe that its economic interests would be served best by a low federal tariff.

Although Calhoun and Lowndes advocated the tariff of 1816, they made it very clear that the needs of national defense alone justified it. Repaying the national debt and financing the national army required higher taxes. Moreover, the possibility of war with a maritime power forced the United States to manufacture supplies for itself. "Had we the means of attaining an immediate naval ascendancy," argued Calhoun, ". . . the policy recommended . . . would be very questionable."[8]

The moderate nature of the proposed duties, no less than the national military necessity, enabled Carolina nationalists to favor the tariff. The duties, while designed to be protective, were actually too low to protect. Rates on cottons and woolens were set at 25 percent ad valorem, with an automatic reduction to 20 percent in 1819. Still, South Carolina's congressional delegation, led by Lowndes, voted heavily to reduce cotton and woolen duties immediately to the 20-percent level and to slice iron duties in half. When these efforts failed, Carolina congressmen supported the tariff by a slim four-to-three margin, with two representatives abstaining.[9]

In view of the planters' traditional crusade for free trade, the delegation's vote for the tariff of 1816 provides a striking illustration of South Carolina's commitment to nationalism in the postwar period. But it is equally significant that the vote was close and

8 Calhoun, *Papers*, I, 351–2; *Annals of Congress*, 14 Cong., I sess., pp. 516–22; Wiltse, *Calhoun: Nationalist*, pp. 121–2. For a superb analysis see Norris W. Preyer, "Southern Support of the Tariff of 1816—A Reappraisal," *Journal of Southern History*, XXV (Aug. 1959), 306–22.

9 *Annals of Congress*, 14 Cong., I sess., pp. 1313, 1326, 1336–7, 1347–8, 1352.

that Lowndes, a nationalist, tried to lower the duties. Even in the heyday of South Carolina's infatuation with nationalism, planters had misgivings about a mildly protective tariff.

Four years later South Carolina nationalists strongly opposed a somewhat higher tariff. The proposed Baldwin Tariff of 1820, which the House passed but the Senate tabled, would have raised cotton and woolen duties to 33⅓ percent ad valorem. Lowndes delivered a major address against the proposal, and his South Carolina colleagues voted against it almost unanimously. In Charleston Robert Y. Hayne, a rising younger nationalist, led the public protest against the bill. According to Henry L. Pinckney, Calhoun also "openly opposed . . . the tariff introduced by Mr. Baldwin."[10]

But in the early 1820's South Carolina nationalists never believed that their opposition to higher tariffs conflicted with their commitment to American nationalism. High protective tariffs, like piecemeal internal improvements, did not seem "truly national." Instead of promoting the general welfare, a high tariff would help some groups and hurt others, creating "jealousies" and "hostilities," putting "in jeopardy the peace and harmony of the whole union."[11]

Most South Carolina planters enthusiastically endorsed the Calhoun-Lowndes variety of nationalism. Carolinians had been eager for war in 1812, and they rejoiced at the upsurge of patriotism which accompanied the peace. South Carolina planters participated fully in the national economic prosperity, and South Carolina statesmen held high positions in Congress and in the cabinet. The interests of the state seemed inextricably linked with the destiny of America; and the Calhoun-Lowndes program appeared perfectly contrived to ward off foreign enemies without endangering southern interests. As James Hamilton, Jr., later rather ruefully described it, "there was something in the picture of a magnificent government, invincible in war, beneficent in peace, holding in exact equipoise the scales of justice, presiding

---

[10] *Ibid.*, 16 Cong., 1 sess., II, 2115–40; *City Gazette*, Sept. 16, 1820; *Charleston Mercury*, Feb. 19, 1824.

[11] Hayne, *Speech . . . Against the Tariff . . .* (Charleston, 1824), p. 3.

over all, sustaining all, protecting all, with neither the power nor inclination to do injury to any, well calculated to fascinate the imagination."[12]

But one South Carolina dissenter made up in determination what he lacked in followers. No one in American politics—not even North Carolina's Nathaniel Macon or Virginia's John Randolph —fought harder than United States Senator William Smith to preserve inviolate the states' rights faith during the years when Calhoun Republicans advocated economic nationalism.

Born in York County in 1762, educated at tiny Mt. Zion College, Smith had frittered away his youth as a gay young blade before marriage and consuming ambition turned him toward a respectable legal career. Elected a South Carolina judge in 1808, the ardent Jeffersonian attained prominence as a somewhat tyrannical but scrupulously fair jurist. In 1816 he was elected to the United States Senate as the upcountry's candidate, defeating James J. Pringle of Charleston.

In Washington Smith soon engaged the attention of visitors who lined the tiny Senate gallery. Of medium height, with a portly build and an unpretentious manner, the new senator from South Carolina had the angelic face and wide-eyed stare of an innocent child. Seldom have appearances so completely belied the man. In an age when fiery personal controversies often dominated national politics, Smith stood second to no one in the malignity with which he carried on a personal attack. Rude and sarcastic in public debate, ill-natured and insolent in private relations, he was fully capable of turning petty slights into lifelong feuds. Politicians went out of their way to avoid crossing swords with the vituperative senator from South Carolina.

Yet at the same time, Smith was perhaps the most committed ideologue in American politics. No Calvinist ever placed more faith in the text of the Bible than Smith bestowed on the words of the Constitution; and indeed he espoused the states' rights creed with an unmistakably evangelical fervor. The Jeffersonian drift toward Hamiltonian nationalism seemed to him a major political calamity; and he dedicated his career to recapturing the

[12] *Southern Patriot,* July 9, 1830.

pristine purity of the original faith. At once a petty schemer and a moral crusader, a vindictive fighter and a fervent reformer, old William Smith was a curious cross between a brawling frontiersman and a Bible-belt divine.

Smith had not been in Congress for many months before Calhoun became the special object of his attack. Smith was more than twenty years older than Calhoun, and he expected the young secretary of war to defer to his leadership. He may also have anticipated a Monroe appointment as minister to Russia. But Henry Middleton secured the ministership, perhaps on Calhoun's recommendation. Meanwhile Calhoun ignored Smith, continued to espouse nationalism, and vaulted higher in national prominence. By 1818, seething at these fancied rebuffs, Smith had set out to destroy Calhoun's career with all the determination of an aging and ambitious politician whose ideas and services have been thrust aside by a new generation.[13]

Smith recruited a devoted band of South Carolina allies, particularly in the upcountry east of the Congaree. Thomas Cooper, David R. Williams, Stephen D. Miller, and Josiah Evans were as dedicated as William Smith to the states' rights cause. By 1821 nationalists and Smithites were engaged in a lively public debate on the merits of the Calhoun-Lowndes program. Lowndes and Hayne, however, rivaled Smith and Cooper in denouncing the proposed tariff of 1820. The national bank was not an important issue in South Carolina in the 1820's. The most significant ideological disputes between the two developing factions concerned federal internal improvements and the nationalists' "broad construction" of the federal Constitution.

The Calhoun-Lowndes nationalists favored a few national roads because of national military necessity. At the same time, South Carolina nationalists repudiated piecemeal, local appropriations because of the economic consequences to their own state. Smith and his cohorts, on the other hand, considered allegedly national projects as illegitimate as explicitly local schemes. The Smithites

[13] Perry Diary, entry entitled "Sketch of my Life" and entry for Apr. 28, 1850, NC; Perry, *Reminiscences of Public Men* (Philadelphia, 1883), pp. 8off.; John B. O'Neall, *Biographical Sketches of the Bench and Bar of South Carolina* (2 vols.; Charleston, 1859), I, 106ff.

never believed that a few paved roads would be of decisive military value. The only certain effect of the great "national" schemes, they maintained, would be to drain away the prosperity of South Carolina planters. Since the state had no pending projects which required federal aid, the planters' dollars would bolster the economy of other, richer states. Since improvement schemes swallowed up much of the federal government's funds, the public debt would remain unpaid despite ever-rising tariffs. At best, "national" roads would perpetuate onerous present tariffs. At worst, improvement schemes would force the passage of still higher duties.

The debate over internal improvements, like most early-nine-teenth-century disputes between nationalists and sectionalists, turned into an argument over the Constitution. Smith and Calhoun agreed that in the constitutional compact of 1787, the contracting agents had delegated some of their power to the federal govern-ment and had reserved the rest for the continued use of the several states. The delegated powers included not only a series of enumerated powers but also several vague, elastic prerogatives. The enumerated power "to raise and support armies" was clear enough. But the vague authority "to lay and collect taxes . . . to . . . provide for the common defense and general welfare" was puzzling. The crucial prerogative to pass laws "necessary and proper for carrying into execution" the enumerated powers was even more debatable.

Broad constructionists, such as Calhoun, believed that the enig-matic elastic clauses could be stretched to give Congress additional authority to meet new problems. The "common defense and general welfare" clause meant that Congress could appropriate money for any "truly national" purpose. The "necessary and proper" clause signified that Congress could assume any preroga-tive connected with the enumerated powers. For example, Con-gress could constitutionally charter a national bank or finance internal improvements (neither of which is an enumerated power) because a bank would help collect taxes and roads would further common defense (both of which are enumerated).

Strict constructionists, such as William Smith, on the other

hand, believed that Congress possessed only the expressly enumerated prerogatives; the elastic clauses gave no additional authority.
The enumerated powers alone defined the ways in which Congress
could promote "the common defense and general welfare." The
"necessary and proper" clause gave Congress authority to use
means indispensably needed to carry out enumerated powers. The
national bank charter was unconstitutional because taxes could be
collected without a bank. Internal-improvement projects were
unconstitutional because the power to appropriate money for
building roads and canals was not one of the enumerated powers
which determined how Congress could further the "common
defense and general welfare."

South Carolina nationalists believed that strict construction
made the Constitution sterile and confining rather than dynamic
and viable; it took away from the government that creative ability
to solve new problems in new ways which would alone enable
the nation, and the Constitution, to endure. The Smith faction
believed that broad construction destroyed the essence of constitutional government and threatened the reserved rights of the
states. Constitutions in general were written to restrain majorities.
The American Constitution in particular was designed to check
federal encroachments on powers retained by the states. If a
simple majority in Congress could exercise any power which it
claimed was related to enumerated powers or conducive to the
general welfare, the Constitution was at the mercy of popular
majorities instead of restraining them. The federal government
could seize reserved rights which states had never consented to
give up.[14]

From 1816 to 1823 Smith and his followers made little progress
arguing against federal internal improvements and broad construction of the Constitution in South Carolina. A Smith supporter,
Pleasant May of Chesterfield, shrewdly seeking to turn the
planters' opposition to higher tariffs into opposition to broad
construction, introduced a resolution in the 1820 state House of

[14] The best sources on the debate between nationalists and Smithites are [McDuffie],
National and States Rights Considered by "One of the People" . . . (Charleston,
1821); Cassius [pseud.], *An Examination of Mr. Calhoun's Economy* . . . (n.p.,
1823); [Thomas Cooper], *Consolidation* . . . (Columbia, 1824).

Representatives proclaiming protective tariffs unconstitutional. A select committee, however, reported against the resolution and was sustained by the House. The committee called the tariff "premature and pernicious," but argued that "among the powers expressly given up by the states and vested in Congress by the Constitution is the very one of enacting all laws relating to commerce." The committee also deprecated "the consequences likely to result from the practice, unfortunately become too common, of arraying upon questions of national policy, the states as distinct and independent sovereigns, in opposition to, or what is much the same thing, with a view to exercise a control over, the General Government." A year later a special committee of the state House of Representatives, headed by Hamilton, noted that "they apprehend no danger from the exercise of the powers which the people of the United States have confided to Congress." The South Carolina legislature could not have repudiated William Smith's states' rights principles more emphatically.[15]

If Smith lacked widespread support in South Carolina, he soon acquired the backing of William H. Crawford in Washington. Crawford is an obscure figure compared to his rivals in the "Era of Good Feeling." To contemporaries, however, he seemed a leading spirit of the age. A huge, hulking man, with a handsome face, a coarse manner, and a shrewd sense of political realities, Crawford had pushed his way from obscure frontier origins to high federal office in the early nineteenth century. Successively a United States senator, a minister to France, a secretary of war, and a secretary of the treasury, he had come surprisingly close to wresting the Republican presidential nomination from James Monroe in 1816. Now secretary of the treasury under Monroe, Crawford was determined to bring his distinguished career to a climax by securing a term in the White House.

The alliance between Crawford and Smith was a political inevitability. Both men favored states' rights principles, and each cherished an abiding hatred for Calhoun. Crawford, Calhoun's most bitter rival for the presidency, would have liked nothing

<hr/>

15 Herman V. Ames (ed.), *State Documents on Federal Relations* . . . (Philadelphia, 1906), pp. 91, 134–5.

better than to have captured his opponent's home state. Meanwhile Smith would have relished using the South Carolina patronage thrown his way by a Crawford administration to destroy his bright young tormentor.

Crawford's alliance with Calhoun's most powerful South Carolina rival added more bitterness to the fiercest feud in Washington. If Crawford, a Georgian, was elected President—and in the early 1820's he seemed ahead of the field—Calhoun's immediate political prospects would be slim, for a coalition between two leaders of the Deep South could never control the nation's politics. On the other hand, if Calhoun was defeated by John Quincy Adams, Henry Clay, or Andrew Jackson, he could hope to join the new administration and to secure the next election.

The Calhoun-Crawford struggle naturally focused on Calhoun's army scheme. As secretary of war, Calhoun favored a large military corps. As secretary of the treasury, Crawford favored tight economy and a smaller army. The War of 1812, by demonstrating the need for military preparedness, presented Calhoun with a decisive advantage. But the Panic of 1819 created a demand for lower taxes and gave Crawford his opening. Urging the need for retrenchment and the potential danger of standing armies, Crawfordites sliced the army in half and successfully opposed several of Monroe's military appointments. No one in Washington gloated more than William Smith over John C. Calhoun's embarrassments.[16]

Smith's alliance with Crawford was a political master stroke nationally, but it made him more unpopular in his own state. Crawfordites themselves admitted that most South Carolinians considered the secretary of the treasury "a sort of unfeeling monster." As a native son of the brawling Georgia frontier, Crawford seemed faintly uncouth to cultivated tidewater patricians. And as an opponent of a large army so soon after the War of 1812, Crawford seemed likely to endanger national security in his quest for political power. Most South Carolinians preferred to rally behind a nationalist from their own state, like Calhoun or Lowndes.

---

[16] Wiltse, *Calhoun: Nationalist*, pp. 203–27; *Annals of Congress*, 16 Cong., 1 sess., II, 1607–11, 17 Cong., 1 sess., II, *passim*.

The Smithites' connection with Crawford's presidential campaign loomed as a formidable handicap when Carolina nationalists selected Hayne to oppose Smith in the 1822 senatorial election.[17]

Hayne's meteoric rise rivaled Calhoun's. Born in 1791 to a respected but impoverished old Colleton family, Hayne grew up with an aunt in Beaufort and studied law in Charleston when the family could not afford to send him to college. An ambitious young man with an aptitude for practical enterprise, he quickly mastered the intricacies of the law. And as the scion of a distinguished tidewater family, he easily assumed the stance of a cultivated lowcountry gentleman.

This combination of well-bred gentility and hard-working practicality was a perfect formula for gaining quick entrance into the tidewater aristocracy; and Hayne's career was a Horatio Alger saga from the beginning. A protégé of Langdon Cheves, perhaps Charleston's richest lawyer, Hayne won admittance to the bar before he was twenty-one and immediately took over Cheves' huge practice when that South Carolina "war hawk" left to serve in the fateful Congress of 1812. A year later the rising young lawyer married Frances Henrietta Pinckney, daughter of Charles Pinckney, the wealthy rice planter and leading lowcountry politician. Before he was twenty-three, the lad who could not afford college controlled one of Charleston's largest law firms and was married to one of the tidewater's richest heiresses. After his first wife died in 1819, Hayne soon acquired another fortune by marrying Rebecca Motte Alston.

Political prominence also came quickly. First elected to the state legislature in 1814 at the head of the Charleston ticket, he was re-elected every two years until, in 1818, he was elevated to the speaker's chair and then chosen attorney general. Boyish-looking, with carelessly worn sandy hair and full, rosy cheeks, Hayne looked the part of an exuberant young nationalist; he gestured too much, spoke too fast, and sometimes analyzed too sloppily. His tastes ran to the practical rather than the philosophic;

---

[17] *To the People of South Carolina. An Address . . . in which the claims of William H. Crawford are Impartially Canvassed* (n.p., 1824) ; *Cheraw Intelligencer*, July 16, 1824; *Southern Patriot*, Dec. 16, 1822; *Charleston Courier*, March 1, 1823.

and when he engaged in a purely metaphysical debate, he some-times lost his way. The defect would become obvious during Hayne's great debate with Daniel Webster in 1830.

Lacking Calhoun's flair for political theory, Hayne also lacked Hamilton's zest for political management. Always the cultivated gentleman, he tended to shun party intrigue and demagogic oratory, and members of his own party occasionally found him aloof. In the end, Hayne's political talents would prove to be solid rather than brilliant; and after his famous encounter with Daniel Webster, he would slowly fade into relative political ob-scurity. But in 1822 Hayne's enthusiastic nationalism, his spark-ling deportment, and his sensitivity to the lowcountry's moods made him an ideal candidate to oppose Smith's bid for re-election to the United States Senate.[18]

The Hayne-Smith election marked the early climax of the nationalist-Smithite conflict, and it was preceded by a bitter campaign. As usual, the electioneering took place in the legislature rather than on the hustings. Voters were almost never trusted with a choice between candidates pledged to Smith or Hayne. When the legislators gathered in Columbia, it quickly became ob-vious that Hayne could not be defeated by a candidate who both opposed economic nationalism and supported William Crawford. In the last days before the election, the Smithites, led by Stephen Miller and Josiah Evans, desperately tried to deny that their beleaguered candidate was committed to Crawford. It was to no avail. When the votes were counted, Hayne had triumphed, ninety-one to seventy-four. By ousting Smith from the Senate, nationalists had dealt the proponents of states' rights another crushing setback. Old Smith himself was reduced to storming around the country, denouncing the alleged partisanship of the South Carolina press, and vowing to gain his revenge from John C. Calhoun.[19]

[18] Perry Diary, entry entitled "Sketch of my Life," NC; *City Gazette,* March 12, 1829; Pierce Butler to Hammond, Dec. 18, 1832, Hammond Papers, LC; Jervey, *Hayne, passim.*

[19] *Southern Patriot,* Dec. 16, 1822; Senate Journal, 1822, p. 47, South Carolina Arch.; *City Gazette,* Feb. 14, 27, 1823.

3

The nationalist-Smithite conflict constitutes the main theme of South Carolina's political history from 1816 to 1823. But it would be a mistake to imagine anything like a clean-cut two-party struggle. The South Carolina legislature was split into a number of loose factions, and many—perhaps most—politicians remained independent of all of them. The diffuse nature of state political alignments was well illustrated at an important caucus of the South Carolina legislators in December 1821. The caucus, called to indicate South Carolina's preference for the presidency, selected neither Calhoun nor Crawford but rather Lowndes as its candidate.

South Carolina's nomination of Lowndes was such a serious blow to Calhoun that one suspects the hand of Smith must have been involved in the caucus. But extensive surviving evidence indicates that Smithites boycotted the proceedings. The caucus involved strictly an intramural conflict between lowcountry nationalists loyal to Lowndes and upcountry nationalists who favored Calhoun; and it showed that South Carolina politicians were as much divided by the old conflict between tidewater and piedmont as by the new controversy between nationalists and Smithites. Lowndes' nomination was engineered by the same lowcountry nationalists—Hamilton, Hayne, Daniel Huger, and William Drayton—who became leading Calhounites after Lowndes died in 1822. The caucus left no doubt that it disagreed on candidates rather than principles. After voting fifty-eight to fifty-four to nominate Lowndes, the legislators unanimously resolved that a proper nominee should eschew "sectional divisions," and should be "brought forth truly, strongly, and indubitably as the NATIONAL CANDIDATE."[20]

The nomination of Lowndes is only the most important indication of the absence of a two-party structure in South Carolina politics in the early 1820's. One significant upcountry faction, led by Alexander Speer, paid little heed to national issues or candidates.

[20] William Lowndes Papers, 1821–2, NC; *Pendleton Messenger,* Jan. 23, 1822; Wiltse, *Calhoun: Nationalist,* p. 237.

The Speer group concentrated on cutting the state budget in order to cut state taxes. In Charleston three factions existed, and until late in 1824 none was pledged to Crawford. The Mercury Junto, named after its newspaper, the *Charleston Mercury*, supported Lowndes, then Calhoun, then Jackson, for the presidency. The Courier party, named after its organ, the *Charleston Courier*, and composed of the mercantile community, espoused neo-Federalist principles and favored John Quincy Adams. The Geddes faction, led by former Governor John Geddes, backed Calhoun and toyed with supporting Jackson before reluctantly entering the Crawford camp in late 1824. Prior to 1823 South Carolina's politics were characterized by a qualified belief in economic nationalism, a firm opposition to William Crawford, and a lack of statewide political parties.[21]

4

In the mid-1820's a series of threatening events turned most South Carolinians against the broad-construction principles advocated by Calhoun-Lowndes nationalists. As one contemporary explained it, "the tariff of 1824, and some movements in regard to the slave population, then seemed for the first time, to create a lurking suspicion that, in her attachment to the general government the State had perhaps, not been sufficiently vigilant in the maintenance of her own rights, and in the protection of her peculiar interests."[22]

In the 1824 Congress, American industrialists, concerned over the defeat of the 1820 tariff and the pressure of foreign competition, demanded further protection for their products. Despite outcries from the South, protectionists pushed the tariff through Congress, raising woolen and cotton duties from 25 percent to 33⅓ percent and increasing other duties proportionately.

In 1824, as in 1820, nationalists led South Carolina's fight against the tariff. In Charleston Henry L. Pinckney's *Mercury* for a time urged Carolinians to cease importing northern goods. In Washington Congressmen McDuffie and Hamilton and Senator Hayne all

---

[21] *Charleston Mercury, Charleston Courier, City Gazette,* 1823–4; Grayson Autobiography, p. 346; Calhoun to Poinsett, July 8, 1824, Poinsett Papers.
[22] *Columbia Telescope,* Nov. 27, 1829.

gave excellent antitariff orations. Indeed, by 1824 South Carolina nationalists had formulated many of the arguments against protection which they would use as nullifiers.[23]

The Carolinians, as apostles of Adam Smith's view of economics, assumed that individuals, if left free to pursue their own self-interest, would inevitably further the general interest. An "invisible hand" would direct capitalists to the investments most profitable for themselves and most beneficial to the economy. If factories were profitable investments, entrepreneurs would create them. If manufactories were unprofitable, governmental intervention could not salvage them. By protecting inefficient industries, the government prevented capitalists from seeking more advantageous investments and thereby slowed down the nation's economic growth.

If tariffs hurt the entire economy, continued the Carolinians, they could ruin southern planters. An avowed purpose of protection was to prevent foreigners from underselling domestic manufacturers, forcing southerners to buy goods at propped-up prices. Other producers could at least hope that higher income would compensate for higher prices. Manufacturers, sugar planters, and lead miners could all expect higher incomes from their protected products. Laborers might be paid higher wages, and farmers selling food to urban dwellers might receive higher prices. But South Carolina planters, selling only a fraction of their staples in the domestic market, could not benefit from protection.

Indeed—and this was the crucial point—tariffs would inevitably destroy foreign demand for rice and cotton. Foreign governments might impose high tariffs on American exports in retaliation. Even if retaliatory duties were eschewed, foreigners would buy rice and cotton from other lands if they could not sell their goods in American markets. England, in particular, would encourage Brazil and Egypt to produce more bales of cotton. At best, Europeans would buy southern staples at lower prices. At worst, cotton and rice would find no foreign market at all.[24]

[23] *Charleston Mercury,* March 20, 1824.
[24] Hayne, *Speech* . . . *1824;* Hamilton, *Speech of Mr. Hamilton* . . . *1824* (Washington, D.C., 1824).

By 1824, with the threat of war receding and their state's economy depressed, most South Carolinians regarded these prospects with dismay. Upland cotton producers had already suffered through five years of deteriorating economic conditions, and the declining upcountry wagon trade had impoverished mechanics and retailers in Charleston. Meanwhile lowcountry luxury cotton planters had not yet discovered that they could escape the consequences of the upcountry cotton glut by adopting more sophisticated agricultural techniques. Producers throughout the state considered themselves "at the very crisis of their fate," and it seemed no time to run the risk of losing British markets.

South Carolina's opposition to the tariff of 1824 was tame compared to what would come later. Calhounites claimed that the new tariff would aggravate an already existing depression; no one blamed hard times on previous tariffs. Hamilton and Hayne both briefly claimed that protection was unconstitutional, but their argument seemed thrown in as an afterthought. And McDuffie closed his antitariff oration with a patriotic statement that he would soon have cause to regret. If Congress passed the tariff, he promised, "I shall, as bound by my allegiance, submit to it as one of the laws of my country. I have endeavored, with zeal and fidelity, to discharge my duty as a Representative. I trust I shall never be found wanting in my duty as a citizen." South Carolinians called numerous public meetings in the fall of 1824, not to protest against the tariff, but to leap enthusiastically upon the presidential bandwagon of General Andrew Jackson, who had supported the new duties.[25]

5

The rise of the slavery issue produced more immediate excitement among planters who lived in the South Carolina lowcountry. In 1820 tidewater gentlemen had been nervous but not acutely distressed when Congress discussed slavery during the Missouri Controversy. Lowndes, the lowcountry's revered political leader, worked hard for a moderate compromise, and a majority of his Carolina colleagues favored the final settlement. Charleston news-

[25] *Annals of Congress*, 18 Cong., 1 sess., II, 2426.

papers did their best to keep the issue out of the public eye. When the Compromise was at last enacted, Calhoun professed to "sincerely believe" that the issue had been settled "forever"[26]—the view of many nationalists.

One lowcountry leader, however, shunned moderation during the first national crisis over the slavery issue. In the national House of Representatives, Charles Pinckney of Charleston gave a major oration against the Missouri Compromise. Pinckney, a leading figure in lowcountry politics for over a generation, had been a prominent member of the Constitutional Convention in 1787. Drawing on his memories of the proceedings, the Charleston congressman maintained that the Founding Fathers had given Congress no authority over the Negro issue. Settling the Missouri dispute, he argued, was "very unimportant" compared with "keeping the hands of Congress from touching the question of slavery." If Congress established its right to consider the subject, he warned, "there is no knowing to what length it may be carried."[27]

In 1820 most South Carolina planters were inclined toward the optimism of Calhoun rather than the forebodings of Pinckney. The outburst of antislavery "fanaticism," however alarming in itself, seemed an aberrant storm which would soon blow over. But after the Denmark Vesey Conspiracy in 1822, the tidewater gentry had grim second thoughts about congressional slavery debates. It seemed clear that "the unreflecting zeal of the North and East" had directly animated "Vesey in his hellish efforts"; and in retrospect the Missouri Controversy appeared to be a harrowing event. Charles Pinckney's doctrines, although rejected in 1820, had become lowcountry dogma by 1823. As Whitemarsh Seabrook summed up the mood at tidewater in the mid-1820's, "whoever remembers the inflammatory speeches on the Missouri bill, must be aware, that no subject, in which the question of slavery may be directly or incidentally introduced, can be canvassed, without the most malevolent and serious excitement."[28]

---

[26] *Ibid.*, 16 Cong., 1 sess., II, 1586; Calhoun to Charles Tait, Oct. 1, 1821, "Letters from John C. Calhoun to Charles Tait," *Gulf State Historical Magazine,* I (Sept. 1902), 102–4.

[27] *Annals of Congress,* 16 Cong., 1 sess., II, 1310–29. See also S[tephen] Elliott to William Elliott, July 27, 1820, Elliott-Gonzales Papers.

[28] *Concise View,* pp. 11–14. See also Holland, *Refutation of the Calumnies,* pp. 8–10.

Since the gentry's post-1822 anxiety about slavery debates often centered around fear of slave revolts, it is important to understand the nature of their apprehensions. Few planters—even in the lowcountry—ever believed that a servile insurrection could succeed. But a series of unsuccessful conspiracies—like the Vesey affair—seemed entirely plausible. The quasi-assimilated slaves of the lowcountry, with their huge numerical majority and their susceptibility to the voodoo of countless Gullah Jacks, appeared likely to respond again and again to congressional lectures on the Rights of Man. Any such series of conspiracies could make the Carolina lowcountry an unnerving area in which to live.

Moreover, a number of revolts could slowly demoralize a community already plagued by grave misgivings about slavery. Few planters could continue to salve their consciences with myths about Sambos if trusted Negroes tried again and again to murder their masters. Even loyal servants would arouse vague apprehensions; and kindly masters would find themselves reaching more often for the lash. A slave revolt had a unique capacity to sweep away all illusions and to force planters to confront the ugliness in their system. Furthermore, congressional debates, by raising questions about the permanency and morality of slavery, could again destroy public confidence in the institution and thereby undermine an effective fight against abolition.

As leading South Carolinians emphasized in the 1820's, the problem of public confidence in slavery seemed in part a crucial economic question. Continual apprehensions about the safety, morality, and permanency of the institution could cause many planters to sell their slaves. A wave of slave auctions would produce "a rapid deterioration of property"; and a sharp drop of slave prices could bankrupt the many planters who relied on selling a few bondsmen to escape onerous debts. In the end, universal bankruptcy would erode the already shaken morale of the South and would lead to the triumph of the abolitionists. Thus in the years when lowcountry planters first came face to face with the slavery issue, they feared that a small number of congressional fanatics, "by disturbing the security of our property" and "by spreading a moral poison through the land," might reduce the South to the necessity "of *consenting* almost to any terms that may be prescribed."[29]

South Carolinians believed that the Constitution was, in Hayne's phrase, "the very 'Ark of the Covenant,' in which alone we will find safety." Slavery was so clearly within the states' reserved rights, and the Constitution so explicitly restricted congressional authority to the delegated powers, that if the Constitution was preserved inviolate, Congress could never touch slavery. As Charles Pinckney urged during the Missouri Crisis, "On the subject of the Constitution, no compromise ought ever to be made."[30]

This extreme commitment to constitutional salvation made Pinckney, Hayne, and other lowcountry nationalists the weirdest of broad constructionists. Many clauses of the Constitution, if interpreted with the slightest latitude, gave Congress at least the power to debate slavery. If Congress can appropriate money for anything it deems in the general welfare, William Smith liked to ask, why can't a northern majority appropriate funds to abolish slavery? After 1822 any indication that the federal government might interfere with slavery made the lowcountry fertile ground for strict-construction doctrines. The signs were not long in coming.

In the wake of the Vesey Conspiracy, the overriding objective of Charleston aristocrats was to seal off their slaves from any contact with "incendiary" ideas. Congressional slavery debates appeared to be the most important way in which slaves were exposed to the idea of freedom. But the lowcountry gentry was also distressed by the slaves' relationships with colored seamen from outside the state.

The seamen problem arose because ships from northern states and foreign lands often docked at Charleston harbor for several days. In 1822 Negro sailors who stepped ashore had free run of the city. This permissive arrangement invited contact between northern Negro abolitionists and the lowcountry slaves. It also

---

[29] See Hayne's speeches in *Register of Debates*, 19 Cong., 1 sess., pp. 165–6, 19 Cong., 2 sess., p. 329; Seabrook, *Concise View;* [Turnbull], *The Crisis;* Arthur P. Hayne to Jackson, Nov. 11, 1835, Jackson Papers, LC.

[30] *Register of Debates*, 19 Cong., 2 sess., p. 329; *Annals of Congress*, 16 Cong., 1 sess., II, 1328.

allowed colored seamen from San Domingo to stride through the streets of Charleston.

The gentry had long regarded these visitors with suspicion. Ever since the days when slavemasters by the hundreds had fled to Charleston to escape the vengeance of their bondsmen, Carolinians had retained a vivid memory of the San Domingo uprisings. Thus planters were dismayed when they learned that Denmark Vesey had used the West Indies example in his harangues to the slaves. The rebel chief had supposedly also promised his followers that San Domingans "would come over and cut up the white people, if we only made the motion here first." One archconspirator did his best to keep Vesey's promise. Monday Gell, the towering blacksmith who had directed the Ebo wing of the Vesey rebels, admitted that he had tried to secure help from the San Domingan government by handing letters to Negro seamen in Charleston. Henry W. De Saussure summed up the tidewater's apprehensions:

I fear this kind of property is fast losing its value on the Sea Coast; for its vicinity to the W. I. Islands, and the great intercourse with them, must introduce among our slaves many of those who have been engaged in scenes of blood in the West Indies, who will beguile our slaves into rebellion with false hopes. . . .[31]

The lowcountry's concern about foreign Negro "agitators" led the South Carolina legislature, in December 1822, to enact a law requiring all colored seamen to be seized and jailed while their ships remained in Charleston harbor. From the beginning the law invited trouble with the federal government. Imprisoning Negro seamen violated an agreement between the United States and Great Britain giving inhabitants of the two nations free access to each other's ports. Early in 1823 England protested to Secretary of State John Quincy Adams, and Adams may have persuaded Charlestonians to suspend the law. At any rate, by mid-1823 Negroes from San Domingo were again discoursing with South Carolina slaves in the streets of Charleston.[32]

[31] Kennedy and Parker, *Official Report*, pp. 62, 96–7; De Saussure to Poinsett, July 6, 1822, Poinsett Papers.
[32] *Statutes at Large*, VII, 461–6; Phillip Hamer, "Great Britain, the United States, and the Negro Seamen Acts, 1822–1848," *Journal of Southern History*, I (Feb. 1935), 3–28.

But tidewater planters were in no mood to tolerate a continued suspension of the seamen law. On July 24, 1823, the gentry met in Charleston's St. Andrew's Hall, and in one of the most revealing events of the period, they formed the South Carolina Association. Leading tidewater planters became officers of the Charleston Association, and auxiliaries were formed throughout the lowcountry. The South Carolina Association was destined to become a permanent ante bellum institution, serving as an eternal watchdog over the slaves and as a fertile source of southern radicalism.

The association's prime purpose was to ensure that civil authorities enforced the Negro laws. Members of the organization elected permanent standing committees, and the committees supervised the day-to-day administration of the Black Codes. Committee members kept a close eye on the slaves and insisted upon arrests at the slightest provocation. The standing committees reported back to the gentry at the association's annual meetings; and these well-attended meetings were one of the great occasions of the year in Charleston. The formation and continued vitality of this extralegal, law-enforcing organization of private citizens indicate better than anything else the tidewater's concern about slave revolts in the years after 1822.[33]

The South Carolina Association had no sooner been formed than it demanded that Charleston's sheriff enforce the seamen law. As a result, a Jamaican free Negro, Harry Elkinson, was imprisoned until his ship left Charleston. Elkinson applied to United States Supreme Court Justice William Johnson for a writ of habeas corpus, and the latter immediately called a hearing. Elkinson's case was simple and logical: the United States Constitution decreed that "all treaties made . . . under the authority of the United States, shall be the supreme law of the land." The seamen law violated the Anglo-American treaty. Therefore the law was unconstitutional and the defendant should be released.

Benjamin F. Hunt and Isaac E. Holmes, arguing for the association, admitted that the law violated the treaty but argued that the treaty violated the Constitution. The national government's

33 *Charleston Courier*, July 24, 1823; *Charleston Mercury*, Aug. 3, 1825.

power to make treaties and pass laws extended only to the delegated powers. State governments, since they retained the reserved powers, remained sovereign. A government which could not protect itself against internal revolution was no longer sovereign. Hence federal action which infringed on a state's police power was unconstitutional. Thus the Negro seamen law or any act necessary to avoid servile insurrection took precedence over any federal treaty.

Johnson denied Elkinson's petition on a legal technicality: the Negro was held under state law, and the Supreme Court's authority to issue writs extended only to federal prisoners. But in a famous obiter dictum, Johnson brilliantly refuted the Carolina argument. The Constitution, he argued, explicitly made federal laws and treaties "the supreme law of the land." Yet if a state could pass any law, in defiance of federal authority, which it deemed "necessary" for internal safety, state law became "the supreme law of the land." Johnson asked, "Where is this to land us? Is it not asserting the right in each state to throw off the federal Constitution at its will and pleasure?"[34]

The decision created a sensation. As Seabrook paraphrased Johnson's logic, "South Carolina possesses no right to enact laws, guarding against the corruption and consequent insubordination of her slaves." The opinion, wrote another Charlestonian, "brought full to my recollection, the wretched fugitives from San Domingo. I cannot but remember that the first cause of these misfortunes, was the interference of their distant supreme government with their internal domestic regulations, with which it had no sympathies."[35]

Despite the decision, Carolinians continued to jail Negro seamen, and British protests continued to embarrass Secretary of

[34] [Turnbull and Holmes], *Caroliniensis on the Arrest of a British Seaman;* [Benjamin F. Hunt], *The Argument of . . . Hunt in the Case of . . . a British Seaman . . .* (Charleston, 1823); [William Johnson], *The Opinion of . . . Johnson . . . in the Case . . . of the British Seamen . . .* (Charleston, 1823); Donald G. Morgan, *Justice William Johnson: The First Dissenter* (Columbia, 1954), pp. 192ff.; Morgan, "Justice William Johnson on the Treaty-Making Power," *George Washington Law Review,* XXII (Dec. 1953), 259–77.

[35] Seabrook, *Concise View,* p. 7; all Charleston papers, Aug. and Sept. 1823, esp. *Charleston Courier,* Sept. 16, 1823.

State Adams. In May 1824 Adams asked United States Attorney General William Wirt to write an opinion on the seamen law. Wirt trenchantly argued that the law violated both the treaty with England and Congress' exclusive power to regulate commerce. In July Adams sent the British protests and the Wirt essay on to South Carolina Governor John L. Wilson, with the request that "the inconvenience complained of will be remedied by the legislature of the State of South Carolina."[36]

Although the two houses of the 1824 state legislature could not agree on the tone which should be adopted, they concurred in defying Adams. "The duty of the state to guard against insubordination or insurrection," resolved the Senate, ". . . is paramount to all *laws*, all *treaties*, all *constitutions*. It arises from the supreme and permanent law of . . . self-preservation; and will never, by this state, be renounced, compromised, controlled or participated with any power whatever." The House added, "The measures directed towards colored persons brought within the territory of this state, are simply part of a general system of domestic police, defensible as such, and absolutely necessary to ensure the safety of the citizens." South Carolina continued to imprison Negro seamen despite sporadic federal protest. Years later Hayne rightly claimed that the state had successfully nullified federal law in the Seamen Controversy.[37]

He might have added that Judge Johnson's opinion and John Quincy Adams' letter raised the basic nullification issues in South Carolina for the first time. In 1823 South Carolinians relied on the reserved rights of the states to nullify a federal treaty which they judged interfered with internal safety. In 1832 South Carolinians used the same reserved rights to nullify a federal law which they judged unconstitutional. The Negro Seamen Controversy, in short, served lowcountry gentlemen as a powerful lesson on the necessity for adopting strict-construction principles if the federal government was to be prevented from touching the slavery issue. As the South Carolina Association put it in 1825, "The State Sover-

---

[36] *Charleston Mercury*, Dec. 8, 1824.
[37] Ames (ed.), *Federal Documents*, p. 207; Elkinson MS, Legaré Papers; *Southern Patriot*, Dec. 15, 1824; *Hayne's Fourth of July Oration . . . 1831* (Charleston, 1831), p. 31.

eignties—the ark to which we must ultimately look to our safety. Let it not be engulfed in the constructive powers of Congress."[38]

The Ohio Resolutions of 1824 again made slaveholders aware of the potential danger in broad construction. In January 1824 the Ohio legislature recommended to the states and to Congress a mild plan of emancipation. The Ohioans admitted that slavery was a "national" evil and urged that "the states of this Union ought mutually to participate in the duties and burthens of removing it." The capstone of the Ohio proposal, which required southern consent before federal action, was a national law freeing all slaves born after enactment when they reached the age of twenty-one if they agreed to foreign colonization. Eight other northern states endorsed the Ohio plan. Six southern states repudiated it.[39]

The dangerous implication of the Ohio plan, like the distressing aspect of the seamen case, was that the federal government could constitutionally interfere with slavery. Congress could at least discuss the proposition before southern states approved it, and a new congressional debate might bring on further servile unrest. Governor Wilson sent the resolution to the 1824 legislature with a covering message insisting on "a firm determination to resist, at the threshold, every invasion of our domestic tranquility." The Senate termed the Ohio proposal "a very strange and ill-advised communication" and protested against "any claim of right, of the United States, to interfere, in any manner whatever," with slavery. The House called on the governor to inform the Ohio legislature "that the people of this state will adhere to a system, descended to them from their ancestors, and now inseparably connected with their social and political existence."[40]

6

Thus by 1824 South Carolina planters had several reasons to regret their old commitment to nationalist dogmas. The Ohio

[38] *Charleston Mercury*, May 30, 1825.
[39] Ames (ed.), *Federal Documents*, pp. 203–4.
[40] *Ibid.*, pp. 204–8. John M. Lofton, *Insurrection in South Carolina: The Turbulent World of Denmark Vesey* (Yellow Springs, Ohio, 1964), ch. 13, contains a good discussion of the immediate political consequences of the Vesey affair. Since these chapters were completed before Lofton's book was published, I unfortunately did not have the benefit of using his analysis.

Resolutions, the Negro Seamen Controversy, and the tariff of 1824 seemed to threaten South Carolina's most vital interests. Meanwhile the danger of foreign war had slipped away, and both the Denmark Vesey Conspiracy and the deepening economic depression had led planters to concentrate on their own peculiar concerns. For the first time since 1816, William Smith's cause had a chance to prevail.

The Smithites lost no time in making the most of their opportunity. Thomas Cooper's excellent pamphlet *Consolidation* presented the case against Calhoun's dogmas, and Stephen Miller introduced resolutions in the state Senate of 1824, stating the principle of strict construction and proclaiming protective tariffs and internal improvements unconstitutional. David R. Williams brilliantly supported the Miller Resolutions, and the Senate passed them despite the vigorous protest of Calhounite leader Eldred Simkins. The House, however, tabled both the Miller Resolutions and the nationalist counterresolutions introduced by Samuel Prioleau, brother-in-law of James Hamilton, Jr., and a Calhounite.[41]

The events of 1825 ensured the triumph of the Miller Resolutions. Congressional appropriations continued to spiral; several more northern states endorsed the Ohio Resolutions; Rufus King introduced resolutions in the United States Senate urging that public land revenues be used to emancipate the slaves. Meanwhile Seabrook's important pamphlet *A Concise View of the Critical Situation and Future Prospects of the Slaveholding States in Relation to their Colored Population* alerted more tidewater planters to the impending dangers. Most important of all, a gigantic English cotton speculation subjected prices to the worst battering of the decade; upland cotton fell from thirty-two cents in June to thirteen cents in October. Once again South Carolina's interests seemed threatened at every turn.[42]

When the state legislature met at the end of the year, Smith,

---

[41] Phillip F. Wild, "South Carolina Politics: 1816-1833" (unpubl. diss., Univ. of Pennsylvania, 1949), p. 221; *Camden Journal*, Dec. 4, 1830; Ames (ed.), *Federal Documents*, pp. 136–40. Ames erroneously states that the House passed the Prioleau Resolutions.

[42] Governor Richard Manning's Message of Dec. 12, 1825, Williams-Chestnut-Manning Papers.

now a member of the state House of Representatives, called up the Miller Resolutions of 1824, which subsequently became known as the Smith Resolutions of 1825. After several days of debate and vigorous protests from Calhounites, the House passed the resolutions, seventy-three to twenty-eight. The Senate concurred, twenty-nine to fourteen.[43]

Probably the lowcountry opted for strict construction more because of apprehensions about slavery than concern about tariffs. Surely the upcountry was less concerned about Negro seamen and more upset about the protective principle. Smithite speeches emphasized both dangers. As Smith himself put it, "that paragraph of the Constitution which authorizes Congress to provide for the 'general welfare' . . . has given you a Tariff, by which you are taxed to support manufacturers that are wallowing in wealth. And it will, as soon as the Northern States . . . have finished internal improvements, rend your government asunder, or make your slaves your masters."[44]

Meanwhile the changing national alliances of South Carolina politicians enabled Smith to take personal advantage of his legislative triumph. Calhoun, unexpectedly swamped by Andrew Jackson in the contest for Pennsylvania's support, had bowed out of the 1824 presidential election, settling for an uncontested election to the vice-presidency. Crawford's campaign had lost its momentum when he suffered a stroke; by 1825 he was out of national politics. No presidential candidate received a majority of the 1824 electoral votes, which threw the election into the House of Representatives. When Henry Clay gave his support to John Quincy Adams, the New Englander triumphed and named Clay as his secretary of state. Opponents of the new administration soon formed a new party dedicated to furthering the presidential ambitions of Andrew Jackson.

The Adams-Clay alliance, the hero of New Orleans' great popularity in South Carolina, and Calhoun's personal predilec-

---

[43] Wild, "South Carolina Politics," ch. 10; *Southern Patriot*, Dec. 19, 1825.
[44] *Charleston Mercury*, Dec. 14, 1824; *Camden Journal*, Feb. 11, 1826; *City Gazette*, March 1, 1826; *Edgefield Hive*, March 5, 1830; *Statutes at Large*, I, 228–9. Sixty-four percent of the coastal legislators and sixty-seven percent of the other members voted for the Smith Resolutions.

tions quickly brought him into the Jackson coalition. Calhoun was a prime critic of the "corrupt bargain" by which Adams and Clay allegedly came to power. Soon the capital enjoyed the rare treat of observing a newspaper war between the President and the Vice President.

Calhoun's central place in the Jackson camp left former Crawfordites like William Smith in a quandary. In reality, Smithites had little choice. Entering a party which Calhoun might dominate was wormwood and gall. But as apostles of states' rights, they could hardly support such nationalists as Adams and Clay. More important, Jackson retained his popularity in South Carolina, and Smith, who had already lost one election by favoring Crawford, had no wish to drag himself under again by supporting Adams.

Free of the Crawford contamination, firmly allied with Old Hickory, William Smith, prophet of the newly popular states' rights ideology, squeezed by the nationalists' Daniel Huger, eighty-three to eighty-one, in the 1826 United States Senate election. Smith raced to Washington on the first coach and could find only one circumstance to mar his vindication. "Do you know, sir," Smith later told Huger, "that Calhoun, on my return to the Senate of the United States, treated me with so much kindness and consideration that I could not hate him as I wished to do."[45]

If Smith's principles had triumphed and Smith himself had been returned to the United States Senate, his faction had in no sense destroyed the Calhoun party. Loose factional organization and the nebulous relationship between issues and elections prevented anything like a sweeping Smithite victory. Several factions continued to exist in 1826, and such important politicians as William Campbell Preston and William Harper remained somewhat independent of all of them. The death of William Lowndes and of John Geddes dissolved their coalitions in a decade when politics revolved primarily around personalities. Lowndes' supporters transferred their loyalties to Calhoun and formed the lowcountry wing of Calhoun's Mercury Junto. Geddes' followers,

[45] T. J. Withers to Hammond, Aug. 26, 1826, Hammond Papers, LC; *Charleston Courier*, Dec. 4, 1826; Perry, *Reminiscences* (1883 ed.), pp. 8off.

despite their short connection with the Smith faction, tended to support Charleston's Courier party. The four surviving factions included the Calhoun faction, or Mercury Junto, strongest in the upcountry along the Savannah and in Charleston; the Smith faction, strongest in the upcountry east of the Congaree; the Speer faction, an upcountry crowd which continued to ignore national issues and to concentrate on paring the state budget; and finally, the Courier party in Charleston, which still attracted merchants and supported John Quincy Adams.[46]

Elections in the state legislature too continued to be decided more on personalities than on issues. The same legislature which overwhelmingly passed the Smith Resolutions chose a nationalist, Richard Manning, as the new governor of the state; selected another nationalist, John B. O'Neall, to be speaker of the House; and gave the majority of its votes to two other nationalists, Daniel Huger and Warren L. Davis, rather than the states' rights candidate, John Gaillard, on the first ballot in the senatorial election of 1824. The legislature of 1826, which would prove in 1827 to be more overwhelmingly in favor of states' rights principles, came within two votes of electing Huger over Smith in their vigorously contested race for the United States Senate. The legislature of 1828, a militant states' rights body, elected a still nationalistic O'Neall to an important judgeship over a powerful Smithite, Josiah Evans.[47]

The nationalist–states' rights controversy had even less effect on popular elections to Congress and to the legislature. The Calhounites' Congressmen McDuffie, Hamilton, and Drayton were re-elected without opposition in 1826. Calhounites and Smithites split the two congressional elections they contested— the nationalist Warren L. Davis defeated John L. Wilson, and

[46] Manning to Harper, March 9, 1826, Williams-Chestnut-Manning Papers; Preston to Thompson, March 4, 1826, Thompson Papers, LC; City Gazette for 1826, esp. Sept. 2, 1826.

[47] Ibid., Dec. 7, 1824; Pendleton Messenger, Dec. 31, 1828; David R. Williams to Miller, Jan. 5, 1829, Williams Papers, SC. If the vote in the senatorial election of 1826 had exactly paralleled the vote on the Smith Resolutions of 1825, Smith would have smashed Huger 102–52! In fact the crucial issue was not the new constitutional issues but rather the old sectional rivalry; a Huger victory would have given the lowcountry both seats in the United States Senate. Withers to Hammond, Aug. 26, 1826, Hammond Papers, LC; City Gazette, Oct. 9, 1826.

the Smithite William D. Martin defeated Andrew Govan. Elections to the state legislature of 1826 were usually uncontested. On the rare occasions when a Calhoun candidate faced a Smith supporter, personal factors rather than the states' rights issue tended to decide the contest.[48]

In 1828 the electorate, finally responding to an ideological issue, failed to return half the state legislators. The victor, however, was neither Calhoun nor Smith but Alexander Speer! Speer's decade-long fight to cut the state budget finally triumphed when the populace exploded at a $10,000 appropriation to get Thomas Jefferson's daughter out of debt. Speaker O'Neall was unseated by his constituents, and the new legislature reduced the budget 20 percent. The retrenchment campaign of 1828 is one of the best indications of the irrelevance of the Calhoun-Smith issues in deciding popular elections in the 1820's.[49]

The Calhoun-Smith conflict remained a superficial clash between legislative factions rather than an organized party struggle for the electorate's support because, despite the fury of the legislative debates and the importance of the constitutional principles discussed, policy differences were remarkably few. After 1819 both factions opposed higher tariffs, and after 1822 they both maintained an unbending position on the slavery issue. Moreover, the Calhounites, although theoretically favoring "national" internal improvements, had denounced as "local" almost every project proposed since 1824. These disagreements never seemed serious enough to justify the supposed risks involved in taking a decision to the people. As events in the 1830's would show, only a fundamental clash over policy could overcome the patricians' profound distrust of demagogues, electioneering, and popular political parties.

48 For example, the contest between the Smithite John Taylor and the nationalist Wade Hampton for the state Senate, won by Hampton, was primarily a personal campaign between Columbia's two leading families. Perry, *Reminiscences of Public Men, with Speeches and Addresses* (Greenville, 1889), p. 109. The Georgetown senatorial contest between Smithite John L. Wilson and nationalist Henry L. Middleton, won by Wilson, was fought over Wilson's alleged personal corruption. *Georgetown Gazette,* July and Oct. 1826.

49 *United States Telegraph,* Jan. 3, 1827; *Southern Patriot,* Nov. 27, 1828; O'Neall, *Biographical Sketches,* I, xxi–xxii.

7

The events of 1827 made sectionalists out of the Calhoun nationalists. The American Colonization Society's request for congressional aid, the woolen manufacturers' attempt to procure
higher duties, and the Harrisburgh Convention's organization of
the protectionist movement drew firm resistance from Hayne,
Pinckney, McDuffie, and Hamilton and an increasingly violent
response from their state.

In 1827 the American Colonization Society dispatched a petition to Congress which inaugurated its campaign for a federal
appropriation. The petition, which Hayne and Smith adamantly
opposed in the United States Senate, was the subject of intense
excitement along the South Carolina coast. The Colonization
Society represented the conservative wing of the antislavery movement—and was patronized by many who opposed abolition. All
colonizers hoped to send free Negroes back to Africa. Those who
favored abolition hoped that resistance to emancipation would
lessen when freedman could be colonized. The society's immediate aims were innocuous enough; some southerners hoped to
strengthen slavery by removing troublesome free Negroes. The
society's project also seemed totally impracticable. At first glance,
a petition from the inept colonizers seems unlikely to rouse the
rage of even so tense a region as the South Carolina seaboard.

But to tidewater aristocrats, the colonization petition seemed
the fatal "entering wedge," which, if not met at the "threshold,"
would clear the way for abolition. A colonization appropriation
would set the vital constitutional precedent, for if Congress could
promote the general welfare by colonizing free Negroes, it could
also promote the general welfare by freeing Negro slaves. "The
only safety of the Southern States," Hayne argued, "is to be
found in the want of power on the part of the Federal Government to touch the subject at all."[50]

Lowcountry planters also suspected that colonization was a
front for northern "fanatics." Abolitionists had enough sense to
realize that "any sudden effort . . . is . . . unwise. . . . It is their

[50] *Register of Debates*, 19 Cong., 2 sess., pp. 289, 329.

policy then, that one cautious and apparently innocent measure shall insensibly succeed another." Colonization was a preliminary agitation, designed to set precedents and to weaken slaveholders. When the main blow came, the South would be supine and defenseless.[51]

The South Carolina radicals vowed never to tolerate congressional discussion of colonization. A debate on colonization would inevitably turn into a debate on slavery; and a renewed discussion of the slavery issue might intensify the guilt and fear which afflicted the gentry. Robert J. Turnbull summarized the situation:

The claims of the Colonization Society can not possibly be discussed, without giving to Congress an occasion, *officially* to express its opinion against slavery as an *evil*. . . . The interference of Congress . . . would alarm the timid amongst us. It would cause those, who are wavering and in doubt, to give up their opinions. It would deter capitalists from investments in plantations and negroes. . . . As regards our domestics, the effects upon their minds, by any such opinion by the National Legislature, would be such, as to fill us all with the DEEPEST apprehensions.[52]

The gentry's sensitivity to developments in England also heightened its fear of the American Colonization Society. Carolina aristocrats read the best English journals, and they had long been aware of William Wilberforce's increasingly successful campaign against slavery in the British West Indies. By 1827 Wilberforce seemed certain to prevail.

Lowcountry planters feared that the impending triumph of English "fanaticism" would pave the way for a vigorous anti-slavery effort in America. They also saw an ominous parallel between the early tactics of Wilberforce and the possible strategy of the colonizers. When Wilberforce first proposed abolishing the slave trade, Turnbull wrote, he was "even *more cautious* than the Colonization Society. He took especial care not to profess that the abolition of the slave trade was but the *first* step towards an object which he then most deeply had at heart." The discussion of the slave trade had inevitably led to a debate on

[51] Seabrook, *A Concise View*, p. 13; *Southern Times*, Apr. 19, 1830; *SR*, I (Feb. 1828), 221, 229–30; *Charleston Mercury*, Apr. 24, 1830.
[52] *The Crisis*, pp. 129–30.

slavery. For over three decades, the "nervous" and "uneasy" West Indies planters, desponding over "the perpetual agitation of this question in and out of Parliament," had watched helplessly while slave prices dropped. "Should the British Government choose to purchase them," exclaimed Hayne, "it will be the easiest thing in nature so to shake the public confidence in that species of property, as to reduce their value to nothing." The lesson seemed clear enough. Unless the Negro question was kept out of Congress, the plight of the West Indies slaveholders would foreshadow the fate in store for the American South.[53]

Thus both the Wilberforce example and their own anxiety about discussing slavery caused tidewater planters to conjure the apparently innocuous colonization petition into a grave threat to southern interests. In December 1827 the South Carolina legislature summed up the lowcountry's concern in a militant report against colonization. "Should Congress claim the power to discuss and take a vote upon any question connected with domestic slavery," proclaimed the legislature,

. . . it will be neither more nor less than the commencement of a system by which the peculiar policy of South Carolina, upon which is predicated her resources and her prosperity, will be shaken to its foundations. . . . It is a subject upon which no citizen of South Carolina needs instruction. One common feeling inspires us all with a firm determination not to submit to a species of legislation which would light up such fires of intestine commotion in our borders as ultimately to consume our country.[54]

South Carolina's response to the colonization petition—like the earlier reaction to the Ohio Resolutions—is of considerable importance in understanding not only the Nullification Crisis of 1832 but also the ensuing era of sectional controversy. Some historians have contended that if northern reformers had offered constructive abolition proposals instead of vituperative antislavery attacks, slavery might have been abolished without a civil war. But the schemes which South Carolina opposed so rigidly in the 1820's were mild suggestions offered a decade before the major

---

[53] *Ibid.*, p. 128; *Register of Debates*, 19 Cong., 2 sess., p. 329.
[54] Quoted in Houston, *Critical Study*, pp. 51–2.

abolitionist onslaught. Indeed, some proslavery leaders feared moderate propositions more than violent attacks, for scrupulous planters might be attracted to a plausible means of emancipating their slaves. As one leading editor remarked on the Colonization Society:

> If slave property is made insecure—if the quiet and content of the Negroe [sic] is chased away—if the timid, among our own people, catch the alarm, and, by their weakness, assist the effect of injuring our property and lessening our safety—we owe it, not to the wild fanatics, whose notions our people can in no sort adopt—but to that other and subtler plan, which, while equally impracticable as to what it pretends to aim at, yet allures men into it, merely by seeming to offer a middle way.[55]

Emancipation involved the kind of massive social revolution which, in a democracy, must be preceded by months or years of searching debate. And the events of the 1820's demonstrate that South Carolina planters had too great a sense of their society's anxieties and weaknesses—too deep a fear that their institutions could be shattered by words—to tolerate discussion, much less action. The Carolinians, in Jefferson's incisive phrase, had the wolf by the ears, and even tame suggestions made them all the more defensive.

In 1827 the United States Senate quickly tabled the colonization petition. Congress, however, almost passed the woolens bill. The bill, which would have raised the tariff on imported woolens from 33⅓ percent to approximately 50 percent of the actual value, passed the House despite angry protests from South Carolina congressmen. McDuffie, a violent nationalist fast becoming a militant southerner, called the duties "more justly obnoxious" than the English taxes which justified the American Revolution. "This government," he warned, "cannot exist under a system of taxation which perverts the powers granted for national objects to the oppression of one part of the Union for the benefit of another." In the Senate a tie vote left the bill's fate up to the casting vote of the Vice President, and Calhoun, formerly the most convinced nationalist in South Carolina, voted to table it.[56]

[55] *Columbia Telescope*, Aug. 20, 1833.
[56] *Register of Debates*, 19 Cong., 2 sess., pp. 496, 1000ff.

Evidence soon accumulated that Calhoun's vote had only postponed a protectionist victory. In the summer of 1827, a tariff convention at Harrisburgh, Pennsylvania, resolved to seek more adequate protection for all major industrial products and for such raw materials as sugar, hemp, and lead. Eastern protectionists bid for western support by offering votes for roads in exchange for votes for tariffs. For the first time, thousands of Carolinians suspected that a majority—perhaps a permanent majority—of northerners were determined to exploit the southern minority.

8

In 1824 South Carolinians had been somewhat apprehensive. In 1827, acutely alarmed, they trooped to public meetings, heard vituperative orations, read violent editorials, and served notice to the nation that South Carolina would not tolerate majority tyranny. The man most responsible for creating the new militancy was Robert J. Turnbull, a lowcountry planter and pamphleteer, whose series of essays, *The Crisis*, made him a hero of the nullification campaign.

The cosmopolitan product of a cosmopolitan marriage, Turnbull was born in Florida, raised in Charleston, and educated in England. His Scottish father, Dr. Andrew Turnbull, received the best medical education in Europe, practiced on the Continent, and married a beautiful, talented Grecian. Migrating to America as director of a colony at St. Augustine, the elder Turnbull was routed by a series of revolutions before he sought asylum and affluence as a Charleston physician. Robert, the second son, was trained as a lawyer, built an extensive Charleston practice before he was forty, and then abandoned the bar to become a sea-island planter. An ex-Federalist, Turnbull had traced in his own career the steps by which the slavery issue made strict constructionists of tidewater planters. A member of the Court of Magistrates and Freemen, which tried the Vesey conspirators, the sea-islander wrote the Negro seamen law, was a founder and subsequently a secretary of the South Carolina Association, and, with Isaac E. Holmes, penned a series of articles challenging Justice Johnson's opinion in the Negro seamen case. The colonization petition was the final blow, and it set Turnbull to writing the famous *Crisis* essays.[57]

Turnbull presented a cogent case for strict construction and a careful analysis of the inexpediency of internal improvements and protective tariffs. *The Crisis* provides compelling evidence that tidewater planters who worried most about slavery also worried about protective tariffs—particularly about the possibility of retaliation. But Turnbull believed that colonization posed a more decided threat to South Carolina interests. Tariffs and improvement schemes were dangerous chiefly because "acquiescence in these measures, on the part of the State sovereignties, sanctions . . . the constitutional right to legislate on the local concerns of the States." The "general welfare" clause would serve abolitionists as well as road builders:

. . . these words "general welfare" are becoming every day more and more important to the folks, who are now so peaceably raising their cotton and rice, between the *Little Pedee* and the *Savannah*. The question, it must be recollected, is not simply, whether we are to have a foreign commerce. It is not whether we are to have splendid national works, in which we have no interest, executed chiefly at our cost. . . . It is not whether we are to be taxed without end. . . . But the still more interesting question is, whether the institutions of our forefathers . . . are to be preserved . . . free from the rude hands of innovators and enthusiasts, and from the molestation or interference of any legislative power on earth but our own? Or whether, like the weak, the dependent, and the unfortunate colonists of the West-Indies, we are to drag on a miserable state of political existence, constantly vibrating between our hopes and our fears, as to what a Congress may do towards us, without any accurate knowledge of our probable fate, and without a hope of successful resistance.[58]

The solution? As a sovereign state, South Carolina should forcibly resist federal laws which encroached on the reserved rights of the states. "To talk . . . of resistance to the tariff, by all *constitutional* means, is to talk to no purpose. . . . Let us say distinctly to Congress, 'HANDS OFF'—mind your *own* business. . . . It is not

---

[57] Turnbull MS, NC; Hamilton, *An Eulogium on . . . Robert J. Turnbull . . .* (Charleston, 1834).

[58] *The Crisis*, pp. 12–14, 64, 139.

a case for reasoning or for negotiation. It must be a *word* and a *blow*."[59]

Turnbull's essays, first printed in the *Charleston Mercury* and later collected and republished as a widely read pamphlet, created a furor in lowcountry South Carolina. As James Hamilton, Jr., later described it, "*The Crisis* was the first bugle-call to the South to rally. Its notes struck upon the public ear with a shrill, yet full volume, that aroused us from the deep trance in which we had long slumbered." Still, as Turnbull himself admitted, colonization was an inflammatory issue only at tidewater. Just as the upcountry had worried more about the tariff than about the Seamen Controversy in 1824, so the uplanders were more distressed by the woolens bill than by the colonization petition in 1827.[60]

If Turnbull was the great lowcountry publicist in 1827, Thomas Cooper was the archradical in the uplands. Cooper, president of South Carolina College and a leader of the Smith faction, delivered a major oration in Columbia on July 2, 1827, which touched off the militant phase of the upcountry's antitariff crusade. Throughout the remainder of the year, and throughout the ensuing decade, he would continue to be one of the most extreme advocates of states' rights principles in South Carolina politics.

On superficial examination, Cooper's credentials as a leading South Carolina politician seem curious indeed. Unlike every other major political leader in the state, he was neither a native of the South nor a large southern slaveholder. But Cooper was not the sort of man who needed the spur of self-interest to throw himself into a fight. An incurable agitator throughout his career, he battled the authorities on both sides of the Atlantic in a long and colorful crusade which ran the gamut from liberalism to reaction.

Cooper first gained notoriety in the early 1790's amidst the passions aroused by the French Revolution. Although previously only a well-born, well-educated, conventional English liberal, he dared to give public praise to the Jacobins' crusade. Upon being denounced by Edmund Burke in the House of Commons in 1792, Cooper lashed back in a famous pamphlet which subjected lords

[59] *Ibid.,* pp. 137, 151.
[60] *Ibid.,* p. 128; Hamilton, *Eulogium on Turnbull,* p. 15.

and clergy to scathing attack. In the ensuing months, he found the conservative reaction in England less and less congenial, and he also had no use for the terror developing in France. The more sober form of democracy practiced in America seemed best suited to his tastes, and he sailed for Philadelphia in 1794.

When Cooper arrived in the United States, the clash between Jeffersonians and Federalists was moving toward its climax. By 1799 the transplanted English liberal was in the thick of the campaign. As a vitriolic exponent of the Jeffersonian cause, he excited the anger of the Federalist camp, and was briefly imprisoned in 1800 for violating the notorious Sedition Law. After his release he stayed on in Pennsylvania, and in 1804 was honored with a place on the Pennsylvania bench.

Cooper was not destined to enjoy his new office for long. In the early nineteenth century Pennsylvania's more radical democrats were seeking judicial reforms, and Cooper became a special target of the radicals' attack. After handing down some allegedly arbitrary decisions, he suffered the indignity of an overwhelming vote of censure, and was driven from the bench in 1811. Even in America, Thomas Cooper sadly concluded, a purely democratic government inevitably went to Jacobinical extremes.

Temporarily renouncing his political career, Cooper decided to make his way in the academic community. He lectured on chemistry at Carlisle College and the University of Pennsylvania from 1811 to 1819, and in 1820 was called to an attractive professorship at South Carolina College. The following year the college trustees elected him president. He remained in Columbia until his death in 1839.

The years in South Carolina brought Cooper perhaps more happiness and certainly more power than he had ever known before. Until the mid-1830's, the college prospered under his management, and after his encounter with Pennsylvania radicals, he applauded the aristocratic features in South Carolina's style of democracy. Soon Cooper was in the forefront of those who were using the old Jeffersonian creed to shore up the southern way of life. An early proslavery writer and a mordant critic of the tariff, this liberal-turned-reactionary spread the states' rights dogmas in countless editorials, pamphlets, and orations throughout the nullification era.

In 1832 Cooper was seventy-three years old, and his afflictions left him stooped over his cane and often gasping for breath. But he possessed more energy than the youngsters who gathered in his classrooms. Working daily from six in the morning until ten at night, the fiery little Englishman managed to find time not only to prepare his lectures and to run the college but also to lead the Columbia nullifiers and to continue his lifelong war against the clerical orders. As he hurried through the streets of Columbia he seemed, as one visitor described him, "the oddest sight that ever was: an accurate description of him would be deemed a burlesque on humanity: short legs, stooping, hump back, slovenly dressed, & wearing an old white hat. He rides a small bob-tail, pacing horse . . . as if the Devil was making off with his last load." In a generation when many South Carolina politicians had attended the college, Cooper was probably even more important than Smith in urging the gentry to repudiate the nationalist heresies Calhoun preached.[61]

In his famous oration on July 2, 1827, at a huge antitariff meeting in Columbia, Cooper reminded his listeners that protective tariffs were already transferring southern wealth to northern pockets, "and wealth is power. Every year of submission rivets the chains upon us, and we shall go on, remonstrating, complaining, and reluctantly submitting, 'till the remedy now in our power, will be looked up to in vain." He spelled out the economic consequences of a higher protective tariff and predicted that Congress would soon enact the woolens bill. He then came to his climax with words that were noted with alarm across the land. "We shall," declared Cooper, "before long, be compelled to calculate the value of our union; and to inquire of what use to us is this most unequal alliance?" At Hamburg two days later, McDuffie was almost as extreme. "This Union," he cried, "cannot exist twenty years under a system of policy, which looks to a perpetual tampering with the great pecuniary interests of society, by laws which invade the rights and affect the distribution of property."[62]

If South Carolina really intended to defy the federal government, it seemed necessary to consult with other slaveholding states. Columbia's citizens called for an immediate southern convention. Several upcountry meetings endorsed the Columbia proposal in the late summer of 1827. But most Carolinians were not ready for southern conventions or the Cooper-Turnbull doctrines. If future prospects looked ominous, federal usurpations had not yet significantly begun. Carolinians also hoped that Jackson, if elected President in 1828, would rescue the country from Adams' nationalism, particularly if Calhoun could control the new administration. The state legislature merely adopted another remonstrance, upholding strict construction and denouncing protective tariffs, internal improvements, and colonization appropriations.[63]

9

The 1827 uproar helps to explain the 1828 militancy; South Carolina was on the verge of radical action before the Tariff of Abominations was passed. The states' rights campaign of 1827 is also significant because Calhoun nationalists led rather than resisted it. But the Calhounites' sectionalism in 1827 was as qualified as their nationalism in 1816. The old Carolina nationalists continued to endorse the United States bank; they failed to repudiate "truly national" internal improvements (and continued to oppose piecemeal projects); they still affirmed that protective tariffs were legitimate if a war was imminent and if essential industries required support. Even their sectionalism was, in an important sense, nationalistic, for Calhoun and his followers were convinced that high tariffs and slavery agitation, if not checked, would dissolve the Union. Since Carolina nationalists clung to fragments of their former program, the petty, factional strife

---

[62] *Charleston Mercury*, July 18–21, 1827; Cooper to Van Buren, Apr. 11, 1827, Van Buren Papers, LC; *United States Telegraph*, July 21, 1827.
[63] *Charleston Mercury*, Aug. 29, 1827; *Statutes at Large*, I, 230–42.

between Calhounites and Smithites continued until well into 1830.[64]

Still, the vestiges of continuity cannot hide the reality of fundamental change. In 1816 South Carolinians had been caught up in a wave of economic prosperity and exuberant nationalism; they had even thrown some support behind a mildly protective tariff. By 1827, with their slaves apparently restless and their economy seriously depressed, planters were beginning to place loyalty to their section over loyalty to their nation. McDuffie had traveled a long way in a short time from his stridently national pamphlet, "One of the People," in 1821 to his patently sectional Hamburg oration of 1827; Henry L. Pinckney, whose Clariosophic Oration in 1825 was a classic statement of American nationalism, was publishing Turnbull and defending Cooper two years later; Hamilton, who had written the nationalist resolution of 1821, helped to whip up excitement over the woolens bill; Hayne, who had resisted the furor over the seamen law, led the campaign against the American Colonization Society; even Calhoun was flirting with nullification in 1827. It would not be long before young Carolina hotspurs like James H. Hammond would be proudly proclaiming that they loved South Carolina better than they loved the Union.[65]

Even while renouncing their old broad construction principles, Calhounites claimed that nationalism had changed as much as its South Carolina proponents. To an extent, they had a point. "If then, we are inconsistent," wrote Henry L. Pinckney, "let it be remembered at all events that we have only changed from being friendly to a system which we once imagined would be *national*, to the opponents of a system which we are now convinced is *sectional* and *corrupt*." As nationalists, Calhounites had always argued that national laws must affect each section equally. As sectionalists, they never ceased proclaiming that protective tariffs, piecemeal internal-improvement projects, and antislavery agita-

---

[64] *Charleston Mercury*, Apr. 30, 1830; *Charleston Courier*, July 14, 1827; *SR*, II (Nov. 1828), 600; McDuffie, *Speech of Mr. McDuffie . . . May 28, 1832* (Washington, D.C., 1832), p. 4.
[65] *Southern Times*, May 28, 1831.

tion were so avowedly sectional as to destroy the nation itself. Calhounites rightfully claimed that supporting 20-percent duties in 1816 did not preclude opposing 50-percent duties in 1827, that supporting a few great national works did not conflict with opposing hundreds of local projects.[66]

The South Carolina version of economic nationalism, in short, was always qualified and soon abandoned largely because it was too disinterested and too much the product of a temporary military crisis. South Carolina had little to gain from a national economic policy. Clay and Adams nationalism, on the other hand, while equally patriotic, was also designed to serve the desires of important economic interests. The great problem of the Republic before 1820 was to survive in an era of fierce European war. After 1820 American politics were increasingly dominated by conflicts over tariffs, banks, and the ominous slavery issue. To Clay and Adams, and to the economic interests which supported them, economic nationalism seemed more attractive than ever in the 1820's. The harder they pushed the doctrine, however, and the more the threat of war receded, the more South Carolinians found nationalism fundamentally "changed." As the South Carolina depression deepened and the state's anxiety about slavery grew the expanding federal government came to seem dangerous rather than benevolent. By 1825 a majority of South Carolinians had renounced broad construction. By 1827 even Calhounites were seeking new theories to solve the problems of a new era in American history.

66 *Charleston Mercury*, Feb. 20, 1830.

5

The Emergence of a Theory, 1828

The congressional session of 1827–8 marks a great turning point in South Carolina's evolution from nationalism to sectionalism. The events in Congress made the old nationalist-Smith issues seem ever more irrelevant, as Calhounites, such as Hamilton and McDuffie, raged at the legislative fruits of broad construction. Wherever South Carolinians turned during the dismal congressional session, it seemed impossible to escape signs of a hostile and tyrannical majority. Debates on slavery broke out in the House, the American Colonization Society stepped up its campaign for federal aid, and internal-improvement appropriations continued to mount. Worst of all, the highest American pre-Civil War tariff was enacted, and South Carolinians contributed their votes to sustain the most flagrant of the abominations.

2

At the beginning of the 1827–8 session, the ubiquitous slavery issue once again demonstrated its capacity to provoke South Carolinians to rage at trifles. For almost the entire month of January 1828 the House of Representatives was consumed by debate over a routine private petition from Marigny D'Auterive requesting government compensation for war-damaged property. The trouble was that the property turned out to be a slave, and that raised the question of whether men could be thought of as property in a nation conceived on natural rights. By granting

D'Auterive's petition, a few northern congressmen claimed, the House would mock the foundations of the Republic.

South Carolina representatives, led by William Drayton of Charleston, came to the defense of the petitioner. The United States Constitution, argued Drayton, both sanctioned chattel slavery and provided that private property could not be taken for public use without due compensation. Thus D'Auterive's request had the clearest sanction. If Congress seriously proposed to discuss "whether the master has a right of property in his slave," Drayton added, no southerner "would remain in this Hall." And if masters held their "slaves at the mercy of the Government," South Carolinians would have no choice but "to calculate upon the value of the Union."[1]

In Charleston leading newspaper editors spread the alarm and applauded the defiance which marked Drayton's stand. Northern opposition to D'Auterive's petition, Henry L. Pinckney's *Mercury* admitted, was the work of a very few "benevolent, misguided men." But in a community like the South Carolina lowcountry, the danger of antislavery ideas bore little relation to the strength of the "fanatics." "The weakest agent who has access to a powder magazine," warned Pinckney, "may create an explosion, as great as the best concerted undermining." Congressional sanction for the notion that men could not be property would inevitably "shake the Union to its centre," added Jacob Cardoza's *Southern Patriot*.[2]

In late January the House granted D'Auterive's petition. The vote, however, was close, and at least one important South Carolinian found little solace in the victory. "The extraordinary debate in Congress," wrote Judge William Harper in Charleston's sober *Southern Review*, has "conjured up a spirit" which would hereafter prove "difficult, perhaps impossible, to lay." Harper brooded over recent events—higher tariffs, expanding internal improvements, the Missouri Crisis, the Seamen Controversy, the colonization uproar. Yet "none of the disagreeable and irritating topics, that have, for a few years past, been agitated in Con-

[1] *Register of Debates*, 20 Cong., 1 sess., I, 971.
[2] *Charleston Mercury*, Jan. 29, 1828; *Southern Patriot*, Jan. 14, 1828.

gress," he claimed, ". . . have done as much mischief, as . . . this trifling claim." Only one course could be adopted, he warned, "whenever such a subject shall, either directly or incidentally, be made a matter of serious consideration."[3]

3

After the House had disposed of Marigny D'Auterive's petition, the representatives settled down to long months of wrangling over a new protective tariff. The longer debate continued, the more it became obvious that the crusade for protection had assumed the aspects of an irresistible movement. Miners and hemp growers, sugar planters and wool producers, joined manufacturers in clamoring for higher duties. Industrial lobbyists swarmed around the capital, promising votes to politicians and bounties to their constituents. Congressmen in both parties were responding to the pressure; the only question seemed to be who would grant the most concessions. South Carolinians could be pardoned for believing that they faced a voracious and permanent majority.

Yet the success of the lobbyists bore little relation to the economic power of their employers. In 1828 the Industrial Revolution was only beginning to transform the economy of the nation. For another half century, the average American would remain a rural entrepreneur who sold agricultural goods in international markets. And while southerners contributed more than westerners to the antitariff cause, agrarians in both sections tended to share an exporter's distaste for restricting foreign commerce.

The protectionists' strength was more a political phenomenon than an inevitable product of inexorable economic forces. In order to triumph in the imminent presidential election, the politicians behind Jackson as well as the proponents of Adams had to win such doubtful manufacturing states as Pennsylvania and New York. In addition, both parties sought to gain support from the various special interests seeking protection for raw materials.

Southern and western opponents of the tariff, on the other hand, seemed firmly lodged in the Jackson camp. It appeared that most westerners would never turn against a frontier idol like Old

[3] *SR*, I (Feb. 1828), 232.

Hickory and that most southerners could never support a New England nationalist like John Quincy Adams. Hence Martin Van Buren and fellow northeastern Jacksonians felt free to bid against Adams for the support of protectionists. The tariff, as one observer noted, had been "changed into a machine for manufacturing Presidents, instead of broadcloths, and bed blankets."[4]

Faced with this impossible situation, South Carolina congressmen clutched at desperate remedies to save themselves from higher duties. The only hope, as some South Carolinians saw it, was to drive a wedge between those who wanted protection for raw materials and those who sought protection for manufactured products. By keeping duties on raw wool at high levels, for example, southerners hoped to make the tariff obnoxious to woolen manufacturers. By maintaining high rates on foreign molasses, Carolinians hoped to force New England rum distillers to oppose the bill. Thus the South would vote with protection-minded producers of raw materials to keep high rates on nonindustrial products. Southerners would then vote with New England manufacturers to defeat the entire Bill of Abominations.

The obvious risk in this strategy was that industrialists might prefer an imperfect bill to no bill at all. If manufacturers should vote for the final tariff despite shored-up rates on raw materials, slaveholders would succeed in saddling unnecessarily high taxes on the nation. George McDuffie correctly termed such a strategy "fighting the devil with fire," and the plot culminated in total disaster. Again and again, southern representatives voted against amendments to lower rates on raw materials. But enough northern Jacksonians, including such Van Burenites as Silas Wright, voted to lower enough of the duties so that industrialists managed to swallow the entire unseemly concoction. The tariff of 1828 was the law of the land, and South Carolinians were the authors of its worst abominations.

Calhounites later claimed that Van Buren was in on their conspiracy and had betrayed them. Van Buren always denied the accusation and Calhoun never proved it; the debacle was proba-

---

[4] Quoted in Robert V. Remini, *The Election of Andrew Jackson* (Philadelphia and New York, 1963), p. 172.

bly a southern plot which backfired rather than a sabotaged Jacksonian stratagem. At any rate, the embarrassing incident won Van Buren his share of enemies in South Carolina and convinced many nullifiers that the Jackson party would never lower the duties.[5]

In the four years of ensuing agitation, South Carolinians reiterated that the new tariff was doubly pernicious. First of all, it raised approximate import duties from 33⅓ percent to 50 percent despite the continued deterioration of South Carolina's economy. Second, it allegedly violated the clauses of the Constitution which prevented further congressional slavery debates.

The Carolinians' constitutional argument against the tariff could not be based on the customary premises of strict constructionists. States' rights purists usually rested their case on the exact language in the Constitution. This textual analysis gave the criterion of constitutionality a simple clarity; any particular power was or was not explicitly enumerated in the fundamental law. But since the Founding Fathers had expressly authorized Congress to pass duties and to regulate commerce, antitariff polemicists had to retreat to the highly tenuous principle of legislative intent. Congress, they were forced to argue, not only was restricted to using powers explicitly granted but also could use these enumerated powers only with the intention of gaining objectives sanctioned in the constitutional text. The power to tax was granted in order to raise revenue. Congress received no authority to encourage industrial enterprise. And so by passing a protective tariff aimed at aiding manufacturers instead of raising a revenue, Congress had exceeded its legitimate prerogatives.

This constitutional perversion, continued South Carolinians, was particularly flagrant because the illegitimately assumed authority destroyed the constitutionally granted power. Since the tariff of 1828 was designed to protect industry, it intentionally

[5] The fortunes of the southern plot can be followed in *Register of Debates,* 20 Cong., 1 sess., *passim.* See also John C. Calhoun, *Works* . . . , Richard Crallé, ed. (6 vols.; New York, 1854–7), III, 47–51; McDuffie in *Congressional Globe,* 28 Cong., 1 sess., appendix, p. 747; John A Garraty, *Silas Wright* (New York, 1949), ch. 3; Remini, *Martin Van Buren and the Making of the Democratic Party* (New York, 1959), ch. 12.

reduced imports and thereby restricted the revenue which duties were supposed to raise. The Tariff of Abominations destroyed the commerce which Congress was charged with regulating.

Congressional discretion to pervert "power from an object intended, to one not intended," like the unlimited authority to provide for the general welfare, would give the federal government infinite opportunity to disregard constitutional restraints and to seize reserved rights. If the majority could use "the right of laying duties, not only to raise revenue, but to regulate the industry of the country," warned Calhoun, taxes could be employed to further "any purpose that the majority may think to be for the general welfare." Encouragement could be offered "to the Colonization Society, as well as to cotton and woolen manufacturers." Indeed, the constitutional precedent set by the tariff of 1828 might lend authority to a direct assault on slavery itself.[6]

The South Carolinians' constitutional case against protection was an ingenious argument which attracted planters worried about slavery as well as agrarians concerned about depression and united them in a campaign against the Bill of Abominations. But outside South Carolina, the logic usually left even strict-construction Democrats shaking their heads. In the last analysis, the argument was undermined by the premise on which it was based. Since the criterion of constitutionality was the intent of the legislature, Calhounites were shouldered with the impossible task of demonstrating the real motives of protariff groups. Nullifiers never proved probably never could have proved—that most supporters of the bill intended to reduce revenue and to destroy commerce. Only a minority of congressmen spoke on the tariff, and many professed mixed motives. Some representatives considered the tariff a revenue bill with only incidental protection afforded a few industries. Other statesmen—including Andrew Jackson—maintained that national defense still required protective tariffs.

If the constitutional argument against protection seems dubious in retrospect, it seemed compelling to most South Carolinians at the time. The new tariff, they urged, opened the door for con-

6 Calhoun, *Works,* I, 3; VI, 89, 131.

gressional slavery debates. Many planters were also convinced that the new 50-percent rates would lead to economic disaster. South Carolina, then, had no intention of submitting to the Bill of Abominations. But the Calhounites, in particular, were ensnared in a difficult dilemma. As conspicuous leaders of the Jackson party, they could sabotage Old Hickory's national campaign by waxing radical on the tariff. Yet as enraged planters, well aware that many Jacksonians favored the tariff, Carolina hotheads suspected that radical action alone would obtain redress.

The Carolinians continued to support Jackson partly because they hoped that Calhoun, who was running for re-election to the vice-presidency on the Jackson ticket, could control Old Hickory's administration. By 1828 it was already clear that Martin Van Buren, the dapper little New York politician whose superb political tactics had won him the epithet the "Little Magician," was Calhoun's chief rival for Jackson's affections and the presidential succession. Van Buren had supported the tariff of 1828, and his triumph would bolster Jackson's earlier commitment to protection. But a Calhoun victory might push Jackson into an antitariff crusade.

The South Carolinians' continued loyalty to Andrew Jackson was augmented by their implacable opposition to John Quincy Adams. Whereas Jackson was mildly in favor of protective tariffs, Adams ranked with Henry Clay as a leading proponent of the American system. The President had also been suspect on the subject of slavery even before his administration began. As secretary of state he had aroused antagonism by requesting repeal of the Negro seamen law; and because he was a New Englander, he could never be trusted to handle the problem with care. The South Carolinians' suspicions increased when President Adams named Rufus King, the antislavery leader in the Missouri debates, to be his minister to England. And to the lowcountry gentry, the Adams administration reached its lowest point when the President proposed American participation in the Panama Congress of Spanish-American nations in 1826.

The Panama Congress raised again the specter of San Domingo. Negroes from Haiti were scheduled to attend the meetings, and the San Domingan revolt might be discussed. South Carolinians considered American involvement in such "incendiary" deliberations to be as disastrous as another congressional slavery debate; in foreign as well as in domestic affairs, discussion of slavery had to be avoided. In the midst of the Panama debate, Robert Y. Hayne warned:

The question of slavery must be considered and treated entirely as a DOMESTIC QUESTION. . . . It is a matter, Mr. President, for ourselves. To touch it at all, is to violate our most sacred rights—to put in jeopardy our dearest interests—the peace of our country—the safety of our families, our altars, and our firesides. . . . Let me solemnly declare, once for all, that the Southern States never will permit, and never can permit, any interference, whatever, in their domestic concerns, and that the very day on which the unhallowed attempt shall be made by the authorities of the Federal Government, we will consider ourselves as driven from the Union.[7]

In addition to disliking Adams' tariff and slavery policies, some South Carolinians believed, apparently sincerely, that the President was the type of political broker who could subvert the democratic process. In national as in state politics, Carolina patricians detested political managers who used demagoguery to delude the "rabble" and patronage to control the politicians. When Crawford sought support from a congressional caucus, Calhounites denounced him for hoping "to attain favor, not by placing himself on principles and policy distinctly avowed and steadily persued, but by political dexterity and management." Where Crawford failed, South Carolinians believed, Adams succeeded. The New Englander bought the presidency by promising patronage to congressmen in general and the secretary of state portfolio to Clay in particular. "Power improperly acquired" was promptly "improperly used." Adams and Clay, as Carolinians saw it, switched from buying up politicians to buying up "whole sections of country by bounties in the shape of protecting duties, and by appropriations of money from the public treasure, and of lands from the public domain."[8]

---

[7] *Register of Debates*, 19 Cong., 1 sess., pp. 165–6; *Charleston Mercury*, March 31, May 2, July 19, Aug. 12, 1826.

[8] Calhoun to Jackson, June 4, 1826, Jackson, *Correspondence* . . . , John Spencer Bassett and J. Franklin Jameson, eds. (7 vols.; Washington, D.C., 1926–35), III, 304–5; Calhoun to John McLean, Sept. 3, 1827, McLean Papers, LC; *United States Telegraph*, July 21, 1827.

Jackson, on the other hand, was a slaveholder himself, and would scrupulously avoid interfering with the peculiar institution. A patriotic general, not a scheming spoilsman, he would rescue the Republic from the grip of corruption, patronage, and partisanship. Calhounites also nourished hopes that Old Hickory could be converted into an antitariff crusader. As a tariff proponent in 1824 and the leader of a coalition containing many protectionists, Jackson would, at best, begin his administration with a neutral position on the subject. But in an age which considered treasury surpluses to be an economic vice, tariff revenues had to be matched by governmental expenditures. If South Carolina congressmen could hold down appropriations, the President might be forced to turn against the protectionists.

In 1828 Carolinians had reason to believe that federal expenditures might soon be reduced. The repayment of the public debt, which required half the federal government's annual revenues, was nearing completion. If Jackson insisted on a prompt payment of the debt, and if he opposed new federal projects, budgetary surpluses would develop before the 1832 elections.

As Calhounite strategists saw it, a coalition between southern and western Jacksonians could ensure these objectives. Since many slaveholders dreamed of moving to virgin territories, the South could join the West in urging free public lands. Since many westerners sold their goods in international markets, the two sections could unite in opposing protective tariffs. The pressure to end land sales and to lower the tariff, in turn, would compel President Jackson to favor tight-fisted economizing. The South-West alliance was a particularly cherished scheme of Duff Green, the Missouri-born moderate whose national newspaper, the *United States Telegraph*, was dedicated to furthering Calhoun's presidential prospects.

Yet if Calhounites remained Jackson supporters in 1828, few of them shared Green's euphoria about a new adminstration. South Carolina radicals tended to overlook the temporary political considerations which led to the passage of the Bill of Abominations. The tariff of 1828, they believed, was the final demonstration of the South's minority position in the nation. Northern economic groups had formed a permanent majority and had appointed the South paymaster of the system. Tariffs were designed to drain away southern wealth and appropriations to fill northern pockets. Southern representation in Congress and participation in elections gave a veneer of legitimacy to majority exploitation. Only a minority check on majority tyranny could save the South—and the Union.[9]

Given this conception of a permanent northern majority, such Calhounites as McDuffie always regarded a South-West alliance as more of a beguiling dream than a distinct possibility. The South could offer the West only free public land in an era when land was cheap anyway. The Northeast could offer millions of dollars for needed roads to the seaboard. The prospective repayment of the national debt, many Carolinians feared, offered equally little hope for tariff redress. Most politicians, including many Jacksonians, had already demonstrated a genius for finding internal-improvement projects, and there was always the possibility that surplus federal revenue would be distributed among the states ("the point in my opinion of the greatest danger," warned Calhoun[10]).

The problem for the Calhounites was to develop a radical remedy without destroying the slim hope of Jacksonian redress. As soon as the Congress of 1828 passed the tariff, the Carolinians caucused and agreed to explore the possibility of a united southern protest. Most southern representatives, however, refused to sanction immediate resistance, and the Carolina delegation met again to determine a unilateral course of action. South Carolina was, fatefully, going it alone even before her congressmen left Washington.

The second meeting, a tempestuous secret caucus at Hayne's house, was marked by radical talk and conservative action. Hamilton threatened to resign his seat in protest; McDuffie fulminated against the Union; Hayne inquired if federal troops would be allowed to march through southern states on their way to put

9 See, for example, *Charleston Mercury*, June 25, 1828; Hamilton, *A Speech . . . Delivered at Walterborough . . .* (Charleston, 1828).
10 Calhoun to Preston, Jan. 6, 1829, Virginia Carrington Scrapbook.

down a rebellion in South Carolina. But moderates were as conspicuous as militants. William Smith refused to attend; his colleague, Thomas Mitchell, looked on silently; William Drayton, long a member of the Calhoun party but already distressed by his cohorts' new radicalism, admitted that the tariff was oppressive, but argued that disunion would be a calamity. Hamilton, McDuffie, and Hayne soon agreed that Carolina militancy might prevent Jackson's triumph. They decided to delay radical discussions and to soothe constituents' tempers until Old Hickory and Calhoun were safely elected.[11]

4

The South Carolina representatives came home in the summer of 1828 to a state on fire, and McDuffie, more than anyone else, chafed at the restraints imposed by the caucus. Soon the stormy congressman was campaigning up and down the state, calling for resistance at the risk, as Duff Green saw it, "of destroying his party" and losing "the elections in the west."[12]

Violence was nothing new to George McDuffie; his passion as a nullifier in the thirties matched his vehemence as a nationalist in the twenties. Born in upcountry Georgia in 1788, the son of impoverished Scottish immigrants, he was orphaned early and was supporting himself as a farm laborer and store clerk when, as a ten-year-old boy, he wandered into the Augusta store of James Calhoun, a brother of John C. Calhoun. More or less adopted by the Calhouns and ever fanatically grateful and loyal to them, McDuffie was passed on to William Calhoun in Abbeville when James's store failed in Augusta. The brilliant orphan studied at Moses Waddel's famous academy, where he set numerous school records, and at South Carolina College, where he was first in his class and gave an oration titled, ironically, "An Oration on the Stability of the Government of the United States." After admission to the bar he became Eldred Simkins' law partner, was elected to the legislature in 1818, and was elevated to Simkins' seat in Congress in 1820.

---

[11] *Charleston Courier*, Nov. 7, 22, 1828; *Charleston Mercury*, Nov. 10, 1828.
[12] Green to Calhoun, Aug. 10, 1828, Green Papers, LC.

In the House of Representatives, McDuffie won renown as a leading exponent of Calhounite nationalism. Few congressmen favored a more expansive view of federal power, and no one else so effectively challenged the extreme versions of the states' rights creed. McDuffie relished attacking that "climax of political heresies," the notion that a state could nullify federal law. Nullification, he wrote in 1821, was "incompatible with the very notion of government" and would lead "directly into a scene of anarchy and blood." An attempt to "prohibit the officers of the general government, under heavy penalties, from collecting the 'taxes, duties, impost and excises' . . . would be the very case which the [constitutional] convention had in view, when they made provisions for 'calling forth the militia to enforce the laws of the Union.' "[13]

In the early 1820's a South Carolina nationalist who adored Calhoun could not escape frequent encounters with Crawford; and in the hands of McDuffie, the crusade for nationalism turned into a slashing attack on the Crawford faction. It was this partisan aspect of McDuffie's rhetoric which led to the most important incident in the young congressman's career. In July 1821 a "Trio" of Georgia Crawfordites were filling the *Milledgeville Gazette* with long essays on the folly of nationalism. McDuffie, employing the columns of the *Georgia Advertiser*, undertook the task of answering the "Trio"; and with characteristic abandon, he denounced his opponents in vitriolic terms. Colonel William Cumming, the leader of the "Trio," demanded satisfaction on the dueling ground, which delighted the fiery McDuffie.

Calhounites viewed the contest with grave forebodings. McDuffie was an inexperienced duelist and Cumming was a crack shot; the South Carolina nationalists never ceased believing that the "Trio" affair was from first to last a Crawfordite plot to assassinate McDuffie.

No such premeditated murder was involved, but the duel itself turned into a one-sided slaughter. After McDuffie fired ineptly into the dirt, Cumming's ball caught the Carolinian in the side and lodged near his spine. For hours McDuffie's life was despaired

13 [McDuffie], *One of the People*, pp. 16–18.

of, and although he eventually recovered, the wound continued to fester in his back, slowly destroying his nerves and making him a paralytic wreck. Within a few months, Cumming and McDuffie again squared off on the dueling ground, and this time McDuffie emerged with a shattered arm to show for his courage.

Previously a warm, affable, engaging man, McDuffie became, after the duels, irritable, austere, and forbidding. He was not, as William J. Grayson remarked with gargantuan understatement, "what Dr. Johnson called a clubbable man." Even at tea parties, McDuffie kept his own counsel; and on the floor of the legislature, he held himself apart from the lighthearted chatter of his compatriots. Sitting motionless near the speaker's chair, he brooded for hours, a stern, ugly, slovenly man, endlessly wrapped in his own ruminations.

But when McDuffie rose to speak, his real nature came out. Weaving awkwardly around the platform, he relentlessly pounded out his message, punctuating each phrase with harsh and fitful gestures and commanding attention by the vehemence of his manner. As one observer described it, "he hesitates and stammers; he screams and bawls; he thumps and stumps like a mad man in Bedlam."[14]

In the years after 1827, McDuffie's oratorical passions came more and more to be enlisted against the nationalist creeds he had done so much to popularize. A large cotton planter himself, and the representative of the most impoverished upcountry region in South Carolina, he looked askance at the high-tariff proposals of the late 1820's. McDuffie also deplored channeling "national" internal-improvement funds into the coffers of "local" canal and turnpike companies. The Tariff of Abominations, enacted as the Carolina depression entered its second decade, seemed the last straw, and it led McDuffie to reconsider the old heresy of nullification.

The nullifiers' leading orator never considered the remedy any more than a sugar-coated version of secession. As in the early 1820's he knew that state veto was likely to end in war, but by the early 1830's revolution was what he was praying for.

[14] *Columbia Telescope,* Apr. 16, 1833.

Wherever he spoke, in Congress or on the stump, McDuffie left no doubts about his commitment to extremes. "Sir," he would shout, at his auditors and at the nation,

South Carolina is oppressed [a thump]. A tyrant majority sucks her life blood from her [a dreadful thump]. Yes, sir [a pause], yes, sir, a tyrant [a thump] majority unappeased [arms aloft], unappeasable [horrid scream], has persecuted and persecutes us [a stamp on the floor]. We appeal to them [low and quick], but we appeal in vain [loud and quick]. We turn to our brethren of the north [low, with a shaking of the head], and pray them to protect us [a thump], but we t-u-r-n in v-a-i-n [prolonged, and a thump]. They heap coals of fire on our heads [with immense rapidity]—they give us burden on burden; they tax us more and more [very rapid, slam-bang, slam—a hideous noise]. We turn to our brethren of the south [slow with a solemn, thoughtful air]. We work with them; we fight with them; we vote with them; we petition with them [common voice and manner]; but the tyrant majority has no ears, no eyes, no form [quick], deaf [long pause], sightless [pause], inexorable [slow, slow]. Despairing [a thump], we resort to the rights [a pause] which God [a pause] and nature has given us [thump, thump, thump]. . . .

As the nullification campaign drew toward its climax McDuffie himself, with his shattered nerves and wild manner, seemed to many Americans a living embodiment of the wrath of the nullifiers.[15]

Although incapable of maintaining the silence which the South Carolina caucus had agreed on at Hayne's house in Washington, McDuffie compromised a bit by advocating somewhat conservative proposals in 1828. Along with Senator William Smith and Congressman William Martin, McDuffie endorsed a prohibitive state excise tax on all northern goods. And in a famous harangue in Columbia, he tore off his northern broadcloth coat, declaring it fit only for the livery of slaves. Thereafter, many South Carolina politicians appeared in public dressed proudly in homespun and urged their constituents to cease importing the goods of tariff states. Daniel Huger refused to eat northern

15 *Ibid.*; Grayson Autobiography, p. 166; *Charleston Mercury,* June 12, 1822; *United States Telegraph,* May 30, 1831; O'Neall, *Biographical Sketches,* II, 463ff.; Perry, *Reminiscences* (1883 ed.), pp. 74ff.; Edwin L. Green, *George McDuffie* (Columbia, 1936).

potatoes; Waddy Thompson rejected a feast of Kentucky pork; an overseer was dismissed for buying a Kentucky horse.[16] Despite the ostentatious parade of men dressed in homespun, nonimportation was a feeble gesture. As it was a voluntary program, the apathy of moderates could easily sabotage it. Hurting Kentucky livestock producers, who opposed the tariff, put little pressure on Kentucky hemp growers, who favored it. And if only slaves wore broadcloth in South Carolina, the demand for northern goods expanded elsewhere. Aristocratic Carolinians found the program galling as well as impotent. Henry L. Pinckney called homespun a "badge of degradation," and to Hamilton, nonintercourse smacked of "a sullen acquiescence in the wrong."[17]

McDuffie's excise tax seemed equally ineffectual. The proposal, designed to destroy the interstate commerce Congress was supposed to regulate, came with particularly bad grace from Carolinians who considered the tariff unconstitutional because it destroyed foreign commerce. Moreover, if the tax might hurt northerners, it would surely hurt southerners, forcing importers to buy foreign goods at the high-tariff price. Some South Carolinians, led by David R. Williams, proposed building southern factories to end northern industrial supremacy. But with heavy debts and a limited number of banks, South Carolina obviously lacked the capital, to say nothing of the managerial experience, needed to industrialize.[18]

Militant Carolinians were driven back step by step to the defiance Turnbull had proposed a year earlier. The radicals' campaign began, appropriately, in Colleton, the most violent area in lowcountry South Carolina, in a movement engineered, appropriately, by Robert Barnwell Rhett, the greatest of all the fire-eaters. In June 1828 Rhett proposed, and a Colleton public meeting accepted, a militant "address" urging Governor John

[16] Charleston Mercury, June 25, July 18, Aug. 8, Oct. 1, 1828; Edgefield Hive, Oct. 16, 1830; Henry T. Thompson, Waddy Thompson . . . (Washington, D.C., 1935), pp. 4–5.
[17] Charleston Mercury, July 30, 1828; Hamilton, Speech at Walterborough, p. 19.
[18] Harvey T. Cook, The Life and Legacy of David Rogerson Williams (New York, 1916), pp. 246–52, 330–1; Greenville Republican, July 26, 1828; Pendleton Messenger, Jan. 9, 1828.

Taylor to call an immediate session of the state legislature. The Colleton Address did not recommend specific measures, but demanded that South Carolina "resist. Not secretly, as timid Thieves or skulking Smugglers—not in companies and associations, like money chafferers or stock jobbers—not separately & individually, as if this were ours and not our Country's cause—but openly, fairly, fearlessly and unitedly." Henry L. Pinckney called the address "the political creed, the popular feeling, and probably the determined policy of South Carolina." Moderates differed, and they applauded when Taylor refused to call the legislature. The *Edgefield Hive* proclaimed that " 'the bare apprehension of disunion is sufficient to drive us into a severe fit of moderation;' " the *Greenville Republican* warned the tidewater aristocrats that "if they could succeed in separating South Carolina from the Union, *we* will separate from South Carolina."[19]

Yet tempers at the tidewater continued to rise. In July a meeting of wealthy sea-island planters in Colleton asked again for an immediate legislative session and proclaimed that "Adhesion of the State of South Carolina to the Union should depend on the unconditional repeal . . . of the Tariff Laws . . . so far as they conflict with the constitutional rights of our citizens." Two anonymous correspondents—"Sidney" and "Colleton"—discoursed on nullification in the *Mercury* throughout July. In late September a huge public barbecue in Abbeville, attended by Hayne and Hamilton and addressed by McDuffie, endorsed state veto. In early October a Pendleton meeting, which Hayne and Warren Davis addressed, seconded the Abbeville resolutions. On October 28, in Walterborough, Hamilton, at last able to break his "sullen silence" with Jackson safely elected, launched the formal nullification campaign.[20]

Carolina's oppressions gave McDuffie an uncontrollable urge to orate; they aroused in Hamilton the irresistible itch to manage.

---

[19] *Charleston Mercury*, June 18, 1828; *Pendleton Messenger*, July 30, 1828; *City Gazette*, July 9, 1828; *Greenville Republican*, July 19, 1828. Rhett, born Robert Barnwell Smith, did not change his name until after the crisis of 1832. I have adopted the expedient of calling him Rhett throughout the period.

[20] *Southern Patriot*, July 5, 1828; *Charleston Mercury* and *Pendleton Messenger*, Oct. 1828, *passim;* Hamilton to Van Buren, Sept. 7, 1828, Van Buren Papers.

Dapper little "Jimmy," the most fabulous character in low-country politics, had been looking for a movement to direct ever since the Lowndes presidential boom had collapsed. The nullification campaign gave him every opportunity to exercise a tact and ingenuity which rivaled Van Buren's.

As far back as his comrades could remember, Hamilton had been trained to play the role of a model lowcountry gentleman. He was born in 1786, the son of a wealthy rice planter who had distinguished himself as aide to George Washington during the Revolutionary War. Like many other scions of rich tidewater families, Hamilton was educated mainly in Newport, Rhode Island, where his parents went to play when the malaria struck. After studying law under Daniel Huger in Charleston, he was admitted to the bar in 1810, served as a major in the War of 1812, and came home to marry Elizabeth Heyward, richest rice heiress in the lowcountry, and to take over William Drayton's huge law practice. Meanwhile he climbed to the top in low-country politics, serving as an important state legislator in the early twenties, as intendent of Charleston during the Vesey Conspiracy, and upon Lowndes' retirement in 1823, as congressman from the tidewater districts.

In his subsequent national and state career, Hamilton continued to seem, at least on the surface, a polished exemplar of the aristocratic manner. His close friend, John Randolph of Roanoke, dubbed him the "Bayard of the South," and Hamilton lived up to the reputation on the dueling ground and in the drawing room. During his fourteen duels, he amassed the perfect record—always wounding but never killing the men who dared to insult his honor. Hamilton was also the most sought-after assistant in southern dueling circles. Men clamored to have him for a second and to use his services to patch up an affair of honor. The ladies found him no less enchanting. Small, tending toward corpulence, with thick wavy hair and the most captivating manner, Hamilton added wit and gaiety to any social function.

Yet Hamilton's courtly manner rarely went very deep; it was largely a matter of bearing, style, and deportment. At the time he became known as the mirror of chivalry, Hamilton was addicted to the Yankee entrepreneurial activities which Charleston patricians most despised. During the Nullification Controversy, his zest for political management represented the antithesis of the disinterested posture a true gentleman was expected to maintain. In the later 1830's Hamilton courted infamy recklessly by becoming a money-grubbing businessman, banker, and merchant, the biggest capitalist to be found in genteel old Charleston. For a time, his enterprises flourished. But he had spread himself too thin; and after he had passed through the Panic of 1837, his debts surpassed his assets by over $200,000.

For the rest of his life, Hamilton became an American pioneer, trying to find in the West the fortune which had eluded him in Charleston. In the 1830's he had lent over $100,000 to the Republic of Texas. In the 1840's he made the Lone Star State his home.. He wandered over the globe to represent Texans in diplomatic capitals, lobbied for Texas bondholders during the Compromise of 1850, and always prayed that his adopted state would someday get him out of debt. In 1857, upon hearing that he could recover $35,000 by coming to Texas, he set sail on the first ship for Galveston. But when his ship collided with another, he was pitched into the sea, and upon tossing his life preserver to a mother and child, he disappeared from view. Hamilton died as he had lived, at once both a Yankee entrepreneur sailing after illusive fortune and an honorable "cavalier" courting death with chivalric gestures.

During the years of the Nullification Controversy, Hamilton's inveterate restlessness, his business speculations, his Texas exploits, all lay well in the future. His energies centered on the South Carolina political scene, and he played the game with the joy of a politico and the intensity of an ideologue. Determined to end the debilitating South Carolina depression, and anxious to prevent a re-enactment of the Vesey affair, in which he had played so prominent a part, Hamilton may have been the most dedicated of nullifiers. With his genius for political intrigue and his reputation as the soul of chivalry, he was the perfect man to break the lowcountry political rules, to rally the "rabble" and organize the machine, to become a beloved South Carolina version of the detested Martin Van Buren.[21]

In his important address at Walterborough in late October 1828, Hamilton publicly repudiated his old nationalism and warned his fellow aristocrats that northern majorities would never voluntarily stop feasting on southern riches. "Your task-master," warned Hamilton, "must soon become a tyrant, from the very abuses and corruptions of the system, without the bowels of compassion, or a jot of human sympathy." Moderate remedies would be ineffectual. Hence "after all, we must come back to Mr. Jefferson's plain, practical and downright principle, as our 'rightful remedy'—a *nullification* by the State . . . of the 'unauthorized act.' "[22]

Hamilton forwarded his speech to Jackson and to Henry Lee, a friend of Old Hickory's. Soon Hamilton's covering letter to Lee reached the President-elect. "I send you my speech at Walterborough," wrote the great lowcountry politician. "And I cannot but say to all who may find fault with it—'if this be treason then make the most of it.' " Eighteen months later Hamilton was writing to Van Buren, "if you think that this confederacy either can or ought to last under the conjoint operation of the tariff & internal improvements, understood & enforced as Mr. Clay & Mr. Adams' doctrines would justify . . . I can only say that we differ in opinion."[23]

Contemporaries accused Hamilton, McDuffie, and their cohorts of embracing nullification because Jackson refused them patronage and favored Van Buren over Calhoun. The notion persists in historical literature. The reverse is true. Hamilton and his compatriots could barely contain themselves until Old Hickory was elected; and they proceeded to destroy their chances for patronage and to help defeat Calhoun by waxing radical long before the crisis

[21] Grayson Autobiography, p. 234; Hamilton Papers, NC, *passim;* Hammond Diary, entry for March 6, 1842, Hammond Papers, LC; J. G. deR. Hamilton, "James Hamilton, Jr.," Allen Johnson and Dumas Malone (eds.), *Dictionary of American Biography* (20 vols.; New York, 1928–36), VIII, 187–8.

[22] *Speech at Walterborough*, pp. 7, 19.

[23] Hamilton to Lee, Nov. 15, 1828, Hamilton to Jackson, Nov. 15, 1828, Jackson Papers; Hamilton to Van Buren, May 27, 1830, Van Buren Papers.

of the first Jackson administration. Jackson told both Hamilton and Amos Kendall that he intended to give South Carolinians high governmental posts until deterred by their "ultra tariff violence." Hamilton confessed to the new President "that the cause of my exclusion I regarded as the highest compliment of my life." As Hayne pointed out in 1831, "a more pliant course" would surely have brought the highest national offices—"heads of their departments, their Supreme Judiciary, or their splendid foreign missions"—within the grasp of leading Calhounites.[24]

Another contemporary accusation, that Calhounites embraced nullification prematurely because of Smith's victories in South Carolina, has only slightly more substance. Of course the passage of the Smith Resolutions in 1825 demonstrated to all South Carolina statesmen that the state's rendezvous with nationalism had come to an end. No doubt the Calhounites' shift toward sectionalism in 1827 represented partly an attempt to blunt the force of the Smithite onslaught. In 1828 South Carolina's anti-tariff excitement forced all aspiring politicians to war against protection.

But denouncing tariffs was one thing; supporting nullification was another. The fact is that popular pressures were not strong enough in the late 1820's to force politicians to carry strict-construction dogmas to extremes. Nullification was rarely an issue in the legislative elections of 1828. The Hamilton-McDuffie public campaign aimed at arousing the legislators rather than rallying the electorate; and the voters, in turn, were more concerned about unseating those representatives who had favored a $10,000 state appropriation for Thomas Jefferson's daughter. When the legislature met at the end of 1828, nullification was rejected by overwhelming majorities. No Carolinian could hope to defeat McDuffie or Hamilton in a congressional race in the late 1820's. Hayne was re-elected United States Senator unanimously in 1828 despite his efforts to delay militant agitation. Smith retained the support of many nullifiers until well into 1830 although he never

[24] Hayne, *Fourth of July Oration, 1831*, p. 35; Hamilton to Van Buren, May 7, 1830, Van Buren Papers; Kendall to Francis Blair [March 7], 1829, Blair-Lee Papers, Princeton. I am indebted to Charles G. Sellers, Jr., for the latter citation.

endorsed the remedy. Drayton was unopposed for re-election to his Charleston congressional seat in 1830 although he opposed state veto.

In short, fire-eating was good politics but not yet necessary politics in South Carolina in 1828. South Carolinians who wished to pursue a course of enlightened self-interest in national politics could still afford to muffle their opinions in the hopes of prospering at the hands of Jackson. The point is crucial: such Calhounites as Hamilton and McDuffie became militants at the risk of losing national political control—and before state political pressures forced their hand—because, right or wrong, they believed in the necessity for radical opposition.

Calhoun's motives are more obscure. On the eve of his re-election to the vice-presidency, his presidential prospects were already showing signs of collapsing as prematurely as they had begun. During the Adams administration the Carolinian found his earlier synthesis of national, state, and personal interests cracking at every turn. In December 1825 Calhoun had secretly attacked the extreme statement of nationalism in Adams' first annual message. By August 1827 he had privately embraced nullification. "The despotism founded on combined geographical interest," he wrote to Littleton Walker Tazewell, "admits of but one effectual remedy, a veto on the part of the local interest, or under our system, on the part of the states."[25]

By accepting the principle of state veto, Calhoun turned away not only from his earlier faith in expansive nationalism but also from his former commitment to government by majority rule. During the prenullification phase of his career, Calhoun often argued that the principle of periodic elections would adequately safeguard the American experiment in self-government. Representatives might be corrupt, but the people were incorruptible. As long as the populace retained control over those who governed, democracy would remain the most viable form of government.[26]

[25] Calhoun to J. G. Swift, Dec. 11, 1825, Swift Papers, New York Pub. Lib.; Calhoun to Tazewell, Aug. 25, 1827, Calhoun Papers, LC.
[26] Calhoun to McLean, May 29, 1827, McLean Papers.

But in his letters to Tazewell in late 1827, and in his later writings, Calhoun expressed severe doubts about the inherent wisdom and virtue of the people and repudiated a strict reliance on periodic elections and majority rule. Man, argued Calhoun in the post-1827 phase of his career, "is so constituted, that his direct or individual affections are stronger than his sympathetic or social feelings." As a result, a group of men with similar interests is always more self-interested than disinterested. In a democracy, therefore, if one portion of the community contains a numerical majority, it will "pervert its powers to oppress, and plunder the other." If no one interest can muster a majority, "a combination will be formed between those whose interests are most alike." In both cases, legislative edict will soon transfer minority riches into majority pockets, a form of legal plunder which rivals the exactions of a despotic prince. Periodic elections are of no help to the hapless minority, for the tyranny of legislative majorities reflects the selfishness of popular majorities; the problem lies in the community, not among the rulers. As Calhoun wrote Virgil Maxcy in 1831, "the rule of the majority and the right of suffrage are good things, but they alone are not sufficient to guard liberty, as experience will teach us."[27]

The exploitation of permanent minorities, then, inevitably followed from the rule of numerical majorities. But a system of minority veto, which Calhoun called a government of the *concurrent* majority, would end the tyranny of numbers. If each interest had to *concur* for any law to pass, selfishness would be unsuccessful, and the great pressure groups would become disinterested compromisers in the legislative chambers. Since Calhoun believed that each interest controlled at least one state, he maintained that the acceptance of state veto would create a national government of the concurrent majority.

Until Hamilton and McDuffie forced him into the open in the late summer of 1831, Calhoun managed to remain publicly aloof from the nullifiers' campaign. But during this period of silence, there can be no doubt about his intellectual commitment

[27] Calhoun, *Works*, I, 3–16; Calhoun to Maxcy, Aug. 6, 1831, Galloway-Maxcy Markoe Papers, LC.

to the doctrine. Calhoun was probably first attracted to nullification because of the economic hardships which afflicted South Carolina. But after working with the theory for a time, his commitment came closer to resembling an author's pride in his own artistic achievement. Calhoun had the sort of mind which gloried in abstractions, and he was fascinated by the intricate difficulties of developing a theory of state veto. "I see and feel, deeply feel, the difficulties which you have so clearly stated," he wrote Tazewell in November 1827. "I know not that they can be surmounted, but am unwilling to consider them as insuperable. I have given to them much thought during the summer, but confess I do not see my way clearly." When Calhoun had finally systematized the doctrine, he was not modest about his contribution to political philosophy. After finishing one essay on nullification, the Vice President wrote that it "will forever settle the question, at least, as far as reason has anything to do with settling political questions." Calhoun made every effort to convince his national political supporters of the efficacy of nullification. Sometimes he was a bit arrogant in addressing his friends. "I think that, in forming your opinions, in the midst of your laborious occupations, you have not sufficiently reflected on the complex nature of our government," he wrote to Supreme Court Justice John McLean. Occasionally he betrayed considerable guilt about keeping his opinion secret. "As I have no reason to disguise any sentiment, I ever entertained," he wrote in 1830, "I have come to the conclusion, that I owe it as a duty to myself & the publick to place my sentiments in relation to it, before the publick."[28]

This intense intellectual commitment to nullification raises serious questions about Calhoun's political sincerity. An ideologue, one would think, should be crusading for his cause instead of concealing it. A definitive statement of the Vice President's motives is impossible, for the problem is complex and the surviving

[28] Calhoun to Tazewell, Nov. 9, 1827, Calhoun Papers, LC; Calhoun to Patrick Noble, September 10, 1832, original in the possession of Mrs. Forest Farley, Austin, Tex., copy held by the John C. Calhoun Coll., SC; Calhoun to Samuel Ingham, Oct. 30, 1830, Calhoun Papers, SC; Calhoun to [McLean], Oct. 4, 1828, McLean Papers; Calhoun to J. C. McDonald, June 29, 1830, Calhoun Papers, Brown.

evidence sketchy. Some tentative conclusions, however, can be essayed.

Certainly Calhoun was a fiercely ambitious politician; and like most public men in the Age of Jackson, he was eager for his chance to serve in the White House. In 1828 his prospects seemed promising enough if he could dampen the spirits of the South Carolina hotheads. Most Americans considered nullification another name for secession and believed that minority veto would destroy government by majority rule. By proclaiming his belief in nullification, Calhoun would throw away his presidential chances and hand control of the Jackson party to Martin Van Buren. The Vice President understandably preferred maintaining a discreet silence to committing political suicide.

Yet Calhoun's passion for the presidency, and consequently his reluctance to announce his commitment to minority veto, was not entirely a matter of personal ambition. The Vice President clearly hoped he could use his power as heir apparent in the Jackson administration, and later as President in his own right, to gain a lower tariff without resorting to nullification. The combination of presidential pressure and the threat of nullification might bring the majority to yield; and if minority veto was put into practice, the remedy would be more likely to prosper with Calhoun administering the laws. The Vice President had reason to believe that he could best serve the nullifiers' cause by remaining apart from their crusade.

Finally, and perhaps most important, Calhoun's reluctance to come out for nullification was caused by the nature of the impossible problem he tried so hard to solve. Calhoun clearly saw that northern abolitionists, if not checked, would eventually lead the South to secede. Other men—Clay, Polk, Webster, Van Buren—hoped that compromise would solve the growing sectional controversy. But Calhoun—agreeing for once with William Lloyd Garrison—believed that compromise would only postpone the moment of decision. The problem was too severe to be avoided; and the true statesman must develop means of resolving the basic issue once and for all. Since Calhoun could not—and knew his fellow southerners would not—accept the abolition of slavery, he believed that the Union could be saved only by giving the South permanent security against northern abolitionists. Nullification was the country's best—probably its only—hope.

Yet if South Carolina nullified before the nation saw the virtues of the remedy, Calhoun might be trapped in an intolerable vicious circle. The one mechanism which could save the Union might bring on a premature civil war. The better part of wisdom seemed to be a campaign of public education before the state took its stand. As Calhoun wrote Francis W. Pickens in 1831, "as much time should be afforded as . . . possible before the State & the Union . . . take sides *finally*."[29]

Thus in the period between 1827 and 1831 Calhoun believed that he could best serve both his personal ambitions and his political principles by a policy of silence. By muffling his opinions, the Vice President hoped to gain national political power; and with the Jackson party at his command, he might be able to lower the tariff without resorting to nullification. If minority veto had to be employed, Calhoun could hope to stop federal armies from marching into South Carolina. And, finally, the Vice President's four-year silence was in part his first prudent response to the dangers inherent in using a potentially revolutionary measure to achieve strictly conservative ends.

But if Calhoun kept his own counsel until well into 1831, he still made a decisive contribution to the developing nullification crusade. As a result of the Hamilton-McDuffie public campaign in the fall of 1828, the legislature was sure to consider the remedy upon convening at the end of the year. Deliberations would be facilitated if representatives had access to a clear formulation of the doctrine. While Turnbull had advocated state veto in 1827 and Hamilton had defended it at Walterborough, neither had developed the theory systematically. In the fall of 1828 William Campbell Preston asked Calhoun to write an extended essay on nullification for the enlightenment of the legislators. The Vice President agreed on the condition that his authorship would be kept secret. Calhoun's long *Exposition* (1828), although

---

[29] Calhoun to Pickens, Aug. 1, 1831, L. W. Smith Coll., Morristown [N.J.] National Historical Park.

written "in great haste, and under perpetual interruption," remains one of the most lucid statements of the South Carolina doctrine.[30]

5

The theory of nullification was in part only an extreme application of strict-construction postulates. No clause in the Constitution expressly delegates *final* authority to determine constitutional questions to the Supreme Court or to any other branch of the general government. The federal courts are given jurisdiction over "all cases, in law and equity, arising under this Constitution, the laws of the United States, and treaties made, or which shall be made, under their authority." The federal "Constitution, and the laws of the United States which shall be made in pursuance thereof; and all treaties made, or which shall be made, under the authority of the United States" are declared "the supreme law of the land." Most Americans believed that these clauses gave the Supreme Court final authority over whether particular United States laws were indeed "made in pursuance" of the Constitution.

The nullifiers, on the other hand, maintained that the Court's prerogative to *hear* federal cases did not mean *final* authority to decide them. Moreover, the supremacy of federal law did not prove that the Supreme Court had *ultimate* discretion over what was constitutional. The Founding Fathers would have expressly enumerated such a vital power if they had intended to delegate it. The final authority to declare laws unconstitutional, the nullifiers concluded, was a reserved right retained by each state.

But the doctrine of nullification usually involved far more than a narrow-minded quibble about words in the fundamental law. During the Nullification Crisis, as during all the great sectional controversies of the mid-nineteenth century, the most inventive explorations of American political thought often took the form of a discourse on the meaning of the federal Constitution. It could not have been otherwise. The Constitution ranks

[30] Calhoun to Preston, Jan. 6, 1829, Virginia Carrington Scrapbook; Calhoun to Preston, Nov. 21, 1828, Calhoun Papers, SC.

with the Declaration of Independence as a practical embodiment of the American political faith; and when enlightened commentators analyzed the text, they reconsidered some of the central ambiguities in the idea of democracy.

Calhoun's formulation of the nullification doctrine is intelligible only against the background of the Lockean social-contract theory and the Anglo-American conception of sovereignty. The ratification of the Constitution was a manifestation of America's commitment to John Locke's contractual theory. Locke's theory, in turn, was an attempt to solve a classic conundrum in political theory: how can a government possess the coercive force necessary to enforce its laws without becoming an illegitimate tyranny? Locke assumed that governmental power became legitimate when the community consented to its exercise. Coercive force could not be considered tyrannical when it was used to enforce the will of the governed.[31]

But as contractual theorists realized, if each citizen had to consent to each law, governments could no longer enforce their edicts. Gaining political legitimacy would require surrendering the power to govern at all.

To escape this difficulty, Lockeans distinguished between an initial, higher, constitution-making stage and a subsequent, more mundane, lawmaking stage. In the initial social contract, members of a community consented to a constitution, thereby establishing a particular form of government and giving it certain powers. When they ratified a constitution, contracting agents also renounced their right to consent to laws passed within the sphere of the power granted. By investing a government with certain general prerogatives, the governed avoided the anarchical consequences of requiring everyone to assent to each specific law.

Americans took John Locke's social-contract theory more seriously than did the English. As a result, American theorists altered William Blackstone's theory of sovereignty. The Blackstonian thesis, widely accepted in late-eighteenth-century England, maintained that sovereignty referred to the absolute power

---

[31] I am simplifying for the sake of clarity. Locke also assumed that human laws, to be legitimate, must be in accord with natural laws.

of an unlimited government to command allegiance from its sub-jects. As Blackstone defined it, "there is and must be . . . a supreme, irresistible, absolute, uncontrolled authority, in which . . . the rights of sovereignty reside." Citizens owed uncondi-tional obedience to edicts of their sovereign, and since by defi-nition there could be only one sovereign, men owed absolute allegiance to one government.[32]

Absolute sovereignty in the Blackstonian sense obviously did not exist in America. Governmental power was divided among federal, state, and municipal authorities. Moreover, according to the Lockean formula, governments were limited to exercising the powers which the governed had delegated in the constitutional compact. But if the essence of Blackstonian sovereignty was lost, the word was retained. To the extent that an American govern-ment exercised any legitimate authority, it was said to be sov-ereign and its citizens were said to owe it allegiance. Americans were ruled by several sovereigns, and they owed allegiance to several governments.

The federal Constitution preserved both the social-contract theory and the changed definition of sovereignty. By restrain-ing majorities to exercising those powers which the contracting parties had agreed to delegate, the Constitution helped maintain the principle of the consent of the governed. By defining the powers of the federal government and expressly reserving the remaining powers for the use of the states, the fundamental text helped safeguard the division of sovereign powers.

The doctrine of nullification could be derived from two dif-ferent theories of the Constitution. One group of nullifiers based their case on the principle of divided sovereignty. They main-tained that the state government, as a co-department in one unified governmental system, could check federal encroachments and preserve its own share of sovereignty. Other nullifiers based their argument on the principle that the governed are supreme

[32] I am simplifying again. Blackstone assumed that the sovereign had absolute practical power, but he maintained that it *ought* to observe moral restraints. For an excellent discussion of the Anglo-American conception of sovereignty, see Bernard Bailyn (ed.), *Pamphlets of the American Revolution, 1750–1776* (4 vols. planned, 1 publ., Cambridge, Mass., 1965–   ), I, 115–38.

over a constitution to which they consent. These nullifiers urged that a state convention, the contracting party which had originally ratified the Constitution, could veto federal laws which assumed power the people had never agreed to delegate. Calhoun's decisive intellectual contribution was to seize the second, and by far the better, of the two alternatives and to buttress it with a clever reformulation of the American theory of sovereignty.

The co-department theorists maintained that balanced power necessarily implied mutual authority to check abuses. The Constitution made both the federal and state governments sovereign in their own sphere. Yet if one sovereign was given exclusive rights to judge what powers belonged to each, divided sovereignty would be an empty constitutional gesture. As Calhoun put it during his brief flirtation with the co-department thesis, "to divide power nominally, without giving to each party the means of protecting its share, is really not to divide it at all."[33]

The fatal weakness of the co-department theory was that it left the federal government no less sovereign than state governments. The same logic which gave state authorities power to nullify federal law gave federal authorities power to veto state law—including a law nullifying federal enactments. The problem was crucial because co-department theorists assumed that disputed power would lead to an appeal for a constitutional amendment. Three-fourths of the states, by amending the Constitution, could end a constitutional stalemate. But would the federal government be presumed right unless the state government could procure a constitutional amendment? Or would a nullifying state remain the final judge unless it was overruled by three-fourths of the others? The difficulty of procuring so large a majority made the question crucial, and the theory of sovereign co-departments left the answer enigmatic.

Moreover, a citizen of a nullifying state was also a citizen of the federal government. Divided sovereignty meant divided allegiance and, in case of conflict, a unionist could legitimately obey national rather than state authorities.

---

[33] Calhoun to [McLean], Oct. 4, 1828, McLean Papers. For a particularly good statement of the co-department thesis, see *Evening Post*, Nov. 3, 1831.

Section 25 of the Judiciary Act of 1789 was the supreme practical obstacle to the co-department theory. This section, which permitted the United States Supreme Court to overrule a state court's decision involving the Constitution, made the federal government final judge of contested powers. In the early nineteenth century defenders of states' rights, led by Chief Justice Spencer Roane of the Virginia Supreme Court, conducted a vigorous campaign against this section and its use by the great nationalist of the United States Supreme Court, Chief Justice John Marshall. For a time in 1827, Calhoun embraced the co-department thesis and considered joining the crusade against Section 25.[34] But he soon realized that if Section 25 gave control to the federal government, its repeal would establish the supremacy of state governments. The case for repeal of Section 25, like all nullification arguments based on the co-department thesis, floundered on the principle of divided sovereignty.

By 1828 Calhoun almost always argued that nullification was a power of a state convention in its capacity as the original ratifying body, not a power of a state government in its capacity as a co-department.[35] The crucial error of the Spencer Roane school, he believed, was to divide sovereignty and to give it to governments. Returning to the Blackstonian definition, the Vice President maintained that sovereignty could only mean uncontrollable power and was therefore indivisible. As Calhoun explained to Congress in 1833, "we might just as well speak of half a square, or of half a triangle, as of half a sovereign."[36]

In England Blackstone had located unlimited sovereignty in Parliament's absolute lawmaking authority. But in America, Calhoun argued, governments were not sovereign because constitutions limited them. Constitutions were not sovereign, for they could be changed or negated by the governed. The American

---

[34] Calhoun to Tazewell, Aug. 25, 1827, Calhoun Papers, LC.

[35] The 1828 McLean letter cited above is a conspicuous exception, and Calhoun slipped once in the *Exposition*. *Works*, VI, 42–3. But by 1831 he had renounced the co-department thesis completely. *Ibid.*, VI, 94–124. Calhoun returned to a modified version of the co-department argument in "Discourse on the Constitution and Government of the United States," published after his death. *Ibid.*, I, 111ff.

[36] *Ibid.*, II, 232.

sovereign could be only the people in their capacity of making, amending, and destroying constitutions.[37]

Calhoun's explication of allegiance followed logically from his view of sovereignty. Nullifiers drew a sharp distinction between allegiance owed *absolutely* to the sovereign which formed the constitution and obedience owed *conditionally* to agencies which made the laws. Just as one *obeyed* a European policeman as long as the sovereign state delegated him authority, so one *obeyed* an American government as long as the sovereign community entrusted it with power. But in both cases, allegiance owed to the sovereign superseded obedience owed to its agent.

The great danger of American government, Calhoun believed, was that the distinction between constitution-making and lawmaking would be lost. Under the guise of enacting the laws, an agent might change the Constitution by seizing power which the people had never consented to delegate. This development would have a series of consequences. A simple lawmaking majority altering the Constitution would destroy the provision of the fundamental law calling for constitutional amendment by three-fourths majorities. With majorities riding roughshod over the Constitution, minorities would have no protection against the tyranny of number. And since assaults on the social contract would undermine the consent of the governed, democracy would become as illegitimate as any form of government.

The critical weapon with which agents became sovereign, Calhoun continued, was the ultimate power to decide constitutional questions. Unlimited power to interpret the Constitution meant unlimited power to alter it, for constitutions could be transformed as easily by constitutional construction as by constitutional amendment. The Supreme Court—no less than any other branch of the central agency—could be controlled by the majority. Calhoun explained that "to confide the power to the Judiciary to determine finally and conclusively what powers are delegated and what reserved, would be, in reality, to confide it to the majority, whose agents they are. . . ." Constitutions would

[37] *Ibid.,* VI, 36–7.

be subject "to the will of the very majority against which the protection was intended."[38]

The distinction between constitution-making and lawmaking, then, could be saved only by keeping final constitutional jurisdiction away from all branches of the governmental agency. The sovereign who created the fundamental law could maintain the constitution's supremacy over his agent, and his own supremacy over the constitution, only by retaining the right to nullify laws which exceeded the sphere of the power granted.

Since the nature of constitution-making sovereignty implied ultimate constitutional discretion, Calhoun merely had to demonstrate that a state convention was the party which had ratified the fundamental law in order to demonstrate its right to nullify. Before the federal Constitution was ratified, he argued, each state was clearly sovereign. The colonies had revolted from England as separate communities rather than in an inseparable union; the Articles of Confederation explicitly recognized the sovereignty of the states; states voted in the Constitutional Convention; and most important, each state had given individual consent to the constitutional covenant. In forming the Republic, the contracting conventions had created a federal agency with a few governmental powers but with no authority to change the Constitution. Each state convention remained sovereign and retained the authority to nullify unconstitutional laws their agency passed.[39]

Calhoun's clever formulation of the nullification theory solved all the problems raised by the co-department thesis. Since a sovereign state was superior to an agency it created, a nullification edict was the law of the land unless the federal government secured a constitutional amendment. If a contest developed between the national agency and a nullifying convention, a unionist clearly had to follow the convention, to which he owed absolute allegiance, rather than the federal government, to which he owed conditional obedience. The Supreme Court, as a part of the agency, could not negate an action of a sovereign convention.

[38] *Ibid.*, VI, 71–2.
[39] Calhoun's theory is most clearly stated in his "Letter to Governor Hamilton," but is well developed in all his great essays of the nullification era. *Ibid.*, VI, 1–209, esp. 114–93.

Calhoun's theory, although rejected by some nullifiers and mis-understood by others, gave the nullification movement an attractive and compelling rationale. Intellectual clarity—particularly for a cause as obscure as nullification—is not the least reason for political success. After Calhoun had developed the doctrine, other nullifiers gained the immense intellectual security of being able to answer their critics with arguments based squarely on cherished American principles. Did nullifiers repudiate majority rule? No, but majorities possessed only the authority which the governed had consented to surrender. Wouldn't nullification inevitably lead to anarchy if governments had no authority to enforce the laws? No, government would merely lose power to enforce those laws which they had had no constitutional right to pass. Did nullifiers deny the supremacy of federal law when they insisted on the absolute power of a state? No, but they argued that a constitution-making sovereign must always be superior to a lawmaking agent. James Hammond, who had been writing nullification editorials by the dozens, remarked after reading one of Calhoun's major essays:

I have never read such a production. It does seem to me to make everything as clear as a sunbeam. What a mind he has. No man in America—I think I may say no man alive is equal to him in powers of analysis & profound philosophical reasonings. . . . His positions on a question almost as threadbare to *my* understanding as the Fourth of July theme are most of them new, & as sound & as forcible as they are original.[40]

But if Calhoun put the case for nullification as soundly as possible, and reassured young men like Hammond in the process, he had a remarkable tendency to destroy the positions he tried hardest to establish. First, his theory attempted to preserve the mechanism of constitutional amendment, as laid down in the constitutional compact, by stopping the federal government from seizing the states' reserved rights. But the Constitution would be changed as completely if states blocked the use of powers they had contracted to delegate. If nullification would have ended

---

[40] Hammond to Isaac Hayne, Aug. 21, 1831, Hammond Papers, SC. See also William Harper, *Judge Harper's Speech . . . April 1, 1832, Explaining . . . Nullification* (Charleston, 1832), p. 9.

constitutional alterations by federal majorities, it would, in practice, have permitted constitutional alterations by single states.[41]

Second, Calhoun's theory, although premised on the notion of undivided sovereignty, established two sovereigns. The nullifiers' insistence that constitution-makers are sovereign left states with something less than absolute authority. By Calhoun's own definitions, although the governmental authority delegated by the states created only a federal agency, the power to amend the Constitution established a national sovereign community. A constituted majority of three-fourths of the states could change the fundamental text without the assent of each supposedly sovereign state. The contracting party which had ratified the Constitution had yielded part of its sovereignty to a new community in consenting to the social compact.

By the 1850's southern extremists realized that an unqualified endorsement of the power of constitutional amendment would negate undivided state sovereignty. But in the 1830's nullifiers often admitted that the national sovereign community could change the fundamental text in whatever way it liked. The way Calhoun put it in his draft of the *Exposition* is significant enough:

> ... by an express provision of the Constitution, it may be amended or changed by three fourths of the States; and thus each State, by assenting to the Constitution with this provision, has modified its original right as a sovereign, of making its individual consent necessary to any change in its political condition; and, by becoming a member of the Union, has placed this important power in the hands of three fourths of the States—in whom the highest power known to the Constitution actually resides.[42]

The *Exposition* as printed by the South Carolina legislature completely contradicted the logic of undivided sovereignty. The legislature changed Calhoun's phrase "has modified its original right as a sovereign" to read "has surrendered its original right as a sovereign." The *Exposition* as printed also altered Calhoun's

---

[41] Calhoun admitted this fallacy but sought, I think unsuccessfully, to minimize it. *Works,* VI, 177ff.

[42] *Ibid.,* VI, 36–7, 50. Calhoun repeated the error in his later nullification essays. *Ibid.,* VI, 173, 180.

final phrase, "in whom the highest power known to the Constitution actually resides," to "in which the sovereignty of the union . . . does now actually reside"! Calhoun's draft, to some extent, and the legislature's *Exposition*, with no qualifications, not only argued that sovereignty was divided but also came close to admitting that the national sovereign community had the greater share.[43]

The best unionist theorists took advantage of the nullifiers' inconsistency. In the most intriguing debates of the nullification period, Judge John Richardson employed the fallacy to outargue both Stephen Miller and William Harper at successive public meetings in 1830. Instead of checking the abolitionists, Richardson argued, nullification, by surrendering sovereignty to a three-fourths majority, handed northern "fanatics" the right to abolish slavery and to outlaw secession! This was merely the practical consequence of

The absurdity of assuming the right to nullify the Federal laws, as a *sovereign right reserved to the State;* and at the same time, of submitting that sovereign power, which is in itself, *uncontrollable from abroad,* to be controlled by three-fourths of the States. . . .[44]

Miller answered ineffectually, that

I do not see much force in this view, since we are *now* at the mercy of three-fourths—this is what we bargained for—I will submit to whatever three-fourths say shall be the rule, since this is my contract, and I will be governed thereby. Our only security now is the moral sense of the three-fourths.[45]

In late 1831 a unionist could correctly point out that "Judge R's . . . reply to CHANCELLOR HARPER, is to this day, unanswered—'response sans replique.'" Even in 1832, Harper, who was the most skillful dialectician in the nullification movement next to Calhoun, was arguing that South Carolina's "faith is bound to submit to any alteration of the compact that may be made with the concurrence of three-fourths of the members of

[43] *Exposition and Protest Reported by the Special Committee of the House of Representatives* . . . (Columbia, 1829), pp. 26–7.
[44] *City Gazette,* Sept. 14, 1830; *Proceedings of the States Rights Meeting in Columbia, S.C. on the Twentieth of September, 1830* (Columbia, 1830), pp. 18–42.
[45] *Camden Journal,* Sept. 25, 1830.

the confederacy." By 1834, although Abram Blanding, a unionist, could still use the three-fourths argument with compelling effect, important fire-eaters, such as Robert Barnwell Rhett, were beginning to throw qualifications around the power of constitutional amendment.[46]

Of course the division of indivisible sovereignty was the kind of theoretical inconsistency which Calhoun, a practical politician, could afford to ignore. In 1832 southern slaveholders controlled far more than one-fourth of the states. If a three-fourths majority could alone enact emancipation, the South seemed safe enough. In addition, Carolina radicals were proposing nullification, not secession. They could rest content with just the assertion of the right to secede in case a three-fourths majority reversed a nullifying state. Indeed, debating secession, and consequently appearing too radical, was highly inexpedient in 1832. The nullifiers may have decided that the defeat in logic that John Richardson inflicted was less harmful than were the political consequences of answering his argument.

But the unguarded theoretical admissions characterizing the nullifiers' statements on the power of constitutional amendment evidenced more than the caution of practical politicians. As a rule, proponents of a new political theory stumble badly—and revealingly—over the most serious intellectual problems they face. No matter how a theorist chose to define sovereignty in America, he would have had trouble establishing an absolute sovereign. In America the power to make constitutions has been divided no less than the power to govern. Calhoun seized on the initial constitution-making body as his absolute sovereign, but the subsequent amending body was equally sovereign in Calhoun's own sense. Given this situation, initial inconsistencies, if not inevitable, were at least likely.

In the overall perspective of southern intellectual history, the nullification debates served as an important rehearsal in which the fatal contradiction in Calhoun's theory of sovereignty was

[46] *City Gazette,* Aug. 18, 1831; Harper, *Speech, April 1, 1832,* p. 8; *A Catechism on the Tariff for the Use of Plain People of Common Sense* (Charleston, 1831), p. 35. The 1834 debate over the three-fourths clause can be followed in *Book of Allegiance; or a Report of the Arguments . . . On the Oath of Allegiance . . .* (Columbia, 1834).

at last discovered. Militant secessionists later reformulated the doctrine to explain away the disastrous implications in the power of amendment. The new explanation was based on the principle of implied consent. If a three-fourths majority amended the Constitution despite the wishes of a single state, the secessionists argued, a state could give its implicit consent by remaining inside the Union. If a dissenting state wished to exercise its sovereignty, it could reject the amendment by seceding from the Union.

Whatever the merits of this latter-day doctrine as a defense of secession, it would have offered no solution to the troubles of the nullifiers. The essence of nullification, and where it differed most profoundly from secession, lay in the affirmation that a state retained its sovereign power to act while it remained in the Union. Since a sovereign by definition had absolute authority, a state should have had limitless authority to protect minorities in any way it liked without leaving the Union to do so. Yet unless and until the Union was dissolved, the secessionists' theory of constitutional amendment gave minorities no check on the unlimited authority of a three-fourths majority. And unless the sovereign state opted for disunion, it could do no more than grovel haplessly before the mighty power of the constitutional amenders. The retention of an absolute right to secede, in short, could not disguise the fact that a state had temporarily given away a large portion of its constitution-making sovereignty when it delegated the power of constitutional amendment.

In addition to dividing indivisible sovereignty, Calhoun unwittingly united his own irreconcilable opposites, sovereignty and government. In passing judgment on a legal case—particularly in enacting means of carrying out a decision—a sovereign nullifying convention would exercise *governmental* authority. The Nullification Ordinance of 1832 was no different from a Supreme Court decision in its judging of constitutional issues and no different from a congressional law in its provisions for enforcing the judgment. The process of deciding constitutional issues was inevitably the twilight zone where government and sovereignty (in Calhoun's sense) became indistinguishable. Calhoun may have been right that governments, in exercising their power to govern under a constitution, could change the fundamental text by constitutional construction. But he missed the equally obvious point that the sovereign which formed the constitution would exercise governmental power when it sat in judgment on alleged constitutional changes.

By plunging his sovereign into government, Calhoun unintentionally established an American version of a Blackstonian despot. Calhoun had embraced Blackstone's concept of absolute sovereignty, but had rejected the Englishman's notion that sovereigns must govern. If governments became sovereign, constitutions would no longer protect minorities. Calhoun's sovereign convention was, of course, Blackstonian with a difference. In its relations with the rest of the Union, a nullification convention could do no more than negate law. But insofar as the sovereign could govern, it was by definition absolute, and it was capable of repressing a dissenting minority within the state. In the end, the theory of nullification succeeded in establishing the majority despotism on the state level which it sought to destroy nationally. The nullifiers' bitter post 1832 controversy with the South Carolina unionists was a direct result of this theoretical weakness.

The theory of nullification not only would have permitted nullifiers to usurp the liberties of unionists but also would have perpetuated the tyranny of white men over the slaves. If a planter-dominated majority in any southern state could veto laws passed by a reform-minded majority in Congress, there remained little hope of passing antislavery legislation. Expressed in more theoretical terms, a system of minority veto would allow exploiting classes to block the positive legislation which alone could aid certain hapless minorities. Of all the ironies in which nullifiers trapped themselves, none surpasses the fact that their idea of minority veto was designed to bolster a notorious form of majority exploitation.

Calhoun also destroyed the theory of contractual consent which he had attempted to salvage. The genius of the Lockean thesis was to establish consent without risking anarchy. In contracting to give up a general power, the governed agreed to obey particular laws of which they disapproved. To Calhoun, of course, the danger in this formula was that a specific law could violate the consent of the governed by assuming a prerogative not included in the social contract. The doctrine of nullification averted this difficulty by permitting each contracting agent to judge whether individual laws exceeded the delegated authority. But this solution, by re-establishing the right of a portion of the community to negate particular laws, brought the social-contract theory full circle. In the name of protecting the original compact to which the governed had consented, Calhoun destroyed the power of governments to enforce laws and thereby returned society to the very state of nature which had produced the need for a compact in the first place. Put another way, by resurrecting absolute sovereignty and giving it to a single state rather than to the national government, Calhoun created a wildly revolutionary doctrine in the name of conserving the Union.[47]

Thus the theory of nullification was a veritable snarl of contradictions. Calhoun stopped constitutional revisions by the federal government and then permitted constitutional alterations by single states; he divided sovereignty after arguing for an absolute sovereign; he rigidly separated and then unwittingly reunited sovereignty and government; he protected national minority rights and then permitted state majority tyranny; he defended the consent of the governed at the expense of destroying the power to govern; he proposed conserving the Union with principles which would have destroyed it.

In the face of these manifold inconsistencies, the wonder is that Calhoun's claim to greatness has so often been based on the supposed rigor of his political logic. His real genius lay in identification of problems rather than in consistency of analysis. What makes his thought always interesting is his capacity to seek out and to wrestle with the usually unexamined ambiguities in the American Lockean faith. Calhoun was clearly right, for example, that the consent of the governed and the power to govern be-

[47] My analysis of Calhoun's role in the Nullification Controversy and of his theory of nullification has been greatly influenced by the brilliant essays of Louis Hartz. See Hartz, "South Carolina vs. the United States," in Daniel Aaron (ed.), *America in Crisis* (New York, 1952), pp. 73–91; Hartz, *The Liberal Tradition in America* . . . (New York, 1955), ch. 6.

come difficult to reconcile when a minority seeks to withhold its consent. The political theory of the secession crisis was to be devoted to this theme. The distinction between constitution-making and lawmaking can become more nebulous in practice than it ought to be in theory. Many aspects of the fundamental law *can* be changed as much by constitutional construction as by constitutional amendment. Finally, few democrats would deny that a written constitution and a balance of power could some-day fail to restrain a majority on the rampage.

The crabbed logic of nullification offered remedies more injurious than the problems it sought to cure. But when Calhoun formulated the doctrine for the South Carolina legislature in the fall of 1828, he established his credentials as one of the most trenchant critics of the American political tradition.

6

When the legislature convened at Columbia for its regular session in late November 1828, the radicals, led by Whitemarsh Seabrook, William Harper, and William Campbell Preston, advocated calling for a nullification convention in 1829. During the debate over the proposal, some nullifiers pointed to the economic disaster in store for cotton planters. Others emphasized the indirect danger to slavery.

The most revealing aspect of the debate, however, was the indication that the lowcountry's sensitivity to the slavery issue was spreading to the upland. The intimate social contact between the gentry in the two sections was having an effect; and planters in the piedmont were coming to rival planters at tidewater in their instinctive dread of slavery debates. Thompson T. Player of Fairfield, one of the most important upcountry legislators, summed up well the piedmont's new apprehension:

Altho, Mr. Chairman, our pecuniary interests are so prejudiced by this system as to be inseparable from its discussion, they are not so much the gist of the controversy as to be thrust into the foreground of debate. . . . The most imposing truth in regard to the scheme of taxing us to pamper others, has already been brought with appropriate solemnity to the view of this committee, and requires no additional views to confirm it. It is, that the present measure is only preparatory to ulterior movements, destined by fanatics and abolitionists to subvert the institutions and established policy of the Southern country, to gratify their capricious and pretended charities.[48]

Although Player and other radicals emphasized the financial consequences of tariffs and the future danger to slavery, they could convince few legislators to vote for nullification in 1828. Some representatives continued to hope that Calhoun would control the Jackson administration. Even more legislators, the moderate William Elliott reported, would have proceeded "to a direct defiance of the General Government if they were sure of the cooperation of the Southern States."[49] The forces of moderation held the upper hand in 1828.

The conservatives' clever tactics and the nullifiers' internal divisions turned inevitable defeat into a rout. Benjamin F. Dunkin of Charleston, a moderate who was elected speaker of the House, shrewdly invoked old sectional rivalries to scare some tidewater politicians away from voting for nullification. As the sovereign community, a convention, he warned, would have full power to reapportion legislative seats and could take away the tidewater's disproportionate control.[50]

Meanwhile nullifiers squabbled among themselves about the proper way to veto the tariff. Player's group preferred immediate nullification by the state legislature. Some of his cohorts favored legislative nullification on the co-department theory. Others accepted Calhoun's logic, but believed that the people of South Carolina had delegated their power as a sovereign community to the state legislature.

Calhoun's theory, on the other hand, clearly pointed toward nullification by a convention. South Carolina's constitution gave only "legislative authority" to the legislature. By Calhoun's definitions, legislative, or lawmaking, powers specifically excluded sovereign, or constitution-making, powers. Most nullifiers, well aware that the strongest possible theory would increase southern

---

[48] *Columbia Telescope,* Feb. 13, 1829.
[49] Elliott to Mrs. Elliott, Dec. 14, 1828, Elliott-Gonzales Papers.
[50] *Charleston Mercury,* Dec. 12, 1828; *Columbia Telescope,* Feb. 13, 1829.

support and decrease national resistance, believed that the delay and inconvenience of nullification by convention was a small price to pay for added intellectual cogency. However, Player, and probably others, disagreed strongly enough to vote against the conventionists.

The state constitution required a two-thirds majority of both houses to call a convention. The conventionists of 1828 lost by almost a two-thirds majority, 41–80, in the House, and never brought the issue to a recorded vote in the Senate. The legislature also failed to adopt the *Exposition*, which Calhoun had drafted and which a legislative committee headed by Preston had revised and presented. The legislature merely passed a strong protest and agreed to print 5,000 copies of the *Exposition*.[51]

The document as printed contained significant alterations of Calhoun's text. Since some radicals favored nullification by the legislature, Preston's committee omitted the Vice President's argument for nullification by convention. The committee also blurred, without rejecting, Calhoun's distinction between sovereign and government. The changes in phrasing were all for the worst. The *Exposition* as printed was an untenable amalgam of several theories of nullification.[52] In subsequent years the most perceptive unionists used the flagrant errors in the printed essay to smash the argument for nullification. In every case, the flaws attacked were the textual changes by which the legislative committee had marred Calhoun's careful argument.[53]

7

Calhoun, although distressed by the committee's stylistic alterations, was pleased with the legislature's moderate action. "We cannot expect a sturdy and powerful resistance," wrote the Vice President, "till the nature of the disease and its fatal consequences, if not arrested, come to be generally understood. . . ." He believed

[51] For the vote on a convention, see House Journal, 1829, p. 127, South Carolina Arch.

[52] One of the best examples is quoted above, pp. 167–8. Compare also Calhoun's draft in *Works*, VI, 1ff., with the printed pamphlet, esp. *Works*, p. 36, lines 14–15, with pamphlet, p. 26, lines 25–6; *Works*, p. 46, with pamphlet, pp. 32–3; *Works*, p. 41, lines 23–30, with pamphlet, p. 30, lines 3–10.

[53] *Book of Allegiance*, pp. 53–4, 127, 175; *Greenville Mountaineer*, Jan. 25, 1834.

that South Carolina could obtain redress peacefully by educating the nation; recognition "that the final remedy under the constitution is in the hands of the state," he wrote, would "go far to affect the remedy of itself." In case the North refused to bow to the theory of nullification, "there would be a strange lack of spirit and sense in the state, if it did not apply it. . . . Never was there a more inspiring cause; relief from grievous oppression, restoring the Constitution to its original purity."[54]

Others, equally inspired by the cause, were distressed by the delay in adopting it. In March 1829 Warren Davis, congressman from Calhoun's district, told his constituents that "I have but little hope of remedy through the voluntary agency of Congress. . . . What people ever yet obtained justice, by whining and whimpering like a great miss from boarding school . . . you *cannot respect a thing that creeps and licks the dust!!!*" A July 4 public meeting at Walterborough was equally disappointed. "Our State Legislature of 1828," toasted the Colleton gentry. "The people asked it for bread, and received a stone." By early 1830 the revolutionary doctrine of nullification, slipping into the hands of South Carolina fire-eaters, was showing signs of wrecking the presidential campaign of the moderate who had so ingeniously formulated it.[55]

[54] Calhoun to Preston, Jan. 6, 1829, Virginia Carrington Scrapbook.
[55] *Pendleton Messenger*, Apr. 15, 1829; *Charleston Mercury*, July 10, 1829.

6

Nullification Defeated,
1829–1830

The year 1829 was one of uneasy quiet in South Carolina. With the state committed to a final appeal to Jackson for redress, and with the first Jacksonian congress scheduled to convene in December, political controversy was temporarily adjourned. Editors filled their sheets with sentimental homilies, and only the shrieks of peddlers enlivened the monotony of court day. But two important events in Charleston testified to the continued tension in 1829 and contributed later to the party alignments of 1832.

?

The East Bay merchants, it will be remembered, built a railroad to Hamburg in the late 1820's and early 1830's to protect Charleston's share of the Savannah River trade. Charleston financiers first organized the railroad company in late 1827 and procured a charter from the state legislature in December 1828. Neither the legislators nor the planters, however, showed much interest in buying stock. The "closed fist" of South Carolina drove "the Company to the doors of Congress." William Aiken and Alexander Black journeyed to Washington in January 1829 to ask Congress to purchase $250,000 in company stock. The directors argued that the railroad would connect two states, promote the national defense, and give South Carolina its share of federal appropriations.[1]

[1] *Charleston Courier*, March 5, Dec. 31, 1829.

The railroad petition, tabled in Congress in early 1829, inspired vigorous opposition when the South Carolina legislature met at the end of the year. The nullifiers, led by Robert Barnwell Rhett and William Preston, orated on the hypocrisy of fighting the American system with one hand and seeking its benefits with the other. The radicals also deplored the petition's effect in dividing the state and corrupting its political opinions. Rhett and Preston proceeded to secure a House resolution "requesting" Carolina representatives "to oppose with all their zeal" internal-improvement projects "and particularly all such appropriations, for the benefit of South Carolina or any of her citizens."[2]

When the railroad renewed its plea for a state appropriation at the 1829 session, the legislature responded with an inadequate $100,000 loan, payable in seven years and subject to rigid qualifications. The company could borrow $10,000 each time $30,000 was paid (as opposed to pledged) by private subscribers if the entire railroad property was assigned as security. The merchants promptly organized a public meeting in Charleston for January 1, 1830. The Charlestonians renounced the state loan and adopted a resolution urging the company to apply again for a congressional appropriation.[3]

The renewed congressional petition disgusted radicals throughout the state. The company's request, the Colleton gentry resolved, gives Carolina's sanction to the principle that "we now hold our property, not by the tenure of the Constitution, but by the *mere permission* of the majority in Congress." The *Columbia Telescope* declared that "the City of Charleston now, *is in fact* a colony of Yankee speculators, cherishing not a spark of Southern feeling." In Washington Hayne and Drayton agreed to present the petition, but warned that they would oppose it. The company decided that a vigorous nationalist presentation would increase the chance of congressional approval. And so South Carolina's mortification doubled when the embarrassing petition was introduced in the Senate by none other than Daniel Webster.[4]

[2] House Journal, 1829, p. 65; *Columbia Telescope*, Dec. 1, 1829; *Southern Patriot*, Dec. 3, 1829.

[3] Senate Journal, 1829, pp. 119–20, 142, 150–1; *Charleston Courier*, Jan. 4, 1830; *City Gazette*, Jan. 8, 1830.

[4] *Charleston Mercury*, Feb. 2, 11, 1830; *Columbia Telescope*, Feb. 5, 1830;

The company never received national aid and eventually accepted the state loan. By 1832 tracks to Hamburg were almost completed. But plans for a railroad to Cincinnati excited attention before the Hamburg line was finished. The 1829 petition marked the beginning of the East Bay's interest in federal internal-improvement appropriations.

The railroad controversy demonstrates an important point: Clay's nationalism better served the economic interests of the Charleston mercantile community than Calhoun's sectionalism. In the pre-1828 decade of canal and road construction, South Carolina projects had been intrastate improvements which had not needed congressional aid. But in the post-1828 era of railroad construction, East Bay financiers hoped that interstate projects, terminating in Charleston and partially financed by federal grants, would provide them with a highway of trade to the West. In addition, the Bank of the United States performed valued services in foreign and domestic exchange for the Charleston merchants.

The merchants' attitude toward protective tariffs, on the other hand, ranged from qualified approbation to mild dissent. Some merchants, realizing that protection was an integral part of Clay's American system, favored the tariff. Others, believing the tariff partly responsible for the planters' decreased ability to buy goods, opposed protection. Yet East Bay financiers realized that depleted piedmont soil and expanding cotton production were principally responsible for the planters' financial embarrassments. Since Charleston merchants imported few goods directly from Europe, tariffs hardly disturbed their external trade. Thus the merchants' qualms about protective tariffs never balanced their approval of other parts of the American system. The East Bay had every reason to oppose nullification.[5]

If the 1829 railroad controversy disposed the mercantile community toward moderation, the 1829 intendent election inclined the lower class toward nullification. Although the October

---

Charleston Courier, Jan. 26, 1830; *Register of Debates,* 21 Cong., 1 sess., I, 21–2; Preston to Thompson, n.d. [Jan. 1830], Thompson Papers, DU.

[5] The merchants' ambivalence toward the tariff can be followed in the *Charleston Courier,* particularly in 1828. After 1828 the *Courier* realized the inexpediency of defending the protective system. But the merchants' mildly protariff views sporadically emerged.

state legislature elections occurred every two years, the September Charleston city elections took place annually. The 1829 intendent election, pitting the Mercury Junto's Henry L. Pinckney against the Courier party's Thomas S. Grimké, was the most important city election of the decade.

Grimké, Charleston's representative in the South Carolina Senate, was at once the most committed figure in state politics and the least suited to be a politician. Like Charles Sumner of Massachusetts, he lived for his principles, and he could never dream of compromising with the eternal truths. An enthusiastic reformer in a state wedded to reaction, he carried his principles down the path toward political isolation.

From the day he emerged as a leading public figure, the ascetic Grimké displayed a compulsion to place the dictates of obligation over the indulgence of private desire. After becoming a learned and enthusiastic classicist, he turned against Greek and Latin studies because he supposed the ancients preached unchristian doctrine. Although eager for a career in the ministry, he became a lawyer out of duty to his father, the well-known Judge Grimké. He confessed to disliking the law, but stayed with the profession because of a sense of responsibility to his ever-growing famliy.

Disinterested benevolence remained the business of his life. An intense little man, frail, emaciated, overworked, Grimké had the kind of long, narrow, aesthetic face El Greco would have liked to paint. He walked the streets dressed like a pauper. By wearing shabby clothes, he pointed out, he was "enabled to give away more. Every dollar saved in this way is an additional sum for the poor." The generous Charlestonian annually gave away over half his personal income.[6]

Grimké's overwhelming sense of obligation was directed more toward public reform than private charity. Although far from an advocate of Christian perfectionism, he was distressed by the imperfections in a nation which claimed to be Christian. At one time or another, he could be found anywhere in the land, engaged in the great campaigns of the northeastern benevolent

[6] James H. Smith, *Eulogium on . . . Grimké . . .* (Charleston, 1835), p. 9.

empire. The movements for women's rights, educational reform, temperance, and universal peace all profited from his support. Occasionally Grimké's crusades took on a more personal cast and a wildly improbable air. When, for example, he developed a passion for simplified spelling, he thought nothing of printing the most serious essays with every silent *e* omitted. One newspaper correspondent caught the eccentric image which Grimké sometimes projected in a delightful spoof on the reforming Charlestonian. "Mr. Grimké," wrote the correspondent,

> has come lately to the conclusion that the practice among the male sex of wearing pantaloons in the summer season, is extremely disagreeable and therefore unnatural, and therefore contrary to *human duty*. In accordance with this opinion, he has appeared for several days past in King Street in petticoats of striped gingham. To render the dress still more cool, it is made to reach just below the knees, and is worn with the old fashioned hoops.[7]

But there was nothing humorous about Grimké's most important concerns. His extended essays on the fallacies of nullification rank among the most brilliant statements any unionist produced. Moreover, unlike every other leading politician in the state, he was at least willing to think about ending human slavery. While opposed to immediate emancipation, he cautiously supported the American Colonization Society and prayed that someday all Negroes would be freed. It would not take much to make a Grimké into an abolitionist, and this was what ultimately happened to Thomas' renowned younger sisters, Angelina and Sarah.[8]

The first famous oration in which Grimké proclaimed his principles in defiance of political consequences was delivered, ironically, in the interests of conservatism. In September 1828 Charleston's large, predominantly lower-class Irish population organized a public meeting in support of Daniel O'Connell and the movement for Ireland's independence. After many of Charleston's leaders paid their tribute to the indomitable O'Connell,

[7] *United States Telegraph*, May 5, 1834.
[8] The best biographical sketches of Grinké are in *ibid., passim*, and in Merle Curti, "Thomas Smith Grimké," Johnson and Malone (eds.), *Dictionary of American Biography*, VII, 635–6.

Grimké shocked the patricians and angered the Irish by a vigorous dissent. The audacious Charlestonian "compared the people of Ireland to the blacks" of Carolina and maintained that the tidewater gentry was the last group which should sanction rebellion![9]

The political recklessness of the 1828 oration was exceeded by Grimké's 1829 election-eve letter. After further angering "plebeians" by denouncing grog shops, Grimké went on to proclaim, in the heart of the embittered lowcountry, qualified approbation of the Colonization Society, opposition to Jackson, and support of protective tariffs. Grimké's independent bearing gained him the personal admiration of opponents, but won the Courier party few votes in Charleston.[10]

Henry Laurens Pinckney was the South Carolina politician best equipped to take advantage of Grimké's eccentricities. Grandson of Henry Laurens, merchant prince of the revolutionary era, son of Charles Pinckney, the leading planter and politician, H. L. Pinckney inherited a fortune in rice plantations and then acquired his own reputation as editor of the *Charleston Mercury*. The short, squat, thickset editor was not well liked by the gentry but was the favorite of the mechanics. Pinckney was always careful to defend Irish causes in his paper and to preside over Irish meetings on St. Patrick's day. This policy paid dividends in 1829 when the *Irishman and Southern Democrat*, a violently antinullification sheet, supported Pinckney and helped him win control of the city government.[11]

The city elections thus increased Pinckney's personal following among Charleston's lower class. The contest also convinced most South Carolina moderates that they would continue to suffer political defeats if they persisted in supporting such men as Grimké and the principles of protection and colonization. In the elections of 1830 and 1832, the moderates were to demonstrate that they had learned at least this lesson.

[9] [Charleston] *Irishman and Southern Democrat*, Sept. 5, 1829, July 17, 1830.
[10] *Charleston Courier*, Sept. 5, 1829.
[11] Prior, "History of the *Charleston Mercury*," pp. 83ff., 101–2, 192–3; Stephen Elliott to William Elliott, July 27, 1830, Elliott-Gonzales Papers; J. H. Cornish Diary, entry for December 14, 1839, NC.

3

On the eve of the congressional session of 1829–30, South Carolina radicals found themselves once again trapped in the classic dilemma extremists face who are not quite sure that moderation will fail. Just as they might have wrecked Jackson's presidential campaign by screaming for nullification in 1828, so the Calhounites could victimize a budding South-West alliance by opting for extremes in 1830. If southern radicals expected to win support from the West, their best strategy was to avoid discussion of nullification, to emphasize free public lands, to hasten repayment of the public debt, and to hope that an overflowing treasury would bring Jackson to lower the tariff. This was the policy urged day after day in Duff Green's *United States Telegraph*.

Yet such radicals as Hamilton and McDuffie continued to suspect that the majority would relent only when nullification was put into practice. The more extreme nullifiers questioned whether a South-West alliance would flourish, doubted that they could force a fast repayment of the debt, and feared that if budgetary surpluses developed, Jackson would favor distributing the excess funds for the use of the states.

Should South Carolina appeal once again to the sense of the majority? Or should the radicals throw their energies into an attempt at minority veto? The new Congress had scarcely begun deliberations when the famed Hayne-Webster debate made the strategic dilemma painfully obvious.

The encounter between Hayne and Webster was the first of those senatorial forensic contests which caught the imagination of the American public in the pre-Civil War era. The nullification issues raised questions about the future of the Republic which seemed more significant than normal congressional topics. And the spectacle itself was of epic proportions. Swarthy gentlemen and gaily dressed ladies crammed into the tiny semicircular Senate chamber, lining the galleries, spilling over onto the legislative floor, and someone snatching up even Hayne's seat when the

Carolinian rose to speak. Those fortunate enough to find a decent vantage point saw some of the great figures in American politics: Robert Y. Hayne, youthful and debonair, dressed to fight the tariff in a handsome suit of homespun; Thomas Hart Benton, "Old Bullion Benton," dedicated to watching over the interests of the West; John C. Calhoun, presiding over the debates, staring intently at the drama unfolding below.

It was Daniel Webster, however, who soon commanded the scene. The New Englander's massive size and craggy face, his smoldering eyes and jutting brows, all exuded greatness; and his blue-tailed coat with shining brass buttons seemed a perfect match for the richness of his rhetoric. Webster in the full tide of oratory was an awesome performer, and in 1830 he seemed, in Emerson's phrase, like a "great cannon loaded to the lips." No wonder that a half century later, men would still be boasting to their grandchildren that they had seen the "grand, God-like Daniel" put Hayne to rout.[12]

In late December 1829 Samuel Foot of Connecticut precipitated the Hayne-Webster debate by introducing a resolution calling for an inquiry into limiting the sale of public lands. The Foot Resolution threatened the South-West alliance, and senators from both sections rushed to the attack. Benton, speaking for the West, denounced the resolution; Hayne, speaking for the South, followed with an eloquent plea for a more liberal land policy. Hayne's first oration was fully in the Duff Green tradition, implicitly assuming that the South could escape minority status within the system of majority rule by forming a new governing coalition.

Hayne's first address was also one of the more ironic events of the nullification era. Cheap southwestern land was a more fundamental cause of South Carolina's cotton depression than protective tariffs. When more virgin territory was devoted to cotton, more bales flooded the market, and overproduction sent prices plunging no matter what happened to protective duties. As one astute observer wrote, at the same time Hayne "was

---

[12] Ralph Waldo Emerson, *Journals* . . . , E. W. Emerson and W. E. Forbes, eds. (10 vols.; Boston, 1909–14), VII, 87.

laboring with an ardor and ability seldom surpassed, in endeavoring to relieve the South from the unequal operation of the tariff, he was supporting a measure infinitely more destructive to the interests of his constituents."[13]

Webster answered his opponent by shifting the grounds of debate. Hayne had opposed high payments for public lands partly because the receipts would give the federal government "a fund for corruption—fatal to the sovereignty and independence of the states." To the great New England nationalist, Hayne's words raised the specter of "Consolidation!—That perpetual cry, both of terror and delusion—consolidation!" Webster argued that federal appropriations were a source of improvement, not "a fund of corruption," and painted glowing pictures of an active, beneficent national government.

Webster's oration challenged the Carolina doctrines, and Hayne was forced to defend state veto rather than debate public lands. Although the Carolinian gave a competent address on nullification, he made one serious error which demonstrated again Calhoun's intellectual supremacy among the nullifiers. Hayne left the implication that a state legislature, with its merely governing power, rather than a state convention, as a constitution-making sovereign, could nullify federal law. Yet Hayne's argument, however imprecise, was fully in the McDuffie-Hamilton tradition that the South could best end majority tyranny by exercising minority veto.

Webster, in his second reply to Hayne, used the Carolinian's unfortunate logical slip to refute the argument for nullification. Webster also outlined the nationalist theory of the Constitution. The nullifiers, he said, erred in thinking that the states were older than the Union. The American colonies had revolted from England in a united crusade rather than as separate states. Moreover, the people of the United States, as one community, rather than the people of several states, in separate communities, had ratified the Constitution. The nullifiers erred again, according to Webster, in affirming that the states retained absolute sovereignty after ratification of the Constitution. By consenting to the fundamental

[13] *Edgefield Hive*, Aug. 13, 1830.

law, the people had divided sovereignty between the state and federal governments. The Constitution also proclaimed federal law supreme. The supremacy of federal law necessarily implied a Supreme Court with final constitutional jurisdiction. Therefore, concluded Webster, a state could neither nullify a federal law nor secede from the Union.

Yet constitutional polemics were the least important part of Webster's oration. The New Englander's prime contribution was to use Hayne's advocacy of minority veto to weaken the South-West alliance which the Carolinian had initially tried to further. The West cared more for majority rule and for the federal Union than for cheap public lands. In the packed Senate galleries, and across the land, westerners, and most Americans, thrilled to Webster's peroration:

> When my eyes shall be turned to behold, for the last time, the sun in heaven, may I not see him shining on the broken and dishonored fragments of a once glorious Union. . . . Let their last feeble and lingering glance, rather, behold the gorgeous ensign of the republic . . . blazing on all its ample folds, as they float over the sea and over the land . . . Liberty and Union, now and forever, one and inseparable.[14]

The Hayne-Webster debate reveals the nullifiers at the cross-roads. By continuing to work hopefully within the old system of shifting majority coalitions, as in Hayne's first oration, Calhounites obscured the necessity for immediate nullification. By supporting nullification, as in Hayne's second oration, Calhounites weakened the possibility of achieving the victory within the majoritarian tradition. As the 1830 session progressed, Jackson's stand on issues, Van Buren's victory over Calhoun, the defeat of McDuffie's tariff proposals, and the emergence of a Colonization Society bill all caused Carolina hotheads to turn decisively in the direction of minority veto.

4

From the beginning of the Jackson administration, Carolinians could not afford the cocky faith in Calhoun's triumph which pervaded the *United States Telegraph*. The new cabinet con-

[14] *Register of Debates,* 21 Cong., 1 sess., I, 3–4, 11, 22–7, 31–41, 43–80.

tained several Calhounites. But Van Buren was installed as secretary of state, Calhoun failed to obtain jobs for several friends, and Jackson, in his inaugural address, was enigmatic on the tariff. By September 1829 the Vice President, morbidly suspicious of Van Buren's "arts and intrigues," "deeply" apprehended "that the choice of the chief magistrate will finally be placed at the disposition of the executive power itself, through a corrupt system to be founded on the abuse of the power and patronage of the government." In his annual message to Congress in December, Jackson endorsed the protective principle and advocated a distribution of the surplus revenue to the states on the basis of population after the public debt was retired. Privately Jackson wrote that he had found Van Buren "everything that I could desire him to be, and believe him not only deserving *my* confidence, but the *confidence* of the *Nation*. . . . I wish I could say as much for Mr. Calhoun."[15]

Both personal factors and political principles gave the Little Magician his quick triumph. Van Buren lost no time in securing Jackson's personal affections. While Calhoun presided over his South Carolina plantation throughout much of 1829, Van Buren, who had learned to ride horseback for the occasion, beguiled the old general on delightful early-morning rides through Washington.

Calhoun also contracted a case of "Eaton Malaria," a disease of the drawing room which for a moment dominated the nation's politics. In the scurrilous 1828 presidential election, Adams propagandists had vilified Aunt Rachel, Jackson's beloved pipe-smoking spouse, for marrying Old Hickory before her divorce from a frontier scoundrel had become final. Mrs. Jackson had died soon after the election, and the grief-stricken old general, blaming her death on malignant gossips, would brook no attack on innocent females.

Jackson had no sooner arrived in Washington than he discovered a new plot against feminine virtue. On New Year's Day 1829 John H. Eaton, Jackson's close friend and the incoming

---

[15] Calhoun to McLean, Sept. 22, 1829, McLean Papers; Jackson to John Overton, Dec. 31, 1829, Jackson, *Correspondence*, IV, 108–9.

secretary of war, had married the former Peggy O'Neale, daughter of a Washington tavern keeper. Eaton had often stayed at the O'Neale tavern and rumors had spread of their illicit relationship. Peggy's husband, a naval purser named Timberlake, had committed suicide in the fall of 1828, and tongues wagged more. Jackson, who had known and liked Peggy for years, advised Eaton to marry her in order to silence the gossips. The marriage inspired the crudest ribaldry. As one leading New Yorker wrote, "There is a vulgar saying of some vulgar man, I believe Swift, on such unions—about using a certain household . . . and then putting it on one's head."[16]

Peggy's notoriety inspired feminine hauteur as well as masculine hilarity. The matrons of Washington, led by Floride Bonneau Calhoun, who, unluckily for the Vice President, was enjoying one of her rare winters in the capital, decided to snub the new Mrs. Eaton. Mrs. Calhoun refused to return Peggy's call, and other cabinet wives followed suit.

Jackson, angered by the petticoat brigade, pontifically pronounced Peggy "chaste as a virgin" and applauded when Van Buren, blissfully unmarried, ostentatiously paid her many courtesies. At first the President blamed Henry Clay for the monstrous plot. But Jackson, with the help of some early-morning hints from his favorite riding companion, soon identified Calhoun as the culprit. By October 1830 the President had convinced himself that the Vice President was persecuting Peggy Eaton in order to renew the assault on Rachel Jackson.[17]

Calhoun was no sooner caught in the snares of the drawing room than he re-encountered the rancors of the Seminole Campaign. In 1818 Jackson, then a frontier general, had invaded Spanish Florida in an effort to stop the ravages of the Seminole Indians. Although the invasion expressly violated Calhoun's War Department orders, Jackson claimed the attack was authorized by a letter from President James Monroe. Monroe never remembered sending the letter.

In the privacy of a cabinet meeting, Calhoun had demanded

---

[16] C. C. Cambreleng to Van Buren, Jan. 1, 1829, Van Buren Papers.
[17] Jackson to Mary Eastin, Oct. 24, 1830, Jackson, *Correspondence*, IV, 186–8.

an inquiry into Jackson's insubordination. The secretary of war's plea had been rejected for diplomatic reasons outlined by Secretary of State Adams. Subsequently Clay and Crawford partisans in Congress had attacked Calhoun's War Department for Jackson's invasion. Thus Old Hickory, who was morbidly sensitive to the charge of being a lawless frontier general, had gained the mistaken notion that Calhoun was his prime defender. Calhoun, a bit deviously, did nothing to alter Jackson's opinion.

In 1828 Jackson was given an old letter Monroe had written to Calhoun, which the Vice President claimed was stolen from his files. The Monroe letter hinted at Calhoun's cabinet maneuvers. Jackson was on the point of asking for an explanation when both men tacitly agreed that political expediency required the matter to be dropped.[18]

In November 1829 Jackson was given proof instead of hints, and this time political expediency allowed the old hero to give free rein to his anger. Crawford climaxed his bitter feud with Calhoun by informing the President, at first indirectly, then directly, of the true nature of the Seminole cabinet discussions. In May 1830 Jackson, now persuaded of Calhoun's treachery, demanded an explanation. A long private correspondence ensued, but the controversy did not become public until the following year.[19]

Personal antagonism partly caused and greatly embittered the Calhoun-Jackson split. Yet even without the Little Magician's new proficiency on horseback, the Eaton Malaria, and the Seminole Controversy, it is hard to see how Calhoun could have triumphed over Van Buren. The President and Vice President differed almost completely on the constitutional principles and the political reforms which the new administration should attempt to further.

Jackson, like Van Buren, accepted a far more limited version of the states' rights, strict-construction doctrines than Calhoun espoused. The President believed the tariff constitutional and considered nullification the ultimate heresy. Jackson had spent a life-

[18] Calhoun to Jackson, Apr. 30, July 10, 1828, Jackson to Calhoun, May 25, 1828, *ibid.*, III, 400, 404–6, 413–15.

[19] The correspondence can be conveniently studied in Calhoun, *Works*, VI, appendix. The best account of the personal disputes between Calhoun and Jackson is in Charles M. Wiltse, *John C. Calhoun, Nullifier: 1829–1839* (Indianapolis, 1949).

time, as he saw it, protecting American democracy against Englishmen and Indians, and he could never approve a successor who might tear down majority rule. "In all Republics the voice of a majority must prevail," Jackson wrote Hayne in 1831. ". . . assert that a state may declare acts passed by congress inoperative and void, and revolution . . . must be looked for and expected."[20] As Jackson's famed Jefferson Day toast would reveal, Calhoun's secrecy was of no avail. Old Hickory, like many others in Washington, was convinced that Calhoun believed in nullification.

Jackson and Calhoun differed almost as much on governmental policies as on constitutional principles. In 1828 the Vice President was vehemently against the protective tariff and mildly in favor of the national bank. The President, as did Van Buren, mildly approved of the tariff and detested the bank. Calhoun considered the tariff the crucial issue because he regarded the conflict between North and South as the overriding national problem. But Jackson was more disturbed by the monster bank because he was distressed about the capitalists and stock jobbers who supposedly made profits by spewing forth paper money instead of producing a material product. The President was determined to stop rich, moneyed interests from using government funds to secure paper profits at the expense of the people. Jackson could tolerate the tariff, one suspects, because industrial capitalists made a finished product instead of "gambling" with paper money and because manufacturers did not employ funds from the public treasury. A national bank, on the other hand, gave paper profits to "a *few Monied Capitalists,* who are trading upon our revenue, and enjoy the benefit of it, to the exclusion of the many." A national debt, Jackson believed, was "a curse to a republic" because "it is calculated to raise around the administration a moneyed aristocracy."[21]

The early ideological differences between Calhoun and Jackson

[20] Jackson to Hayne, Feb. 8, 1831, Jackson, *Correspondence,* IV, 241–3.
[21] Jackson to L. H. Colman, Apr. 26, 1824, Jackson to Moses Dawson, July 17, 1830, *ibid.,* III, 249–51, IV, 161–2. For a fine discussion of Jackson's dislike for the "money power," see Marvin Meyers, *The Jacksonian Persuasion* . . . (Stanford, 1957), ch. 2.

became particularly evident on the question of distributing the federal surplus to the states after the national debt was paid. Jackson vigorously favored distribution; Calhoun adamantly opposed it. For Jackson, retiring the debt, and thereby stopping the moneyed interests from employing the people's funds, was an important end in itself. Repayment, Jackson believed, was stalled by logrolling internal-improvement appropriations. The President hoped to hold down present expenditures by offering the enticing future alternative of distributing the surplus revenue in the postdebt era. Distribution would hasten repayment.[22]

For Calhoun, on the other hand, retiring the debt was only a means of lowering the tariff. Once the debt was repaid, expanding federal surpluses would force the government to cut taxes. But if the surplus was distributed, the federal government would retain an excuse for high tariffs. Distribution would destroy the reason for repayment.

Even without the national debt, Jackson opposed logrolling appropriations. The President considered federal appropriations for local projects unconstitutional. He also feared that congressional appropriations would be divided unequally. To Jackson, equal division meant division according to population. Distributing surplus revenue to the states on the basis of their population would ensure equal use of national funds.[23]

But Calhoun considered distribution according to population completely unequal. The majority North would continue to drain away the wealth of the minority South. Jackson's distribution would institutionalize the worst evils of Adams' nationalism.

Thus any interpretation of the Calhoun-Jackson split which concentrates only on personal feuds misses the larger significance of the issues at stake. The President and Vice President clashed over crucial matters of public policy no less than over petticoat politics and old Indian wars. As Jackson summed up their many ideological disagreements:

[22] Jackson to Overton, Dec. 31, 1827, Jackson, Correspondence, IV, 108–9.

[23] Jackson's program can best be studied in his messages to Congress. See James D. Richardson (ed.), *A Compilation of the Messages and Papers of the Presidents* (11 vols.; Washington, D.C., 1897–1909), II, 999–1121. Distributing the surplus revenue is a major and neglected theme in the early Jackson messages.

Mr. Calhoun objects to the apportionment of the surplus revenue among the several states, after the public debt is paid. He is also, silent on the Bank question, and is believed to have encouraged the introduction and adoption of the Resolutions in the South Carolina Legislature relative to the Tariff.[24]

The increasing tension between Calhoun and Jackson became blatantly public at the April 13, 1830, Jefferson Day dinner. Although the dinner was another attempt to bolster the South-West majoritarian alliance, several of the prepared toasts seemed to celebrate the doctrine of minority veto. Jackson, either before he came to the dinner or after he read the prepared toasts, saw his duty and scribbled out his own toast. Glaring at Calhoun, signaling the boisterous crowd to rise, the President toasted "Our Federal Union—It must be preserved." With Van Buren standing on a chair so as not to miss an instant of his triumph, and the crowd now deathly still, the Vice President, as if in a trance, his hand shaking so "that a little of the amber fluid trickled down the side" of the glass, gathered his thoughts. His reply, when it came, was an anticlimax: "The Union—Next to our liberties the most dear." Moments later, George McDuffie was more blunt: "The memory of Patrick Henry: The first American statesman who had the soul to feel, and the courage to declare, in the face of armed tyranny, that there is no treason in resisting oppression."[25]

The Jefferson Day toasts indicated the trend of events but did not proclaim a final breach in the Jackson party. The Calhounites remained Jacksonians and continued to argue that Jackson would never coerce a nullifying state. Many newspaper editors claimed that Jackson meant that the Union must be preserved by maintaining strict construction. Still, Jackson's messages to Congress seemed to remove any chance that South Carolina would gain a lower tariff with the President's help. And the Jefferson Day dinner clearly destroyed all hope that John C. Calhoun would vault to the presidency with the benign approval of Andrew Jackson.

5

McDuffie toasted the memory of Patrick Henry at the Jefferson Day dinner partly because his own tariff proposals had met with

[24] Jackson to Overton, Dec. 31, 1829, Jackson, *Correspondence,* IV, 108-9.
[25] *Columbia Telescope,* Apr. 30, 1830.

ignominious defeat in the House of Representatives. On February 5, 1830, McDuffie, as chairman of the Ways and Means Committee, introduced a bill to repeal many of the 1828 and 1824 rates. The Carolinian's proposal represented the minimal redress which his state would accept. Three days later, the House voted, 107–79, to table the bill without debate.[26]

The angry McDuffie resorted to parliamentary tricks to gain the floor. When a bill to reform the method of collecting the tariff reached the House, McDuffie, arguing that lower rates would make for easier enforcement, proposed an amendment to cut the duties. The Carolinian demanded the right to be heard in support of his own amendment and proceeded to blaze away at the protectionists for two hours. The tariff, proclaimed McDuffie, forced southerners to deposit in the customhouse the proceeds of fully forty out of every one hundred bales of cotton produced![27]

The protectionists could not allow McDuffie's charge to remain unanswered, and so the tariff debate was on again. The 1830 Congress was not disposed to repeal the Tariff of Abominations. But the debate, by giving national publicity to the forty-bale theory, inspired greater antitariff excitement in South Carolina. McDuffie's theory itself became an important cause of the Nullification Controversy.

The genius of the forty-bale theory was that it explained in disarmingly simple terms exactly why protective tariffs were responsible for the collapse of the upcountry cotton economy. Various Carolinians had presented elements of the thesis in 1828. But before 1830, antitariff leaders—including McDuffie in 1824— had argued that protective duties were ultimately paid by consumers in the form of higher prices for manufactured products. The Carolinians had claimed—essentially correctly—that the tariff was more oppressive for southern consumers, who usually received no compensating benefits, than for northern consumers, who sometimes received higher incomes. The Carolinians had also argued— again cogently—that tariffs would hurt cotton prices in the future if retaliatory foreign duties or declining American imports cut

[26] *Register of Debates*, 21 Cong., 1 sess., I, 555–7.
[27] *Ibid.*, II, 819.

the European demand for the southern staple.[28] But in the forty-bale theory, McDuffie tried to establish the absurd position that the tariff was ultimately paid by southern producers in the form of plunging cotton prices no matter what happened to foreign tariffs or American imports.

The forty-bale theory was based on the notion that all the confusion about protective tariffs stemmed from one misleading fallacy. Southern producers assumed that the cash they received for their crop was derived from the sale of cotton in England. But in reality, claimed McDuffie, England shipped manufactured goods rather than cash across the Atlantic to pay for cotton. As a result, the money dispatched to southern cotton planters was the proceeds of the sale of English manufactured goods in America. To take a hypothetical example, the planter exchanged his one hundred bales of cotton for one hundred pieces of cloth in Europe, and exchanged the European cloth for cash in America. The process was obscured by the intervention of merchants. But the merchants were merely agents who traded the raw cotton in Europe, sold the manufactured cloth in America, and forwarded the proceeds to the planter.

Since foreign trade essentially involved an exchange of raw cotton for manufactured cloth, continued McDuffie, a protective tariff cut the exchangeable value of the southern staple. If no tariff was in effect, the planter could send his one hundred bales abroad and sell his one hundred pieces of cloth at home. But if a 40-percent tariff was enacted, the planter would have to pay forty pieces of cloth at the customhouse and would have only sixty pieces left to sell.

The planter could not pass the tax on to consumers by charging higher prices for the surviving sixty pieces. McDuffie believed that the price of a commodity was dependent on the iron laws of supply and demand. Prices went up if the amount of goods available declined or if the amount of money in the economy increased. Tariffs did not change the domestic price because they had no effect on either the supply of cloth or the amount of money.

[28] *SR*, II (Nov. 1828), 578; *Pendleton Messenger*, July 16, 1828; Calhoun, *Works*, VI, 1–25; *Register of Debates*, 18 Cong., 2 sess., I, 253.

Imagine an economy with one hundred dollars available to purchase cloth and one hundred pieces imported. A 40-percent tariff would neither augment nor decrease the one hundred dollars purchasers would use. Since the government would sell the forty pieces and the planter his sixty pieces, one hundred pieces of cloth would remain on the market. Thus the planter would receive sixty dollars for his sixty pieces. The intervention of merchants again obscured the process. But the merchants remained no more than agents who sold the one hundred pieces of cloth for one hundred dollars, handed forty dollars to the customs collector, and passed the loss on to the cotton planter by dispatching only sixty dollars. Therefore, McDuffie triumphantly concluded, a 40-percent tariff robbed the planter of forty bales per hundred![29]

The forty-bale theory was poor economics—but superb propaganda—because it grossly simplified both foreign trade and the domestic market. First, Anglo-American commerce involved more than a simple bartering of raw cotton for manufactured goods. American merchants could—and did—import items not subject to American tariffs, or accept bills of exchange, useful in buying nonprotected goods in the Indies and the Orient, or take cash credits, needed to pay back debts owed Europeans, or import specie, desperately needed by American banks. In fact, raw cotton not only paid for manufactured goods but also helped support the entire structure of American international finance. American merchants, whether acting as agents for planters or as independent entrepreneurs, were not importing cloth at a 40-percent loss with many profitable alternatives available.

Second, the price structure of the American domestic economy was more flexible than the iron law of supply and demand indicated. To borrow McDuffie's own example, the one hundred

[29] McDuffie changed the forty-bale theory constantly. His theory was sometimes more formidable, and sometimes more fallacious, than the version presented here. I have chosen to ignore the vicissitudes of McDuffie's reasoning and to describe the theory as popular propagandists used it. The forty-bale thesis contributed more to the nullifiers' victory than to economic theory. For a good example of the propaganda version of the McDuffie thesis, see *A Catechism on the Tariff for . . . Plain People of Common Sense*. His versions can be followed in McDuffie, . . . *Speeches . . . April and May, 1830* (Washington, D.C., 1830) ; *Speech . . . May 19, 1831* (Charleston, 1831) ; *Speech, May 28, 1832; Second Speech . . . June, 1832* (Washington, D.C., 1832).

dollars chasing the cloth was not the only money in the economy. Since cloth and other protected manufactured goods were often necessities or desirable luxuries, consumers bought them at higher prices, employing dollars they would otherwise have spent on other items. The notion that manufactured goods were imported at a 40-percent loss, in short, was as absurd as the notion that manufactured goods alone could be imported.

Yet the forty-bale theory, however invalid intellectually, was of great importance politically. A simple-minded theory of economic affairs can have a profound impact on individuals facing economic disaster. Just as "Coin Harvey's" nostrums later drove populist-minded farmers to seek their salvation in the free-silver cause, so the forty-bale theory led scores of South Carolinians to place their faith in the antitariff movement. After McDuffie had popularized his theory, the most ignorant cotton planter, mechanic, or retailer could adroitly explain how the tariff had caused South Carolina's depression. Even in the lowcountry, Hamilton, a sophisticated planter, instinctively employed the forty-bale theory to explain a temporary decline in rice prices or to account for the persistence of debts contracted in the days of prosperity. William Elliott ruefully admitted to his sea-island constituency, "You are as persuaded as if you saw it—that the manufacturer actually invades your barns, and plunders you of 40, out of every 100 bales that you produce."[30]

6

The presentation of the first Colonization Society bill, as well as Calhoun's defeat and McDuffie's tariff theory, increased the militancy of South Carolina radicals as the congressional session progressed. Previously the American Colonization Society had petitioned for congressional aid without presenting concrete proposals. But in April 1830 Charles F. Mercer of Virginia introduced a bill calling for federal contributions of $25 to $35 per free Negro colonized, up to $50,000 per year. For a tense moment, South Carolinians feared that the "deed of blood and murder" would

[30] Hamilton to Van Buren, Nov. 16, 1829, Van Buren Papers; Elliott, *Address to the People of St. Helena Parish* (Charleston, 1832), p. 4.

"pass the house by a considerable majority, and . . . receive the
concurrence of the Senate."[31]

In 1827 the colonization petition had aroused consternation only
at tidewater. In 1830 the Mercer bill provoked excitement throughout the state. In the lowcountry, the *Winyaw Intelligencer* proclaimed that "the mask is now thrown off; and a direct attack
made upon us. . . . We are at the feet of the majority, who, having
destroyed the Constitution, are now prepared to crush us with
its fragments." The *Charleston Mercury* warned that the "object" of the northern "fanatics" was to "colonize the free, and
excite dissatisfaction in the bond. Then regulate slavery—inflame
discontent to madness—render the property equally valueless and
dangerous—and then abolish it entirely. Charles C. Pinckney wrote
with "mingled indignation and sorrow" that the Mercer bill veri-
fied "all that has been predicted as to the gradual course of en-
croachment by the northern party on our domestic system. . . .
There is no longer any reason for hesitation what course we ought
to pursue."[32]

The upcountry was almost as militant. The *Edgefield Carolinian*
warned that "if we have now to pay for the transportation of
those that are free, we shall soon have to pay for the emancipation of slaves, that they may be transported." The *Cheraw Republican* termed the scheme "a tragedy . . . which must cause
the stoutest heart to quake." In Columbia James Hammond's
Southern Times called the bill "murderous. It ruins our property;
it breaks down our individual rights; it destroys our political
security; it sweeps away our Constitution; it dissolves our Union; it annihilates the last hope of self government on earth."
Benjamin F. Perry, the unionist leader of the most moderate
section in South Carolina, asserted that if Mercer's scheme passed,
"we may well begin to 'calculate the value of this Union.' . . .
As dearly as we love this Union . . . we love still more dearly our
rights, our liberties, and our preservation."[33]

[31] *Charleston Mercury*, May 3, 1830; *Southern Times*, Apr. 19, 1830.
[32] *Winyaw Intelligencer*, May 1, 1830; *Charleston Mercury*, Apr. 12, 24, 27, 28,
May 1, 17, 1830.
[33] *Ibid.*, Apr. 30, May 3, 1830; *Southern Times*, Apr. 19, Oct. 17, 1830; *Greenville Mountaineer*, Apr. 30, 1830.

The House of Representatives soon tabled the Mercer bill. But lowcountry planters believed, as the *Winyaw Intelligencer* pointed out, that "the mere bringing forward [of] such a measure" was "not to be tolerated." The bill seemed a culmination of that decade of "fanaticism"—the Seamen Controversy, the Ohio Resolutions, the Panama discussions, the colonization petition, the D'Auterive petition—which had afflicted the Carolina lowcountry since the Missouri Controversy. None of these events had involved more than a few days of talk, yet the pattern seemed disturbing enough. Moreover, the Georgetown Conspiracy in 1829 appeared to demonstrate again that a modicum of discussion led to servile unrest. The colonization "threat" of 1830 served to intensify the tidewater's conviction that constitutional principles had to be established which would preclude the development of "incendiary" debates.[34]

It is this persistent tendency to take alarm at innocuous attacks which explains why lowcountry nullifiers alluded to the Mercer bill throughout the South Carolina election campaign of 1830. Congressman William J. Grayson, for example, carefully pointed out to his tidewater constituency that "if the tariff were oppressive merely" patience "might well be deemed a virtue. . . . But you assert it to be unconstitutional. This it is that authorizes and requires you to act. . . . Allow Congress to make their will the limit of their power, and prepare to see it exercised in a shape, the very shadow of which must strike you with horror." In Barnwell Representative Angus Patterson, a leading state legislator, echoed Grayson's admonition. "If the Tariff were all we had to fear," he counseled,

I might be disposed to advise longer delay. . . . [But] one of the avowed objects of the Tariff, is to favor free labor, as it is called, at the expense of slave labor—to render the latter species of labor unprofitable and indeed valueless, and thereby incline and force us to assent to a system of emancipation, through the agency of the General Government. Have not several of our sister States already instructed their Senators and Representatives in Congress, to urge such a measure? Nay have not we ourselves been invited by these States to cooperate? And was there not before Congress at its last

[34] *Winyaw Intelligencer,* May 1, 1830.

session, a Bill bearing directly on this measure? This question will be pressed upon as sure as we exist, and on the same grounds, and by the same arguments by which the Tariff was imposed.

If South Carolina yielded "full supremacy" to the northern majority, added Congressman Robert Barnwell, ". . . there are some changes in the very forms of our *domestic* policy, to which they could scarcely persuade us quietly to submit. And there are no changes, however vital and subversive of our most absolute rights, which fanaticism and misguided philanthropy would not attempt."[35]

7

Thus as the 1830 congressional session progressed, Jackson's doctrines, Van Buren's supremacy, McDuffie's defeat, and the Mercer bill increased the nullifiers' conviction that continued majority rule would mean permanent southern oppression. But to genuine radicals, slight concessions are always worse than total defeats. As Congress worked toward adjournment, several tariff reductions and Jackson's Maysville veto gave South Carolina moderates renewed faith that redress could be achieved without radical action.

Jackson, in his December annual message, had suggested that the tariff could be modified and protection still maintained if Congress lowered only the duties on imports "which can not come in competition with our own products." In the late spring of 1830 Congress responded by lowering duties not only on such unprotected items as tea and coffee but also on such protected articles as salt and molasses. Annual revenue from the tariff, well over $20 million in 1830, was cut approximately $4.5 million, with about one-fifth of the reductions covering protected items.

The prospect of decreased federal revenue was brightened even more by Jackson's opposition to logrolling federal expenditures. Federal appropriations for internal improvements almost doubled in Old Hickory's first term. But Jackson's 1830 Maysville veto gave the expanding system a decided check. The Maysville road,

[35] *Charleston Mercury,* July 31, Aug. 10, 18, 1830. See also Hayne in *Southern Patriot,* July 7, 1830.

while part of the national Cumberland system, lay wholly within Kentucky. On May 27 Jackson, arguing that the road was local rather than "national in . . . character," vetoed a bill granting federal aid to the project.

To nullifiers, the reductions and the veto were "nothing but sugar plums to pacify children." The modified duties only made the tariff "more satisfactory to the Manufacturing states." Rates on goods northerners bought were lowered; duties on the great northern products—iron, cottons, woolens—remained the same. "The overwhelming majority" against "Mr. McDuffie's motion to repeal the Tariff of 1828 and 1824" left "no ground for any confident expectation that the system will be broken up."[36]

The nullifiers also believed that the Maysville veto, laudable in itself, offered equally little cause for rejoicing. Renouncing their earlier qualified approval of internal improvements, the Calhounites attacked Jackson for approving schemes of "national importance." "Language like this" only forced the majority to find "more plausible objects of improvement." More important, Jackson, in his veto message, endorsed the protective principle, denied the connection between improvement appropriations and protective duties, and advocated a distribution of the surplus reserve. The message upheld the principles against which South Carolina was contending.[37]

The Carolina moderates, on the other hand, agreed with Judge John Richardson that "had J. C. Calhoun or Langdon Cheves, been President of the United States, neither could have done more in the first session of Congress than Gen. Jackson has done." Piecemeal tariff reduction might succeed where overall reform had failed. The protectionists had already lost the "*sweetening*" of Louisiana molasses and the "*seasoning*" of New York salt. Furthermore, Jackson's Maysville veto, if insufficiently "*tight-laced*" in language, was eminently efficient in practice.[38]

---

[36] *Edgefield Hive*, Sept. 17, 1830; *Proceedings of the Meeting in Columbia, September 20, 1830*, p. 18; *Southern Patriot*, July 7, 1830.
[37] *Winyaw Intelligencer*, June 12, 16, 1830; *Proceedings of the Meeting . . .*, p. 18.
[38] *Camden Journal*, June 12, Sept. 11, 1830; *The Debate in the South Carolina Legislature in December, 1830 . . .* (Columbia, 1831), p. 105.

Even such a radical as Congressman James Blair, who had "believed . . . that South Carolina had no alternative but to redress her own wrongs" before "the last few days of the session," now hoped that the state would "give Congress and the Administration, time to improve on the good beginning they have so recently made." At worst the delay would give South Carolina time to "hoard up arms" in case recent hopes proved "vain and delusive."[39] Such cogent arguments augured ill for the success of the nullification crusade of 1830.

8

The campaign of 1830 was noticeable for the militancy with which it began and the equivocations with which it ended. In the winter and early spring of 1830, several correspondents in piedmont newspapers cast caution to the winds and declaimed on secession. Visitors to Charleston found the tidewater gentry "*more* undisguised in the expression of their real sentiments. . . . Many openly avow that they not only think it time to calculate the value of the Union but that they *have calculated* it—and with them it has been found wanting."[40]

Undisguised radicalism remained in full force when nullifiers congregated for their first public meeting of the year, a giant July 1 dinner held in Charleston and organized by Hamilton. Although the celebration was ostensibly called to welcome Robert Y. Hayne and William Drayton back from Congress, Hamilton had caused "sudden" and "violent" excitement by making it "distinctly understood that those who go to the dinner declare themselves in favour of some interposition of State Sovereignty." The boisterous dinner, which Hamilton proudly described as "the largest most enthusiastic & splendid public festival ever given at the South," featured "some indiscreetly warm toasts & sentiments." Turnbull, Hayne, Hamilton, and Henry L. Pinckney all gave crusading speeches, to the delight of the militant gentry.[41]

39 *Camden Journal,* July 10, Sept. 4, 1830.

40 *Southern Times* and *Columbia Telescope,* Jan. through May 1830, esp. *Columbia Telescope,* Apr. 23, 1830; I. W. Hayne to Hammond, June 29, 1830, Hammond Papers, LC.

41 *Ibid.*; Hamilton to Van Buren, Sept. 20, 1830, Van Buren Papers.

Yet in the first moments of excitement, the difficulties ahead were already ominously clear. Drayton's vigorous speech against radical action was no more disturbing than Judge Daniel Huger's conspicuous absence; the Charleston wing of the Calhoun party was splitting apart. More important, the radicals failed to agree on a remedy. At the dinner, Langdon Cheves, a famous South Carolinian who had recently returned to his home state, denounced the nullifiers no less warmly than he had the northerners.

Cheves' alienation from the gentry was both very new and very old in 1830. For many years he had been one of the tidewater's most respected and wealthy leaders. But Cheves, an extremely sensitive man who never quite forgot his plebeian origins, poor education, and early financial struggles, had always remained somewhat aloof from lowcountry society.

Born in Abbeville in 1776, Cheves moved with his family to Charleston as a youth and soon became a merchant's clerk. After a defective early education, he studied law with William Marshall and was admitted to the bar in 1797. Before long the young lawyer's great abilities and scrupulous integrity became a Charleston legend. As a lowcountry saying went, if you have a good case, take it to Langdon Cheves, if a bad one, take it to William Drayton. In 1808 the state legislature elected the revered Cheves attorney general; in 1810 Charleston honored him with a seat in Congress; in 1814 the House of Representatives selected him speaker. Few careers in American politics seemed so promising.

Yet after 1814 Cheves slowly retreated from national and state politics. In 1816 he left Congress and secured a state judgeship. In 1819 he resigned from the bench to become head of the Bank of the United States. In 1823 he left the bank to become an obscure Pennsylvania lawyer. Returning to South Carolina as a Savannah River planter in 1829, he completed his political isolation by his independent stand in the Nullification Controversy. Stout, bald, with a massive, ruddy face, Langdon Cheves had, in body and mind, the "marble solidity" of the man who stands alone.[42]

In his oration on July 1 at the nullifiers' own dinner, Cheves

---

[42] Perry, *Reminiscences* (1883 ed.), pp. 241ff.; O'Neall, *Biographical Sketches*, I, 133–9; Grayson Autobiography, p. 237.

proclaimed the necessity for radical action, but challenged the practicality of resistance by a single state. He urged the planters to eschew state veto and to seek a southern convention. "Any measure by one of the suffering states, alone," warned the respected lawyer, "will be a measure of feebleness, subject to many hazards. Any union among the same States, will be a measure of strength, almost of certain strength."[43]

To Carolina moderates, Cheves' proposal for a southern convention, by raising specters of extreme southern resistance, seemed almost as "radically erroneous" as the nullifiers' doctrine of extreme Carolina resistance. Drayton lamented that Cheves, "who could have done so much good, should according to my views have aided in doing so much evil."[44]

To Carolina radicals, on the other hand, a southern convention seemed certain to destroy all hope of effective resistance. Other slaveholding states were obviously less excited than South Carolina. United action would lead to interminable, probably fatal, delays.

Cheves' speech, although repudiated by both moderates and nullifiers, raised some important questions. Why were South Carolinians more radical than other southerners? How did Carolina hotheads expect nullification to succeed without the endorsement of other slaveholding states?

Nullification had some support in most southern states. John Floyd's political faction and Richard Crallé's Richmond newspaper advocated the South Carolina doctrines in Virginia. Some tidewater planters and several piedmont regions endorsed the remedy in Georgia. In Alabama future United States Senator Dixon H. Lewis was a conspicuous proponent of nullification. These exceptions aside, slaveholding regions usually opposed the remedy. The problem was that the factors which led South Carolina to nullify were less important in other southern states.

First, most other regions in the South, either accustomed to hard times or enjoying economic prosperity, were not so distressed by tariffs. Rural depression in the Old South took place

[43] *Charleston Mercury*, Oct. 5, 1830.
[44] Drayton to Poinsett, Oct. 13, 1830, Poinsett Papers.

at different times in different regions. Virginians and North Carolinians had been struggling to raise tobacco on thin soil for generations. They were neither surprised at the hard times of the 1820's nor prone to blame them entirely on tariffs. South Carolinians, and to some extent piedmont Georgians, had led the first great wave of frontier cotton planting. Faced with depleted soil and low prices after a generation of prosperity, they reacted angrily to the galling experience of pecuniary embarrassment in the 1820's. Meanwhile some of upcountry Georgia and most of Alabama, Mississippi, and Louisiana were enjoying the second great expansion of frontier cotton planting in the twenties. The southwestern planters, like all frontiersmen, had their booms and their busts. Yet fresher soil was a decided economic advantage. And so in the decade of nullification, South Carolina experienced a rural depression which had first affected Virginia and North Carolina much earlier and would affect the southwestern states somewhat later.

Second, states possessing a less concentrated Negro population were less tense about slavery and not so worried about abolitionists. Such areas as the Louisiana delta and the Georgia seaboard had above-average proportions of slaves. But the South Carolina lowcountry had a far more widespread and massive Negro population, and, in the 1820's, far more experience with servile conspiracies.

Third, the close relationship between tidewater and piedmont, which helped inflame planters in both sections of South Carolina, was relatively absent in other southern states in the 1820's. In Virginia and North Carolina the conflict between upcountry farmers and lowcountry planters remained as fierce as it had been in South Carolina earlier in the century. In Georgia, Alabama, Mississippi, and Louisiana settlements were too recent and society too mobile for strong channels of communication to develop.

Thus South Carolina's combination of internal unity, heavy concentration of slaves, and new experience with economic depression was unique in the South in the 1820's and 1830's. Significantly, Georgia, the state which came closest to possessing these characteristics, was least opposed to nullification.

Leading nullifiers "never calculated on the cooperation of the other states until we have taken some definite step." But if other slaveholders were presented with a choice between making "common cause with South Carolina" or aiding "in putting her down by violence," they "would from necessity if . . . not from feeling take their stations at our side." As William Preston lucidly explained the reason for the nullifiers' confidence: "the slave question will be the real issue—All others will be absorbed in it. The hypocrisy of the north & the fears of the South will combine to bring us to the same result, and will Louisiana cling to her sugar and give up her negroes?"[45]

To Cheves, however, "the argument that in a cause common to many, some one shall rush ahead and supersede the free deliberation and volition of the rest, is a monstrous violation of good sense, good logic and . . . good fellowship." Unilateral action would disgust and offend the other states. "What apology can we make to the other states and to posterity," he asked, "if we shall put at hazard these great questions on our own single strength and they shall be doomed by our weakness and rashness to fail?"[46] Hamilton's dinner had unleashed some sobering questions as well as a radical crusade.

9

In 1830 the radicals, in their determination to nullify the tariff, and the moderates, in their determination to stop radical action, were willing to break the rules of South Carolina politics by rallying the people in pre-election debates. "The state became," in Grayson's phrase, ". . . a great talking and eating machine." Wherever planters congregated—at markets, courts, musters, shooting matches, and religious revivals—radicals and moderates debated the Carolina doctrines. Immense barbecues and intense stump speaking were "in the full tide of successful experiment," and "the appetites and lungs of the conflicting parties never failed, nor faltered."[47]

[45] Preston to Thompson, Feb. 14, 1830, Preston Papers, SC; Hamilton to Richard Crallé, Jan. 15, 1833, Crallé Papers, Clemson College; William Harper, *Speech, April 1, 1832*, p. 2.
[46] *Occasional Reviews*, I, 19–20.
[47] Grayson Autobiography, pp. 168–70; John N. Banillon to John Seibels, Sept. 5, 1830, Seibels Family Papers, SC.

As debate progressed the nullifiers retreated. Most South Carolinians were heartened by concessions already won and distressed by the state's internal divisions and external isolation. Most important, moderates raised "a war whoop of disunion."[48] The people, unschooled in the subtleties of nullification, failed to see how negating a law fell short of revolution. In the popular mind, nullification conjured up scenes of a fierce civil war, and the nullifiers seemed bloody "Jacobins."

Some nullifiers were, in fact, "Jacobins." Such men as Warren Davis, Thomas Cooper, and George McDuffie probably favored nullification as a means of achieving disunion. James Hammond exaggerated only a little when he concluded in 1850 that "*only a few* of the older nullifiers regarded it as any more than a *form* of *secession*."[49]

Other nullifiers, such as Calhoun, Hayne, and Hammond himself, were conservatives who believed that protectionists and abolitionists, unless checked by nullification, would eventually drive the South out of the Union. In the perspective of the Civil War, these nullifiers appear to be excellent prophets and genuine conservatives. Yet even Calhoun was morbidly aware of the risk of disunion. The remedy would be peaceful only if the government abstained from enforcing the laws. And in view of the way Jackson and the nation regarded the doctrine, nullification seemed more likely to terminate in revolution.

The "Jacobin" label was, then, depending on the nullifier, relatively accurate. Still, the nullifiers, understanding the political effect of the detested label and perhaps stung by its accuracy, desperately tried to prove they were the true conservatives. The argument that nullification was old and conservative rather than new and revolutionary turned on historical precedent. Francis W. Pickens, in his widely read "Hampden" essays, found dozens of supposed precedents, including South Carolina's nullification

---

[48] The phrase is Hamilton's. Hamilton to Van Buren, Sept. 20, 1830, Van Buren Papers.

[49] Preston to Hammond, July 24, 1830, Hammond Papers, LC; O'Neall, *Biographical Sketches*, II, 466; Hammond to N. B. Tucker, March 5, 1850, quoted in Robert Tucker, "James Henry Hammond, South Carolinian" (unpubl. diss., Univ. of N.C., 1958), p. 42.

of treaties protecting Negro seamen. The more important alleged precedents involved Madison and Jefferson's Virginia and Kentucky Resolutions. South Carolina debates on the proper interpretation of the federal Constitution often turned into debates on the true meaning of the Jeffersonian Resolutions.[50]

In 1798, amid one of those war hysterias in which Congress has periodically infringed on the civil liberties the nation is seeking to preserve, a strongly Federalist Congress enacted the Alien and Sedition Laws. The laws gave President John Adams, a Federalist, authority to expel dangerous foreigners and to prosecute critical opponents. Adams seldom used his new powers. But for a time, Jefferson and Madison feared that the Federalists would stifle Jeffersonian criticism and subvert democratic elections.

From 1798 to 1800 Madison and Jefferson penned, and the Virginia and Kentucky legislatures adopted, a series of resolutions declaring the Alien and Sedition Laws unconstitutional and proclaiming a series of principles which Calhoun used in his nullification theory. The Constitution, declared the resolutions, limited the federal government to powers delegated by the contracting states; "the government created by this compact was not made the exclusive or final judge of the extent of the powers delegated . . . since that would have made its discretion and not the Constitution the measure of its powers"; and so "each party has an equal right to judge for itself, as well of infractions as of the mode and measure of redress."

The Virginia and Kentucky Resolutions remained unenforced declarations of opinion. Jefferson was elected President in 1800, and the Alien and Sedition Laws were allowed to lapse. The resolutions soon became revered documents in the Jeffersonian tradition of civil liberties. Yet their meaning was enigmatic. Did

[50] [Pickens], *The Genuine Book of Nullification* . . . (Charleston, 1831). My interpretation of the Virginia and Kentucky Resolutions leans heavily on the excellent article by Adrienne Koch and Harry Ammon, "The Virginia and Kentucky Resolutions, An Episode in Jefferson's and Madison's Defense of Civil Liberties," *The William and Mary Quarterly,* 3rd Series, V (Apr. 1948), 145–76, and on the solid review by Merrill D. Peterson, *The Jefferson Image in the American Mind* (New York, 1960), pp. 51–66.

they sanction remonstrance or secession or Calhoun's version of nullification?

To nullifiers, the 1798 Virginia and Kentucky Resolutions, and particularly the 1799 Kentucky Resolutions, established the doctrine that a state could veto a law and remain within the Union. Their argument was weakened, however, by the fact that no one knew whether Jefferson wrote the 1799 Kentucky Resolutions, the most radical of the documents and the only one containing the fatal word "nullification." So nullifiers considered it a stroke of providence when, in 1832, Jefferson's draft of the 1799 resolutions was discovered and printed in Richmond. Jefferson's draft was more radical than the printed resolutions. Calhoun later gleefully remarked that "had it been possible for him to have had access to the manuscript, he might well have been suspected of plagiarism." Since Thomas Jefferson recognized and used nullification as a peaceful and conservative remedy, the doctrine could hardly be "Jacobinical."[51]

The unionists, frustrated by the enigmatic phrases of Jefferson, sometimes privately denounced him. Virginia's best politician, wrote Daniel Huger, "was Washington who knew nothing of mystics— The worst was Jefferson who was full of them." Hugh Legaré expressed his exasperation more bluntly. "The politics of the immortal Jefferson! Pish!"[52]

The moderates need not have despaired. Madison's 1830 essay, declaring that the resolutions sanctioned only remonstrance, more than balanced the discovery of Jefferson's 1799 draft.[53] In the ensuing South Carolina debates, unionists successfully argued that Jefferson's doctrines did not sanction Calhoun's. In retrospect, it seems evident that the Virginia and Kentucky Resolutions were a precedent either for remonstrance or for secession, but not for South Carolina's version of nullification.

The debate over the meaning of the resolutions started with their authors. Madison, who wrote the milder Virginia Resolutions, believed that the Old Dominion's legislature merely en-

[51] *Pendleton Messenger*, March 28, 1832; Peterson, *Jeffersonian Mind*, p. 57.

[52] Huger to Drayton, Jan. 11, 1833, Drayton Papers; Legaré to Isaac Holmes, Oct. 2, 1832, Legaré, *Writings*, I, 207.

[53] *Charleston Courier*, Oct. 20, 1830.

dorsed a remonstrance to Congress and to other state legislatures. In his "Report of 1800," written for the Virginia legislature, Madison distinguished between the Virginia Resolutions and judicial decisions which are "carried into immediate effect by force." The resolutions merely expressed an opinion, "unaccompanied with any other effect than what they may produce on opinion by exciting reflection."[54]

While Jefferson's meaning in the more radical Kentucky Resolutions is elusive, the surviving evidence tends to indicate that he considered the resolutions a justification of secession. In the 1799 draft, which nullifiers celebrated so joyously, Jefferson called nullification a "natural" right; in Jeffersonian rhetoric, a "natural" remedy involved revolutionary crusades rather than civil reforms. In a 1799 letter to Madison, Jefferson advised his cohort to use the resolutions to defend the right "to sever ourselves from . . . the Union . . . rather than give up the rights of self government." Finally, in his First Inaugural Address in early 1801, Jefferson declared that "absolute acquiescence in the decisions of the majority, [is] the vital principle of republics, from which there is no appeal but to force." Neither Madison nor Jefferson appears to have believed that a state could veto a law and remain in the Union.[55]

The nullifiers of 1832 also differed from the remonstrators of 1798 in the type of law they were opposing and the broader philosophy they were defending. As John Richardson pointed out in 1830, the Alien and Sedition Laws, which threatened "personal liberty," were different from the Tariff of Abominations, which threatened only "the rights of property."[56] Madison and Jefferson feared that the Alien and Sedition Laws would end the free discussions and open debates which must precede a truly democratic election. Unless minorities had power to take their case to the people, they believed, majorities would have no right to rule the Republic. The Virginia and Kentucky Resolutions were at least intended to preserve the sanctity of majority rule

---

[54] Koch and Ammon, *loc. cit.*, p. 173.
[55] *Ibid.*, pp. 157, 165–6; Richardson (ed.), *Messages and Papers*, I, 311.
[56] *City Gazette*, Sept. 14, 1830.

by protecting the electoral process which made it legitimate. In this sense, when South Carolinians claimed that a minority could negate economic legislation passed by a fairly elected majority, they repudiated a critical aspect of the resolutions.

Nullifiers, in short, could not escape the Jacobin label by posing as heirs to the revered Jeffersonian tradition. The old documents were too ambiguous, the precedent too uncertain. As the debates of 1830 progressed, and the "war whoops of disunion" grew louder, nullifiers laid new claim to the mantle of conservatism by diluting their doctrine to the point of absurdity. Nullification, as explained by Congressmen Warren Davis and George McDuffie, involved nothing more radical than a simple trial by jury!

The McDuffie-Davis trial-by-jury theory depended on the merchants' method of paying duties. Instead of carrying cash to the customs office, merchants usually signed a bond promising to pay the tax within a given period. If a merchant believed the bond fraudulent, he could refuse to meet the obligation. The government would sue the defaulting merchant and bring the case to trial in a South Carolina federal court. A merchant could demand a jury trial and then defend his failure to pay the tax by attacking the legitimacy of the bond.

McDuffie and Davis urged Carolinians to call a convention and nullify the tariff, "thereby absolving our citizens from all its supposed obligations." An importing merchant could then refuse to pay his bond, "throw his case before a Jury of the State," and claim the bond void because the convention had declared the tariff unconstitutional. "I do not believe that a Jury (not packed) could be found in any District of the State, who would find a verdict for the Government," wrote Davis. "An oppressive and tyrannical law, that is driving almost to madness a generous, patriotic and highminded people, would be seen *annulled, avoided*, and *made harmless* by the quiet and peaceful intervention of 'trial by jury.' "[57]

The McDuffie-Davis plan represented a significant retreat from the earlier version of nullification. In 1828 radicals had relin-

[57] *Greenville Mountaineer*, Aug. 13, 1830; *Charleston Courier*, Aug. 28, 1830.

quished voluntary boycott of northern goods partly because the moderates' noncompliance wrecked the scheme. One important advantage of nullification, they had then argued, was that everyone in the state could be commanded and compelled to cease obeying the law. Yet the nullification-by-jury scheme proposed in 1830 was fully as voluntary as the nonimportation plan tried in 1828. The East Bay merchants, who opposed nullification almost unanimously, could voluntarily choose to pay the duties, and Charleston juries could voluntarily find verdicts against defaulting merchants. This sort of nullification seemed likely to "terminate as did the plan of wearing homespun, without affording the least shadow of a remedy for our wrongs."[58]

The McDuffie-Davis scheme also raised serious legal problems. Many lawyers believed that the constitutional argument would never come before a jury. South Carolina common law, they argued, gave judges exclusive authority to determine the law and juries only power to decide the facts. More important, nullification by jury invited legal chaos. Since no higher federal court allegedly had jurisdiction after a sovereign nullification convention had spoken, the decisions of local juries could not be appealed. And with the community badly divided over nullification, local juries would—Warren Davis notwithstanding—decide differently. As William Drayton pointed out, "the persons and property of our citizens, instead of being protected by uniform rules, would depend upon the varying opinions of different jurors, uncontrolled by precedents or principles." Of course the problem could be neatly solved—as Stephen Miller suggested in an indiscreet moment—by packing Davis' unpacked juries. But then nullifiers would become Jacobins again![59]

In short, nullification without some form of compulsion, and an aura of radicalism, was impossible. As Benjamin F. Perry noted after reviewing McDuffie's scheme, "the doctrines of *Nullification* seem to have been given up." By the fall, the nullifiers, having already surrendered the essence, came close to abandoning the form. Instead of advocating nullification, they urged that the

[58] *Ibid.*, Aug. 13, 1830; *Edgefield Hive*, Sept. 16, 1830.
[59] *Southern Patriot*, Nov. 23, 1831; *Camden Journal*, Sept. 25, 1830.

state legislature call an unpledged convention. A South Carolina convention, argued the radicals, could petition Congress for a redress of grievances, and a remonstrance from the people in convention assembled might have an impact which legislative remonstrances had lacked. Alternatively, a convention could proclaim essential principles or propose constitutional amendments. The radicals minimized the chance that a convention would adopt nullification. James Hamilton, Jr., conceded that probably "the public mind is not sufficiently informed of the true character and probable consequence of a veto on the part of the State . . . to authorize that measure being considered as one of the probable or legitimate acts of convention."[60]

By the October elections, the nullifiers' equivocations had blurred the issues which their public campaign had initially tried to clarify. The populace was rarely given a choice between nullifiers and unionists. More often, conventionists ran against anticonventionists. To add to the confusion, some important nullifiers, including Calhoun, sought to delay radical action by opposing a convention. Meanwhile some major conventionists deplored nullification and sought only a stronger remonstrance. By election day, the division between conventionists and anticonventionists paralleled only vaguely the division between nullifiers and unionists.[61]

Many voters were not even offered a clear choice between conventionists and anticonventionists. In some districts, the two developing parties failed to nominate full slates of opposing candidates. In others, potential legislators ignored the convention issue, and elections turned "upon some little local matters, prejudices & personal partialities." When the contest was over, observers despaired of "designating Members in relation to the question of Convention . . . with anything like certainty."[62]

[60] *Greenville Mountaineer*, Sept. 17, 1830; *Southern Times*, Aug. 26, 1830; *Charleston Mercury*, Sept. 29, 1830; Hayne to Van Buren, Oct. 23, 1830, Van Buren Papers.
[61] Calhoun to Samuel Ingham, Oct. 30, 1830, Calhoun Papers, SC; *Winyaw Intelligencer*, Sept. 25, 1830; *Camden Journal*, Sept. 4, 1831; Perry, *Reminiscences* (1889 ed.), pp. 207–9.
[62] Joseph N. Whitner to Hammond, July 22, 1830, Hammond Papers, LC; *Greenville Mountaineer*, Oct. 15, 1830; *Charleston Mercury*, Nov. 2, 1830; *Camden Journal*, Nov. 20, 1830.

Despite the initial uncertainty about the opinions of victorious candidates, the election of 1830 vindicated the nullifiers' strategy of equivocation. When an unpledged convention was the issue at stake, the radicals won their share of seats. When a clear division between nullifiers and unionists occurred, the radicals invariably lost. Abbeville, for example, a severely depressed up-country cotton district, voted for nullification by a two-to-one margin in 1832. Yet in 1830, with the two emerging parties debating nullification rather than convention, unionists elected their entire ticket. If the radicals had dared to base their statewide campaign on nullification in 1830, a unionist electoral landslide would have swept them away.

The nullifiers' strategic retreat not only salvaged the election of 1830 but also diluted the emerging revolution in the nature of South Carolina politics. When the 1830 campaign began, the sharp public debates had promised to create clear popular parties which would give plebeians a decisive choice between public policies. When the campaign ended, the obscure programs and diluted tickets often allowed the masses only the usual decision between aristocrats. Once again the final policy decision would rest with the patricians. In this sense, the 1830 campaign marks an important period of transition in the change from the old personal politics to the emerging ideological parties.

10

Although popular parties remained half formed at the October legislative elections, the Smith and Calhoun factions split apart and two coherent legislative parties developed when the legislators convened in November. The new party structure became spectacularly evident in the bitter senatorial election between William Smith and Stephen D. Miller, the two leading members of the old Smith faction.

The split betwen Miller and Smith in 1830 was foreshadowed by the conflicting stands Miller and David R. Williams took in 1828. Williams, in a series of widely read public letters, urged that the old Smithite fight for strict construction had been waged to save rather than destroy democracy and the Union. Williams opposed all schemes for forcible resistance ("my eyes have been nearly blistered by looking on such a project on paper") and urged the propriety of an appeal "to the sense of the majority." Minorities have constitutional rights, concluded Williams, but "that the majority ought to rule, is a principle on which all our institutions are bottomed."[63]

To Miller, on the other hand, the strict-construction assumption that "the constitution must govern the majority" required forcible minority resistance to "unregulated Despotism. . . . Tell me not that a majority in Congress must govern," Miller argued. "This is the wedge which . . . will sooner or later split the Union asunder."[64]

Although private letters between Williams and Miller became increasingly disputatious after 1828, they remained close friends and political allies. Until late in 1830, Smithite newspapers continued to snipe at the Calhounites. But Miller's messages as governor were almost as radical as Hamilton's speech at Walterborough, and the governor's August 1830 Statesburg Speech must have embarrassed even McDuffie. Meanwhile Smith remained ominously silent on the subject of convention and nullification.

As early as June 1830, Calhounites, thinking it probable "that Judge Smith will be moderate," hoped that Miller could "be indirectly & judiciously flattered . . . to run for the Senate" against his cohort. The support of the Calhoun faction and "a part of his own party will elect him," wrote Francis Pickens. "Their party will then be divided, & we will have the power of the state in our own hands."[65]

Hamilton, a master at tactful flattery, undertook the task of beguiling Miller. The Calhounites, Hamilton wrote Miller, had discouraged any opposition to Smith in their own faction. "But I cannot shut my eyes to the evident dissatisfaction of some of the Judge's old friends at his present sentiments & his probable course," Hamilton added. With "serious misgivings" about Smith

[63] *City Gazette,* Aug. 27, 1828.
[64] *Ibid.,* Sept. 24, 1828.
[65] Pickens to Hammond, June 26, 1830, Hammond Papers, LC. See also Pickens to Hammond, July 14, 1830, Hammond Papers; Preston to Thompson, July 4, 1830, Preston Papers.

growing in "his own section of country," perhaps the judge
would step aside and allow both factions to elect Miller unanimously.[66]

By late August Miller was nibbling at the bait; in mid-November Smith, in his Yorkville Address, came out vehemently against
a convention. With a debate and vote on convention imminent
in the legislature, the more radical Smithites could no longer
afford to back their old leader. Miller was perhaps the only man
in South Carolina capable of defeating Smith and was surely the
candidate most likely to give former Smithite's a respected place
in the convention party. Twice Miller refused to run because of
his long association with Smith. Finally, a paper signed by Miller's
old cohorts, claiming the right to use him for the benefit of the
country, compelled him to give up his "scruples."[67]

Smith's supporters proceeded to denounce Miller as a traitor
to his party, a self-seeking politico who brushed aside close friendships in his drive for personal power. Miller partisans pointed out
that Smith had sold almost all his Carolina property, had bought
huge cotton tracts in Alabama, and had purchased a sugar plantation in Louisiana. Smith had lost his taste for a crusade against the
tariff, concluded the conventionists, because he benefited from
the sugar duties and because "nineteen-twentieths of his immense
property lies beyond the limits of the state."[68]

Some conventionists, remembering that Smith had led the
states' rights crusade in the days when South Carolina was infatuated with nationalism, nostalgically cast a ballot for the
beleaguered old partisan. Others, such as Thomas Jefferson
Withers, a devoted Smith protégé and the editor of the *Columbia
Telescope*, remained aloof from the painful contest. Despite the
bitter insults and the old loyalties, the Smith-Miller clash was
fundamentally a conflict between the new legislative parties. "I
have little doubt that in a week, if a doorkeeper is to be elected,
an enquiry will be made whether he is for or against Convention,"

[66] Hamilton to Miller, Aug. 9, 1830, Chestnut-Manning-Miller Papers; Hamilton
to Miller, Aug. 17, 1830, Hamilton Papers; Hamilton to Van Buren, Sept. 20, 1830,
Van Buren Papers.
[67] *Charleston Courier*, Nov. 13, 15, 1830; *Winyaw Intelligencer*, Jan. 4, 1832.
[68] *Southern Times*, Nov. 18, 1830.

wrote one observer. As the party battle progressed the conventionists' slim numerical majority and superior legislative organization became increasingly obvious. "We are not organized and drilled as well as the ultras," admitted one moderate sadly. In the end, Miller triumphed, eighty-one to seventy-seven, and joined Hayne in the United States Senate.[69]

Miller's victory signified the Calhounites' gains from the factional reorganization. The Calhoun faction was weakened by the loss of several prominent Charlestonians, including Daniel Huger, William Drayton, Joel Poinsett, and James L. Petigru. Alexander Speer's old faction and Charleston's Courier party also cast their lot with the South Carolina moderates. These changes, however, were more than offset by the permanent destruction of the old Smith faction. In addition to Senator Miller and his large personal following in the Sumter and Marion districts, the Calhounites gained a host of upcountry Smithites, including Thomas Cooper and his powerful Columbia cabal. In late 1830 David R. Williams was killed by falling timbers while working on a Pee Dee River project. In late 1831 Smith migrated to Alabama, virtually ending his checkered career in Carolina politics. Secondary politicians, such as Congressmen James Blair, Starling Tucker, and Thomas Mitchell, took control of Smith's crippled faction. Leadership of the statewide unionist movement passed, fatefully, to Charleston ex-Calhounites—Poinsett and Huger—archconservatives who were, as we will see, ill-equipped to lead a popular political party.

South Carolina historians have often described the passage of the earlier Smith Resolutions as the "Revolution of 1825." But the real "revolution" took place in 1830. The 1825 resolutions, although marking an important point in South Carolina's evolution toward sectionalism, neither disrupted the old factional alignments nor established the undisputed primacy of Smith. The 1830 convention issue, on the other hand, split the old factions, produced the beginnings of a two-party struggle in popular elections, and established strict party organizations in the state legislature.

[69] Perry, *Reminiscences* (1883 ed.), p. 223; *Charleston Courier*, Nov. 30, Dec. 3, 1830; *Greenville Mountaineer*, Dec. 3, 1830.

The two developing parties proved transitory. After the Nullification Controversy was over, personal factions again dominated state politics. But in the 1820's Smith had held his own against Calhoun. In the fifteen years after 1835, with the Smith faction irretrievably smashed, Calhounites maintained almost despotic control. The ramifications of the "Revolution of 1830" continued a decade and a half after the resolution of the nullification issues.

11

In 1830 the superior organization which had helped give Miller his triumph was even more telling in other legislative elections. Hamilton, seeking an official position from which to mastermind the radicals' crusade, had been lining up votes for governor since 1828. Meanwhile the moderates disputed over the merits of rival candidates throughout 1830. At the last minute, the anticonventionists unenthusiastically managed to unite behind Richard Manning, a former governor and one of the few upcountry seceders from the Calhoun faction. Hamilton won easily, ninety-three to sixty-seven. Henry L. Pinckney was elected speaker of the House against token opposition.[70]

The debate over calling an unpledged convention lasted for almost two weeks, with William Preston leading the radicals and Daniel Huger directing the moderates. The debate revealed more clearly that the convention party was an amalgam of those who favored a more effective remonstrance and those who favored immediate nullification. Huger, seeing the chance to split his opponents, jeered at the nullifiers for evading the real issue and proposed an amendment declaring that a state had no right to nullify federal law. Robert Barnwell Rhett instantly recognized the danger and hissed out scorn at Huger for trying to make "a bugaboo of nullification." Huger challenged, Rhett accepted, and the House of Representatives adjourned in an uproar. The war of words seemed about to end in tragedy on the dueling ground.[71]

As so often happened with the gentry of the Old South, the affair was settled with gestures instead of pistols. The next morn-

[70] *Southern Times*, Nov. 23, 1830.
[71] *Debate in the South Carolina Legislature, December, 1830, passim;* Perry, *Reminiscences* (1883 ed.), pp. 129–30.

ing Rhett declared he had meant no insult, and Huger deigned to accept the explanation. The conventionists proceeded to use parliamentary tricks to avoid the divisive vote on nullification. Other efforts to split the conventionists failed, significantly, because the anticonventionists were even less united. The House voted for a convention, sixty to fifty-six; the Senate favored a convention, twenty-three to eighteen. The respective margins were well short of the required two-thirds majority, and only a minority of the legislators advocated immediate nullification. Yet the conventionists, by achieving a simple majority, had gained an important propaganda victory.[72]

For the nullifiers, the legislative proceedings marked a promising end to a discouraging year. Throughout 1830 Hamilton and others had been equally distressed by the strength of northern majorities and the moderation of Carolina planters. By excellent strategy in the popular elections and solid organization during the legislative session, the radicals had avoided a disastrous defeat and had won control of the state government. The majority of Carolinians, however, remained hopeful of congressional redress and fearful of radical action. Nullifiers had contained their losses. But they had not yet converted their state.

[72] For a full discussion of the conventionists' parliamentary tricks and their opponents' defective organization, see William W. Freehling, "The Nullification Controversy in South Carolina" (Ann Arbor: Univ. Microfilms, 1965), pp. 312–13, nn. 112–13.

7

Nullification Victorious, 1831–1832

In mid-1831 the nullifiers' campaign reached its decisive turning point, shifting from the equivocations of 1830 and the confusion of early 1831 to a sustained, organized effort to convert South Carolina. The crusade, expertly managed by Hamilton, produced an organized political "association," forced Calhoun to declare his opinions, educated the populace, and, partly because of the unionists' poor campaigning, swept the 1832 elections.

2

The early months of 1831 were depressing times for all South Carolina politicians. The disputes in Congress distressed the moderates; the apathy in South Carolina alarmed the radicals; the break with Jackson upset Calhoun. An uneasy tension hung over state politics, as leaders of differing persuasions sought to break free of the confusion which preceded the great campaign for nullification.

Even moderates who had rejoiced at the concessions won in May 1830 professed concern over Congress' deliberations in the winter of 1830–1. Instead of following up on his Maysville Road veto, Andrew Jackson gave his approval to several acts increasing internal-improvement appropriations. And instead of gaining further piecemeal tariff reductions, James Blair found himself fighting to preserve the concessions previously granted. When tariffites tried to rescind the 1830 reduction on salt, Blair warned

Congress that "if this proposition should succeed, *the time* for argument will *have passed away*." William Nuckolls, Blair's moderate Carolina colleague, declared that if Congress went backward, South Carolina would resist, "peacefully if we can, forcibly if we must." The subsequent defeat of higher salt duties was small recompense for the diminished hope of majority redress.[1]

For Calhoun, the continued evidence of northern tyranny was no less distressing than Jackson's increasing hostility. Earlier their relations had suddenly improved. In late 1830 the President had informed Van Buren that the estrangement from Calhoun had ended; the Vice President would be invited to dinner. The Little Magician, ever imperturbable, blandly offered his congratulations. But Calhoun promptly blundered away any chance for a comeback. The Vice President, always the optimist, apparently transformed the invitation into a triumph and determined to finish off his opponents before they could retreat. Convinced that the Seminole correspondence would establish his own loyalty and Van Buren's treachery to the interests of Jackson, Calhoun decided to publish the hitherto-secret letters.

The Calhounites gathered together the bulky correspondence and asked John Eaton to inform the President of the prospective publication. Evidently Eaton, determined to avenge his maligned wife, never mentioned the subject to Jackson. At any rate, when the pamphlet appeared in February 1831, the President flew into one of his famed rages. "They have cut their own throats," Jackson exploded.[2]

The Little Magician administered the final blow by promptly pulling one of his more audacious maneuvers. Pleading his desire to save Jackson from a renewal of the unhappy controversy, Van Buren submitted his resignation as secretary of state. By late spring the entire cabinet had been maneuvered into resigning. The reconstituted cabinet contained no Calhounites, and Van Buren was appointed ambassador to England. The wily New Yorker, accepting his ministership after Congress adjourned, gaily sailed off for his rendezvous at the Court of St. James without Senate confirmation.

[1] *Charleston Mercury,* Feb. 11, 17, 1831; *Evening Post,* Dec. 30, 1831.
[2] Jackson to Charles Love, March 7, 1831, Jackson, *Correspondence,* IV, 245-6.

When Congress reconvened the following winter, Calhoun had his revenge. In late January 1832 a tie vote in the Senate permitted him to spike Van Buren's appointment by voting against confirmation. "It will kill him, sir, kill him dead. He will never kick, sir, never kick," declared an angry Calhoun. Senator Thomas Hart Benton, who recorded the statement, differed from the conclusion. "You have broken a minister, and elected a Vice-President," remarked the Missourian. Jackson's explosion vindicated Benton's judgment. "By the Eternal," shouted the President, "I'll smash them." John Randolph of Roanoke gleefully observed that "Calhoun, by this time, must be in Hell. . . . He is self mutilated like the Fanatic that emasculated Himself."[3]

Calhoun considered himself a leading presidential candidate in the spring of 1831 despite his break with Jackson. In a memorable conversation with James Hammond in March 1831, the Vice President explained his strategy. Both major parties, Calhoun told Hammond, would seen break up, and neither Jackson nor Van Buren nor Clay could step into the vacuum. By espousing his old limited nationalistic program, Calhoun hoped to sweep the 1832 election. The tariff would be lowered to please the South, but a "liberal protection" on "some of the most important articles" would appease the North. A constitutional amendment authorizing internal improvements would satisfy strict constructionists, and roads and canals, financed by public-land sales, would win the West. Hammond denounced the scheme. But in late May 1831 Calhoun continued to promise his friends that "I will in the coming contest act second to no one." He remained convinced that "I never stood stronger."[4]

Calhoun's strategy depended on Carolina's moderation; a renewed radical campaign would scare away conservative national support. The nullifiers, however, had no intention of settling for a moderate national compromise. Radicals, including Governor Hamilton, had long since given up safeguarding Calhoun's ex-

[3] Benton, *Thirty Years View* (2 vols.; New York, 1854–6), I, 215–19; Marquis James, *Andrew Jackson, Portrait of a President* (Indianapolis, 1937), p. 296; Randolph to Jackson, March 28, 1832, Jackson, *Correspondence*, IV, 425–9.

[4] Memorandum by Hammond, March 18, 1831, Hamilton to Hammond, June 11, 1831, in "Letters on the Nullification Movement in South Carolina," *AHR*, VI (July 1901), 741–7; Calhoun to Van Deventer, May 25, 1831, quoted in Capers, *Calhoun*, p. 143; Calhoun to Ingham, July 31, 1831, Andre DeCoppet Coll., Princeton.

tremely dubious prospects. On the contrary, Hamilton was distressed by South Carolina's inertia; for despite the Jackson-Calhoun controversy and the events in Congress, the nullifiers' campaign showed fatal signs of lagging in the early months of 1831. By the beginning of May, Hamilton, desperately "aware of the great peril of permitting public feeling to collapse," was casting about for a way to "rally on some firm ground and then stand manfully to our arms." In mid-May McDuffie's "'chance" visit to Charleston finally gave Hamilton an opportunity to organize one of his patented public dinners and to initiate the sustained crusade which would convulse Carolina politics until the election of 1832.[5]

The Charlestonians who streamed into St. Andrew's Hall on May 19 were treated to one of McDuffie's most memorable orations. The speech, although studded with fire-eating phrases, was more a reasoned analysis than a stump harangue. As Hamilton reported, McDuffie's "gigantic effort" was masterfully adapted "to the crisis and the community in which it was delivered." After presenting a sophisticated version of the forty-bale theory, McDuffie termed the tariff a "system of stupendous oppression under which we are steadily and rapidly sinking into utter and hopeless ruin." Urging that "no human power of argument and eloquence" would be "of any avail against the mere brute force of superior numbers," he called on Carolinians to stand on their sovereignty and attacked those who maintained the "utterly ridiculous" notion that nullification would end in "blood-shed and civil war."

At the same time, McDuffie, anticipating the nullifiers' strategy in the coming campaign, implicitly admitted the possibility of violence and heaped scorn on those who preferred tyranny to disunion. "The Union, such as the majority have made it," he declared, "is a foul monster, which those who worship, after seeing its deformity, are worthy of their chains." Revolution involved danger. But "shall we be frightened by mere phantoms of blood, when our ancestors, for less cause, encountered the dreadful reality? Great God! are we the descendants of those ancestors;

[5] Hamilton to Hammond, May 3, 1831, *AHR*, VI, 745.

are we freemen; are we men—grown men—to be frightened from the discharge of our most sacred duty, and the vindication of our most sacred rights, by the mere nursery tales of raw-heads and bloody-bones, which even the women of our country laugh to scorn?"[6]

The Carolina opponents of nullification almost rejoiced at McDuffie's speech. The "nursery tales of raw-heads and bloody-bones" was the sort of Jacobinical cant unionists never allowed the community to forget. But Calhoun and Duff Green shuddered at the "untimely agitation." Publicly the *United States Telegraph* denounced the proceedings and denied Calhoun's involvement. Privately Green wrote Hamilton, asking "civilly," "if we were all crazy at McDuffie's dinner."[7]

Calhoun was equally upset. The Vice President warned Hamilton that the affair was in "every way imprudent," and confessed to northern allies that "I feel its embarrassment as well on my own account, as of that of my friends." Well aware that the McDuffie dinner brought "matters to a crisis," Calhoun knew that "I must meet it, promptly and manfully."[8]

Yet as June and the first weeks in July passed, Calhoun remained publicly silent on nullification. The Vice President did all he could "to keep things quiet." But quieting the community and controlling the fire-eaters proved "impossible."[9] With Charleston in an uproar over the McDuffie rally, Hamilton and his colleagues whipped up excitement. In early June both Charleston parties planned separate Fourth of July celebrations. And the events of Independence Day demonstrated that the nullifiers' campaign had reached the proverbial point of no return.

On the morning of the fourth, the Charleston nullifiers marched to the Circular Church to hear Hayne give the traditional noon

[6] Hamilton to Hammond, May 21, 1831, *ibid.*, VI, 745–6; McDuffie, *Speech, May 19, 1831, passim.*

[7] *United States Telegraph,* May 30, June 3, 1831; Hamilton to Hammond, June 11, 1831, *AHR*, VI, 747.

[8] Calhoun to Virgil Maxcy, June 16, 1831, Galloway-Maxcy-Markoe Papers; Calhoun to Samuel Ingham, June 16, 1831, Calhoun, *Correspondence . . .* , J. Franklin Jameson (ed.), in *Annual Report of the American Historical Association for the Year 1899* (2 vols.; Washington, D.C., 1900), II, 294–5.

[9] Calhoun to Ingham, July 31, 1831, DeCoppet Coll.

oration. Hayne, like McDuffie, denounced the tariff and urged the legitimacy of nullification, but admitted that the remedy "may possibly lead" to disunion. The northern majority would be forced to choose between giving up the exploitation and giving up the Union. "Nullification is better than Secession," declared Hayne, "simply because it presents the alternative to the other side." In the evening, nullifiers met again to eat a sumptuous feast and hear fire-eating addresses by Pinckney, Hamilton, Turnbull, and Hayne.[10]

Meanwhile the unionists paraded to the First Presbyterian Church to listen to an excellent oration by William Drayton. At the unionist evening banquet, Hugh Legaré, James Petigru, Thomas Mitchell, and Daniel Huger all castigated nullification. Most important, the unionists, with great rejoicing, heard a special public letter from Jackson. The President hoped that the "declarations inconsistent with an attachment to the Union . . . were the effect of momentary excitement, not deliberate design," and warned that "he should also see that high and sacred duties which must and will, at all hazards, be performed, present an insurmountable barrier to the success of any plan of disorganization." The wording was oblique but the meaning unmistakable: President Jackson equated nullification and secession, and would countenance no plan of disunion.[11]

The Fourth of July celebrations raised the specter of Jacobinism more clearly than ever before. Hayne had admitted that the federal government might resist nullification and Jackson had affirmed that he would; how, then, could the remedy be peaceful? Unionist newspapers teemed with prophecies of disaster, and nullifiers had to move quickly. On July 12, 1831, the Charleston nullifiers met at Fayolle's Hall, created a statewide States Rights and Free Trade Association, and called on other districts to create local chapters. The association had the avowed object of unifying the nullifiers'

[10] Hayne, *Fourth of July Oration, 1831*, esp. p. 33; *Proceedings of the Celebration of the 4th, July, 1831, at Charleston* . . . (Charleston, 1831), *passim.*

[11] Jackson to John Stoney *et al.*, June 14, 1831, Drayton, *An Oration Delivered* . . . *on* . . . *July 4, 1831* . . . (Charleston, 1831), pp. 54–5; Jackson to "Robert Oliver" [Joel Poinsett], Oct. 26, 1830, Jackson to Charles Webb, Sept. 5, 1831, Jackson, *Correspondence,* IV, 191, 345; Jackson to Webb, draft copy, Sept. 2, 1831, Jackson Papers.

campaign, distributing propaganda, and arranging meetings. By establishing a popular political club dedicated to educating and exciting the "rabble," the nullifiers had deliberately violated all the unwritten rules which had long preserved the quasi-aristocratic nature of South Carolina democracy.[12]

As the nullifiers' crusade grew more intense, the pressure on Calhoun became irresistible. Unionists clamored to know his position, and nullifiers declared that "*if Mr. Calhoun . . . will go . . . with South Carolina, well and good; if not, South Carolina does not go with Mr. Calhoun.*" Even such devoted Calhoun partisans as Hammond threatened to send the Vice President "into coventries with old Smith" unless he came "down flatfooted upon Nullification."[13]

Hammond need not have worried. Calhoun, while extremely reluctant to renounce secrecy, had no intention of denouncing nullification. Hamilton and McDuffie were, after all, pushing him toward avowing a doctrine which was peculiarly his own, which he had accepted privately in 1827, at least as early as any other Carolinian, and which he was proud of having formulated in the 1828 *Exposition.* Once the younger nullifiers had precipitated the crisis, Calhoun had to make the most of it. "Relaxation now," he realized, "would be fatal." Calhoun believed that radicals who desired secession could destroy nullification as completely as moderates who proposed submission; by joining the crusade, he hoped to restrain the disunionists. Personal considerations may have been as compelling as disinterested convictions. Although Calhoun was reluctant to antagonize his national following, he could hardly repudiate his Carolina party. Moreover, Calhoun perhaps hoped that if he became more explicitly southern, the South would push him harder for the presidency. Late in July he at last issued his famous Fort Hill Letter, announcing to the nation his belief in nullification.[14]

[12] *Charleston Mercury,* July 14, 27, 1831. Hamilton's States Rights and Free Trade Association should not be confused with the South Carolina Association, the organization formed in 1823 to enforce the black codes.
[13] *Columbia Telescope,* June 10, 1831; Hammond to Hamilton, July 28, 1831, Hammond Papers, SC.
[14] Calhoun to Pickens, Aug. 1, 1831, L. W. Smith Coll.; Calhoun to Ingham, July 31, 1831, DeCoppet Coll.; Calhoun, *Works,* VI, 59ff.

In one sense, Calhoun found the public declaration a relief. Harboring political secrets had never quite squared with his high-minded sense of political ethics. "When you come to read the paper," he wrote Samuel Ingham, "I hope you will at least think I have done right in coming out."[15]

In every other way, Calhoun regretted being forced into the open. Historians have often argued that Calhoun declared for nullification only after he realized that his presidential campaign was crushed. But this interpretation ignores Calhoun's capacity to delude himself about his own political prospects. The Vice President's abstracted view of the world rendered him at once acutely aware of long-range historical trends and sometimes blinded to his day-to-day environment. When the insensitivity to immediate circumstances was united with wishful thinking about tenure in the White House, Calhoun's distortions reached comic proportions. The reluctance to issue the Fort Hill Letter is a case in point. In late July 1831 Calhoun was loath to declare his allegiance to nullification, partly because he continued to harbor the illusion that his 1832 presidential prospects were promising. A week after publishing the fateful essay he still considered "Jackson's fall . . . almost certain" and believed "Van Buren's prospects . . . hopeless." With a "period of great confusion" imminent, the prospect of "separation from those I so much esteem" was "painful."[16]

In addition, Calhoun feared that the South Carolina radicals had moved too soon. Redress could still be obtained, he believed, by appealing to the sense of the majority. Even when writing such a militant nullifier as Pickens, Calhoun declared that his "opinion was decidedly against active operations this summer," and confessed his "regret" at being "forced" from "a silent & retired position."[17]

For Calhoun, the collapse of presidential prospects was a shat-

[15] Calhoun to Ingham, July 31, 1831, DeCoppet Coll.
[16] Calhoun to Charles J. McDonald, Aug. 4, 1831, Calhoun Coll., New York Pub. Lib.; Calhoun to Maxcy, Aug. 6, 1831, Galloway-Maxcy-Markoe Papers. For a more astonishing example of Calhoun's naïveté about his presidential prospects, see Calhoun to Ingham, May 27, 1832, Calhoun Papers, SC.
[17] Calhoun to Pickens, Aug. 1, 1831, Smith Coll.

tering experience. The bright young man who had always enjoyed success at last endured the agony of overwhelming setback. The signs of his despair were visible everywhere: in the slouch of his shoulders as he paced the Senate corridors, in his increasing tendency to make conversations into soliloquies, in his long dirges on the decline of the Republic. "The times are so sadly changed in a few years," he wrote in early 1832. "I never suspected that a people could so sadly degenerate." Henry Clay scribbled out the classic Calhoun caricature: "tall, careworn, with furrowed brow, haggard and intensely gazing, looking as if he were dissecting the last abstraction which sprung from a metaphysician's brain, and muttering to himself, in half-uttered tones, 'This is indeed a real crisis.' " Calhoun's taste for abstractions, always present, became obsessive. Giving an oration, with his graying hair standing bolt upright, his hawklike eyes defying dissenters, his bony finger emphasizing the unadorned syllogisms, he could easily have been mistaken for a professor of mathematics. He would spend the rest of his life combating the inexorable fate which John McLean sadly penned in late 1831: "Our friend Calhoun is gone, I fear, forever."[18]

In Calhoun's eyes the nullification campaign took on expanding objectives, at once more disinterested and more personal. He saw himself once again as the disinterested statesman fighting the demagogical spoilsmen. Jackson seemed more foully corrupt than Adams, Van Buren a more scheming manipulator than Crawford. But South Carolina, by nullifying the tariff, could cut governmental income, thereby decreasing executive patronage and ending the supremacy of spoilsmen. For Calhoun, one suspects, nullification was in part a means of creating a nation in which a Calhoun rather than a Van Buren, the philosopher-statesman rather than the party manager, would again have a chance to be President of the United States.[19]

If South Carolina helped push Calhoun into avowing nullifica-

[18] Calhoun to Pickens, March 2, 1832, Calhoun Papers, DU; McLean to Samuel Gouverneur, Sept. 25, 1831, William Meigs, *Life of John C. Calhoun* (2 vols.; New York, 1917), I, 361. Clay is quoted in Richard Hofstadter, *The American Political Tradition* . . . (Vintage ed.; New York, 1955), p. 74.

[19] Calhoun to McLean, Sept. 22, 1829, McLean Papers; Calhoun to the Committee . . . , Sept. 5, 1836, *Pendleton Messenger*, Sept. 30, 1836.

tion, Calhoun helped push South Carolina into voting for it. When Calhoun entered the canvass, his state was still extremely suspicious of nullification. In the long and arduous campaign ahead, no one else could have so successfully persuaded the timid and fearful that the remedy was both rightful and peaceful. Calhoun's massive prestige and conservative essays perfectly complemented Hamilton's managerial genius and McDuffie's wild oratory. Benjamin F. Perry's conclusion was accurate: "Mr. Calhoun was the author of nullification in South Carolina, but Governor Hamilton made it a success throughout the state."[20] Still, in an election where a change of a few votes in key districts would have upset the nullifiers' two-thirds majority, Calhoun surely helped Hamilton prevail.

Hamilton's great contribution, as Perry also noted, was to make the association an effective political club in the fall of 1831. Under the governor's supervision, almost every district in the state formed an association, and almost every local club held monthly meetings. With membership open to anyone upon payment of one dollar, the association meetings became popular social events where the poorest farmer and the richest planter met together to curse the northerners.

For many Carolinians, the association meetings were most important as social events. The monthly rallies were a welcome relief from the loneliness, boredom, and tedium of life in rural Carolina. For certain dispossessed groups, membership in the association also eased acute social frustrations. The slaveless farmer, the small slaveholder, the Charleston mechanic, and the lowcountry cadet class, although becoming nullifiers in part because of financial difficulties, also found joining the association a welcome relief from social tensions which economic depression had made particularly severe.

The nonslaveholders and small slaveholders who lived in planting areas often were consumed by the desire to match the estates of neighboring aristocrats. As an upcountry slaveholder described the jealousy, "a rich planter lives sumptuously, and his less wealthy neighbor thinks as he is equal he can live as well, he goes in debt

[20] *Reminiscences* (1883 ed.), p. 143.

to do so, and ruin follows as a consequence." Hard times not only brought ruinous debts but also acute frustrations. Depression, noted one observer, "altogether removes the prospect of their increasing their prosperity" and thus of becoming planters. But the association meetings for a moment obliterated the class differences. As Perry wrote, "many persons have joined the rank of the nullifiers in order to get into a company a little above their accustomed circle. . . . [Particularly] those who were ambitious of belonging to the Chivalry."[21]

For Charleston's white mechanics, depression brought an increasingly desperate competition with the detested Negro laborers. But by joining the association, the mechanics became respectable white Carolinians, differentiated from the Negroes and somewhat respected by the planters. As a Charleston unionist ruefully described the process, we see "men, who, in quiet times, are scarcely seen when the sun shines, whose habits and pursuits confine them to the sinks and stews of the obscure allies, and by places of the city, parading our streets arm in arm with the great and the wealthy . . . and in turn these men treading the avenues of vice and dissipation. . . . Nullifiers take care to make the support of their cause itself, a substitute for every other title to respect and confidence."[22]

The younger sons of lowcountry planters were the prime casualties of the tidewater's paradoxical commitment to both capitalistic enterprise and an anticapitalistic attitude. With the "respectable" professions overcrowded, and with their fathers unable to give them plantations to manage, the cadet class preferred a life of dissipated idleness to "working" at "degraded" jobs. Yet Charleston aristocrats respected entrepreneurial success enough to disdain able young men who squandered their fathers' savings. Too poor to afford gentility but too genteel to go to work, the lowcountry cadet class suffered from a painful erosion of morale. By joining the association and cheering on the nullifiers, the younger sons could temporarily escape from the tug of conflicting

21 Furman Plantation Journal, p. 179; Camden Journal, Oct. 27, 1827; Perry Diary, entry for July 29, 1833, NC; Daniel Huger to Perry, Apr. 17, 1832, Perry Papers, Alabama Arch.
22 Quoted in Greenville Mountaineer, Dec. 3, 1831.

values and become, like their fathers, chivalrous Carolinians, members of the great planting community. Charleston newspapers often noted that no group so often flaunted its membership in the association and its claim to chivalry.[23]

Hamilton's association, in short, resembled an exclusive social club which suddenly opens its doors to men who had despaired of entering. At a time when economic depression erected impassable obstacles for everyone seeking wealth and prestige, the gentry had seemingly invited the impoverished to share all the trappings of power. No wonder that farmers and mechanics, petty slaveholders and aristocratic sons, all eagerly anticipated the monthly gatherings of the Carolina elect.

The association's central planning enhanced the effectiveness of local meetings. Hamilton organized two spirited statewide conventions during the winter of 1831–2. In December of 1831, 112 delegates, representing thirty districts, met at Columbia during the legislative session. The convention set up machinery for financing, printing, and distributing tracts, and listened to militant orations by B. J. Earle and Robert J. Turnbull. In February 1832, 183 delegates, representing thirty-six districts, met at Charleston during race week. The Charleston convention, a splendid affair which attracted thousands of spectators to its meetings, perfected the statewide propaganda network and featured fire-eating addresses by A. P. Butler, Turnbull, Hamilton, Henry L. Pinckney, and William Preston. As one exuberant participant exclaimed, "It was the true spirit of '76." The two conventions, by establishing internal unity and engendering fervent dedication, contributed vitally to the growing strength of the nullification movement.[24]

Hamilton, determined to maintain the party's new momentum, traversed the state in the spring of 1832, ostensibly to review the militia, actually to direct the association. In a state which treasured martial glory as the highest chivalric virtue, he made an impressive spectacle, riding in his small military carriage, drawn by his two dock-tailed gray cobs from Vermont, followed by his mounted

[23] For some good examples, see *Charleston Courier,* March 24, 1830, Feb. 16, 1833.
[24] *Charleston Mercury* and *Evening Post,* Dec. 8–20, 1831, Feb. 18–28, 1832, *passim; Pendleton Messenger,* Feb. 29, 1832; *Proceedings of the Convention, February, 1832.*

servant riding the handsome parade horse. After flattering the citizenry by attending the muster, there was always time to make speeches, distribute propaganda, and soothe tempers.[25]

The association's monthly pamphlets grew steadily more effective under Hamilton's skilled direction. The governor insisted on "the expediency of giving to these publications a more popular and less abstract character . . . that they may be brought down to the comprehension of every freeman in the South who is able to read what it so much behooves him to learn." Two tracts in particular, featuring "A Dialogue Between a Merchant and a Planter," explained the mysteries of the forty-bale robbery and the lawful negation of laws in language which must have been comprehensible to even the least educated red-neck. All in all, the association had launched the most extensive campaign to educate the populace in political and economic principles which was ever attempted in ante bellum South Carolina.[26]

The most important challenge awaiting Hamilton's association was to answer the unionist charge that nullification would lead to civil war. After Jackson's letter to the Fourth of July unionist celebration, nullifiers realized that they must meet the question head on. Radicals ceased discoursing on unpacked juries and stopped discussing an unpledged convention. Frankly avowing nullification, they minimized the dangers of violence and ridiculed the "cowards" who feared it.

The nullifiers insisted that Jackson could not use force without specific congressional sanction. Although the federal Constitution designates the President "commander in chief" of the state militias when they are "called into the actual service of the United States," Congress alone is given power "to provide for calling forth the militia." In the late eighteenth century, Congress had given the President authority to suppress an insurrection *in* a state. The nullifiers claimed, however, that nullification involved legal resistance, not illegal insurrection. If the tyrannical Jackson should confuse the Carolina doctrines with lawless force, continued the

---

[25] J. G. deR. Hamilton, "James Hamilton, Jr.," pp. 20–1, Hamilton Papers.
[26] *Proceedings of the Convention, February, 1832*, p. 5. See also *A Catechism on the Tariff for . . . Plain People of Common Sense.*

radicals, the insurrection would be *of* a state, not *in* a state. Jackson would be compelled to ask Congress for further authority if he wished to use the militia to suppress nullification.[27]

Once Jackson sent the problem to Congress, the same selfish principle in man which made nullification necessary would make the remedy successful. Disunion and coercion would cost northerners "far more than all their factories are worth." Just as other southern states would join South Carolina rather than endanger slave property, so a northern majority would abandon protective tariffs rather than risk southern secession. Jackson could not and Congress would not start a civil war.[28]

Jackson's own actions led many Carolinians, including some unionists, to wonder if he would use force even if he could. In 1832 Georgia "nullified" an important Supreme Court decision and the President did nothing to "enforce the laws." Jackson in practice, it seemed, was not altogether the same as Jackson in theory.

The Court's decision marked the climax of a touchy controversy between Georgia and the federal government over the rights of Indian tribes within the state's borders. The federal government, employing its constitutional prerogatives of making treaties and regulating commerce, had long maintained exclusive authority over the Indians and had usually cajoled or forced tribes to move westward, out of the way of ambitious frontiersmen. But in Georgia the Creeks and Cherokees had no intention of moving, and restless planters hungered for Indian lands.

In the years before Jackson came to power, President John Quincy Adams and Governor George M. Troup had clashed over the Creeks. President Adams had periodically threatened to use armed force to keep white surveyors off Creek land. Governor Troup had warned that federal intervention would produce civil war and had prepared Georgia's army to defend state "sovereignty." Ultimately the messy problem was neatly solved at the expense of the hapless Indians: the Creeks were sent off to new lands beyond the Mississippi.

[27] For a good example, see *Charleston Mercury*, May 28, 1831.
[28] See, for example, Henry L. Pinckney as quoted in *Proceedings of the Celebration, July 4, 1831*, p. 68.

The Jackson administration was confronted by a crisis over the Cherokees. In 1827 the Cherokees in Georgia declared themselves an "independent nation" and adopted a written constitution. The Georgians annulled the constitution and seized the lands. The Cherokees subsequently filed suit in the United States Supreme Court, asking for an injunction restraining the white men. The Court, in an 1831 decision, *Cherokee Nation* v. *Georgia,* denied the petition on technical grounds: the Indians, although possessing unquestioned right to their lands, had no right to sue in federal courts.

A year later, in *Worchester* v. *Georgia,* the Court explicitly denied Georgia authority within Cherokee boundaries. The Georgians had required every white man who lived in Cherokee territory to obtain a Georgia license. When Georgia used the law to convict a pack of New England missionaries, Samuel A. Worchester and Elizor Butler, two of the condemned men, appealed to the Supreme Court. Although Georgia refused to appear before the Court, Chief Justice John Marshall, speaking for the majority, ordered the prisoners released because the law was unconstitutional. The Cherokee nation, declared Marshall, was a distinct political community, and within its boundaries "the laws of Georgia can have no force."

Both Georgia and Jackson ignored the ruling. The President, who had dodged his share of Seminole bullets and liked his Indians better dead than alive, is reputed to have said, "John Marshall has made his decision, now let him enforce it." The remark, even if apocryphal, accurately describes Jackson's actions. The President failed to enforce the decision. Georgia eventually released the missionaries and the Indians finally agreed to depart for the West.[29]

Georgia's "nullification" of Marshall's decision did not set a clear precedent for South Carolina's nullification of the tariff. The Georgians eschewed constitutional polemics and relied on crude defiance. Moreover, Georgia's "nullification" affected only Indians in the state, whereas South Carolina's veto would have disrupted a national revenue system. Some constitutional historians have argued that Jackson's course was far from inconsistent. A Presi-

[29] The best account of the controversy is in Wilson Lumkin, *The Removal of the Cherokee Indians from Georgia* (2 vols.; New York, 1907).

dent, after all, has some discretion about *how* to enforce the laws, and Jackson chose to end the dispute by removing the Indians.

To South Carolinians, however, the crucial point was that Georgia had defied a law and Jackson had acquiesced. "Georgia on a very recent occasion, nullified a decision of the Supreme Court," wrote one leading upcountry editor. "Do we see Gen. Jackson taking any *coercive* measures to *enforce* that decision? Is not the principle precisely the same with South Carolina? Is the Tariff act more of a Supreme law than a Supreme Court decision?" Some unionists also wondered if Jackson could be "depended on," for "the *old man* seems to be more than half a Nullifier himself." Jackson himself may have inadvertently contributed to the diminishing fear of federal coercion, and the increasing chance of nullification's triumph, during the campaign of 1831–2.[30]

By exhibiting President Jackson's "inconsistencies," demonstrating his lack of authority, and stressing a congressional majority's economic interest in avoiding war, the radicals developed a cogent case for the peaceful nature of nullification. But following in the tradition of McDuffie's and Hayne's earlier orations, the radicals admitted that nullification could lead to war. The real question, they insisted, was not whether Jackson intended to dispatch his armies but whether a President could legitimately "coerce" a state. The answer was that the federal government, as a mere agent of sovereign states, could not question the commands of a nullification convention. Armed coercion would be another proof of federal despotism, and "no people can be long free, who will submit to be frightened out of their rights by threats of lawless power."[31]

Nullifiers disdainfully referred to unionists as "submissionists," cowards who would fight neither for their own rights nor for their state's honor. In nullification imagery, the controversy with the federal government became a gigantic duel, and Carolina stood in danger of permitting "our national character for chivalry and honor to be tarnished by degenerating into abject servitude." Leading unionists watched helplessly as "the timid and the time-

---

[30] *Sumter Gazette*, June 16, 1832; Petigru to Legaré, Oct. 29, 1832, Carson, *Petigru*, pp. 102–5.

[31] Harper, *Speech, April 1, 1832*, p. 10; *Sumter Gazette*, Oct. 6, 1832; *Greenville Mountaineer*, March 17, 1832.

serving" slinked into the nullifiers' ranks rather than endure "the finger of scorn" which marked "submission men."[32]

Thus the association not only convinced the dubious but also condemned the "cowardly." By appealing to Mother Carolina's honor, the chivalric Hamilton joined nullification to one of the most cherished concepts Carolinians maintained and made the association a more powerful organization in Carolina politics.

3

From mid-July 1831 through the end of June 1832, the nullifiers' agitation became steadily more intense. In contrast, the unionist campaign, although spurting a bit in late 1831, had almost sputtered out by mid-1832. The nullifiers' organizational superiority, which had been significant during the 1830 legislative session, became decisive in the 1831-2 public campaign.

Unionists held several impressive public rallies in the fall of 1831. Drayton gave one excellent oration in the lowcountry, and the Smith-Blair-Mitchell crowd vilified Miller in the uplands. These exceptions aside, the moderates' campaign lagged. Unionists failed to form rival political clubs, held no regular meetings, did not convene a statewide convention, and developed no propaganda network. As Perry summed up the situation in mid-November 1831, "whilst the 'State Rights' party are constantly engaged in getting up meetings, adopting resolutions, forming societies, and distributing pamphlets and documents, the 'Union party' have been inactive and inert, opposed to public meetings and taking little interest in the politics of their country. Whilst our opponents have established a most perfectly organized party . . . we have hitherto had no concert or system in our movements. The consequence of this is that the Union party are losing ground throughout the State."[33]

[32] *Sumter Gazette*, July 28, 1832; Hamilton in *Proceedings of the Celebration, July 4, 1831*, pp. 23–4; *Greenville Mountaineer*, June 2, 1832; Drayton to Poinsett, Oct. 13, 1830, Poinsett Papers. For an intriguing example of the intimate rhetorical relationship between the code of individual duels and the rationale of state honor see John Lyde Wilson, *The Code of Honor; or Rules For the Government of Principals and Seconds in Duelling* (Charleston, 1838), pp. 3–5.

[33] *Greenville Mountaineer*, Nov. 12, 1831; *City Gazette*, Sept. 9, 1831; *Pendleton Messenger*, Oct. 3, 1832; Richard Yeardon to Isaac Dwight, June 8, 1831, copy in Hamilton Papers; Perry, *Reminiscences* (1889 ed.), p. 210.

Despite Perry's warning, the unionist campaign degenerated. Soon public rallies ceased. In 1832, for example, Charleston unionists held no meetings until mid-June. Occasionally an editor wrote biting editorials and several pamphleteers penned illuminating tracts. But while nullifiers were enlisting in the association and parading with the chivalry, "submissionists" found no clubs to enjoy and few publications to bolster belief. By mid-1832 the unionists' inept campaign had become a critical cause of the nullifiers' mounting strength.

In part, the unionists' destructive inertia was no more than the characteristic sluggishness of conservative movements. The need to convert the community always forces radicals to develop intense campaigns, to use inflammatory language, and to attract the most tempestuous citizens. These methods often give radical crusades initial momentum. Conservatives, on the other hand, can rely on the community's distrust of innovation and can direct soothing appeals to more sober citizens. Hence conservative campaigns often lag a bit.

But the difference between the nullifier and unionist campaigns was too great to be explained wholly in such terms. In part, the nullifiers' crusade was more successful because their leaders were more skilled. No unionist politician compared to James Hamilton, Jr., Thomas Cooper, or Henry L. Pinckney in the ability to organize a political movement. Joel R. Poinsett, who would show marked talents as a politician after nullification was adopted, returned to South Carolina in 1830 after years as minister to Mexico. But Poinsett, angered by fancied slights, took almost no part in the 1831-2 campaign. Daniel R. Huger had too much contempt for electioneering to indulge in it himself; James L. Petigru was too busy prospering at the law to travel around the state; William Smith spent too much time in Alabama to direct Carolina campaigns; Hugh S. Legaré was too jealous of his reputation to risk losing an election. The nature of the campaign might have changed a good deal if Hamilton had happened to be a unionist.[34]

[34] *Niles Register*, XLIII (Dec. 1, 1832), 222; Grayson Autobiography, p. 143; Petigru to Elliott, Sept. 30, 1832, Carson, *Petigru*, p. 96; Legaré to Alfred Huger, Dec. 15, 1834, Legaré, *Writings*, I, 216.

Still, Hamilton himself would have faced difficult, perhaps insuperable, obstacles in unifying the moderates. The two great pressure groups in the nullifiers' ranks—the upcountry cotton planters and the lowcountry rice and luxury cotton producers—shared similar values and enjoyed intimate social contacts. The unionist party, on the other hand, was a motley coalition of disparate types. Yeoman farmers in Greenville had little in common with East Bay merchants in Charleston, and in the lowcountry, unionist planters and lawyers often disliked Yankee entrepreneurs.

Divisive political principles compounded divisive social attitudes. Unionists tried to cover up their policy disagreements by espousing a common platform. According to the unionist argument most commonly developed, the two parties agreed that the tariff was an unconstitutional oppression; they differed on the proper remedy. Whereas nullifiers believed that the majority was permanently corrupt, unionists affirmed that "public opinion, when it settles down, will be right." If South Carolina remonstrated often enough, and hard enough, truth would ultimately prevail. If remonstrance failed, South Carolina could always secede. For the present, the tariff was a lesser evil than disunion, and nullification was secession in disguise.[35]

Unfortunately some unionists disagreed with each of these positions. Many moderates believed the tariff constitutional; others considered the duties expedient; others denied that a state could secede; others wondered if the majority would relent. Since the Grimké debacle in 1829, unionists had posed as ardent Jacksonians. Yet a strong Charleston contingent almost seceded from the party in order to support Henry Clay in the 1832 election. The dispute over Clay was suppressed, but unionists bickered over other issues in public, thereby feeding the nullifiers' superb propaganda.[36]

The unionist divisions became most obvious, and most destructive, in the 1832 controversy over calling a southern convention.

[35] For some good examples, see Drayton, *Oration, July 4, 1831*; C. G. Memminger to Franklin Elmore, March 7, 1830, Memminger Papers, SC.

[36] James Haig to H. A. De Saussure, Apr. 28, 1832, De Saussure to Drayton, May 4, 1832, Drayton Papers; S. C. Jackson to William True, Dec. 14, 1832, S. C. Jackson Papers; *Charleston Mercury*, Sept. 19, 1832.

The scheme, first proposed by Cooper's Columbia cabal in 1827 and widely publicized by Langdon Cheves in 1830, was caught up by the more radical unionists in the spring of 1832. Congressman Blair, distrusting nullification but despairing of majority redress, wrote his constituents in April 1832, suggesting the propriety of working for united southern action. A southern convention, he declared, ought to present the majority with a choice between surrendering protective tariffs or allowing southern secession. The other states, "committed with us," would be "compelled to march 'pari passu' in every movement we make."[37]

Blair's letter provoked the same dispute which Cheves' oration had inspired earlier. Conservative unionists deplored Blair's radical threats; militant nullifiers wondered if Blair really meant "compelled to march with us! Did it occur to the General that we might be compelled to stop with them?"[38]

In 1832, unlike in 1830, unionists pressed the proposal. Blair's scheme, however, was progressively diluted. A large Sumterville public meeting on May 5 called for a southern convention to inform the North of the "true sentiments and opinions" of the South. The question remained whether Blair's sentiments were "true sentiments." A Charleston unionist meeting on June 12 was almost sabotaged by the embarrassing Thomas Grimké. The omnipresent gadfly argued that a southern convention was a dangerous step toward southern secession and, to the joy of the nullifiers, implied that unionists were becoming disunionists. Benjamin F. Hunt answered Grimké by declaring a southern convention a means of cooling off South Carolina; clearly Hunt's sentiments were not Blair's. At ten P.M., with Grimké supporters clamoring to speak, the unionists shut off debate and passed an innocuous resolution endorsing a southern convention limited to advising and consulting.[39]

The Charlestonians would just as soon have dropped the matter, but the Sumterites called for a September statewide unionist convention to endorse the remedy. Conservatives, including Petigru,

---

[37] *Camden Journal,* May 12, 1832.
[38] *Camden and Lancaster Beacon,* May 15, 1832.
[39] *Charleston Mercury,* May 12, 1832; *Southern Patriot,* June 13, 15, 1832.

cynically worked for the scheme. Unionists were risking nothing, Petigru pointed out, for "we may call for [southern] convention as loud as we please; it is not likely the other States will join in convention, as long as they keep down nullification without it."[40]

On September 9, 1832, only a month before the legislative elections, the first unionist convention met in Columbia to consider campaigning for a southern convention. By this time, Cheves himself declared that the proposal came too late to justify an 1832 convention. The moderates split over the proposal, and on the eve of the unionist meetings, Blair, "wrathy . . . about the '*damn party*,' " stormed out of Columbia.[41]

The unionists confirmed Blair's premonitions by adopting an evasive plank which fooled no one. If Virginia, North Carolina, Georgia, Alabama, Mississippi, and Tennessee *all* concurred, declared the unionists, a southern convention would be justified. Tennessee, a mildly antitariff and passionately pro-Jackson border state, obviously would never adopt the proposal; so the resolution was tantamount to rejection. Even Daniel Huger and Smith admitted that the scheme had been rendered nugatory.[42]

Cheves firmly believed that unionists had wrecked their campaign by failing to work for a southern convention. He had a point. Many moderates, although unconvinced by the nullifiers' polemics, voted for nullification because unionists offered no viable alternative. In Cheves' opinion, poor strategy accounted for the failure to propose "some active measure of redress." The party, however, was too deeply divided to agree on anything except opposition to nullification.[43]

Opposition might have been enough if the unionists had organized a counterassociation to propagate their views. But unionists preferred denouncing the nullifiers' club to forming their own. "God forbid that we should recommend a system of counteracting clubs," wrote one influential moderate. ". . . let all the fear-

[40] Petigru to Elliott, Aug. 7, 1832, Carson, *Petigru*, pp. 89–90.
[41] Cheves to Josiah Crosby, Aug. 14, 1832, *Charleston Courier*, Aug. 28, 1832; James L. Clark to Hammond, Sept. 14, 1832, Hammond Papers, LC.
[42] *Southern Patriot*, Sept. 14, 1832; *Evening Post*, Oct. 8–9, 1832.
[43] Cheves to Crosby, Aug. 14, 1832, *Charleston Courier*, Aug. 28, 1832; John L. Hunter to Elliott, Sept. 4, 1832, Elliott-Gonzales Papers.

ful responsibility of *such* an organization rest upon our opponents." Unionists simply could not stomach the system of sustained popular agitation which Hamilton had introduced in South Carolina.[44]

The key to the moderates' hatred of the association is that a clique of high-toned Charleston aristocrats led the unionist party. Charleston merchants and upcountry farmers were the prime interest groups in the unionist movement. Still, such leading unionists as Joel Poinsett, Daniel R. Huger, James L. Petigru, William Elliott, Hugh S. Legaré, Langdon Cheves, William Drayton, and Henry Middleton were as much members of the planter-lawyer lowcountry aristocracy as were such leading nullifiers as James Hamilton, Jr., Robert Y. Hayne, Robert J. Turnbull, Whitemarsh Seabrook, Henry L. Pinckney, Robert Barnwell Rhett, and Robert Barnwell. The nature of the unionist leadership illustrates well the danger of a rigidly deterministic socioeconomic theory of history: some men, for reasons of taste, temperament, and intellect, often vote against the party they are supposed to favor.

The case of the unionist leaders, however, is unusual in that the deviant voters led the party they joined. Charlestonians dominated the unionist movement partly because of their own talents and partly by default. The great leaders of the Smith faction had either died, defected, or departed; the secondary politicians in the faction were too busy attacking Miller to worry about statewide planning. The most respected upcountry leaders —John B. O'Neall, John B. Richardson, and David Johnson— were all state judges. Although they made speeches, they feared that their judicial robes would be stained by more sustained partisan efforts. The old Courier party lacked established statesmen, and prominent politicians in the mountain districts, such as Benjamin F. Perry, were delighted to yield to their lowcountry betters; Perry held Daniel Huger in awe. The Charleston lawyer-planters, with their established reputations and obvious abilities, controlled the party.

[44] *Camden Journal*, Sept. 24, 1831; *City Gazette*, Oct. 11, 1831; *Greenville Mountaineer*, Nov. 12, 1831.

Lowcountry leaders gave the party an archconservative tone because they formed the elite of the tidewater aristocracy. Some leaders, including Huger and Middleton, prided themselves on their exclusive tea parties; others, such as Petigru and Legaré, grew haughty over their rarefied intellectual pursuits. Like Legaré, the clique of leaders "never . . . doubted of the immense superiority of Carolina society" and asked "of heaven only that the little circle I am intimate with in Charleston should be kept together while I live."[45]

The leading unionists, although impassioned defenders of majority rule when debating nullifiers, insisted on the watered-down, Carolina style of democracy. Daniel Huger summed up their convictions in a famous legislative episode. When asked what his constituents thought of a proposed measure, Huger, his huge eyebrows arched, replied, "Think! They will think nothing about it—They expect me to think for them *here*."[46] Hence the unionists' revulsion for Hamilton's political clubs.

The nullifiers, by employing popular agitation, were hardly endorsing the wisdom of popular majorities. Hamilton rivaled Huger in proclaiming the aristocratic dogma that the people should choose leaders rather than determine policies. The nullifiers' commitment to the old order was evident even in the spirit in which they broke from it. Hamilton defended his association as an extraordinary response to an unusual crisis; and immediately after the Nullification Controversy was over, he lost no time in disbanding the organization.[47]

The controversy over the association remained within the South Carolina aristocratic consensus. The difference between the two groups of leaders was primarily one of temperament. Leading nullifiers, instinctively more radical, were more inclined to flare up at northern aggressions and more willing to break temporarily with the unwritten rules of South Carolina politics. Leading unionists,

[45] Legaré to Isaac Holmes, Apr. 8, 1833, Legaré to Alfred Huger, Dec. 15, 1834, Legaré, *Writings*, I, 215, 218. The tone of the unionist leadership can best be observed in *ibid., passim*; Carson, *Petigru, passim*; Daniel Huger's letters to Perry, 1830–4, Perry Papers, Alabama Arch.
[46] O'Neall, *Biographical Sketches*, I, 181.
[47] See above, p. 89; Hamilton, *The Introductory Address of Governor Hamilton . . . August 1, 1831* (Charleston, 1831), esp. pp. 2–3.

instinctively more conservative, tried harder to believe that
northerners would relent and clung tenaciously to old aristocratic
codes. Considering nullification preposterous, leading unionists
gave speeches and wrote articles against it. But they were not
the men to organize the "rabble" into opposing political clubs.

Sometimes unionist leaders denounced the association with
exquisitely wrought phrases of contempt. "I agree that the times
would justify it in us to meet club with club," wrote Petigru.
"But, can we get a gang to oppose robbers, as easily as robbers
unite in gangs? I think not."[48] Cheves expressed the unionists'
conservative persuasions more systematically. He regarded "the
institution of these Associations" as "the most deplorable event
that has fallen upon the Country since we have been an independent people." He had no objection to "occasional public meetings of the people, which express the public sentiment without bias
of party contrivance." The association, however, met "to excite
the people and hurry them on to a definite party object," thereby
inviting that greatest of all evils, "temporary popular delusion."

Worse still, the association required candidates to pledge themselves on issues. "Great national questions" should be decided only
by "unbiased" leaders after "effective deliberations." Ideological
pledges, declared Cheves, are "pernicious and indefensible." The
only pledges the public should require are "in the talent and in the
high and pure moral principles of the persons to whom they may
give their confidence and intrust their rights." The association
could best be opposed by a counterclub, but "God Forbid" that
unionists should form one. The danger would be suppressed only
"at the hazard of raising up an equal or greater evil."[49]

The unionists' conservative persuasions rendered a counterclub
unnecessary as well as dangerous. Considering the nullification
uproar a classic example of the power of insincere politicos to
"delude" the rabble, the unionists took solace in the judgment
that such bogus crusades usually destroyed themselves.[50]

Unionists ridiculed the notion that Calhounites believed in their

[48] Petigru to Elliott, Aug. 7, 1832, Carson, *Petigru*, pp. 89–90.
[49] *Occasional Reviews*, esp. II, 44–5, III, 17, 28–31.
[50] For a superb example, see Daniel Huger to Perry, Apr. 17, 1832, Perry Papers,
Alabama Arch.

absurd remedy. No sincere politician, unionists maintained, could repudiate everything he stood for in less than a dozen years. In 1821 McDuffie had urged that Carolinians meet nullification with bullets and bayonets. Could he now believe that the future of the Republic rested on a negation of the laws? No, the Calhounites' "utter recklessness" fed on nothing more than their boundless and frustrated ambition. "Had John C. Calhoun continued still the friend & favorite of General Jackson," asked Mitchell King, one leading moderate, ". . . who can believe that we should ever have heard . . . of the rightful remedy of nullification from him or any of his tribe?"[51]

Unionists also doubted that the mass of Carolinians sincerely believed in the remedy. The populace suffered from "delusion" and would recover when war threatened. The leaders, according to the unionist formula, would battle over the spoils of victory and split the party. By opposing nullification too strenuously, unionists would hold the opposition together and feed the excitement of the "mob." Since "party agitation" was inherently "artificial," there were great attractions in sitting back and allowing the nullifiers' cabal to collapse.[52]

Thus the unionist leaders, as the most conservative of tidewater aristocrats, accepted political principles which precluded the development of a unionist club as well as permitted apathy and confidence that nullifiers would wreck themselves. In addition, leading unionists, again because they were charter members of the lowcountry aristocracy, often could not escape their share of concern about northern aggressions, and this too vitiated their campaign against the nullifiers. Petigru, Poinsett, and to some extent Huger always believed South Carolina was in an uproar over trifles. Yet Drayton had been denouncing protectionists in unmeasured terms for years; Legaré had been obsessed with abolitionist beginnings since the mid-1820's; Cheves had cooperated with the nullifiers until well into 1831 because of his acute sense of the South's being in danger; Middleton had been an ardent

---

[51] King to Legaré, May 5, 1833, Legaré Papers.

[52] For a good example, see *Charleston Courier*, Apr. 24, 1832. See also Calhoun's intriguing comments on the unionists' misconceptions in Calhoun to Richard Manning, Sept. 1832, Dawes Coll., Amer. Philosophical Soc.

conventionist in 1830 because he hated protectionists and colonizers. As Legaré summarized the divided loyalties of all these leaders, "how could one who deeply felt the injustice of the tariff, answer it to his conscience, if it came to a fight, to take part with the oppressor, merely because his victim felt his wrongs too keenly?"[53]

In the year which began with the Fourth of July, 1831, Charleston celebrations, the unionists failed to develop a sustained crusade which could rival the agitation of Hamilton's powerful association and thereby handed the nullifiers a tremendous advantage. The usual inertia of conservative movements, the lack of leaders comparable to Hamilton, and the party's internal divisions hindered the unionist campaign. But the crucial reason for the unionists' failure was that the great South Carolina spokesmen for majority rule and the American Union had too little faith in the people and too much fear for the South to develop an effective crusade for the principles they professed to cherish.[54]

4

The nullifiers' superior campaign yielded immediate results. Henry L. Pinckney swept the Charleston city elections in September 1831, and radicals dominated the legislative session at the end of the year. The radicals, however, still lacked the two-thirds majority needed to call a state convention.

Some nullifiers, reviving the scheme proposed by Thompson Player in 1828, contemplated vetoing the tariff by a simple legislative majority at the 1831 session.[55] But most radicals remained committed to nullification by convention and concerned only with sweeping the 1832 elections. The great obstacles to a landslide election remained the community's fear of civil war and hope of conservative reform. The association's propaganda rapidly

[53] *Winyaw Intelligencer*, Sept. 25, 29, 1830; Legaré to Alfred Huger, Dec. 15, 1834, Legaré, *Writings*, I, 216; Manning to Swesson Cox, n.d. [Nov. 1828], Williams-Chestnut-Manning Papers.

[54] Historians of the Old South have concentrated on the fire-eaters' successes and given only cursory attention to the unionists' failings. Yet in the pre-Civil War South, as in more recent times, the moderates' apathy was a prime cause of the extremists' triumph. A systematic analysis of ante bellum southern unionism would be an important contribution to our understanding of the coming of the Civil War.

[55] *Greenville Mountaineer*, Sept. 24, 1831.

counteracted the Carolinians' apprehensions. In the fall of 1831 nullifiers set out to demonstrate the futility of conservative redress.

First, radicals made a well-publicized effort to seek relief through the courts. In July 1831 Isaac E. Holmes and Alexander Mazyck, leading members of both the nullification party and the Charleston bar, created a test case by importing a bale of Yorkshire plains. The lawyers swore out a bond for the duties, demonstrated that the rate was prohibitive by selling the bale at a loss, and then refused to pay the bond because the tariff was unconstitutional. James J. Pringle, collector of the Port of Charleston, turned the case over to Edward Frost, federal district attorney for South Carolina. The district attorney, however, refused to prosecute the suit and submitted his resignation to President Jackson.

Frost's position was intriguing. He had long opposed nullification and had withdrawn from the Mercury Junto's legislative ticket in 1830. But Frost considered the tariff unconstitutional and oppressive, and he could not in conscience obstruct a lawful, peaceful measure, like the Holmes test case, "which in the judgment of others may hold out the prospect of relief." In 1832 Frost, although still considering nullification unconstitutional, would join the nullifiers' crusade and lead their Charleston legislative ticket. Remonstrance was ineffective, he then explained; and the nullifiers had adopted "the only plan which was vigorously urged." Frost, in submitting his resignation and supporting the radicals, was the most prominent of the many Carolinians who became nullifiers because the unionists' inept campaign left them nowhere else to go.[56]

Jackson indulged himself in one of his private explosions upon receiving Frost's letter and toyed with the notion of refusing the resignation and impeaching the district attorney. After cooling off, the President decided to accept Frost's resignation, appoint a new district attorney, and send a private agent to spy on "this act of intended Treason." "*The union*," Jackson wrote Van Buren, "*shall be preserved.*" Van Buren, always more cautious, suggested dispensing with the agent.[57]

[56] Frost to [Jackson], n.d. [mid-July 1831], Frost to Henry Deas, Oct. 3, 1832, Frost Papers.
[57] Jackson to Van Buren, July 23, 1831, Jackson, *Correspondence*, IV, 316–17; Van Buren to Jackson, July 29, 1831, Van Buren Papers.

In South Carolina nullifiers offered McDuffie several thousand dollars to come to Charleston and argue the case. He replied that no fee would induce him to risk the country fever, but that to fight the tariff, he would attend for free. The fiery congressman arrived in Charleston on September 17, and two hundred cheering celebrants escorted him from the ferry. Staid old Charleston was in an uproar again.[58]

The trial itself was anticlimactic. McDuffie, noting that the case involved a claim of over twenty dollars, demanded a jury trial for his clients. Judge Thomas Lee, a Carolina unionist, agreed to the request over Petigru's objection. But when McDuffie introduced constitutional arguments in addressing the jury, Petigru again objected and this time was sustained. All questions of law, declared Lee, should be decided by judges, and only questions of facts should be submitted to juries. McDuffie appealed twice, was overruled twice, and then dramatically refused to go on with the case. The jury was left with no choice except to order the bond paid.[59]

When the state legislature convened in mid-November, Governor Hamilton requested, and the legislators passed, a law allowing the introduction of constitutional questions in jury trials. Yet Carolinians were well aware that federal judges could disregard the new law and that local juries could uphold the tariff. The test-bond case of 1831, like the McDuffie-Davis trial-by-jury procedure in 1830, demonstrated the futility of reliance on voluntary measures if the tariff was to be negated through the courts.

The nullifiers, again posing as reasonable reformers, willing to try all constructive suggestions, also sent a large contingent to the October 1831 Philadelphia Anti-Tariff Convention. The proceedings afforded nullifiers little satisfaction, for the convention denounced the tariff but avoided the question of its constitutionality. The Carolina radicals, however, commended the convention's antitariff remonstrance and, with a new Congress convening in December, professed they were delighted to "await the results of this most important and final application."[60]

[58] Samuel Townes to George Townes, Sept. 13, 1831, Townes Family Papers.
[59] *Charleston Mercury*, Sept. 20–2, 1831, *passim; Southern Patriot*, Sept. 28, 1831.
[60] *Charleston Mercury*, Jan. 4, 1832.

Jackson's December 1831 annual message increased the possibility of tariff reform. Jackson dropped all mention of distributing the surplus revenues, noted the approaching repayment of the national debt, and urged the propriety of reducing the tariff. Even nullifiers felt compelled to applaud their enemy in the White House.[61]

The President's argument did not completely contradict his earlier statements. Jackson's position on the tariff had always been enigmatic. In his first annual message, he had endorsed protection but had suggested lower rates on unprotected items. In his letter to the July 4, 1831, Charleston unionist celebration, he had pointed "to the fast approaching extinctions of the public debt, as an event which must necessarily produce modification in the revenue system." And in December 1831 Jackson was no radical fiscal reformer. He deplored South Carolina's demand for an immediate reduction to the 15-percent level and wished "a reduction of the tariff so as to give fair protection to our own labor." Jackson still opposed only excess revenue, not the principle of protection.[62]

Nevertheless, by remaining silent on distribution, and linking repayment of the debt and reduced expenditures with tariff reform, Jackson had implicitly accepted the same South Carolina formula he had gone out of his way to attack in the Maysville Road veto. There is reason to think that the nullifiers' pressure helped produce Jackson's shift; the President wrote Van Buren that the tariff proposal would "annihilate the Nullifiers as they will be left without any pretext of Complaint."[63]

As the congressional session progressed Secretary of the Treasury Louis McLane, Senator Henry Clay, and Representative John Quincy Adams, now chairman of the House Committee on Manufactures, all presented new tariff bills. With tariff reform imminent, Hamilton's association worked hard to establish the proper criterion of an adequate adjustment. The nullifiers, addicted to McDuffie's forty-bale theory, argued that a sharp reduction on iron, cottons, and woolens—the products "exchanged" for southern staples—was needed to bring significant economic relief. The

[61] Richardson (ed.), *Messages and Papers*, II, 1118–19.
[62] Jackson to Van Buren, Dec. 17, 1831, Jackson, *Correspondence*, IV, 383–5.
[63] Nov. 14, 1831, *ibid.*, IV, 373–6.

radicals also urged that only an immediate reduction to at least the 15-percent level would constitute adequate tariff reform. With the unionists almost silent in the crucial months of early 1832, when Congress was deliberating on the tariff, South Carolinians increasingly accepted the nullifiers' formula.[64]

In late June Congress finally passed the tariff of 1832, a modified version of the bill John Quincy Adams had originally introduced. Although the new act sliced tariff revenues about $5 million, only about one-fourth of the reductions applied to protected products; average rates were reduced to approximately 25 percent, but the approximately 50-percent rates on cottons, woolens, and iron were largely retained. The tariff of 1832 was, paradoxically, both lower and more proportionately protective than the tariff of 1828.

A majority of southern representatives, including South Carolina's Mitchell, Blair, and Drayton, voted for the bill. These southerners, although distressed by the continued protective provisions, realized that generally lower rates would make for lower prices. Jackson seemed elated. "The people must now see," he wrote, "that all their grievances are removed, and oppression only exists in the distempered brains of disappointed ambitious men." In South Carolina unionist editors proclaimed the "Glorious News" and presented the "Cheering Intelligence."[65]

To the nullifiers' leaders in Congress, on the other hand, the new tariff proved that any hope for "a returning sense of justice" had "finally and forever vanished." The principle of protection had been retained, and rates on iron, cottons, and woolens—the "exchangeable products"—remained the same. The nullifiers, misled by one of McDuffie's most egregious economic statements, proclaimed that income from protective duties had been *increased* $1 million. The congressional representatives left it up to the people "whether the rights and the liberties which you received as a

[64] Aristides [pseud.], *The Prospects Before Us* . . . (Charleston, 1832); Harper, *Speech, April 1, 1832; Charleston Mercury*, May 11, 1832; McDuffie, *Speech, May 28, 1832*, pp. 4–5.

[65] Blair in *Charleston Courier*, Aug. 10, 1832; Drayton in *City Gazette*, Aug. 23, 1832; Jackson to John Coffee, July 17, 1832, Jackson, *Correspondence*, IV, 462–3; *Camden Journal*, July 21, 1832; *Southern Patriot*, July 5, 1832.

precious inheritance from an illustrious ancestry shall be tamely surrendered without a struggle, or transmitted undiminished to your posterity." Calhoun, who had long tried to restrain his compatriots, now urged them on. "The question is no longer one of free trade, but liberty and despotism," he wrote. "The hope of the country now rests on our gallant little state. Let every Carolinian do his duty."[66]

In the weeks after Congress passed the tariff, unionists finally bestirred themselves. The moderates struggled to demonstrate that the majority had granted significant concessions which belied both the notion of majority tyranny and the need for minority veto. But unionists were doomed by their own previous inertia. In the months when nullifiers' arguments had gone almost unchallenged, the community had been led to accept the fallacious forty-bale assumptions. In the few weeks remaining before the election, moderates had the burden of refuting McDuffie's erroneous figures on the 1832 rates, and had little opportunity to contest the assumptions by which any figures had to be evaluated. In the end, nullifiers were delighted to base their case on the unionists' figures. If the overall tariff was lower, rates on the "exchangeable products" remained the same, and it was these duties which swallowed up the forty bales.[67]

Drayton and others occasionally pointed out that the new tariff helped Carolinians as producers no less than as consumers. Foreign customers exchanged more than cottons, woolens, and iron for the great southern staples, he argued. The lower rates on Cuban coffee, Spanish wines, French silk, and East India tea, for example, all encouraged American imports and thereby increased foreign capacity to buy cotton and rice. The lower rates on East India products, in particular, stimulated a triangular trade which also involved English purchase of southern cotton.[68]

Drayton's thesis was as simple as McDuffie's, and given the

[66] McDuffie, *Second Speech, June, 1832,* p. 4; *Southern Patriot,* Aug. 24, 1832; *Charleston Mercury,* Aug. 4, 1832; Calhoun to Thompson, July 8, 1832, Calhoun Papers, SC.
[67] *Sumter Gazette,* July 7, 1832; Calhoun to C. G. Pegues *et al.,* Sept. 13, 1832, *Evening Post,* Oct. 1, 1832; Hamilton, in *Camden Journal,* Oct. 27, 1832.
[68] *City Gazette,* Aug. 23, 1832; *Charleston Courier,* July 24, 1832.

same sustained agitation, it might have prevailed. But the argument was presented seldom and introduced too late. Despite the passage of a tariff which eased the burden on southern planters, South Carolinians emerged with a renewed conviction that a tyrannical majority ruled the Republic.

5

The failure to win "significant" tariff reform seemed serious enough in itself. The poverty afflicting large parts of South Carolina showed no signs of relenting, and the imminent repayment of the public debt removed the last excuse for tariff oppressions. But in addition, Carolina planters had found renewed reasons to fight against the constitutional principles which protective tariffs embodied, for the slavery problem had taken a dramatic turn for the worse in the 1831–2 period.

On New Year's Day, 1831, William Lloyd Garrison had inaugurated his *Liberator* and had proclaimed to the nation that his views would be heard. Less than eight months later, Nat Turner burned a trail of destruction across the Virginia countryside. For weeks South Carolina communities were paralyzed with fear as wild tales of uprisings spread throughout the state.[69]

Few if any South Carolina slaves were implicated in the Turner affair. Yet the characteristic form of servile unrest involved individual resistance rather than massive revolts. And in the first eight months of 1832, planters thought they saw evidence that at least some Carolina slaves were taking Garrison's pronouncements to heart. Roving bands of Negro desperadoes were loose in the lowcountry swamps; at one point three runaways emerged and strangled William Martin's overseer. A slave in the Marion district murdered his master; another in Lancaster killed his master's daughter; and a Charleston slave ran amok, slashing two white men before he was subdued. The most frightening incident involved a slave cook who poisoned a feast in Sumter on July 4, 1832, killing several celebrants and leaving two hundred others desperately ill.[70]

[69] See above, p. 63.
[70] *City Gazette*, May 19, 26, 1832; *Camden and Lancaster Beacon*, July 18, 1832; *Charleston Courier*, July 16, Aug. 6, 1832.

As was always true during the preliminary phase of the slavery controversy, these disturbances were upsetting not only because of the terror they inspired. Another concern was that in a community which often spoke of slavery with loathing, continual servile conspiracies might lead scrupulous planters to consider emancipating the slaves.

The Nat Turner Revolt seemed to provide evidence that this fear had basis in fact. In January 1832 the Virginia legislature reacted to the Southampton uprising not by devising ways to silence the Garrisonians but by seriously debating the possibility of abolition. To the Carolina gentry, the folly of the Virginia "fanatics" seemed compounded when Maynard Richardson opened his upcountry newspaper for another discussion of slavery.[71] In the wake of Nat Turner, the South appeared, in Hamilton's words, "infested" with misguided "Missionaries"; and this "is nothing to what we shall see," he privately warned Hammond, "if we do not stand manfully at the Safety Valve of Nullification." Or as planters whispered to one another during these first years of facing the issue, "remember the serious discussions in the Virginia Legislature after the petty affair of Southampton, & think what would have been the effect had there been a rebellion more extensive, well concerted & bloody at its outset."[72]

Thus in the period immediately preceding the Nullification Crisis, the South Carolinians' dilemma about discussing slavery became more acute. On the one hand, Garrison's activities seemed to indicate that the South would soon be forced to debate the question in earnest. On the other hand, the Nat Turner Revolt and the Virginia Slavery Debates pointed to the dangers of talking about the issue at all. The uneasiness stemming from this dilemma led Blair to explode in the South Carolina manner when colonization was broached in Congress in the winter of 1832. The same apprehensions led fire-eating orators throughout the state to allude again to the slavery issue during the Fourth of July,

---

[71] See above, pp. 83–5.
[72] Hamilton to Hammond, Jan. 16, 1832, *AHR,* VI, 748–9; Henry J. Nott to Hammond, March 8, 1836, Hammond Papers, LC.

1832, celebrations which kicked off the final phase of the nullifiers' campaign.[73]

Robert J. Turnbull's three-hour harangue in Charleston was the highpoint of the nullifiers' Independence Day festivities. The Charleston Circus was jammed with a sweltering mob of radicals when Turnbull rose to give the traditional noon oration. Striding around the lecture platform and downing pitcher after pitcher of iced lemonade, he warned listeners to shun all thought of submitting to the tyrannical North. A decision to reject nullification, he said, would lead to "exorbitant" increases in the tax "burthens of the South." But "great as is this evil," Turnbull continued, "it is perhaps the least of the evils which attend an abandonment of one iota of the principle in controversy. Our dispute involves questions of the most fearful import to the institutions and tranquility of South Carolina. I fear to name them. The bare thought of these is enough to rouse us to resistance were there no other motives."[74]

6

The last weeks of the 1832 pre-election campaign were charged with tension and bespattered with violence; polite debates often degenerated into frontier brawls. In Greenville in early August, Perry, unionist editor of the *Greenville Mountaineer*, took exception to "a most scurrilous and abusive attack" by Turner Bynum, nullifier editor of *The Sentinel*. Perry challenged, Bynum accepted, and they met at the dueling ground on an upcountry Savannah River island. Perry had been practicing with William Cumming, the Georgian who had so seriously wounded McDuffie

[73] Blair proclaimed that "there had always be . a disposition in that House to agitate the slavery question. It had often been manifested. The next step would be to patronize the Colonization Society; and then, he supposed . . . to appropriate their own money to purchase their own property. He could tell gentlemen, that when they moved that question seriously, they from the South would meet it elsewhere. It would not be disputed in that House, but in the open field, where powder and cannon would be their orators. and their arguments lead and steel." *Register of Debates*, 22 Cong., 1 sess., II, 2340.

[74] G. W. Egleston to Legaré, July 7, 1832, Legaré Papers; Turnbull, *An Oration Delivered . . . on the 4th of July, 1832* . . . (Charleston, 1832); Hemphill, *An Oration Delivered on the Fourth of July, 1832* . . . (Sumterville, 1832); Alexander Bowie, *An Oration Delivered on the Fourth July, 1832* . . . (Abbeville, 1832), esp. pp. 8–9.

in their 1822 duel. Cumming counseled firing "slowly, deliberately," at the count of two, and Perry learned his lesson well. On the count of one, Bynum fired into Perry's coat. On two, Perry shot his man through the hip. A day later Bynum died, the first martyr to the nullification cause.[75]

In Charleston armed mobs roamed the streets almost every night; bloody fights and destructive riots were commonplace. Charleston paupers and seafaring strangers shouted for whoever offered more grog; Hamilton estimated that "300 . . . votes are afloat." Both parties engaged bullies and hired houses. The bullies kidnapped the scum of the rabble, locked them up in the houses, reduced them to inebriation, and carried them to the polls. The procedure reached its climax when P. B. Stanton, a notorious drunkard, sought asylum in a unionist house on Queen Street, harangued against the nullifiers as he sipped his grog, fell asleep at a fourth-story window, and tumbled to his death.[76]

The weekend before the election, the two parties barely escaped an all-out fight in the streets. Unionists marched out of their meeting in Seyle's, eight hundred strong, with white badges on their arms and clubs in their hands, and confronted hundreds of nullifiers. Poinsett and Drayton were hit by bricks and the two sides surged forward. But the leaders quieted the mob, the unionists backed up, and the nullifiers moved on. Charleston returned to the more pedestrian havoc that individual fights and gang wars wrought.[77]

The legislative election was scheduled for October 8 and 9. By the first of the month, both parties had nominated complete tickets; few candidates were equivocating on nullification. For once the final decision lay with the people. Both unionists and nullifiers considered the result highly uncertain. As Petigru wrote,

[75] Perry Diary, pp. 35–6 and entries for Aug. 5, 11, 23, Dec. 4, 1832, NC; Hamilton to Thompson, Aug. 31, 1832, Thompson Papers, SC.

[76] T. W. Johnson to W. C. Storrs, Aug. 17, 1832, Timothy Johnson Papers, SC; John Banillon to John Seibels, Aug. 29, 1832, Seibels Family Papers; Evening Post, Sept. 3, 29, Oct. 3, 1832; Southern Patriot, Sept. 3, Oct. 10, 1832; Hamilton to Thompson, Aug. 31, 1832, Thompson Papers, SC; Jacob Schirmer Diary, entries for Sept. 2, 4, 1832, SCHS.

[77] Mrs. Edward C. Rutledge to Rutledge, Oct. 10, 1832, Rutledge Family Papers, SC; Evening Post, Oct. 9, 1832; Petigru to Legaré, Oct. 29, 1832, Carson, Petigru, pp. 102–5.

"it will be 'touch and go,' as they say, about a convention. If we break their ticket in town, the convention is lost; if we do not, it is perfectly uncertain."[78]

When the returns poured in from throughout the state, the nullifiers' sweeping triumph became apparent. The results were no sooner announced than Charleston Sheriff Jack Irving leaped "upon a table at the door of the State House" and shouted out a proclamation from Governor James Hamilton, Jr. The proclamation, prepared in advance of the election in hopes of victory, called the new legislature into special session on October 20. The nullifiers had won the right to try their remedy, and with the power of the state in their hands, they would brook no further delay.[79]

7

The 1832 election results revealed that the state split along fairly clear lines of economic interests. In Charleston a nullifier party composed primarily of town-dwelling planters, younger gentry, petty shopkeepers, and mechanics defeated a unionist party heavily supported by the East Bay mercantile community.[80] The nullifiers swept the rural area of the tidewater, controlling thirteen of the seventeen parishes and winning 76 percent of the popular votes. The radicals usually controlled the great planting districts in the upcountry. The unionists usually controlled regions where yeoman farmers maintained supremacy.[81] The loyalty of three districts to revered old personal leaders somewhat upset the pattern. Pendleton, which had an unusually low percentage of slaves, voted for the nullifiers probably because it was Calhoun's home district. Kershaw and Darlington, two districts with a relatively large slave population, voted for the unionists

---

[78] Petigru to Elliott, Sept. 28, 1832, *ibid.*, p. 97; John B. Grimball Diary, entry for Oct. 5, 1832.

[79] Petigru to Legaré, Dec. 21, 1832, Carson, *Petigru*, pp. 111–14.

[80] For a description of the Charleston alignments, see Hamilton to Miller, Aug. 9, 1830, Chestnut-Manning-Miller Papers. Unionists often admitted that most mechanics were nullifiers. *Charleston Courier*, Aug. 22, Sept. 22, 1832; *Southern Patriot*, Aug. 14, 1833. Conversely, nullifiers often admitted that most merchants were unionists. *Charleston Mercury*, Aug. 25, 1831; Hamilton to Duff Green, June 8, 1835, Green Papers, LC. This testimony of contemporaries is reinforced by the statistical study of the Charleston political alignments in Appendix B, Part II, below.

[81] See Appendix B, Part I.

probably because they were the home districts of Blair and David R. Williams.[82] In all, the nullifiers controlled almost three-fourths of the Senate and almost four-fifths of the House.

The election was closer than these figures appear to indicate. The nullifiers won less than a two-thirds popular majority, garnering approximately 25,000 compared to the unionists' approximately 17,000 votes. The nullifiers' margin in some districts was extremely thin. In Charleston a shift of sixty-seven votes, or 2.4 percent of those voting, would have given unionists the victory. If Charleston's sixteen members of the House of Representatives had been unionists, nullifiers would not have had the requisite two-thirds majority. In such a tight election, all the events and factors which led Carolinians to vote for nullification were matters of crucial import. The Irish issue in the 1829 Grimké-Pinckney election, the Smith-Miller split in 1830, Hamilton's management, McDuffie's oratory, Cooper's agitation, Calhoun's essays, the association's campaign and its social functions, the unionists' failings, the distaste for being called a submissionist, South Carolina's sense of honor, and perhaps Jackson's handling of the Georgia case were all significant causes of the nullifiers' triumph.

But the question remains, What was the central persuasion, the overriding impulse, which swept a majority of Carolinians to the verge of rebellion in 1832? Put in simple terms, the nullification crusade was produced by two acute problems: protective tariffs and slavery agitation; and to most nullifiers, the separate issues had long since intermeshed in a single pattern of majority tyranny. Of course there were many Carolinians, particularly among the impoverished upcountry cotton producers, Charleston retailers, and Charleston mechanics, who became "nullifyers," as Perry explained, "because they thought the Tariff prevented them from paying their debts."[83]

But leading nullifiers, reflecting the lowcountry's dominant mood, never ceased reiterating that the slavery issue was always in the background and often at the center of their concern. Henry

[82] Although Williams died in 1830, his family remained influential in Darlington, and his son, John, was elected to the state legislature in 1832.

[83] Perry Diary, entry for July 29, 1833, NC.

L. Pinckney, for example, urged that if South Carolina yielded its "opposition to the tariff, internal improvements will revive upon a more extended scale than ever, the Colonization Society will be patronized by Congress, abolition will become the order of the day, and the unhappy South, taxed by the one, drained by the other, and convulsed by the third, will soon become a scene of melancholy desolation and decay, even if it should fortunately escape results still more dreadful to anticipate. . . . the dictate of true wisdom is to arrest these usurpations while they may be arrested: to stop the torrent of oppression, before it accumulates into a mass which can be neither avoided nor resisted." Miller argued that "those States owning Slaves, have a distinct and separate interest from such as have none. With this difference in our institutions we jointly . . . formed our present Constitution; we came into the Union with our slaves, and now the selfish sons of chivalrous parents, would either directly, or indirectly, deprive us of the use of them. Whether this shall be so, is the issue, which is now making up, between the friends of the Constitution and the advocates of General Welfare." William Harper noted that "in contending against the Tariff, I have always felt that we were combatting the symptom instead of the disease. Consolidation is the disease. . . . To-morrow may witness . . . [an attempt] to relieve . . . your free negroes, first; and afterwards, your slaves."[84] Hamilton, McDuffie, and Calhoun fully concurred. James Hamilton, Jr.:

I have always looked to the present contest with the government, on the part of the Southern States, as a battle at the out-posts, by which, if we succeeded in repulsing the enemy, *the citadel would be safe*.

The same doctrines *"of the general welfare"* which enable the general government to tax our industry for the benefit of the industries of other sections of this Union, and to appropriate the common treasure to make roads and canals for them, would authorize the federal government to erect the *peaceful* standard of servile revolt, by establishing colonization offices in our State, to give the bounties for emancipation here, and transportation to Liberia afterwards. The

---

[84] *Proceedings of the Celebration, July 4, 1831,* p. 64; *Camden Journal,* Nov. 28, 1829; *Speeches Delivered in the Convention of the State of South Carolina . . . March, 1833* . . . (Charleston, 1833), p. 50.

last question follows our giving up the battle on the other two, as inevitably as light flows from the sun.[85]

George McDuffie:

Any course of measures which shall hasten the abolition of slavery by destroying the value of slave labor, will bring upon the southern States the greatest political calamity with which they can be afflicted. . . . It is the clear and distinct perception of the irresistible tendency of this protecting system to precipitate us upon this great moral and political catastrophe, that has animated me to raise my warning voice, that my fellow-citizens may foresee, and, foreseeing, avoid the destiny that would otherwise befal them.[86]

John C. Calhoun:

I consider the Tariff, but as the occasion, rather than the real cause of the present unhappy state of things. The truth can no longer be disguised, that the peculiar domestick institutions of the Southern States, and the consequent direction which that and her soil and climate have given to her industry, has placed them in regard to taxation and appropriation in opposite relation to the majority of the Union; against the danger of which, if there be no protective power in the reserved rights of the states, they must in the end be forced to rebel, or submit to have . . . their domestick institutions exhausted by Colonization and other schemes, and themselves & children reduced to wretchedness. Thus situated, the denial of the right of the state to interfere constitutionally in the last resort, more alarms the thinking than all other causes.[87]

The nullifiers' decision to fight the abolitionists indirectly by contending against the tariff raises the obvious question, Why didn't South Carolina meet the slavery issue head on? The obvious answer is that in 1832 there was as yet no political abolitionist movement to fight against. Abolitionists were not yet flooding Congress with antislavery petitions, and committees quickly tabled colonization petitions. Carolinians obsessed with what they regarded as signs of a growing antislavery movement could only wage a preventive crusade against the abolitionists by attacking the protectionists' use of broad construction.

[85] Hamilton to John Taylor *et al.*, Sept. 14, 1830, *Charleston Mercury*, Sept. 29, 1830.
[86] *Speech, May 28, 1832*, p. 34. See also *Speeches Delivered in the Convention, March, 1833*, p. 41.
[87] Calhoun to Virgil Maxcy, Sept. 11, 1830, Galloway-Maxcy-Markoe Papers.

Yet leading nullifiers professed other, more revealing, reasons for choosing a contest against the tariff. First, lower tariffs would aid the defense of slavery. Perhaps the most important fact about the rise of the slavery issue and the decline of South Carolina's economy is that they occurred at precisely the same time; the anxiety depression caused heightened the apprehensions about slavery. The sight of planters going into bankruptcy and Carolinians departing for the West increased that sense of southern weakness which helped make the slavery issue so frightening. To McDuffie, "the most deplorable of all the consequences of this steadily declining state of our pecuniary prosperity, is the moral and political degeneracy which must inevitably result from it." By gaining a lower tariff, nullifiers could at least hope to end the economic decline which might, as Henry L. Pinckney wrote, "even deprive" South Carolina "of the physical ability to act." The connection between the protective tariff as an economic threat and the slavery issue as a future danger became most intimate, and explosive, in such a consideration as this.[88]

Nullifiers also realized that a proslavery crusade would invite external isolation and risk internal revolution. Hamilton considered slavery of all questions "the last on which the South ought to desire to make battle . . . however we might be united at home, we should have few confederates abroad—whereas on the subject of free trade and constitutional rights, we should have allies throughout the civilized world." Angus Patterson expressed perhaps the most important impulse. "The bare discussion of this question," he wrote, "will endanger the peace and safety of the State, and it is principally to avoid that discussion, that I think the State should *now* resort to her inherent and unalienable rights." If it accomplished nothing else, the nullification crusade would surely end that "solicitude as to future consequences" which Turnbull had once called "the worst species of slavery for us to endure." Robert Barnwell Rhett declaimed: "At least it will determine our fate and will relieve the proud mind from the wretched uncertainty of not knowing whether it be bond or free."[89]

[88] McDuffie, *Speech, May 28, 1832*, p. 34; *Charleston Mercury*, Aug. 4, 1830; *S Ag*, II (Apr. 1829), 173–4.
[89] *Charleston Mercury*, July 31, Aug. 18, Sept. 29, 1830, July 14, 1832; [Turnbull], *The Crisis*, p. 138; *Southern Patriot*, Oct. 19, 1830.

Nullifiers, then, considered protective tariffs not only an inherently onerous economic burden but also an integral part of
a pattern of sectional exploitation which would lead to slave
revolts, colonization schemes, and ultimately the abolition of
slavery. The nullification impulse was both a result of the severe
pecuniary distress which afflicted many Carolinians in the 1820's
and an expression of the anxiety surrounding the discussion of
slavery in South Carolina in the years immediately before the
antislavery crusade became part of the national political scene.
Depressed economically, frightened by recurrent slave conspiracies, disturbed by nagging qualms about slavery, threatened by
rising worldwide moral condemnation, South Carolinians had
every reason to dread an encounter with the abolitionists. To
leading Carolina nullifiers, the chance of avoiding the encounter,
lowering the tariff, and winning permanent security seemed
worth the risk of provoking an American civil war.

8

Nullification Nullified, 1832–1833

On October 22 the special session of the new legislature met, received a message from Governor Hamilton demanding an immediate convention, and appointed a joint committee to consider the proposal. The joint committee recommended a convention bill to both houses the next day, and on October 26 the bill became law. The House voted for convention, ninety-six to twenty-five; the Senate concurred, thirty-one to thirteen. Elections for convention delegates would be held on November 12; the Convention would convene in Columbia on November 19; the legislature would meet for its regular session on November 26.[1]

2

The election for convention delegates, conducted with a minimum of debate everywhere, was uncontested in the lowcountry. Tidewater unionists threw away the convention seats of the several coastal parishes they controlled by refusing to present candidates. The Charleston unionists circulated a preconvention letter threatening to split the party if the elected upcountry unionists took their seats. Unionist participation in the Convention, they claimed, would "commit the Party to abide by its decrees." More

[1] *Camden Journal,* Oct. 27, 1832.

important, Charleston unionists, laboring under the same misconceptions which had hampered their campaign from the beginning, argued that the nullification party, like all popular parties, was an "artificial" movement hungry politicos had whipped up. If the nullifiers were unopposed in the Convention, they would inevitably split over the spoils of office. "While party is arrayed against party," wrote a Charlestonian, "the most aspiring can be controlled by the danger of defeat. But when power and office are entirely within the gift of one party, the ambitious, no longer fearing a common enemy, will certainly contend for them among themselves."[2]

The upcountry unionist delegates decided to come to Columbia despite the threats of tidewater leaders. On the evening before the Convention, Daniel Huger, elected a delegate by an upcountry district but sent by Charlestonians to plead against participation, precipitated a stormy and indecisive unionist caucus with a last-minute tirade. "If we take seats in the convention," he argued, "we shall be the means of keeping the Nullification party together." The next morning, however, the unionists voted to attend, and Huger also agreed to take his seat.[3]

Unionist participation gave added luster to a distinguished assemblage of Carolinians. Huger, John O'Neall, David Johnson, Henry Middleton, and Perry were among the unionist delegates; Hayne, Hamilton, McDuffie, Miller, Turnbull, Robert Barnwell, and William Harper attended for the nullifiers. The Convention elected Hamilton president and gave him authority to appoint a committee of twenty-one. The select committee, charged with recommending appropriate measures to the Convention, in turn appointed a working subcommittee dominated by Turnbull, Hayne, McDuffie, and Harper.[4]

While the subcommittee was preparing the Convention's Ordinance and Reports, a caucus of the nullification party debated

[2] Edward McCrady to Joshua Teague, Nov. 2, 1832, *AHR*, VI, 749–50.
[3] Perry, *Reminiscences* (1889 ed.), pp. 214ff.; Perry Diary, entry for Nov. 28, 1832, NC.
[4] The Convention's proceedings are reprinted in *State Papers on Nullification*, pp. 293ff. On the appointment of the subcommittee, see *Pendleton Messenger*, Nov. 28, 1832.

several important policy questions. The movement had always been composed of extremists who viewed nullification as a step toward secession and conservatives who were seeking to avoid disunion forever. When nullification was put into practice, this division was bound to break into the open. The two groups of nullifiers clashed initially over the date on which the Ordinance would take effect. The more radical nullifiers opted for immediate enforcement; the more conservative nullifiers wished to give Congress a final chance to lower the tariff. The caucus compromised on February 1, 1833, as the effective date.

The conservative and radical wings of the party split more sharply over the question of secession. Proposals ran from shunning the matter entirely to declaring that secession would automatically ensue if Congress authorized the use of force. The deadlocked caucus rejected Robert Barnwell's proposed compromise of a mere threat of secession and deferred the problem to the subcommittee of the committee of twenty-one. Hayne and some other leading conservatives joined McDuffie and other radicals in pushing the subcommittee into an unqualified declaration for secession in case of coercion. The decision seemed to indicate that the fire-eaters controlled the nullification party almost as completely as the nullifiers dominated the Convention.[5]

The committee of twenty-one reported on November 22. The Convention was offered the "Report of the Select Committee of Twenty-One," written by Hayne, an "Address to the People of the United States," drafted by Calhoun and revised by McDuffie, an "Address to the People of South Carolina," penned by Turnbull, and finally the Ordinance itself, written by Harper. Hayne and McDuffie's essays were particularly important because they defined the conditions of an adequate settlement. A satisfactory tariff would contain equal duties on protected and unprotected items and a rate of no more than 12 percent. "A protective tariff," wrote McDuffie, "shall no longer be enforced within the limits of South Carolina."[6]

[5] For full reports of the caucus debates, see Butler to Hammond, Nov. 20, 22, 1832, Preston to Hammond, Nov. 21, 1832, Hammond Papers, LC.

[6] *State Papers on Nullification*, p. 71. The four essays can be found in *ibid.*, pp. 1–27, 35–55, 57–71.

The Convention approved the essays and passed the Ordinance within two days. The Ordinance declared the tariffs of 1828 and 1832 unconstitutional, and null and void in South Carolina. After February 1, 1833, proclaimed the Convention, "it shall not be lawful . . . to enforce payment of duties . . . within the limits of this state." The state legislature was charged with passing "such acts as may be necessary to give full effect to this Ordinance." The Convention solemnly declared that "we will consider the passage by Congress of any act authorizing the employment of military or naval force against the State of South Carolina . . . as inconsistent with the longer continuance of South Carolina in the Union."

From the standpoint of the unionists, the provision for a test oath was the most notorious part of the Ordinance. The oath included promises to uphold both the Ordinance and all legislation to sustain it; unionists who refused to take the oath could not hold state office. The nullifiers, however, curbed their opponents' wrath somewhat by delaying the administering of most oaths. Jurors impaneled in a case under the Ordinance, and, excepting legislators, state officials elected *after* the Ordinance was passed, had to take the oath immediately. But officers, again excepting legislators, *previously* elected were required to take the oath only when the legislature demanded it. Since most officials had taken their positions before the Convention met, it would be up to the legislature whether the test oath became a potential or an actual weapon with which to disenfranchise the unionists.[7]

The nullifiers closed the proceedings by giving Hamilton authority to reconvene the Convention and by lining up to sign the engrossed Ordinance. To leading fire-eaters, the final ceremonies marked an inspiring culmination of the long crusade. "There was something so heart-cheering and inspiring in the mode of ratification," declared Turnbull. "The seven patriots and war-worn soldiers of the revolution, going up to sign their names—the crowd around the table—the anxiety to affix their signatures to an instrument, which, like the Declaration of Inde-

[7] The Ordinance can be found in *ibid.*, pp. 28–33.

pendence, was to endure forever—the joy beaming on the countenance of all, that the great work of reform was at last begun."[8]

3

The exhilaration of the last moments of the Convention continued during the first days of the legislative session. Hayne resigned as United States senator and was elected to succeed Hamilton as governor; Calhoun resigned as Vice President and was elected to succeed Hayne as senator. This Carolina version of musical chairs set the stage for the new governor's inaugural address, perhaps the most important oration of the era. Hayne's speech was nothing short of a full-blown statement of state supremacy and indicated in itself how far Calhounites had come from their fervent attachment to the American nation in the years after the War of 1812. "Fellow citizens, THIS IS OUR OWN—OUR NATIVE LAND," declared Hayne.

It is the soil of CAROLINA which has been enriched by the precious blood of our ancestors, shed in defense of those rights and liberties, which we are bound, by every tie divine and human, to transmit unimpaired to our posterity. It is *here* that we have been cherished in youth and sustained in manhood . . . *here* repose the honored bones of our Fathers . . . *here*, when our earthly pilgrimage is over, we hope to sink to rest, on the bosom of our common mother. Bound to our country by such sacred, and endearing ties—let others desert her, if they can, let them revile her, if they will—let them give aid and countenance to her enemies, if they may—but for us, we will STAND OR FALL WITH CAROLINA.[9]

An observer noted 'that Hayne's address contained "a show of patriotism . . . & a *real* eloquence, which gave it *prodigious power*. I never saw greater excitement. I actually saw several of the legislators shedding *tears*. It made *me* feel solemn, for it seemed as if that awful scourge—civil war must *soon* come."[10]

Heady excitement gave way to grim resolution as the odds against the nullifiers' gamble became increasingly apparent. Slaveholders always had less reason than other men to view military

[8] *Speeches Delivered in the Convention, March, 1833*, p. 54. See also Butler to Hammond, Nov. 27, 1832, Hammond Papers, LC.
[9] *Pendleton Messenger*, Dec. 26, 1832.
[10] S. C. Jackson to Truc, Dec. 14, 1832, S. C. Jackson Papers.

invasion with equanimity. During both the Revolutionary and Civil wars, southerners periodically feared that hostile armies would rouse the Negroes to insurrection. It is not surprising, then, that during the heat of the Nullification Crisis, "both parties," as a visitor to Columbia reported, were "afraid that the blacks will take an opportunity in these commotions to cut their throats." Hayne later noted that "the enemies of our institutions (deeming the occasion favorable to their schemes) were industriously employed in circulating incendiary publications amongst us, several of which fell into my own hands."[11]

Meanwhile unfavorable resolutions from other southern states flowed into Columbia. Many slaveholding regions expressed sympathy with South Carolina's opposition to the tariff. A Georgia convention demanded a southern convention, and the Virginia legislature debated the question until almost the end of January. But all southern legislatures reiterated their abhorrence of nullification. The Alabama legislature pronounced the "alarming" scheme "unsound in theory and dangerous in practice"; the Georgia lawmakers believed that the "mischievous policy" was "rash and revolutionary"; the Mississippi representatives denounced South Carolina for acting with "reckless precipitancy." Like the Mississippians, most slaveholders stood "firmly resolved, at whatever sacrifice," to do everything necessary to put down nullification.[12]

South Carolina's isolation was rendered the more dangerous by Jackson's determination to enforce the tariff. The President wasted no time in preparing for action. In early November Jackson sent George Breathitt, brother of the Kentucky governor, to South Carolina, ostensibly as a postal inspector, actually to spy on the nullifiers. The President also transferred several military companies to Fort Moultrie and Castle Pinckney, the federal installations on islands in the Charleston harbor, and ordered General Winfield Scott to take charge of military preparations.[13]

But from the beginning, Jackson displayed that commitment

---

[11] *Ibid.; Camden Journal*, Nov. 30, 1833.
[12] *State Papers on Nullification*, pp. 219–23, 230, 274.
[13] Jackson to Breathitt, Nov. 7, 1832 (2 letters), Jackson to Poinsett, Nov. 7, 1832, Jackson, *Correspondence*, IV, 484–6; *Evening Post*, Feb. 21, 1833; Lewis Cass to Scott, Nov. 18, 1832, *American State Papers; Military Affairs*, V, 159.

to employ force with caution—and to use the army within the law—which was to be the hallmark of his statesmanship during the Nullification Crisis. Federal troops had occupied the Charleston citadel for years. Nevertheless, South Carolina owned the building, and Jackson issued standby orders to relinquish the citadel upon demand. In early December the state legislature requested federal withdrawal, and the citadel troops moved to the island forts. The action had the added advantage of avoiding provocative incidents by putting the waters of Charleston harbor between the federal army and the Carolina mainland.[14]

In early December President Jackson outlined his policy in his annual message to Congress. He declared that nullification would "endanger the integrity of the Union" and expressed hope "that the laws themselves are fully adequate to the suppression of such attempts as may be immediately made." He promised to give Congress "prompt notice" of any "exigency . . . rendering the execution of the existing laws impracticable." For the moment, Jackson obviously believed he needed no further power to put down nullification.

Yet even while announcing his determination to enforce the tariff, Jackson urged Congress to lower the existing rates. Breaking with his earlier position that the 1832 tariff was a thoroughly adequate reform, he attacked the protective system for the first time and argued that "the policy of protection must be ultimately limited to those articles of domestic manufacture which are indispensible to our safety in time of war." Jackson had previously opposed the Bank of the United States partly because it made "the rich richer and the potent more powerful." By late 1832 he had come to see a similar issue in the tariff question. "Those who have vested their capital in manufacturing establishments," he wrote, "can not expect that the people will continue permanently to pay high taxes for their benefit, when the money is not required for any legitimate purpose in the administration of the Government." The advantage of protection was also more than counterbalanced by its tendency "to beget in the minds of a

[14] Alex Macomb to Brevet Major Heileman, Nov. 12, 1832, *ibid.*, V, 158; "Reports and Resolutions of 1832," in *Acts and Resolutions of . . . South Carolina . . . 1832* (Columbia, 1832), p. 29.

large portion of our countrymen a spirit of discontent and jealousy dangerous to the stability of the Union." The December 1832 annual message clearly revealed that southern pressure, and particularly from South Carolina, had helped turn the President into a tariff reformer and had broadened the Jacksonian crusade against special privilege.[15]

Jackson followed up the annual message with his famous Nullification Proclamation of December 10, repudiating both nullification and secession in sweeping terms. The proclamation, drawn up largely by Secretary of State Edward Livingston, endorsed the nationalist interpretation of the Constitution which Webster had espoused for years. The American nation, Jackson asserted, came before the states; the federal Constitution, by creating a strong government, only made more perfect a pre-existing union; a government which could not enforce its laws was a contradiction in terms. "I consider, then," declared the President, "the power to annul a law of the United States, assumed by one State, *incompatible with the existence of the Union, contradicted expressly by the letter of the Constitution, unauthorized by its spirit, inconsistent with every principle on which it was founded, and destructive of the great object for which it was formed.*" He closed by stating that "disunion by armed force is *treason,*" warning that the "First Magistrate can not, if he would, avoid the performance of his duty," and appealing to the nullifiers to "snatch from the archives of your State the disorganizing edict."[16]

Miller sent Jackson's special message on to Columbia by express mail, and the ensuing explosion in the Carolina legislature vindicated McDuffie's prediction that "the Proclamation will be received in South Carolina with universal scorn & contempt as the mad ravings of a drivelling dotard." Robert Barnwell Rhett swore that "if the views contained in the proclamation be correct, our situation is worse than that of the Prussian Boor or the Russian Serf." To Isaac E. Holmes, Jackson's course proved that "we must give up the pen for the sword, and prepare to die in defense of our State." Pickens urged that "if we have not the

---

[15] Richardson (ed.), *Messages and Papers,* II, 1160–2.
[16] *Ibid.,* II, 1203–19.

right of secession, we have the right of glorious rebellion and I am prepared to go into it." The legislature passed strong resolutions, condemning Jackson's position and ordering Governor Hayne to issue a counterproclamation. Hayne's proclamation, although prepared in great haste, was an excellent statement of the case for nullification.[17]

But the nullifiers' anger was tempered with caution; for in addition to the South's rejection of nullification and Jackson's threat of force, the Carolina unionist convention, meeting in Columbia from December 10 to 14, displayed an inclination to bring on a civil war within South Carolina rather than acquiesce in nullification.

The secret of the unionists' increased militancy was the threat of a test oath. Even the most conservative unionists, although dubious about allowing the populace to determine public policy, had great respect for the forms of democracy. Carolina moderates had always attacked the nullifiers for frustrating national majority rule, and they now were prepared to fight for their own minority rights. Legaré, for example, previously one of the most timid of unionists, sounded like a fire-eater after hearing about an imminent test oath. "For the very first time during this whole controversy," Legaré wrote from Europe, "I felt the spirit of civil war burning within me. . . . I fervently prayed that my friends of the Union party would . . . swear that it should never be enforced but at the point of the bayonet. . . . Life under such a tyranny . . . is not worth having."[18]

The nullifiers considered the test oath a logical extension of Calhoun's theory of undivided sovereignty. Since unionists owed undivided allegiance to the sovereign convention and no more than obedience to the federal agency, the Convention could command complete allegiance to any edict. The people had voted to nullify the tariff, and nullification without coercion would be patently idle. The nonimportation scheme of 1828, the McDuffie-Davis trial-by-jury plan of 1830, and the Charleston

[17] McDuffie to [Nicholas Biddle], Dec. 25, 1832, Biddle Papers, LC; *Southern Patriot*, Dec. 20, 1832; *Sumter Gazette*, Dec. 22, 1832; Preston to Miller, Dec. 17, 1832, Chestnut-Manning-Miller Papers; *Statutes at Large*, I, 355–70; *Pendleton Messenger*, Jan. 2, 1833.
[18] Legaré to Holmes, Apr. 8, 1833, Legaré, *Writings*, I, 207–15.

test-bond case of 1831 had all demonstrated that moderates could sabotage voluntary action. Unless a thoroughgoing oath ensured loyalty to the commands of the Convention, unionist judges and juries could wreck nullification.

The unionists, of course, accepted the more conventional American theory of divided governmental sovereignty and believed that the allegiance owed the federal government superseded that owed the state. Swearing allegiance to an Ordinance which nullified the supreme law of the land was equivalent to committing treason. Since unionists could never in conscience take the oath, they were virtually disenfranchised, neither able to "hold office, nor vote for the man of their choice, without throwing away their suffrage." Prominent unionists believed they were fighting for the same principles against the nullifiers that the nullifiers were seeking to secure from the nation; and they considered it remarkable that a convention "called together for the avowed purpose of protecting minorities, could have been capable of passing an act so palpably calculated to oppress them."[19]

When unionists gathered for their December meeting in Columbia, the only debatable question was the extent to which opposition should be carried. Daniel Huger, Joel Poinsett, Randall Hunt, and C. G. Memminger proposed an open, systematic military organization. Judge John B. O'Neall, Judge David Johnson, and ex-Governor Richard Manning, on the other hand, wished to give the nullifiers room to retreat by issuing only a remonstrance against nullification. The issue was finally compromised. The idea of the proposed military organization was watered down by providing for no more than a committee of correspondence, chaired by Joel Poinsett. The meeting also adopted a strong "Remonstrance and Protest" proclaiming "their determination to protect their rights by all legal and constitutional means." Unionists would "maintain the character of peaceable citizens, unless compelled to throw it aside by intolerable oppression."[20]

By mid-December, with the Carolina legislature still deliberating

---

[19] *Greenville Mountaineer*, Jan. 12, 1833; *Southern Patriot*, Feb. 26, 1833.
[20] Huger to Drayton, Dec. 14, 17, 1832, Poinsett to Drayton, Jan. 8, Feb. 3, 1833, Drayton Papers; Manning to Poinsett, March 29, 1833, Poinsett Papers; Perry Diary, entry for Dec. 21, 1832, NC; Perry, *Reminiscences* (1889 ed.), pp. 218–21; Carson, *Petigru*, pp. 108–14.

over measures to make nullification effectual, the obstacles confronting the nullifiers seemed almost insurmountable. Surrounded by a dense and perhaps restless slave population, challenged by a large and hostile Carolina minority, isolated from every other southern state, opposed by a vigorous and determined President, Carolina radicals faced certain disaster if they plunged recklessly on with nullification.

As a result, the nullifiers in the state legislature conducted a series of retreats which made nullification less radical and, in the process, effectively nullified the original Ordinance. Considerable effort was made to placate the unionists. The legislature did nothing to change the Convention's decree that officers elected after the Ordinance was enacted had to take the test oath immediately. As a result, several minor officials were forced to resign when they refused to swear they would enforce the Ordinance. But the nullifiers in the state legislature succeeded in shelving a treason bill under which almost any unionist could have been imprisoned. The legislature made the test oath less odious by requiring officers elected before the Ordinance was enacted to swear allegiance only when their duties involved enforcing nullification. Since most officers took their state positions before the Convention passed the Ordinance, and since nullification was never enforced, few unionists were confronted with the oath. And so the Carolina legislature, like the Nullification Convention before it, made the test oath, for the most part, only a potential threat to the unionists' civil liberties.[21]

In addition to easing unionist rage by softening the test oath, the nullifiers, bidding for southern support, enacted a diluted version of nullification. In one sense, Carolina radicals had found the southern response to nullification faintly encouraging. Nullifiers had always believed, as Hamilton had explained in early 1833, that "the other Southern States would come up and take position by our side" only if "the Genl. Gov't by military coercion should drive us into secession." Throughout the nullification winter, southerners continued to disavow minority veto. Yet

[21] *Statutes at Large*, I, 375–6; *Southern Patriot*, Feb. 26, 1833; *Charleston Mercury*, March 4, 1833; *Charleston Courier*, Apr. 18, 1833; *Camden Journal*, Apr. 20, May 18, 1833.

slaveholders also deplored Jackson's statement against secession in the December proclamation. If nullification led South Carolinians to resort to disunion, the state might no longer stand alone.[22]

The chance of winning southern support depended partly on the way armed combat began. If South Carolina troops used force to seize imported goods, southern sympathies would remain with Jackson. But if federal troops attacked the Charleston citizenry, the South might flock to South Carolina's defense. Thus nullifiers had to stand "greatly on our guard against making the first move." Hamilton reassured allies in other states "that we shall ... put our opponents in the wrong. My life upon it, if a conflict does occur, he strikes the first blow."[23]

Under the terms of the original Nullification Ordinance, Hamilton could not have kept his promise. The November Convention had forbidden the collection of duties within South Carolina and had ordered its agent, the legislature, to pass all acts "necessary to give full effect to this Ordinance." The Convention's edict obviously required legislative provisions for punishing federal officials who collected the duties and Carolina merchants who paid them. But jailing the customs collectors and prohibiting merchants from obeying the law were aggressive acts which would make the nullifiers' cause more unpopular throughout the South.

Thus the nullifiers in the legislature backed away from the iron-clad compulsory nullification which the Convention had decreed and adopted instead a plan they had previously rejected as untenable—the old scheme proposed by McDuffie and Warren Davis in 1830. The voluntary trial-by-jury procedure, however, was now strengthened by the test oath and other provisions. Under the laws passed by the 1832 legislature, merchants were free to pay the duties if they wished. But the legislature provided means by which merchants who voluntarily decided to cooperate with the nullifiers could avoid the duties through the courts. As in

[22] Hamilton to Richard Crallé, Jan. 15, 1833, Crallé Papers, Clemson College; *Charleston Mercury,* Dec. 21, 1832, Jan. 5, 1833.

[23] Preston to Miller, Dec. 17, 1832, Chestnut-Manning-Miller Papers; Hamilton to Crallé, Feb. 6, 1833, Crallé Papers, Clemson College.

the McDuffie-Davis plan, merchants would obtain a tariff bond rather than pay the impost in cash when they took possession of dutiable goods. Importers could then refuse to pay their bonds and when the case came to trial plead that the duties were null and void. With judges and jurors sworn to obey the Ordinance, the importer would be sustained and the bond rendered nugatory.

The legislature tried to protect cooperating importers and to force more tariff cases into the Carolina courts, by authorizing a writ of replevin if the customs officials refused to issue tariff bonds or seized imported goods for noncompliance with the tariff. Writs of replevin had previously been issued when a landlord seized a tenant's property for failure to pay rent. The tenant, upon swearing out a bond on his goods, could direct the sheriff to force the landlord to give them up. The landlord would then have to go to court and defend the original seizure by demonstrating that rent was due. In the case of the tariff, the customs collector, the equivalent of the landlord, would have to defend the original confiscation by claiming that the tariff had not been paid, and the importer, the equivalent of the tenant, could argue that the tariff was unconstitutional. Once again, judges and jurors sworn to obey the Ordinance would decide for the importer. The process was an ingenious way of nullifying the tariff, for in common law a sheriff armed with a writ of replevin had a legal right to use force to obtain goods.

The legislature also strengthened the trial-by-jury process by authorizing a capias in withernam if a customs collector removed an importer's goods and thereby frustrated a sheriff's effort to serve a write of replevin. Under the withernam process, the sheriff, again with clear legal right, could use force to seize the customs collector's personal property up to twice the sworn value of the confiscated goods. The withernam law was another clever maneuver. If Charleston Collector Pringle removed confiscated goods to the island forts, nullifiers could regain the goods only by attacking army installations. But Pringle had hundreds of slaves scattered throughout the state who could be taken for the asking. The collector would then be forced to sue for his property in the

Carolina courts, again before a judge and jury sworn to obey the Ordinance.[24]

The voluntary trial-by-jury procedure, with its replevin and withernam corollaries, seemed adroitly contrived to enlist sympathy throughout the South by forcing Jackson to defy a court if he wished to enforce the tariff. Nullifiers would secure dutiable goods by using accepted common-law procedures; and they would win a decree authorizing nonpayment of the tariff from a sacrosanct jury of their peers. As the *Charleston Mercury* summed up the nullifiers' strategy, "we do not believe that any federal officer will dare attempt to put himself in opposition to our State laws. Our remedy will go on peacefully through our courts; and committing no act of violence ourselves, even Andrew Jackson will be unable to make a pretext for commencing a battle. We will not give him a chance to fight us."[25]

The apparently clever scheme the legislature adopted was in fact a poor excuse for nullification and shows how desperate the nullifiers had become by the end of 1832. Even if nullification had transpired exactly as the nullifiers planned, the rest of the South would hardly have considered South Carolina a lawabiding community. First, the United States Supreme Court had declared that federal courts alone had authority over cases involving seizure of goods for failure to pay federal taxes, making dubious the state's right to issue a writ of replevin in tariff cases. Second, despite the technical legality of the common-law replevin process, the image of a Carolina sheriff crashing into the customhouse was not calculated to make Jackson seem the aggressor. Finally, packed juries and a perjured judge do not ordinarily supply the most respected form of law.

More important, the federal government could choose between a number of techniques to negate the nullifiers' plan. First, Pringle could ignore the confiscation of his property under the withernam law and continue to load federal forts with the nullifiers' imports; in fact, Pringle intended to follow this procedure.[26]

[24] The act for enforcing nullification is in *Statutes at Large*, I, 371–4.
[25] Jan. 1, 1833.
[26] Pringle to Louis McLane, Feb. 18, 1833, "Letters to and from Collectors," Treasury Dept. Records, National Arch.

Second, Congress could require that all duties be paid in cash before merchants gained possession of imports, leaving nullifiers with no bond on which to sue. Third, Congress could authorize moving all customhouses to federal forts or ships. A sheriff might still try to serve a writ of replevin. But breaking into a customhouse was one thing, invading a fort quite another.

Finally, the federal government could appeal all tariff cases to a higher federal court outside South Carolina. The nullifiers, of course, denied the jurisdiction of any higher court, and the Ordinance prohibited any Carolina court from providing a copy of the record of any tariff case. Still, federal courts could contrive to hear an appeal without the original record, and most Americans, including most southerners, granted that higher federal courts could overrule local courts in cases involving the federal Constitution. Jackson could then enforce the laws, not in the name of defying a Carolina court, but rather as a means of carrying out a decree of a higher court.

Even if Jackson adopted none of these measures, the nullifiers could hardly nullify for long. The leading Charleston merchants, almost universally unionists, controlled most of South Carolina's mercantile capital and would cheerfully pay their duties. After five years of sustained agitation, Carolina radicals had progressed little further than the voluntary nonimportation agreements of 1828. In one sense the nullifiers had gone backward. The 1832 procedure depended on the cooperation of the class of Carolinians least disposed to fight the tariff.[27]

The legislature's scheme was as illegitimate theoretically as it was abortive practically. The legislature, a mere agent, could not legitimately negate the decree of the sovereign convention. But the nullifying Convention had outlawed enforcement of the tariff, and the state legislature had permitted almost all duties to be collected. The legislature had no right to make voluntary a remedy which the Convention had declared compulsory.

If the legislators retreated from the Convention's version of nullification, they also created an army to defend the remedy.

---

[27] Pringle to McLane, Jan. 20, 27, 1833, *ibid.;* Henry W. De Saussure to Drayton Jan. 10, 1833, Drayton Papers; *Charleston Courier,* Dec. 25, 1832.

The legislature gave Governor Hayne authority to accept military volunteers, to draft any Carolinian between eighteen and forty-five (including unionists), and to call out the state militia. The legislators approved a $200,000 appropriation for purchasing arms and authorized Hayne to draw an additional $200,000 from the contingent fund.[28]

On December 26 Hayne issued his proclamation asking for volunteers; by the beginning of 1833 the governor and his district commanders were raising, equipping, and training an army. Soldiers constantly drilled in the streets, and for a season Carolina uniforms and blue cockades were standard fare in churches and at tea parties. Over 25,000 men—more than had voted for nullification in the first place—volunteered to defend South Carolina against Jackson's armies.[29]

The volunteer army was more enthusiastic than efficient. The corps suffered from an obvious lack of officers, discipline, and arms. The governor's agents searched the North for weapons, and Hayne established a cannon-ball factory in South Carolina; the nullifiers bought over $100,000 worth of arms in less than three months. But Hayne confessed that the demand for weapons exceeded the supply five times over and that nullifiers would exhaust state funds before purchasing half of what they needed. His lieutenants reported that they would have to use guerrilla tactics in the woods if federal troops marched into South Carolina.[30]

The nullifiers' preparations sometimes seemed ludicrous. One Columbian "witnessed the other day, the turn out of 'The Silver Greys' a company made up of men over forty five. Altho their appearance was not very warlike (many of them, instead of guns on their shoulders, were compelled to carry sticks in their hands to sustain, a trembling and worn out frame) yet it was inspiring.

[28] *Statutes at Large*, VI, 480–1, VIII, 562–4.

[29] S. C. Jackson to Elizabeth Jackson, Jan. 28, 1833, S. C. Jackson Papers; Mary Ann [Taylor] to Marion Singleton, Jan. 6, 1833, Singleton Family Papers, LC; James Chestnut to Drayton, Jan. 20, 1833, Drayton Papers.

[30] *Pendleton Messenger*, Dec. 18, 1833; Hammond to Robert Y. Hayne, Feb. 7, 1833, Robert Y. Hayne to Pickens, Feb. 12, 1833, Hammond to William E. Hayne, Feb. 24, 1833, *AHR*, VII, 95–8, 101–2.

CHARLESTON HARBOR DURING THE NULLIFICATION CRISIS

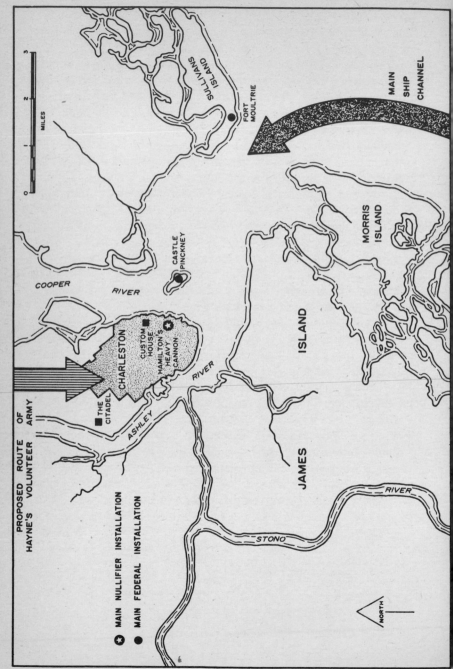

PROPOSED ROUTE OF
HAYNE'S VOLUNTEER ARMY

☆ MAIN NULLIFIER INSTALLATION

● MAIN FEDERAL INSTALLATION

MILES
0   1   2   3

COOPER
RIVER

THE CITADEL

CHARLESTON

CUSTOM HOUSE
HAMILTON'S HEAVY CANNON

ASHLEY RIVER

CASTLE PINCKNEY

SULLIVANS ISLAND

FORT MOULTRIE

MAIN SHIP CHANNEL

MORRIS ISLAND

JAMES ISLAND

STONO RIVER

JAMES RIVER

NORTH

The fire of liberty is not in them wasting with that of life, but still burns bright and steadily in their noble old hearts."[31]

But the Charleston military preparations, supervised by former Governor Hamilton, were not ludicrous at all. Nullifiers had a chance to win an immediate victory over the two badly exposed federal forts. Fort Moultrie had been built on Sullivans Island, and since South Carolina owned part of the island, Hamilton's volunteers could lay siege to the fort. Castle Pinckney, erected on an island only a mile out from Gadsden Wharf, could be battered down by the nullifiers' heavy cannon.[32]

The necessity for a strategy of defense, however, weakened the possibility of quick victory. Many slaveholders considered the raising of Carolina troops fully as aggressive as prohibiting merchants from paying duties. If Hayne sent 25,000 soldiers into Charleston, southerners would rejoice at Jackson's call to the colors. The governor, commanding his army with commendable restraint and caution, also knew that a concentration of troops might precipitate a needless war. Hayne insisted that volunteers train at home and contented himself with preparing for a later march on Charleston. Yet he knew that the state would lose southern support if the federal government instantly crushed all efforts to nullify. And with almost the entire volunteer army drilling in the uplands, Charleston would be vulnerable to a concentrated federal attack.[33]

Hayne attempted to solve the dilemma with his mounted-minutemen plan. The governor asked each district to appoint a small cavalary unit which could race to Charleston on a moment's notice. "If in each District only *one hundred* such men could be secured," wrote Hayne, "we would have the means of throwing 2,500 of the *elite* of the whole State upon a given point in three or four days."[34]

[31] Tandy Walker to G. F. Townes, Feb. 23, 1833, Townes Family Papers.

[32] Thomas Jones to John Boyle, Jan. 28, 1833, Jackson Papers; Hamilton to McDuffie, Feb. 1, 1840, typecopy in Hamilton Papers.

[33] *Pendleton Messenger*, Dec. 18, 1833; O'Neall, *Biographical Sketches*, II, 30–1; William E. Hayne's circular letter to Regional Officers, Jan. 30, 1833, Hammond Papers, LC; Hammond to Robert Y. Hayne, Jan. 23, 1833, *AHR*, VI, 762–4; Poinsett to Drayton, Feb. 3, 1833, Drayton Papers.

[34] Hayne to Pickens, Dec. 26, 1832, *AHR*, VI, 752–5.

To the governor's dismay, the mounted corps was formed at the expense of the regular troops. Some district commanders appointed high officers and many selected important subordinates to be mounted minutemen. Hayne urged his commanders to develop a cavalry elite without damaging the marching brigades. But in the end, the governor was forced to weaken the regular troops by accepting officers as minutemen; there were not enough skilled soldiers to form two separate armies. If Hayne had ordered the minutemen and the marching troops to descend on Charleston in separate waves, the corps would probably have arrived in a mass of confusion.[35]

The flaws in Hayne's minuteman idea, like the general weaknesses of the volunteer army, were symptomatic of the difficulties facing a state engaged in defying the nation. The necessity for winning quick victories without committing aggressive acts had forced the nullifiers to adopt a military strategy which completely overtaxed South Carolina's resources. In the heat of the Nullification Crisis, the extreme caution South Carolina's isolated position required not only dictated a partial surrender of nullification but also weakened the army with which nullifiers hoped to defend the remnants.

4

Meanwhile Joel Poinsett worked hard to recruit and equip unionist volunteers. His efforts were often frustrated by old unionist weaknesses: the petty jealousies of Charleston moderates, the expectation that the people would soon awaken from their "delusion," the reluctance to fight against a Carolina crusade. But Poinsett used the committee of correspondence which the December unionist convention had established to set up "Washington Societies" in many districts, particularly in the yeoman farming areas near the North Carolina border. In all, close to 8,000 unionists volunteered. The total comprised less than one-half of the unionist voters and less than one-third of the nullifiers' army. The nullifiers' greater enthusiasm was evident in their

[35] Hayne to Pickens, Jan. 11, 1833, Hayne to Hammond, Jan. 18, 1833, Hammond to Hayne, Jan. 14, 23, 1833, *AHR*, VI, 758-62.

military preparations, as it had been in their public campaign earlier. If war came, the unionists would have as little chance against the nullifiers as the nullifiers would have against the nation.[36]

Still, Poinsett's volunteers were numerous enough to cause the nullifiers grave concern. Furthermore, unionist recruits were of central importance in Jackson's emerging strategy. In December Congressman Drayton, acting on the advice of Daniel Huger, begged Jackson "not to interfere with our party by affording them the aid of federal troops under existing circumstances." Old Hickory was delighted to comply. Jackson could keep the federal troops at the island forts and could use a civilian marshal's posse composed of South Carolina unionists to enforce the laws. The President sent Poinsett "five thousand stand of musket with corresponding equipments" "to aid the civil authority in the due execution of the law, *wherever called on* as the *posse comitatus*, etc. etc." Jackson wrote Van Buren: "The Union will be preserved and Treators [sic] punished, by a due execution of the laws, by the *Posse comitatus*."[37]

The President's eagerness to employ a civilian posse did not reflect doubts about the legality of using federal troops. Jackson gave no thought to the nullifiers' tenuous distinction between insurrections *in* and insurrections *of* a state. Since nullification would obstruct the enforcement of the laws, he could use authority granted to suppress insurrections. Under the 1795 militia law, the President could call out the state militias "whenever the laws of the United States shall be opposed, or the execution thereof obstructed in any State, by combinations too powerful to be suppressed by the ordinary course of judicial proceedings, or by the powers vested in the Marshals." Before calling out the militias, the President had to issue a proclamation commanding the "insurgents to disperse, and retire to their abodes

[36] Poinsett to Drayton, Dec. 22, 1832, Jan. 8, 1833, Huger to Drayton, Jan. 11, 1833, King to Drayton, Jan. 15, 1833, Drayton Papers; Poinsett to Jackson, Feb. 22, 1833, Jackson, *Correspondence*, V, 21–2.

[37] Hamilton to McDuffie, Feb. 1, 1840, typecopy in Hamilton Papers; Huger to Drayton, Dec. 17, 1832, Drayton Papers; Drayton to Poinsett, Dec. 31, 1832, Poinsett Papers; Jackson to Poinsett, Dec. 2, 9, 1832, Jackson to Van Buren, Dec. 23, 1832, Jackson, *Correspondence*, IV, 493–4, 497–8, 504–5.

within a limited time." Under an 1807 law, the President could employ the United States Army and Navy to enforce the laws if the insurrection justified using the state militias and if he had issued his proclamation warning insurgents to disperse. Although the requirement of issuing prior proclamations could delay military action, Jackson had clear authority to use both the state militia and the federal army to enforce the laws.[38]

Jackson rejoiced at forming a civilian posse, not because he doubted his military authority, but because he was reluctant to use it. The old general remained sensitive to the charge of being a military tyrant, and smothering an insurrection was an unpleasant business. The President was no less aware than the nullifiers were of the danger of antagonizing southern states by appearing the aggressor. Jackson preferred not to use armed force at all, and was determined that if war came, the nullifiers would be clearly to blame. "It is the most earnest wish of the President," Secretary of War Lewis Cass instructed General Winfield Scott, "that the present unhappy difficulties in South Carolina should be terminated without any forcible collision; and it is his determination that if such collision does occur it shall not be justly imputable to the United States."[39]

In addition to forming civilian posses and restraining federal troops, Jackson endorsed ingenious means of avoiding bloodshed, and putting nullifiers in the wrong if hostilities did begin, by enforcing the tariff before imports could be landed on the Charleston docks. Congress had designated Charleston "a port of entry" and had established a customhouse for the port. But the island forts and harbor waters were as much parts of the port as the city itself was. In the judgment of Secretary of the Treasury Louis McLane, a customs collector could perform his duties anywhere within the port of entry.

Thus McLane, with Jackson's blessings, instructed Collector Pringle to move the Charleston customhouse from the mainland to the forts if nullifiers tried to obstruct the enforcement of the

[38] *Annals of Congress,* 3 Cong., 1 and 2 sess., pp. 1508–10, 9 Cong., 2 sess., p. 1286.
[39] Cass to Scott, Jan. 26, 1833, *American State Papers; Military Affairs,* V, 160–1; Scott to Preston, Dec. 14, 1832, Virginia Carrington Scrapbook.

laws. Jackson also put the revenue cutters in the harbor at Pringle's disposal, and McLane told the collector to stop all ships after they had entered the harbor and before they had reached the city. Pringle would then enforce the tariff, taking care to refuse bonds and permits to land goods to any importer who might cooperate with the nullifiers.

McLane derived authority for this maneuver from the 1799 revenue law. The law gave a collector the prerogative of refusing to issue tariff bonds if he questioned the "sureties" of the importer. According to McLane's interpretation, the collector must "be satisfied not only of the solvency of the party but of his sufficiency in other respects, and would not be expected or authorized to accept as surety any individual who should be understood to have formed a determination not to pay the Bond."[40]

The strength of the McLane-Jackson plan was that at least in Charleston, nullifiers were not likely to get their hands on imported goods without either meeting tariff obligations or attacking federal forts. If any suspected nullifier tried to secure a tariff bond instead of paying his duties in cash, Pringle would store his goods in the Charleston customhouse. If nullifiers threatened to use a writ of replevin to gain the confiscated goods, Pringle would move the customhouse to Fort Moultrie or Castle Pinckney.

The McLane-Jackson strategy had certain obvious defects. Pringle had to give out bonds to seemingly loyal merchants, and an importer might use the nullification court procedure after bonds had been issued. Moreover, the state's two other ports of entry, Beaufort and Georgetown, possessed no federal forts to which a customhouse could be moved. These ports were more vulnerable to the replevin process.

In December 1832 Jackson did not worry excessively about these loopholes. If nullifiers obtained tariff bonds or seized imported goods, the President could enforce the laws by employing the marshal's posse. Jackson also gave Pringle unlimited authority to hire civilian customs inspectors. If the nullifiers

<hr />

[40] McLane's instructions to Pringle can be followed in "Letters to and from Collectors," Nov. 13, 1830, to March 10, 1833, pp. 2–63, Treasury Dept. Records. See esp. McLane to Pringle, Nov. 6, 1832.

wished to try their remedy, they would be forced to attack fellow South Carolina civilians.

The restraint which characterized most of Jackson's preparations was almost rendered nugatory by the recklessness of his plan for a precipitous arrest of leading nullifiers. In early December Jackson declared to Van Buren and other correspondents that the "act of raising troops" was "not merely rebellion, but . . . positive treason." Once the President received proof that nullifiers had started to recruit an army, he would "issue my proclamation ordering them to disperse, directing a prosecution against all the leaders for rebellion and Treason, and order a sufficient force as the posse Comitatus of the marshall . . . [to] seize their leaders . . . regardless of the force that surrounds them" and try them for "Treason against the U. States."[41]

Jackson's plan was not totally illegitimate. In one sense, the strategy involved no more than requiring marshals to arrest individuals on suspicion of treason. Yet any such action might have appeared aggressive to the rest of the South and might have provoked an unnecessary war. The plan was altogether out of keeping with the restraint which Jackson demonstrated in other respects throughout the crisis. The aberration may have been little more than the blustering threats with which Old Hickory so often preceded cautious action.

At any rate, Van Buren wrote back that raising troops was not a clear enough case of treason, and Jackson abandoned the scheme. By early January the President planned to issue his proclamation warning insurgents to disperse only when Governor Hayne's army marched on Charleston "in hostile array in opposition to the execution of the laws." Jackson then would employ the marshal's posse to put down the insurrection. Meanwhile Pringle's civilian customs collectors could resist a writ of replevin and the civilian marshal's posse could enforce court orders.[42]

In mid-January the President was forced to alter his strategy.

[41] Jackson to Poinsett, Dec. 9, 1832, Jackson to Van Buren, Dec. 25, 1832, Jackson, *Correspondence*, IV, 497–8, 505–6.
[42] Van Buren to Jackson, Dec. 27, 1832, Jackson to Van Buren, Jan. 13, 1833, Jackson to Poinsett, Jan. 16, 1833, *ibid.*, IV, 506–8; V, 2–6.

The unionists confessed to Jackson that they could supply neither customs inspectors nor a marshal's posse. Poinsett's volunteers feared that without further authority from the federal government than a summons from a marshal, they "would render themselves amenable to the laws of the state, should they fail and be taken prisoners." If Jackson called out the state militia, the unionists "would promptly obey the call." But the volunteers "want to act with a [presidential] commission in their pockets and think without it they will be fighting with a halter about their necks."[43]

In mid-January unionists also had second thoughts about eschewing the protection of federal troops. If 25,000 nullifiers marched into Charleston, city unionists would be at the mercy of their foes. Poinsett still wished no federal intervention "under *existing circumstances*." But he begged Jackson to issue standby orders authorizing federal troops in the island forts to move to the neck "the moment" nullifiers marched toward Charleston. If the President waited to send such orders until he received confirmation that the nullifiers were "in hostile array," warned Poinsett, Hayne's army might capture the city before federal troops received authority to move. By the end of January Daniel Huger, going a step further than Poinsett, wanted Jackson to camp 1,000 troops on the neck *before* the nullifiers marched.[44]

Jackson probably gave Huger's request little consideration. Camping troops on the neck before the nullifiers moved might seem aggressive and might precipitate hostilities. "Your own advice," Jackson pointed out to the unionists, "has been to do nothing to irritate."

Poinsett's plan was more feasible. Jackson himself assumed that a nullifier march on Charleston would require the federal government, in self-defense, to call out a marshal's posse or the state militias. But the President turned down Poinsett too. Allowing the nullifiers to capture Charleston seemed preferable to creating

[43] Poinsett to Jackson, Jan. 16, 1833, *ibid.*, V, 6–7; Poinsett to Drayton, Jan. 16, Feb. 3, 1833, Drayton Papers.
[44] Poinsett to Jackson, Jan. 16, 20, 30, 1833, Jackson, *Correspondence*, V, 7–10, 13–14; Poinsett to Jackson, Jan. 27, 1833, Poinsett to James Smith, Jan. 30, 1833, Jackson Papers; Poinsett to Drayton, Jan. 16, 23, Feb. 2, 1833, Drayton Papers.

any doubt about whether General Scott's troops had acted aggressively. Jackson reassured Poinsett that he would act after the nullifiers moved; the President could do no more. "The nullifiers in your state have placed themselves thus far in the wrong," wrote Jackson. "They must be kept there." Poinsett professed to be satisfied.[45]

From Jackson's viewpoint, unionist refusal to provide a civilian posse or customs inspectors was more distressing than the possibility that nullifiers would capture Charleston. The lack of civilian law-enforcement officials made the defects in the plan for collecting the customs far more important. If nullifiers seized imported goods from the exposed Beaufort and Georgetown customhouses or secured a tariff bond in Charleston despite Pringle's precautions, the laws could be enforced only with federal bayonets.

In his December annual message, Jackson had promised to give "prompt notice . . . to Congress" "should the exigency arise rendering the execution of the existing laws impracticable." Since the unionists' refusal to provide civilian reinforcements for the marshal and customs collector seemed just such an "exigency," on January 16, 1833, President Jackson sent Congress a special message on the South Carolina situation.

The bill which grew out of Jackson's message was often called the "Force Bill" and the message was often termed the "Force Bill Message." Historians have picked up the labels. At this late date an attempt to rechristen the Force Bill would be an exercise in futility. But the discrepancy between title and content must be insisted on. In the main Jackson requested, and Congress provided, means of avoiding the use of force rather than new authority for dragooning South Carolina.

In his special message Jackson explained the replevin and withernam laws, announced that customs inspectors and a civilian posse could not be procured in sufficient numbers, and pointed to the weaknesses in the plan for collecting the tariff before ships reached the mainland. In order to protect the Georgetown and

---

[45] Jackson to Poinsett, Feb. 7, 1833, Poinsett to Jackson, Feb. 22, 1833, Jackson, *Correspondence*, V, 14–16, 21–2.

Beaufort customhouses from the replevin process, Jackson wished permission to store confiscated goods in "floating custom houses" on United States ships off each harbor. In order to stop nullifiers from procuring a tariff bond, Jackson asked to be empowered to collect all duties in cash. He requested authority to begin tariff cases *de novo* in federal circuit courts if Carolina courts refused to forward a copy of the record, to protect a customs collector's property in a withernam action, and to establish jails if the nullifiers refused to house Carolinians imprisoned for violating federal laws.

Congress eventually granted all these requests in the Force Bill. Armed with these new provisions, the President could have enforced the laws in the name of obeying a higher court. Officials could have collected duties in cash before imports reached the Carolina mainland and could have stored confiscated items in ships or forts off the coast. If Carolinians dared to go on with nullification, they would have had to cross harbor waters and invade military installations. The Force Bill Message probed the weakest parts of replevin nullification, making armed resistance to the laws less likely by forcing nullifiers to commit blatantly aggressive acts. Jackson had outmaneuvered his foes.

The military provisions of the Force Bill Message—and of the subsequent Force Bill—possessed little but symbolic importance. Jackson was primarily interested in a congressional declaration specifically approving of the President's use of powers previously granted. Insofar as he asked for new authority, it was to speed up the process by which authority already possessed could be used. The President asked for power to call up the state militias and to use the national army and navy without issuing a prior proclamation warning insurgents to disperse. The federal government could then more quickly come to the rescue of the Charleston unionists and more easily repel a writ of replevin.[46]

Congress eventually gave the President power to use the national army and navy immediately, but reasserted the requirement of a proclamation before calling out the state militia. Congress also gave Jackson the prior symbolic approbation he

[46] Richardson (ed.), *Messages and Papers*, II, 1173–95.

desired by endorsing the use of earlier laws in the current crisis. If Congress had failed to act and Hayne had ordered his army to march, Jackson fully intended to use the authority granted in the 1795 and 1807 laws.[47]

5

As soon as the Force Bill Message was read in Congress, Calhoun, new senator from South Carolina, rose to his feet and asked for unanimous consent to be heard. Since Calhoun had not expected the message, he had not prepared a speech, but for half an hour he lashed away at the old man in the White House. Another great senatorial debate was on.

In the next weeks ladies in trim bonnets and gentlemen in waistcoats once again jammed the tiny Senate gallery, and all over the land Americans eagerly followed reports of the newest oratorical treat. The Force Bill debates excelled the more famous Hayne-Webster debates in intellectual cogency, and the greater national crisis invested them with a heightened sense of drama. George Poindexter of Mississippi gave excellent speeches against the Force Bill, and William Campbell Rives of Virginia ably defended the administration.

The main contest was between Webster and Calhoun, and this time the Carolina senator outargued the New Englander. Calhoun having maneuvered to speak after Webster, seized upon Webster's unguarded admission that nullification might be right if the Constitution was a compact between the states. The historical argument that the nation came before the states was perhaps the weakest (and certainly one of the most unnecessary) parts of the nationalist interpretation, and Calhoun took full advantage of his adversary's mistake. As always, Calhoun matched his unadorned logic against Webster's lush rhetoric and studied his opponent's face for the first sign of dismay. John Randolph of Roanoke, no longer senator from Virginia but still a vigorous foe of nationalism, sat near Calhoun and nodded approbation as the Carolinian carried on the attack. A hat obscured Randolph's

[47] Jackson to Poinsett, Jan. 24, 1833, Jackson to Van Buren, Jan. 25, 1833, Jackson, *Correspondence*, V, 11–13.

view of Webster, and the Virginian's high-pitched squeak was heard even in the galleries demanding, "Take away that hat. I want to see Webster die, muscle by muscle." It was Calhoun's greatest parliamentary triumph.[48]

While Calhoun was declaiming against the Force Bill Van Buren was urging Jackson to give up its military provisions. The President's policy had placed the Little Magician in an uncomfortable position. Van Buren's many southern allies, particularly in Virginia, were restive over his ambiguous position on the tariff, and they might bolt the party rather than swallow Jackson's repudiation of secession and assertion of the right to use force against a departing state. In late December the Little Magician had written Jackson protesting against the statement on secession in the proclamation. In late February Van Buren wrote again, this time arguing that the military provisions of the Force Bill be dropped. Van Buren, ever the pragmatist, could see no reason for splitting the party over purely theoretical issues. If Jackson opposed nullification, ignored secession, and stopped pressing for symbolic military authority, the southern wing of the party would remain as loyal as ever.[49]

Jackson's position had precisely the effect Van Buren feared. A group of states' rights Democrats, led by United States Senator (and future President) John Tyler of Virginia, seceded from the Jackson party. In 1840 Tyler, running for Vice President on the Whig ticket, would help William Henry Harrison defeat Van Buren's bid for re-election to the presidency.

But in the winter of 1832–3, Jackson was annoyed with Van Buren's timidity. South Carolina had threatened secession as well as nullification, and to the President, the permanence of the Union was one of those fundamental questions which a statesman must meet regardless of consequences. Instead of muffling his opinions on secession as Van Buren wished, Jackson went out of his way in the Force Bill Message to answer southern critics of the Nullification Proclamation. The President also refused

[48] *Register of Debates*, 22 Cong., 2 sess., I, 519ff., 553ff., 750ff., 774ff. See the excellent discussion of the debate in Wiltse, *Calhoun: Nullifier*, pp. 186–95.

[49] Van Buren to Jackson, Dec. 27, 1832, Feb. 20, 1833, Jackson, *Correspondence*, IV, 506–8; V, 19–21.

to soften the Force Bill. Nullification, he believed, must be put down at any price.[50]

Although Jackson would not temporize on the South Carolina doctrines, he remained an ardent friend of tariff reform. Putting down nullification by passing the Force Bill, and quieting the South by lowering the tariff, seemed to Jackson the only legitimate way to avoid war without sacrificing principles. In early January the Ways and Means Committee reported the Verplanck bill to the House of Representatives. Jackson and his entire administration stood behind the bill, which would have sliced tariff duties approximately in half by 1834. The proposed rates were double what the Nullification Convention had defined as an adequate settlement, and Hammond and other nullifiers opposed the bill. But Hammond confessed that he thought that a majority of Carolinians would accept the compromise.[51]

With the Verplanck bill under consideration in the House of Representatives, and with the Virginia House of Delegates still debating nullification, Carolina radicals would have completed their isolation from the South by enforcing nullification on February 1. On January 21, nullifiers staged a giant public meeting in Charleston to determine future policy. The meeting urged that "all occasions of conflict . . . should be sedulously avoided" pending the completion of Congress' deliberations on the tariff. In effect, this represented a voluntary agreement among the nullifiers themselves not to take advantage of their own voluntary court procedures until after Congress had adjourned.[52]

Historians have often argued that the public meeting acted without a smattering of legality and grossly violated the theory of absolute sovereignty; a party conclave had suspended the Ordinance of a sovereign convention. On the contrary, the suspension procedure was entirely legitimate. The replevin laws remained in force, and "any importer," as the *Charleston Mercury* pointed out, could "at any time avail himself of them."[53] The body violating the theory of absolute sovereignty was not the

[50] Jackson to Van Buren, Jan. 13, 25, 1833, *ibid.*, V, 2–4, 12–13.
[51] Hammond to [Preston], Jan. 27, 1833, Hammond Papers, LC.
[52] *Evening Post*, Jan. 22, 1833, has a full report of the meeting.
[53] Feb. 19, 1833.

public meeting, which only recommended that individuals voluntarily choose to pay the duties, but the legislature, which had left the matter up to voluntary individual choice in the first place.

The suspension proceedings, like the earlier adoption of voluntary nullification, was a strategic retreat rather than a final surrender. The Charleston public meeting set up a systematic military organization for the city, and Hamilton announced that if the Force Bill passed, he would reconvene the Convention and recommend secession. In addition, the public meeting prepared for a test case in the event that Congress failed to lower the tariff. Since most merchants seemed unwilling to use replevin nullification, the meeting formed the Free Trade Importing Company to import goods without paying the tariff. Hamilton announced that he had sent part of his rice crop to Havana and had ordered the proceeds returned in sugar. He would allow the sugar to go into the customhouse stores and would await events. If the tariff was not satisfactorily adjusted, "he knew that his fellow citizens *would go even to the death with him for his sugar.*" The 3,000 Carolinians jammed into the Circus interrupted him with "a unanimous burst of accord."[54]

Unionists burst out with laughter rather than with applause whenever imitators shouted out "even to the death with Hamilton for his sugar"; thereafter the former governor was known as "Sugar Jimmy." The sugar arrived on the brig *Catherine* in late February. Pringle ordered the ship stopped before it reached Charleston and had twenty-two boxes of Havana sweets tucked away in Fort Moultrie. Petigru "could not resist the sly dig that 'Hamilton imported the sugar to play Hampden with.' "[55]

The resolutions of the Charleston public meeting made February 1, 1833—the "Fatal First," as it was called in South Carolina —a day of irony rather than tragedy. In Columbia a mob of students triumphantly burned Jackson in effigy. In Charleston harbor Jackson's ships stopped almost all possibility of nullification.

[54] *Ibid.*, Jan. 23, 1833.
[55] J. G. deR. Hamilton, "James Hamilton, Jr.," pp. 26–7, Hamilton Papers; Perry, *Reminiscences* (1883 ed.), p. 145; Pringle to McLane, March 1, 1833, Treasury Dept. Records.

Pringle ordered foreign vessels brought to anchor before they reached the city. The collector then issued tariff bonds and permits to land only after receiving full assurance that duties would be paid. The federal government was taking no chances that an aberrant fire-eater would take advantage of the nullification laws despite the wishes of the nullification party. Pringle followed the same procedure with every incoming ship until the Ordinance was rescinded.[56]

Three days after the "Fatal First," Benjamin Watkins Leigh, commissioner from Virginia, arrived in South Carolina and laid his credentials before Governor Hayne. The long debate in the Virginia legislature had finally ended on January 26. The legislature had passed resolutions affirming the principles of 1798 and the right of secession, denouncing the Nullification Ordinance and Jackson's proclamation, and offering to mediate between South Carolina and the nation. Virginia asked Congress to lower the tariff, nullifiers to rescind the Ordinance, and both parties to "abstain from any and all acts, whatever, which may be calculated to disturb the tranquility of the country, or endanger the existence of the Union." Leigh requested that the nullifiers reassemble the Convention and consider the proposals.[57]

Virginia's offer of mediation has often been interpreted as an excuse the nullifiers seized on to suspend the Ordinance. But the Ordinance was suspended *before* Virginia resolved and Leigh arrived. Hamilton had already decided that the Convention must meet to consider Congress' actions, and so he granted Leigh's request. The Virginia mediation offered only the occasion for Hamilton's proclamation reconvening the Nullification Convention after Congress had adjourned.[58]

Leigh soon despaired of restraining the nullifiers. The Verplanck bill had been riddled with amendments in the House and would probably be defeated in the Senate. By late January nullifiers were convinced, as Calhoun wrote from Washington, "that the Force Bill will pass, and the Tariff bill be defeated; at least,

[56] *Southern Patriot,* Feb. 2, 4, 6, 1833.
[57] *State Papers on Nullification,* pp. 327–35.
[58] *Speeches in the Convention, March, 1833,* pp. 12–14.

NULLIFICATION NULLIFIED
291

if not, that it will pass in such a shape, that we cannot accept it, as an adjustment." Hamilton, McDuffie, Hayne, Preston, Cooper, Turnbull, Barnwell, Hammond, and many others were ready—indeed eager—for secession. Among the Carolina citizenry, the shock of imminent disunion had given way to a zealous preparation of arms and ammunition.[59]

But Calhoun, standing almost alone among the leaders of the crusade, opposed that "most fatal of all steps" toward which his state was drifting. Writing to Preston, Hamilton, and Hayne in late January, Calhoun urged that "we must not think of secession, but in the last extremity." If Congress authorized the use of force, counseled the senator, South Carolina must suspend the Ordinance. "A year would make an immense difference in our fortunes," added Calhoun. ". . . I feel confident, we want time only to ensure victory."[60]

Some nullifiers, including Hamilton and McDuffie, undoubtedly thought Calhoun had surrendered. Nullification, like any remedy which threatens war to avoid war, had always been a decided gamble. The choice of nullification rather than remonstrance implied, in case of failure, a decision for secession rather than submission; in this sense, unionists were indeed submissionists and nullifiers always Jacobins. Having taken their state to the brink of war, leading nullifiers were ready to abide by the consequences rather than give up the fight.

To Calhoun, suspension seemed another strategic retreat—a way of preventing secession rather than a means of abandoning nullification. With the passage of the Force Bill and the rejection of tariff reform apparently imminent, this appeared to other nullifiers a distinction without a difference. Yet the crucial point in understanding Calhoun's motives is his insistence on the differ-

[59] Leigh to John Floyd, March 12, 1833, Crallé Papers, LC; Drayton to Poinsett, Feb. 9, 1833, Drayton to Huger, Feb. 19, 1833, Poinsett Papers; Poinsett to Drayton, Jan. 23, 1833, Drayton Papers; Calhoun to Preston, n.d. [late Jan. 1833], Virginia Carrington Scrapbook; Charles McBeth to Robert McBeth, Jan. 26, 1833, McColm-McBeth Coll., SCHS; H. H. Townes to George Townes, Feb. 10, 1833, Townes Family Papers; McDuffie to Armistead Burt, Feb. 19, 1833, McDuffie Papers; I. W. Hayne to Hammond, Jan. 28, Feb. 20, 1833, Preston to Hammond, Jan. 14, 1833, Hammond to Preston, Jan. 27, 1833, Hammond Papers, LC.

[60] Calhoun to Preston, n.d. [late Jan. 1833], Virginia Carrington Scrapbook.

ence at a time when his cohorts had given it up. Calhoun always considered nullification a way of preserving the South *in* the Union, the South *and* the Union. To adopt secession because nullification had failed (and perhaps failed only for the moment) was to surrender the reason for having waged the crusade in the first place.

The notion persists in historical literature that Calhoun was the grand symbol of the Lost Cause, an archetype of the rebellious southerner. This myth, like all important historical myths, has its basis in fact. Calhoun was one of the most militant southern defenders of slavery. But throughout his career as a sectionalist, and particularly in the Nullification Controversy, Calhoun's love of the Union almost balanced his fear for the South; he adopted extreme remedies because he wished to save both nation and section and because he understood the dangers which threatened to destroy them both. Yet he knew that extreme remedies could hasten the cataclysm he was determined to avoid. It was partially this paradoxical understanding of the need for radical action and the danger of revolutionary consequences that led him to devise nullification and then counsel delay; this that led him to urge suspension after bringing South Carolina to the edge of rebellion; this that made him at once the fire-eater and the Hamlet of the Nullification Controversy. And in a wider sense, Calhoun's ambivalent relationship with the South Carolina nullifiers is a classic example of the agonizing dilemmas which often confront a conservative statesman who takes his stand on the brink of war.

6

Calhoun himself soon helped make the argument over secession only a revealing footnote to the drama of nullification. In early February Henry Clay asked the Carolinian to cooperate on a tariff compromise, and Calhoun agreed. On February 12 Clay introduced his bill and Calhoun immediately spoke in favor of it. Clay and Calhoun made strange bedfellows, but both hoped to head off civil war and neither wanted Jackson to receive credit for tariff reform. Clay also realized that his bill would not seriously injure industrialists, and he relished receiving renewed acclaim as the "Great Compromiser."

The Compromise Tariff, a slightly modified form of Clay's bill, passed the House, 119–85, on February 26; the Senate concurred, 29–16, on March 1. The new tariff put many unprotected goods on the free list and provided that rates on protected products would be lowered in gradual stages to the 20-percent level in mid-1842. All duties over 20 percent would be reduced one-tenth of the excess (as opposed to one-tenth of the entire duty) on December 31, 1833; the same cuts would be applied on the last days of 1835, 1837, and 1839; one-half of the remaining excess would be sliced on December 31, 1841, and the residue would be removed on June 30, 1842. The tariff would be highly protective for almost nine more years; the bulk of the reductions would take place in the last six months.[61]

The Compromise Tariff, then, offered far slower reductions than the original Verplanck bill and much less than the minimum demands of the Nullification Convention. The industrial community itself displayed surprisingly little anger about the new rates. Although some leading protectionists opposed the bill, others took solace in the fact that they would have a decade to counterattack before feeling the pinch. No less a textile tycoon than Abbott Lawrence, for example, professed complete satisfaction with Clay's handiwork. Still, considering that the Jackson administration had regarded the tariff of 1832 as a final settlement, the South—and particularly South Carolina—had won significant concessions. The tariff was indeed a compromise.[62]

But there was no compromise on the Force Bill. Most senators and representatives wished to crush nullification once and for all. The Senate approved the bill, 32-1, with many slaveholders, including Henry Clay, boycotting the vote and John Tyler standing proudly alone. The House concurred, 149-48. Jackson had won his fight for the supremacy of national law over the wishes of a single state.[63]

The concluding events of the congressional session marked a great victory for Jackson—probably his greatest victory as President. The triumph had exacted a heavy price. Some southern

[61] *Register of Debates,* 22 Cong., 2 sess., I, 808–9, II, 1810–11.
[62] Lawrence to Clay, March 26, 1833, Clay, *Works . . . ,* Calvin Colton, ed. (7 vols.; New York, 1897), IV, 357–8.
[63] *Register of Debates,* 22 Cong., 2 sess., I, 688, II, 1903.

Democrats were in revolt, and the Clay-Calhoun alliance formed the nucleus of a potent opposition party. The Compromise Tariff was Clay and Calhoun's bill, and the President believed it offered the South too few concessions. The combination of tariff reform and the Force Bill, however, had been Jackson's policy throughout the critical last few weeks of Congress. John Quincy Adams and Webster had opposed lowering the duties; Calhoun, Clay, and Van Buren had opposed the Force Bill. Jackson alone among the nation's leaders had insisted on both measures, and his masterful statesmanship had played a crucial role in gaining the final settlement.

Jackson's superb performance was not without those little ironies which often dog the efforts of the great men in history. By 1832, partly as a result of the Nullification Controversy, Jackson was fully committed to the states' rights, strict-construction economic policies which his Democratic party would espouse for the next generation. But the Nullification Proclamation and the Force Bill Message were based on an ultranationalist version of the origins and permanence of the Constitution. There was no *intellectual* inconsistency in believing, on the one hand, that the federal Union had always been and would ever be a nation, and believing, on the other hand, that the national government could legitimately exercise very few powers. Still, the emotional nationalism Jackson did so much to further could lead to economic nationalism; men who prized the nation could easily be swept up in policies to improve it. In the coming decades, for example, Democrats sometimes became almost indistinguishable from Whigs in their votes on internal improvements. Jackson's nationalism, in the end, would help his opponents' policies to prevail.

More important, Jackson was, after all, a slaveholder, and his beloved Tennessee was a slaveholding state. In less than thirty years President Abraham Lincoln—as nationalistic, as vigorous, and as cautious as Jackson—would have his turn at enforcing the laws and maneuvering for position in Charleston harbor. Lincoln's policy would win widespread support partly because it drew on the tradition Jackson had established in the Nullification Controversy. And in the long and bitter war which followed, Jackson's nationalism would help reduce Tennessee to ashes. Even Andrew Jackson, at the moment of his greatest statesmanship, could not escape the dilemma inherent in being both a mid-nineteenth-century slaveholder and a democratic nationalist.

7

Calhoun spent the time between the adjournment of Congress and the reassembling of the Convention in an open wagon, racing over icy roads to reach Columbia in time to avert revolution. He need not have rushed. Although Turnbull, Thomas Cooper, and a few kindred spirits were still itching to take on the nation, most nullifiers realized that southern support could never be secured after the concessions won in the Compromise Tariff. Even such hotheads as Rhett and McDuffie now favored rescinding the Ordinance.[64]

McDuffie's reasons for accepting compromise were intriguing. The upcountry congressman confessed that he had voted for the tariff with great reluctance. But to the astonishment of unionists, he argued that the clause putting linen, silk, and worsted goods— all unprotected items—on the free list was too important a concession to pass up. The items in question were all exchanged for southern products, and they would increase southern income "15 millions of dollars . . . *per annum.*"[65]

Although McDuffie's figures were as dubious as ever, his new logic was right precisely because the old "exchangeable value" theory was wrong. By 1833 McDuffie had at last come to realize that protected industrial products were not the only goods "exchanged" for southern staples. In terms of the tariff's effect on cotton prices, what counted was the rates on *all* goods, protected or unprotected, shipped to the United States in exchange for southern staples. As McDuffie himself explained it in 1835, "whether these foreign products consist of such articles as are manufactured in this country or not, is a less important consideration, than that

---

[64] Perry, *Reminiscences* (1889 ed.), p. 223; Poinsett to Drayton, Feb. 22, 1833, Drayton Papers; Featherstonhaugh, *Excursion Through the Slave States*, p. 157; *Evening Post,* March 14, 1833; *Speeches in the Convention, March, 1833*, pp. 16, 20, and *passim.*

[65] *Ibid.,* p. 38.

they come from the countries that consume our staples, or from others in exchange for these staples." If he had applied his reasons for accepting the nullification settlement to the prenullification tariff of 1832, he would have been forced to agree with Drayton that the South had won the sort of major concessions which belied the necessity to nullify at all.[66]

The Convention reopened on March 11. Within the week the November Ordinance was repealed, and in a purely symbolic gesture, the Force Bill was nullified. The fire-eaters found the newest nullification a bit absurd. McDuffie sarcastically asked his compatriots "how they proposed to nullify the military provisions of the bill. He thought the army and navy of the United States required something more than an ordinance to nullify them." A few days later "Sugar Jimmy" paid his duties.[67]

The only substantial debate over rescinding the original Ordinance involved the spirit with which the Convention should act. The original committee report recommending repeal called "the late modification of the Tariff, cause for congratulation and triumph." Rhett urged his compatriots to strike out "and triumph." He was sustained.[68]

The revised wording was altogether in order. The nullifiers had cause for congratulation, but hardly a right to proclaim their triumph. The new tariff was a decided victory, although a limited one. The rates had been lowered, but neither so much nor so fast as Carolinians had demanded. And in an important sense, the nullifiers had won because their social theory had failed them. The South would not be in a permanent minority on the tariff for at least another generation. In 1833, as in 1828, far more Americans —in the North and in the South—sold their goods in the international market than produced manufactured items for domestic consumption. The tariff of 1828 had been largely a product of temporary political circumstances. By 1833, with the repayment of the national debt imminent, the majority was bound to reduce the tariff. This is not to deny, however, that tariff reform came

---

[66] *Camden Journal and Southern Whig*, Nov. 28, 1835.
[67] Perry, *Reminiscences* (1889 ed.), p. 228.
[68] *Speeches in the Convention, March, 1833*, p. 21; *State Papers on Nullification*, p. 346.

when it did primarily because of the nullifiers. As Clay confessed to Nicholas Biddle, "If So. Carolina had stood alone, or if she could have been kept separated from the rest of the South in the contest which I apprehended to be impending, I should not have presented the measure which I did."[69]

But the Force Bill overshadowed the Compromise Tariff. Leading nullifiers had entered the crusade partially to win a weapon with which they could avoid an encounter with the abolitionists. And nullification had been irretrievably smashed. The events of the nullification winter had clearly revealed that in the American Republic, the majority would rule; given the stir increasingly visible in the North, majority rule meant that the minority South would have to endure the anxiety being generated by a growing anti-slavery movement. The lowcountry planters could no longer hope to deal with the question indirectly. They would have to discuss slavery openly despite their dense population of blacks and would have to convince themselves that their curse was worth defending. "A people, owning slaves, are mad, or worse than mad, who do not hold their destinies in their own hands," warned Rhett in the March 1833 Convention. Not only your "northern brethren" but also "the whole world are in arms against your institutions," he continued.

Every stride of this Government, over your rights, brings it nearer and nearer to your peculiar policy. . . . Let Gentlemen not be deceived. It is not the Tariff—nor Internal Improvement—nor yet the Force Bill, which constitutes the great evil against which we are contending. . . . These are but the forms in which the despotic nature of the Government is evinced—but it is the despotism which constitutes the evil: and until this Government is made a limited Government . . . there is no liberty—no security for the South.[70]

With the defeat of nullification, the fight against the abolitionists entered a new phase.

[69] Clay to Biddle, Apr. 10, 1833, Biddle Papers.
[70] Speeches in the Convention, March, 1833, pp. 25–6. See also Winyaw Intelligencer, March 6, Apr. 6, 10, 1833; Pendleton Messenger, Apr. 3, 1833; Charleston Mercury, May 31, 1833; United States Telegraph, March 23, 1833.

PART THREE

The Crisis Resolved:
The Direct Defense of Slavery,
1833–1836

For a long while they [the abolitionists] were chiefly men of peculiar and eccentric religious notions. Their first practical and political success arose from the convulsions of the French revolution, which lost to that empire its best colony. Next came the prohibition of the slave trade—the excitement of the Missouri Compromise in this country, and the then deliberate emancipation of the slaves in their colonies by the British government in 1833–4. . . . And what then was the state of opinion in the South? Washington had emancipated his slaves. Jefferson had bitterly denounced the system, and had done all he could to destroy it. . . . The inevitable effect in the South was, that she believed slavery to be an evil—weakness—disgrace—nay a sin. She shrank from the discussion of it. . . . and in fear and trembling she awaited a doom that she deemed inevitable. But a few bold spirits took the question up; they compelled the South to investigate it anew and thoroughly, and what is the result? Why, it would be difficult to find a Southern man who feels the system to be the slightest burthen on his conscience.

—James Henry Hammond, October 29, 1858

9

The Great Reaction

Ante bellum South Carolinians, exercising a religious version of
their vaunted southern hospitality, customarily asked visiting
clergymen to preach their Sunday sermons. But in August 1833
the Columbia Presbyterian Church issued its invitation to the
Reverend John B. Pinney with more than the usual spirit of dutiful
courtesy. Pinney, born in the South and educated at the University
of Georgia, had spent the previous year offering the Gospel to
heathen African tribes. As Columbia citizens walked to church
on August 26, they looked forward to hearing Pinney preach an
orthodox southern sermon on the inevitably barbaric conditions
of Negro life in Africa.

In his afternoon sermon, the visitor treated his hosts to a
discourse on the "moral ruin and spiritual wants" of the heathen
world. Afterward, Pinney attended Francis Goulding's African
Sabbath School and "contrasted the superior advantages our
Negroes enjoy, with the suffering and degradation of the Negroes
in Africa. He told the slaves how much better is their situation
than that of the people he had visited, and exhorted them, by
many considerations, to prize and improve the religious blessings
they possess here." In the evening, the African missionary continued his good work by giving "an account of the degradation,
physical, intellectual, moral and religious, of the African tribes
he had visited." The slaveholders nodded their approval. But in
the gallery, "many" of the slaves, "offended at the accounts Mr.

P. gave of their countrymen in Africa . . . rose and left the house in disgust."

During the last half hour of the evening sermon, the slaveholders' smiles turned to frowns as Pinney launched into a description of the Colonization Society's Liberia colony. The visitor never advocated emancipation or colonization—in fact never mentioned abolition or colonization societies. Still, the white communicants, eying the remaining Negroes in the gallery, shuddered at the allusion to the subject.

As reports on the sermon circulated through Columbia, Pinney's sin became steadily more monstrous. On Monday evening an unofficial town meeting of enraged Columbians (few of whom had heard the sermon) condemned the "incendiary" discourse and warned "that we will not . . . permit the notion [of colonization] to be uttered amongst us; and will punish any attempt to propagate it, no matter how subtly contrived." On Tuesday morning Pinney denounced the resolutions and declared that he would remain in Columbia to defend his sermon. On Tuesday evening the unofficial public meeting reconvened and gave Pinney "official notice . . . that he should leave the Town immediately." The Columbians resolved that "we regard this man as a dangerous character, against whose machinations it is our duty to defend ourselves as against the unholy attempts of the midnight incendiary."

Still not satisfied, a group of slaveholders decided to possess "themselves of the incendiary's person" and to inflict "upon him some token of public indignation, such as might disgrace, without hurting him." The mob, understanding that Pinney would depart on the midnight Augusta coach, "waylaid" the coach at the Columbia bridge and searched eagerly for their victim. But Pinney, apprised of the mob justice which awaited him, spent the evening in hiding at an obscure farm two miles outside the city. The next day he escaped "by private conveyance and a more private road."[1]

The Pinney incident was only one of several dramatic examples

[1] The Pinney incident can best be followed in *Columbia Telescope*, Sept. 1833, *passim*, and in *Charleston Observer*, Sept. 28, Oct. 5, 1833.

of the "Great Reaction" which took place in South Carolina in the years after 1832. With abolitionists rising and nullification defeated, Carolina fire-eaters grimly prepared their state for the direct encounter they had long dreaded and now believed could no longer be avoided. The radicals passed new test oaths in an effort to force unionists to be loyal to the state. They tried to bolster the state militia, to call a southern convention, to tighten control over the bondsmen, and to propagate a proslavery argument. Yet by 1835 the radicals had made little progress. Most Carolinians seemed more susceptible than ever to the guilt and fear which threatened to undermine the defense of slavery.

2

In the perspective of the prenullification period, the most striking aspect of the 1833-6 reaction was that it occurred despite a marked upswing in South Carolina's economy. The nullification impulse had fed on the financial embarrassments which afflicted thousands of producers throughout the 1820's. But the campaign against the abolitionists came during a period of resurgence and diversification of the agricultural order.

The economic renaissance of the mid-1830's was securely based on the rising incomes of South Carolina planters. Upland cotton prices almost doubled from 1831 to 1835; by mid-1836 prime lots of the upcountry staple were selling for twenty cents a pound. Prices of the various brands of luxury cotton increased proportionally, and rice prices, always more stable, climbed 20 percent. As one Carolinian exuberantly proclaimed, "cotton is up to 20 and of course everybody is as rich as Rothschild and can buy what he pleases. Ah this is a great world."[2]

Planters used the return of prosperity not only to save mortgage-ridden estates but also to further that readjustment of the Carolina economy which had commenced in the immediate prenullification period. From 1815 through 1819, agriculturalists had been even more affluent, but instead of investing in banks and factories, they had poured their capital into land and slaves. By 1833, how-

[2] See Appendix A, Table 1, below; R. O. Gage to James M. Gage, Apr. 3, 1836. James M. Gage Papers, NC.

ever, Carolinians had come to a new realization of the need for a more diversified state economy. It was at last becoming patriotic rather than degrading for chivalric gentlemen to take part in manufacturing and mercantile enterprises.

The shift in economic attitudes could be seen most clearly in Charleston's East Bay countinghouses. The fact that outsiders controlled the lucrative import-export trade was one of the heaviest prices Carolinians paid for concentrating capital in planting during the early nineteenth century. Since successful merchants usually left South Carolina rather than risk a bout with yellow fever, the steady profits of East Bay magnates drained out of the state. Prejudices against entrepreneurial activity helped perpetuate the tendency; unemployed sons of declining gentlemen shunned a profession tainted by "Yankee stockjobbing." From the standpoint of fire-eaters, northern influence on the East Bay was dangerous politically as well as costly economically. Northerners were certain to oppose radical southern action and likely to swallow antislavery doctrines.[3]

By 1835 McDuffie and other militant southerners were demanding that Carolinians shed their "mistaken and pernicious . . . prejudice against the mercantile character." Observers noted that "our most eminent men are placing their sons in counting houses on both sides of the Atlantic." Successful planters invested funds in East Bay countinghouses, and struggling aristocrats insisted that their sons go to work. By the late 1830's permanent residents controlled Charleston's mercantile endeavors. One of Charleston's leading merchants was none other than James Hamilton, Jr., the soul of Carolina chivalry.[4]

Hamilton and his fellow Charleston financiers hoped to extend their economic power by securing a share of ocean shipping and winning control of western trade. In 1835 the state legislature lent a hand by chartering three steamship companies with an aggregate capital of over $1 million. The legislators gave bountiful support to the Louisville, Cincinnati, and Charleston Railroad Company in the mid-1830's. The railroad, which Hayne directed until his tragically premature death in 1839, represented South

[3] For an excellent example, see *Charleston Mercury*, Sept. 12, 1835.
[4] *Camden Journal*, Dec. 5, 1835; *The Disabilities of Charleston for Complete and Equal Taxation* . . . (Charleston, 1857), pp. 36–7.

Carolina's greatest effort to tap the trade of the Ohio valley and Hayne's final attempt to secure a lasting economic basis for a South-West political alliance. In 1836 the state legislature subscribed for $1 million of company stock. A year later the legislature agreed to underwrite a $2 million loan.[5]

In addition, the legislators took steps to redress that state banking imbalance which had helped pull down the upcountry economy in the prenullification period. By 1835 the great fall-line towns—Columbia, Camden, Cheraw, and Hamburg—had all won private bank charters. In the spring of 1835, genteel Charleston experienced a spectacular banking orgy; over $90 million were subscribed for $2 million worth of stock in the new Bank of Charleston as rival groups of stockholders fought for control of the board of directors. The bank president turned out to be that new Charleston entrepreneur, James Hamilton, Jr.[6]

In all, private banking capital more than doubled throughout the state from 1831 to 1836, and the combined total of public and private banking capital almost quadrupled in the upcountry. Yet South Carolina banks survived the Panic of 1837 and the low cotton prices of the early forties with no bankruptcies and relatively few specie suspensions. The stability of a banking system which expanded so fast and was so quickly beset by economic depression underscores the overly restricted nature of upcountry banking in the 1820's.

The legislature chartered and Carolinians supported several new textile mills in the mid-1830's. The two largest cotton factories, the Vaucluse Company and the Saluda Manufacturing Company, received charters in 1833 and 1834, respectively, and were producing cloth by the late 1830's. Both companies used slaves extensively and each included planters among its shareholders. A total of seven cotton factories were started in central and lower South Carolina between 1828 and 1838.[7]

[5] *Statutes at Large,* VIII, 409–29; Derrick, *South Carolina Railroad,* chs. 9–12.

[6] *Statutes at Large,* VIII, 58–64, 68–70; Joseph Johnson to Biddle, June 3, 1835, Potter to Biddle, June 13, 1835, Biddle Papers; Hamilton to Green, June 8, 1835, Green Papers.

[7] *Proceedings of the Agricultural Convention,* pp. 235ff.; E. M. Lander, Jr., "Slave Labor in South Carolina Cotton Mills," *Journal of Negro History,* XXXVIII (Apr. 1953), 161–73. The economic renaissance chronicled here is traced in greater detail in Alfred G. Smith, Jr., *Economic Readjustment of an Old Cotton State: South Carolina, 1820–1860* (Columbia, 1958).

The Carolinians' somewhat diversified economic investments in the mid-1830's contrast sharply with their almost exclusive devotion to agriculture in the 1820's. But it would be a mistake to overemphasize the economic readjustment which took place in the years after 1832. Many planters continued to despise Yankee enterprises, and several of the companies so hopefully begun in the mid-1830's had disappeared by 1850.[8] Hayne's railroad company succeeded only in linking up Columbia with the Charleston-Hamburg line; none of the steamship companies sent a single ship to Europe; the Vaucluse and Saluda factories staggered through crisis after crisis. South Carolinians remained addicted to a predominantly agricultural, quasi-colonial economy, and although periodic campaigns for more scientific farming enjoyed marked success, planting techniques often remained wasteful and slovenly.

Yet the Carolina economy was far stronger in the 1840's than it had been in the 1820's. The intrastate railroad system lowered transportation costs; the establishment of resident Charleston merchants eased the severe specie drain; the expanded banking system created a more adequate upcountry circulating medium; the progressively lower tariff perhaps made for lower consumer prices; the improved agricultural techniques led to higher agricultural profits. All in all, Carolinians could afford full confidence in their economy throughout the period of the postnullification reaction.

3

While economic conditions dramatically improved, the threat northern "fanatics" posed grew more serious during the 1833–6 period. In the years when South Carolina had renounced nationalism and embraced nullification, the abolitionist movement, although slowly growing in strength, had been a barely recognizable threat. Few northerners worried excessively about slavery in the 1820's, and those who did usually joined the inept Coloniza-

[8] The old distrust of capitalistic enterprise and the new enthusiasm for Carolina projects sometimes led to ambivalent economic attitudes. See Butler to Hammond, June 23, 1834, Hammond Papers, LC; James Walker to King, Sept. 30, 1839, King Papers, NC.

tion Society. The antiabolitionist impulse behind the nullification crusade was a measure of South Carolina's anxiety about slavery rather than a tribute to the strength of the antislavery movement.

But in the years immediately after 1832, abolitionists became more of a factor on the northern political scene. In New England Garrison and fellow agitators appealed with increasing success to the Quaker and Puritan conscience. In the West Theodore Dwight Weld and other exhorters preached in the wake of Charles G. Finney's religious revival, winning enthusiastic converts to the antislavery crusade. The two wings of the movement joined together to form the American Anti-Slavery Society in December 1833. By 1835 the society, backed by wealthy northerners, such as Arthur and Lewis Tappan, had established hundreds of local chapters and was bombarding Congress with thousands of antislavery petitions.[9]

The growth of an organized antislavery movement seemed the more ominous in the perspective the triumph of English abolitionists supplied. In 1827 Hayne and Turnbull had pointed out that William Wilberforce was gaining ground in England. In 1833 these premonitions were realized when English reformers pushed the Emancipation Bill through Parliament, freeing all slaves in the British West Indies. The lesson of San Domingo was augmented by the example in Britain's colony; "incendiary" ideas could provoke successful slave revolts, and abolitionist movements could gain sweeping legislative victories. And as fire-eaters incessantly warned their followers, if a northern majority ruled the Republic, southern states would be "as virtually colonies as the British West Indies—as much at the mercy of knavish and fanatical speculators, and with no greater security for their liberty and property."[10]

[9] The best account of the Garrisonian abolitionists is in John L. Thomas, *The Liberator: William Lloyd Garrison* (Boston, 1963); the best account of Weld and his followers is in Gilbert H. Barnes, *The Anti-Slavery Impulse, 1830–1844* (New York, 1933). For a solid review of the whole movement, see Filler, *The Crusade Against Slavery.*

[10] *Charleston Mercury*, Sept. 27, 1833. The English Emancipation Bill was, I think, one of the more important reasons for the intensity of the Great Reaction. For some good examples see McDuffie in *Camden Journal and Southern Whig*, Nov. 28, 1835; [Harper], *Anniversary Oration; Delivered . . . December 9, 1835* (Charleston, 1835), p. 8; [Preston], *Speech . . . on the Abolition Question . . . March 1, 1836* (n.p., 1836), pp. 2ff.

Despite the distressing British precedent, many Carolinians, particularly among the unionists, believed that the antislavery movement should be ignored unless it reached formidable proportions. Moderates pointed out that the Carolina radicals were still overreacting to what continued to be a distant threat. By 1835 abolitionists had gained only a few thousand supporters and remained in a tiny minority throughout the nation. Moreover, in the mid-1830's northern mobs carried opposition to the point of suppression, pelting antislavery agitators with rotten eggs and tomatoes, and chasing them out of town before they could secure a hearing. Since northerners wished to let the question sleep, argued opponents of a militant southern stand, "it would be folly and madness in us to disturb its slumbers." As James Blair lucidly expounded the moderates' argument, "suppose you contemplated nothing unfair or violent towards me, and I make it a point to charge you publicly with an intention to rob me and cut my throat, would you not find it difficult to keep your hands off me?"[11]

But most Carolinians, especially in the lowcountry, continued to fear that a small number of "fanatics" could menace an institution like slavery. Furthermore, it seemed dubious that the North would remain antagonistic to the reformers for long. Carolina planters knew in their own hearts the powerful appeal of antislavery ideas, and the English example had taught them how quickly abolitionists could capture an initially hostile nation. "For the first 25 years," Arthur P. Hayne pointed out to President Jackson, "Mr. Wilberforce was repeatedly mobbed in the Streets of London for his fanatical doctrines." But "in less than 25 years," Wilberforce "guided" the English people to take *strong hold upon this their darling abstraction,* viz that as liberty . . . was sweet—so Slavery must be *'a bitter draught'.* . . . *It is not the fanaticks at the North that the South fear,"* Hayne concluded. *"It is this abstract love for liberty, it is that the moral power of all Europe is against us—it is this that the South fears."*[12]

There seemed to be only one solution. The South had to force the issue, to organize the most uncompromising proslavery cam-

[11] Blair to Peter Wiley *et al.,* June 12, 1833, *Charleston Courier,* July 18, 1833.
[12] Hayne to Jackson, Nov. 11, 1835, Jackson Papers.

paign, to compel the North to silence the abolitionists once and for all before it was too late. South Carolinians opted for this solution with considerable misgivings. By pressing the question, planters might bring on more servile conspiracies; and by mounting a crusade in the face of southern supineness, nullifiers might once again find themselves standing alone. Yet despite their fear of the consequences of agitation, most Carolina planters saw no choice but to prepare to meet the question at the threshold.

4

The nullifiers' long-standing uneasiness about confronting the abolitionists lies behind much of the virulence of that test-oath campaign which dominated South Carolina politics in the two years after the Nullification Controversy. Although qualms about bondage were rampant at tidewater, unionist districts appeared more likely to sap a proslavery effort. Unionists had been "disloyal" during the Nullification Crisis, and Yankee merchants and slaveless farmers seemed susceptible to antislavery nostrums. Nullifiers were determined that when the showdown with the abolitionists came, South Carolina would "have the power of commanding the services of its citizens." The best means of avoiding "distracted councils and a divided population," they concluded, was a permanent test oath.[13]

The test oath in the November 1832 Nullification Ordinance had contained pledges to enforce both the Ordinance and all legislation to sustain it. When the March 1833 Convention rescinded the November Ordinance, it repealed the old test oath. A new oath would clearly be an addition to the state constitution. The Carolina constitution provided that only a two-thirds majority of each house in two successive legislatures could enact constitutional amendments. Thus the legislature could not pass an oath quickly or by a simple majority. But a sovereign convention, as the body which had created the constitution, could revise its own handiwork at any time and by any majority. Most nullifiers in the March 1833 Convention hoped to include a new oath in the proposed Ordinance nullifying the Force Bill.

The March Convention, like its November predecessor, ap-

[13] Turnbull in *Speeches Delivered in the Convention, March, 1833*, p. 56.

pointed a select committee of twenty-one to report appropriate measures. The select committee appointed a working subcommittee, chaired by Turnbull. After hours of deliberation, Turnbull's subcommittee recommended to the select committee that the Force Bill Ordinance require all state officers to swear "primary and paramount allegiance" to the "free, sovereign and independent" state of South Carolina.[14]

A majority of the select committee, however, questioned the expediency of pushing ahead with such a thoroughgoing oath. Since unionists continued to believe that the allegiance owed the federal government superseded the allegiance owed the state, Turnbull's wording invited a full-scale revolt. Furthermore, leading nullifiers doubted that they could control their party well enough to procure so harsh an exaction.

The select committee of twenty-one decided to include a diluted version of Turnbull's oath as part of the Ordinance nullifying the Force Bill it reported to the Convention. The proposed oath, which would have been required of all state officers except legislators *hereafter* elected, contained the vague assertion: "I declare that my allegiance is due to the said state, and hereby renounce and abjure all other allegiance incompatible therewith." Since unionists admitted that they owed *some* allegiance to the state, a unionist official could take the oath and deny that the allegiance owed the federal government was "incompatible therewith."[15]

Still, judicial construction could transform vague phrases into a tyrannical oath. Future judges might argue that the oath's meaning depended on the Convention's intent, and a pack of nullifiers could only intend "exclusive" or "paramount" allegiance when they used the fateful word at all. Thus the unionist delegates, led by Perry and O'Neall, demanded that the Convention drop the oath.

The unionist attack intensified the division in the nullification party over the test oath. The most radical group of nullifiers, led by former Governor John L. Wilson, approved of the select committee's vague oath but wished to expand the number of

[14] Perry Diary, entry for March 30, 1833, NC.
[15] *Charleston Courier*, March 18, 1833.

Carolinians required to take it. Wilson argued that the Convention should impose the oath not only on officers hereafter elected but also on officers previously elected. He urged that election managers be allowed to require all *voters* to take the oath.[16]

Meanwhile a more moderate group of nullifiers, led by Miller and Barnwell, hoped to placate the unionists by omitting an oath entirely. The legislature could still pass an oath by constitutional amendment, argued Miller, and unionists would cool off in the two years before an amendment could be ratified. Miller's prospects were increased when the Convention voted to reject Wilson's ultra proposals; the majority of Wilsonians preferred to pass the problem on to the legislature rather than to settle for the select committee's circumscribed oath.

With the breach in the nullification party widening, the unionists' defective strategy became increasingly important. The low-country unionists had refused to run candidates for convention seats in 1832 and had tried to prevent upcountry unionist delegates from attending the November Convention. Now, in February 1833, Poinsett, Petigru, and Daniel Huger issued a circular letter urging unionist delegates to stay away from the March Convention. "The Union is endangered by the fury of party," wrote the Charlestonians, "and the presence of a minority . . . serves only to ensure to the leaders of the majority an unlimited control over their followers." At the last minute, Huger attempted to countermand the previous instructions, but his letter reached some delegates too late to ensure attendance. Only sixteen of the twenty-six unionists came to Columbia.[17]

Despite the meager unionist turnout, the select committee's oath faced rough sledding in the Convention. With the vote on the Force Bill Ordinance imminent, the nullification party caucused and engaged in hours of bitter wrangling. The caucus finally agreed to a substitute amendment, crossing out the select committee's oath but giving the legislature special authority to pass a test oath by a simple majority. Unionists would be placated until

[16] *Ibid.,* March 21, 1833.
[17] Poinsett *et al.* to Perry, Feb. 21, 1833, Huger to Perry, n.d. [postmarked March 4, 1833], Perry Papers, Alabama Arch.; Manning to Poinsett, March 29, 1833, Poinsett Papers.

the legislature met in December, and nullifiers could then enact an oath without securing the two-thirds majorities or enduring the two-year delay required to ratify a constitutional amendment.

At first glance, the caucus decision appeared to be a major concession to the unionists, for an immediate convention oath had been dropped. Yet as Miller remarked to unionist leaders after emerging from the caucus, the nullifiers had actually *"made it a d——d sight worse than it was before."* The select committee's oath had been only potentially tyrannical because of its vague wording. But the caucus added a clear definition of allegiance to the provision that the legislature could require "such allegiance" at any time. According to the amendment proposed by the caucus, "the allegiance of the citizens . . . is due to the . . . State, and . . . obedience only, and not allegiance, is due . . . to any other power or authority, to whom a controul over them has been or may be delegated by the state." The distinction between the absolute allegiance owed a sovereign convention and the conditional obedience owed the federal agency was, of course, the essence of Calhoun's theory of nullification. If the legislature required a pledge of "such allegiance" as a prerequisite to state office, unionists would be virtually disenfranchised.[18]

From the standpoint of most nullifiers, the crucial point was that the convention oath had been discarded and the whole matter turned over to the legislature. The caucus proposal, although potentially stronger, had a better chance of passing than the select-committee oath. The Convention voted, ninety to sixty-one, to strike out the old oath and to add the new proposal to the Force Bill Ordinance.

Despite his waning support among nullification moderates, Miller then moved that all mention of oaths be stricken out of the Ordinance. The sixteen unionists present and eighteen of the thirty supporters of Wilson's ultra views voted with the Miller-Barnwell moderates, and Miller's motion lost by only six votes, seventy-nine to seventy-three. Moments later, the Ordinance was passed and engrossed. Judge David Johnson, one of the least

[18] O'Neall, *Biographical Sketches*, II, 412–13; *Charleston Courier*, March 21, 1833.

excitable unionists, turned to Perry and declared that "you may go home and convert your plowshares into swords and your pruning hooks into spears for we shall have to fight."[19]

But as Perry and O'Neall knew very well, no one would have had to go home and fight if unionists had attended the Convention in full strength. If the ten absent unionist delegates had attended the March Convention, Miller's attempt to drop all mention of oaths would have succeeded by four votes instead of failing by six; if unionists had elected their full complement of convention delegates in November, Miller would have won a landslide victory; if the definition of allegiance and provisions for a legislative oath had been stricken out of the Force Bill Ordinance, the entire 1833-4 test-oath controversy might have been avoided. Few political parties in American history have so directly caused their own misfortunes.[20]

The unionists had miscalculated in every essential. The nullifiers had not divided over the spoils of office but rather over questions of policy; the presence of some unionist delegates had provoked rather than precluded the radicals' schism; the absence of other unionists had prevented the division from becoming disastrous. In a wider sense, the test-oath debacle was the final result of the erroneous assumptions about political parties which had wrecked unionist efforts from the beginning. Since tidewater unionists assumed that a "party" is nothing but a collection of spoilsmen, and that the democratic process cannot withstand an intense public election campaign, they had tended to shy away from effective opposition and to wait for the nullifiers' "cabal" to collapse. In the 1831-2 campaign, unionists had contributed to their own defeat by their aversion to popular agitation. In the angry controversy which followed the defeat of Miller's motion in the March Convention, unionists paid for their distrust of democracy by being forced to wage a two-year crusade to protect their own democratic rights.

[19] *Evening Post*, March 21, 1833; Perry Diary, entry for March 30, 1833, NC. The various roll-call votes on the test oath are recorded in *State Papers on Nullification*, pp. 359–62.

[20] Perry, *Reminiscences* (1889 ed.), p. 228; O'Neall, *Biographical Sketches*, I, 182, II, 17, 413.

5

When the legislature convened in late 1833, nullifiers split again, this time over the expediency of using the special authority granted in the Ordinance. The more conservative nullifiers favored ignoring the Ordinance and passing an oath as a constitutional amendment. The more militant radicals endorsed the amendment but refused to jeopardize state security during the year before which it could be ratified. The fire-eaters believed, in Hamilton's words, that the abolition question was "every day threatening to be moved against us." In the face of this "great public danger," he said, South Carolina could no longer permit "any stand but that of Sovereignty."[21]

Hamilton and his followers considered it dangerous to permit unionists to retain positions in the state militia after Poinsett's "treachery" during the nullification winter. They favored using the special authority granted in the Force Bill Ordinance to require an oath of allegiance from all military officers, effective at once. Oaths for civil officials would be added if and when the legislature of 1834 ratified the constitutional amendment.[22]

The militia oath, as passed by the legislature, was purposely vague. The nullifiers, adopting a strategy Governor Hayne devised, hoped that hazy wording would split the unionists; the oath was written so "that the moderate men of that party could not object to it, and must necessarily separate themselves from the violent and incorrigible." New militia officers were merely required to swear "that I will be faithful and true allegiance bear to the State of South Carolina." Nullifiers often pointed out that other states had more extensive oaths, and some conservative unionists, particularly in Charleston, snapped up the bait. The Charlestonians, led by Poinsett and Petigru, wanted unionist militia officers to take the oath and then declare that the "true" allegiance they had sworn to the state was not incompatible with

---

[21] *Pendleton Messenger,* Jan. 7, 1834.
[22] The debates on the test oath were printed in *Columbia Telescope,* Dec. 1833, *passim;* the legislative proceedings were printed in *Acts and Resolutions . . . 1833* (Columbia, 1833). Calhoun supported the radicals and opted for an immediate oath. Calhoun to Thompson, Oct. 18, 1833, Calhoun Papers, SC.

the "paramount" allegiance owed to the federal government. Petigru, as usual, favored nothing more strenuous than "waiting for the ebb of popular infatuation."[23]

Most unionists, however, believed that individuals had no right to construe the oath for themselves. Although the militia oath itself was harmless enough, it was passed by the authority granted in the Force Bill Ordinance. Thus courts would have to interpret "true" allegiance to mean the exclusive allegiance explicitly defined in the Ordinance.[24]

In the face of this potentially tyrannical oppression, the mountain yeomanry was no longer willing to follow the lead of conservative tidewater aristocrats. Mountaineers had long been dissatisfied with the passive resistance which Petigru preferred. Like yeoman farmers throughout the nation, they relished the spectacle of pre-election campaigns; and they did not share the patricians' fear that democracy would crumble at the hands of demagogues and spoilsmen. The yeomanry had contributed most of Poinsett's troops during the nullification winter, and their representatives had rejected Daniel Huger's plea to return home rather than attend the November Nullification Convention. They were not now disposed to base their liberties on the verbal niceties which Charlestonians thought sufficient.

In the Greenville area, enraged farmers girded for a fight; Petigru expected "border war" unless nullifiers relented. The yeomanry, in meeting after meeting, proclaimed that they would serve under their elected officers and ignore the commands of anyone who swallowed the oath. The more fiery spirits declared that they would not vote in an election under the militia bill and

---

[23] James Jones to Hammond, Apr. 14, 1834, Angus Patterson to Hammond, June 15, 22, 1834, Hammond Papers, LC; *Pendleton Messenger*, March 12, 1834; Petigru to Legaré, Nov. 20, 1833, Petigru to Drayton, March 26, 1834, Carson, *Petigru*, pp. 127, 130; Poinsett to James Campbell, Jan. 10, 1834, Poinsett-Campbell Correspondence, SCHS; *Southern Patriot*, Feb. 3, 1834.

[24] See, for example, *Charleston Courier*, Feb. 9, 1834. The nullifiers occasionally admitted the cogency of the unionists' argument. See *Evening Post*, Jan. 18, 1834. On the other hand, the nullifiers sometimes argued that the militia oath had been passed as a simple legislative act and had no connection with the Ordinance. But the militia oath, as an addition to the pledge in the state Constitution, was more patently unconstitutional if passed under mere lawmaking powers; the legislature would never have enacted the oath if the Convention had not granted the requisite authority. See the nullifiers' and unionists' arguments in *Book of Allegiance, passim*.

would not recognize the results; Perry and other conservative Greenville unionists had their hands full stopping an immediate revolution. But Perry convinced a meeting of 1,500 angry mountaineers in Greenville on February 3, 1834, to attempt legal redress before resorting to armed resistance. A huge gathering in Spartanburg on the same day endorsed Perry's formula, and both meetings demanded a March unionist convention in Greenville. Charleston unionists reluctantly agreed to the call, but sent few delegates. Control of the unionist party was at last slipping into the hands of leaders as determined as the most militant nullifiers.[25]

At the unionist convention in Greenville the moderates managed to maintain precarious control, but only at the expense of agreeing to a systematic military organization. The convention resolved that unionists would eschew military action unless they were denied redress through the courts. If state judges sustained the oath, the party would appeal to the United States Supreme Court; if nullifiers defied the Court's decision, unionists might call out their own "mounted minute-men." A year after the passage of the Compromise Tariff, Carolina radicals faced the possibility of an intrastate civil war and a renewed encounter with the federal government over the theoretical question of allegiance.[26]

While mountaineers began their military preparations test cases on the militia oath were argued in the courts. In Charleston in March 1834 Edward McCready, elected a lieutenant in the Washington Light Infantry, refused to take the oath and sued for his commission. Judge E. H. Bay, a nullifier, upheld the oath and withheld the commission. In Lancaster in April, James McDonald, elected a colonel of the 27th Regiment, also renounced the new oath and demanded his commission. This time Judge John S. Richardson, a unionist, declared the oath unconstitutional and

[25] Petigru to Drayton, March 26, 1834, Carson, *Petigru*, p. 130; Perry Diary, entries for Jan. 17, Feb. 8, March 28, 1834, NC; McDuffie to Thompson, Jan. 24, 1834, Thompson Papers, LC; *Charleston Courier*, March 17, 1834; *Greenville Mountaineer*, January through April, 1834, esp. Feb. 8, 22, 1834.

[26] *Charleston Courier*, March 4, 1834; *Greenville Mountaineer*, March 29, 1834; Hayne to Hammond, March 31, 1834, *AHR*, VII, 115–16; Perry Diary, entry for March 28, 1834, NC; Poinsett to Drayton, June 15, 1834, Drayton Papers; *Charleston Mercury*, May 21, 1834; R. Cunningham to Perry, Apr. 14, 1834, Perry Papers, Alabama Arch.

ordered the commission to be issued. Unionists appealed Bay's decision and nullifiers appealed Richardson's; eventually the state Court of Appeals heard both cases together in Columbia in early May.[27]

Both parties enlisted excellent lawyers, and the counsels treated the judges to the most searching debate on the Carolina doctrines since the Richardson-Harper-Miller contests in 1830. Grimké, Petigru, and Abram Blanding all argued brilliantly for the unionists, and Rhett presented a telling case for the nullifiers.

On June 2 the Court announced its decision. The two unionist judges, O'Neall and David Johnson, declared the militia oath void because the relevant portions of the parent Force Bill Ordinance were unconstitutional. O'Neall argued that the exclusive allegiance defined in the Ordinance violated the United States Constitution. Johnson maintained that the Convention, explicitly called only to fight the tariff, had no right to alter the state constitution after a tariff adjustment had been accepted. Chancellor William Harper, the third judge and only nullifier on the Court, vigorously but futilely dissented.[28]

Thomas Cooper sat in front of the Court, conspicuously scribbling notes as the two unionist judges read their opinions. By afternoon the *Columbia Times and Gazette* was out with a hand-bill denouncing the decision. Fire-eating newspapers termed O'Neall and Johnson's opinions *"corrupt, slavish, stupid"* and demanded that they be *"dragged down from that tribunal."* Governor Hayne was besieged with requests that he ignore the decision, reassert the requirement of the militia oath, call the legislature into immediate session, and urge that the judges be impeached.[29]

Hayne, after hasty conferences with leading nullifiers, decided on a more conciliatory policy. The governor issued a proclamation praising the lawyers on both sides for the skill with which they

[27] Bay's decision was printed in *Book of Allegiance*, pp. 4–11. For Richardson's decision see John S. Richardson, *The Opinion of the Honorable J. S. Richardson, in the Case of McDonald, vs. McMeekin* (Charleston, 1834).

[28] The counsels' arguments and the judges' decisions were printed in *Book of Allegiance*.

[29] *Charleston Courier*, June 6, 9, 11, 1834; Patterson to Hammond, May 2, June 15, 1834, Hammond Papers, LC.

had argued, declaring the decision of the Court the law of the state, and announcing he would issue militia commissions if officers took the innocuous prenullification oath. Hayne explained to correspondents that a two-thirds legislative majority could not be obtained for impeaching the judges or calling a convention. The wisest course was to accept the decision, work hard to win a two-thirds legislative majority in the 1834 popular elections, and ratify the constitutional amendment containing the oath at the end of the year.[30]

The pre-election debate between nullifiers and unionists began almost as soon as O'Neall and Johnson struck down the militia oath. The election issues, however, were obscured by the vagueness of the oath in the proposed constitutional amendment. The wording of the militia oath, harmless in itself, had been necessarily dangerous only because of its connection with the insistence on absolute allegiance in the Force Bill Ordinance. The oath in the proposed constitutional amendment contained the same innocuous wording and would not be passed by authority granted in the Ordinance. If the amendment was ratified, state officials would lose their jobs only if they refused to swear that "I will be faithful, and true allegiance bear, to the State of South Carolina." The question remained whether "true" allegiance meant the nullifiers' conception of "paramount" allegiance or the unionists' conception of "subordinate" allegiance. Judge Johnson, in his opinion voiding the militia oath, had admitted that an amendment containing this wording would be constitutional, and Petigru warned his cohorts that any court would sustain the proposed oath.[31]

Still, most unionists considered the constitutional amendment almost as intolerable as the militia oath. A vague pledge could later become an iron-clad oath in the hands of radical judges. While the amendment was not necessarily connected with the Ordinance, judges could seize upon the March Convention's definition of allegiance as the definitive statement of the nullifiers'

[30] *Pendleton Messenger*, June 25, 1834; Hamilton to Thompson, May 23, 1834, Hamilton Papers; Hayne to Pickens, June 10, 1834, *AHR*, VII, 118–19.
[31] *Book of Allegiance*, p. 248; Petigru to Drayton, July 11, Aug. 12, 1834, Petigru to Legaré, Aug. 1, Sept. 16, 1834, Carson, *Petigru*, pp. 153–61; *Charleston Mercury*, Sept. 4, 20, Oct. 11, 1834.

intentions in subseqent oaths. If unionists took the oath, the mountaineers feared, they would risk committing treason against the United States; if they refused to take it, they would be virtually disenfranchised.

The election of 1834 was contested almost as zealously as the election of 1832; once again street fighting broke out in Charleston. But most nullifiers rejoiced at the concessions won in the Compromise Tariff, and few believed that an unclear pledge of allegiance would disenfranchise the unionists. By mid-September the unionists, having admitted defeat, desperately circulated mammoth petitions against the amendment; in early October nullifiers won more than the requisite two-thirds of the legislative seats.

The remaining question was whether nullifiers dared to pass the amendment in the face of unionist threats. Many mountaineers had wished to fight the militia oath on the battlefield rather than in the courts, and the yeomanry intended to defy the state to enforce the amendment. Unionist legislators demanded that nullifiers accompany the amendment with a resolution declaring that "true" allegiance did not mean "exclusive" or "paramount" allegiance. If the legislature ratified the amendment without approving the resolution, representatives from the mountain districts planned to leave Columbia. Many of their constituents intended to resist tax collectors with shotguns and bayonets.[32]

The unionists' threats intensified the fire-eaters' rage. The more militant nullifiers favored passing not only the amendment but also a resolution declaring that "true" allegiance did indeed mean "exclusive" allegiance. The radicals also hoped to remodel the appeals court and to enact a Draconic treason bill. With nullifiers determined to enforce loyalty in the face of the abolitionists, and unionists determined to secure their own civil liberties, South Carolina was closer than ever to civil war.

As the nullification party deliberated on the proper course of action in December 1834, Hamilton astonished everyone by seizing the role of peacemaker. He sought out Petigru, his old law

---

[32] Petigru to Drayton, Nov. 28, 1834, Petigru to Legaré, Nov. 29, 1834, Carson, *Petigru*, pp. 164–7; George Reese, Jr., to Perry, Oct. 17, 1834, John H. Harrison to Perry, Nov. 28, 1834, Perry Papers, Alabama Arch.; *Southern Patriot*, Nov. 24, 1834; *Pendleton Messenger*, Dec. 3, 1834.

partner, and spent hours hammering out a mutually satisfactory compromise. Hamilton and Petigru agreed that the House Committee on Federal Relations should present, and the legislature adopt, a report declaring that "the allegiance required by the oath . . . is the allegiance which every citizen owes to the State consistently with the Constitution of the United States." Of course neither nullifiers nor unionists believed that the allegiance they owed the state was inconsistent with the allegiance they owed the nation. In this sense, neither Hamilton nor Petigru compromised at all. But both parties were demanding explicit legislative sanction for their own views; and in this perspective, the deliberately vague Hamilton-Petigru wording represented an implicit agreement that the legislature which passed the oath insisted on no specific definition of allegiance. To seal the bargain, Petigru demanded that nullifiers drop all plans to remodel the judiciary and enact a treason bill. Hamilton acquiesced and then promised Petigru "that he was going to work as hard now for peace as ever he did for nullification, at the risk of dividing his party forever."[33]

On December 5 the nullifiers ratified the constitutional amendment. Only the adoption of the compromise wording in the committee report could prevent civil war. Petigru had little trouble convincing unionists to accept the report. But Hamilton faced a formidable task in pacifying the party which he had done so much to enrage; the more fiery nullifiers scorned all thought of compromise. When belaboring individuals in private failed, Hamilton scheduled a party caucus for "the extraordinary hour" of ten A.M. on December 9, hoping that the hard-drinking legislators could not bring themselves to swallow "John Barleycorn" so early in the day.

At twelve noon, when the legislature convened, the caucus was still in progress; at two-thirty P.M., with the legislative galleries packed, the nullifiers finally emerged, and Hamilton flashed a triumphant smile. The House voted, ninety to twenty-eight, to accept the compromise wording in the committee report, and the Senate concurred, thirty-six to four. The dissenters were all incorrigible nullifiers. As the clerk announced the final vote the galleries shook with applause, and amid great rejoicing nullifiers

[33] Petigru to Legaré, Dec. 15, 1834, Carson, *Petigru,* pp. 167–71.

and unionists warmly clasped hands. Subsequently the nullifiers tabled the treason bill and postponed judicial reform; and in a final peace gesture, unionists supported McDuffie's candidacy for governor. Two years after the event, the nullification issues had at last been resolved.[34]

Until the middle of 1835, extremists on both sides half-heartedly tried to keep the controversy alive. A few leading nullifiers claimed that future judges could still construe the new oath as a pledge of absolute allegiance, and a few leading unionists harped on these threats.[35] But the circumstances surrounding the legislative compromise would have made it almost impossible for jurists to argue that the legislature intended to proscribe the unionists. The vague compromise wording could not hide the fact that mountaineers had won close to a complete victory.

All in all, the nullifiers' attempt to enforce state unity by enacting test oaths formed the most unsuccessful part of the postnullification reaction. There had always been a serious inconsistency in the test-oath strategy, for the harder radicals pushed the oath, the more the state became disunited. After two years of intense agitation, the rage of the mountain districts finally convinced the nullifiers that internal state unity could be attained only by convincing rather than by repressing the minority. Radicals never succeeded in proscribing a unionist officer or in disenfranchising a unionist voter. The tragedy of the test-oath controversy was that the Carolina nullifiers, having just waged one of the most impassioned fights for minority rights in American history, had to be taught within their own state that tyrannical majorities have no place in the American theory of self-government.

6

Jackson's troops had posed an awesome threat to Carolina radicals during the Nullification Crisis because of the weakness of

---

[34] Petigru to Chestnut, Dec. 9, 1834, Williams-Chestnut-Manning Papers; Francis Quash to Perry, Nov. 25, 1849, Perry Papers, Alabama Arch.; "Legislative Proceedings" in *Acts and Resolutions . . . 1834* (Columbia, 1834), *passim; Southern Patriot*, Dec. 9, 1834. In 1835 the judiciary was remodeled, but the vote cut across party lines. *Camden Journal*, Dec. 19, 1835.

[35] See, for example, Laurens, *An Oration . . . on the Fourth of July, 1835 . . .* (Charleston, 1835); Perry Diary, entry for Dec. 16, 1834, NC.

Hayne's volunteer army as well as the stand of Poinsett's unionist volunteers. When a showdown with the abolitionists came, nullifiers might need armed force as well as universal loyalty. Thus the radicals' attempt to pass a test oath during the postnullification reaction worked hand in hand with their effort to develop a stronger state army.

The nullifiers' effort to rebuild the militia, like their attempt to pass test oaths, began as early as the March 1833 Convention. McDuffie warned the Convention that "we have greater need to be prepared to defend ourselves against" the abolitionists "than against a foreign enemy"; William Harper urged that "we cannot safely intermit our military preparations"; Rhett declared that "South Carolina must be an armed camp." The Convention responded by exempting the 1832 militia law from the Ordinance repealing the nullification edicts. Governor Hayne retained authority to bolster the state militia and to train a volunteer army.[36]

Two weeks after the Convention adjourned, Hayne issued orders authorizing volunteers to continue their drills. He spent a good part of the spring of 1833 reviewing troops and addressing musters. At the end of the year, he proposed, and the legislature enacted, the omnibus militia bill which contained the test oath. The bill reformed the state's armed forces, integrating the volunteers and the militia and providing a clear-cut chain of command. The legislature granted Hayne's request for a $50,000 appropriation for the purchase of arms.[37]

The military preparations reached their full potential only after McDuffie became governor in December 1834. The fiery upcountryman had refused to stand for re-election to Congress in 1834, for the wound from the 1822 Cumming duel was rankling in his spine, leaving his "whole nervous system . . . in a state of stricture almost amounting to spasm." But McDuffie eagerly undertook the comparatively lighter duties of governor, and the acute paralysis

[36] *Speeches Delivered in the Convention, March, 1833,* pp. 27, 41, 52, 62.
[37] Printed General Orders of J. B. Earle, March 27, 1833, Hammond to J. M. Tyrin, Apr. 5, 1833, Hammond Papers, LC; Hayne to Hammond, May 7, 1833, *AHR,* VII, 115–16; *Evening Post,* Apr. 4, 1833; *Pendleton Messenger,* Dec. 18, 1833; *Acts and Resolutions, 1833,* pp. 13ff., 39–40.

which caused him to "totter in walking like an old man" made him a more violent fire-eater.[38]

In his inaugural address, McDuffie urged that "for a State having the peculiar institutions and occupying the peculiar position of South Carolina to think of preserving her liberties without a vigorous state of military preparations, is that sort of madness with which the heathen gods of antiquity were supposed to afflict a state they had predestined to destruction." Thereafter the governor was obsessed with the state militia. Despite his shattered nerves, he attended every possible muster, exhorting the troops to train zealously for the imminent crisis. "I regard a separation of the slaveholding states from the Union, as . . . absolutely inevitable," McDuffie wrote Hammond in 1836, "and all my efforts for two years past have been devoted to the work of preparing this state for every possible emergency."[39]

By 1836 the Carolina militia, although still rather weak, was stronger than the volunteer army which Hayne had hastily thrown together in early 1833. Throughout the rest of the ante bellum period, and particularly in the 1850's, leading Carolinians built up their arms and trained their troops. When the firing on Fort Sumter finally led to armed combat, the South Carolina militia was at least somewhat prepared for its encounter with Lincoln's armies.

7

During the Nullification Crisis, Carolina radicals had learned not only the necessity for a stronger army and the need to bring unionists to heel. They had also discovered the folly of isolation from the rest of the South. Unless slaveholders from Virginia to Mississippi rallied to the South Carolina standard, nullifiers knew they would continue to fritter away proslavery zeal. By mid-1833 the fear of once again standing alone had led a handful of South Carolina extremists to work for a convention of the southern states.

[38] McDuffie to [?], Apr. 24, 1834, McDuffie Papers; Perry Diary, entry for Aug. 14, 1835, NC; O'Neall, *Biographical Sketches,* II, 467.

[39] *Pendleton Messenger,* Dec. 24, 1834; McDuffie to Hammond, Dec. 19, 1836, Cooper to Hammond, Jan. 8, 1836, Hammond Papers, LC; John Pressly to Perry, Aug. 7, 1835, Perry Papers, Alabama Arch.

The leading advocate of a southern convention in the post-nullification period was Columbia's Thomas Cooper, who was returning to a scheme which was initially his own. Cooper had first proposed a convention during the 1827 campaign, at the same time that he alarmed the nation by calling for a calculation of the value of the Union. While Cooper had then envisioned a southern convention as a way Carolina radicals could awaken the South, he had soon discovered that the scheme might restrain South Carolina. The Carolina unionists, no doubt to Cooper's chagrin, had taken the lesson to heart. In the early 1830's they had called for a southern convention with the hope of sabotaging the nullifiers' crusade. But by April 1833 Cooper had found renewed virtues in the convention idea; and he was soon using it, as McDuffie was training the army, to prepare the South for secession.

The southern convention scheme could have had few more effective champions. In the mid-1830's Cooper was at the height of his political power. Since 1820 he had served his adopted state as a schoolmaster of states' rights, making South Carolina College a hotbed of secession dogma and winning the hearts of a new generation of South Carolinians. By 1835 young planter-politicians, including James H. Hammond, were rising to national power, and they looked first for political advice to their old college mentor.[40]

Furthermore, the changed political conditions in the postnullification period gave Cooper unlimited opportunities to exercise his genius for agitation. The triumph of Wilberforce in England and the rise of organized abolition in America fed the planters' dread of the slavery issue; and the demise of Hamilton's association made South Carolina College an unrivaled institutional device for spreading the Carolina dogmas until Cooper resigned in late 1834. Meanwhile Hamilton's addiction to banking and McDuffie's obsession with the militia removed radicals who had outshone Cooper in the early 1830's. Those nullifiers who had always considered Calhoun too conservative and who now itched to renew their crusade

[40] Cooper's impact on his old students is evident in Hammond Papers, 1835–6, LC. Harold Schultz has pointed out that many of the South Carolina leaders in the 1850's had come of age during the nullification era and had attended the college while Cooper directed it. Schultz, *Nationalism and Sectionalism in South Carolina, 1852–1860* . . . (Durham, 1950), p. 8. See also Hollis, *University of South Carolina*, I, 266–8.

found themselves driven into the arms of the fiery English octogenarian.

No trip to Columbia in 1833 could be complete without a visit to Cooper's study. Strangers found him undaunted by the ravages of age, and cursing the day when South Carolina backed away from enforcing nullification. Bent double like a hook, waving his hearthbrush like a sword, Cooper would denounce the decision to accept compromise rather than secession. "We have lost a fine opportunity, sir, of carrying this State to the highest renoun," he would pant, before polishing off Jackson with the hearthbrush and collapsing into his chair.[41]

In the months after nullification, a southern convention seemed to Cooper the best assurance that no further opportunities would be lost. South Carolinians, he hoped, would not again lose their nerve if they had assurances of extensive southern support. In a carefully organized campaign developed by Cooper's leading lieutenant, Edward Johnston, editor of the *Columbia Telescope*, newspapers throughout the state called for a southern convention during the spring of 1833. Johnston left no doubt in correspondents' minds how Cooperites viewed a convention. "I take it for granted that all know what a Southern Convention means," he wrote to one leading Richmond editor. It would be "the certain forerunner of secession."[42]

Other, more conservative, nullifiers continued to view radical southern action as an attempt to make secession unnecessary; they believed, in Hamilton's words, that their own "salvation & the safety of the Union will be found in the united action of the South." Calhoun once again took the lead in putting Cooper's doctrines to more conservative uses. Calhoun chose his occasion skillfully. Turnbull, the revered lowcountry publicist, had died of country fever in the summer of 1833. The Charleston nullifiers planned a memorial service for November 22, and they decided to use the occasion to stage a massive political rally. Calhoun came down from Pendleton for the occasion, first paying homage to

[41] Featherstonhaugh, *Excursion Through the Slave States*, p. 157.
[42] *Winyaw Intelligencer*, Apr. 23, 1833; *Evening Post*, Apr. 23, 1833; *Charleston Mercury*, May 7, 1833; Johnston to Crallé, Apr. 7, 1833, Crallé Papers, Clemson College.

Turnbull during the morning services at St. Phillips graveyard and then giving the main oration at the evening rally in the Circus. It was his first public appearance in Charleston in at least a decade, and his only formal public oration in South Carolina during the nullification era; the Charlestonians packed into the Circus received him with enthusiastic rejoicing.[43]

Calhoun told them that the Nullification Crisis had yielded only a partial victory. The tariff had been lowered but the Force Bill remained; and "under the fostering encouragement of that Bill, Emancipation Societies had sprung up like mushrooms." Southerners, he continued, must use every effective resistance to the tyrannical law lest the abolitionists overwhelm them all. If other means should fail, "it would be their duty to concentrate the voice of the South" through a southern convention. The convention, if it had to be called, should be used not to secure secession but rather to employ the threat of disunion to bring the North to yield. The South, Calhoun declared, should "plainly announce to their Northern brethren that either the bill or the political connexion must yield—that much as we valued the Union . . . we MUST MAINTAIN OUR LIBERTY." Calhoun clearly valued the liberty to own slaves more than the permanence of the Republic, but he continued to believe what Cooper had long since doubted—that both the South and the Union could be saved.[44]

In the end, neither Cooper's nor Calhoun's conception of a southern convention won widespread support. South Carolina politicians were more interested in the test-oath controversy, and most slaveholders in the rest of the South were sick to death of South Carolina. Had Cooper lived through the years of sectional controversy, he would have rued the day he revived the scheme. In 1850 the South Carolina moderates, once again led by Langdon Cheves and playing on the state's memories of isolation during the Nullification Crisis, would head off secession by espousing a southern convention. The ensuing Nashville Convention would

---

[43] Hamilton to Beverley Tucker, Feb. 17, 1834, typecopy in Hamilton Papers; *Charleston Mercury*, Nov. 25, 1833.

[44] *Charleston Mercury*, November 25, 27, 1833.

For a further discussion of Calhoun's postnullification attachment to the Union, see below, pp. 354–5.

slow down South Carolina's drive toward disunion. As the events of the secession winter would show, Carolina planters could best break up the Union in the style of nullification: by acting independently and precipitating a crisis. For in 1861, unlike in 1833, South Carolinians were not destined to find themselves standing alone.

8

The test-oath controversy, the emphasis on a stronger militia, and the southern convention scheme were all significant parts of the radicals' attempt to strengthen South Carolina for the coming political crisis. But the most important aspect of the postnullification reaction—what made it indeed a Great Reaction—was the conservative philosophy and the repressive policies with which Carolina planters prepared to defend their peculiar institution.

In the years before the Nullification Controversy, many Carolinians had declared slavery a necessary evil and some had called it a positive good. But the most characteristic response to the nascent abolitionist threat in the 1820's was the attempt to silence all public discussion of slavery in South Carolina. Yet the policy of cautious silence in South Carolina could not be reconciled with the strategy of vigorous defense in Washington. Only a well-informed planter class would enthusiastically support a campaign to meet the question at the threshold. The nullification crusade had been, in part, an attempt to check the abolitionists without debating slavery. But from the moment Jackson issued his Nullification Proclamation in December 1832, Carolina publicists conducted an extensive campaign in their own state to convert slaveholders to the proslavery arguments.[45]

Many Carolinians—including such a militant nullifier as David J. McCord—opposed the new policy of open newspaper discussion. Incessant agitation in the South, they feared, would increase the possibility of widespread slave revolts.[46] But proponents of the proslavery argument believed that South Carolina could no longer

---

[45] Note the emergence of a concentrated proslavery campaign in *Evening Post*, Dec. 1832, *passim*.

[46] Johnston to Hammond, Feb. 20, 1836, Hammond Papers, LC; Perry Diary, entry for Aug. 8, 1835, NC. See also the revealing debate between the "South Carolina Nullifier" and Green in *United States Telegraph*, Sept. 3, 1834.

afford the *"apologetical whine"* with which many planters revealed "the false compunctions of an uninformed conscience." Leading Calhounites, among them Duff Green, declared that the South had "most to fear" from the abolitionists' "organized action upon the consciences and fears of the slaveholders themselves." Green called for a massive campaign of public education which would "meet the question in all its bearings. We must satisfy the consciences, we must allay the fears of our people. We must satisfy them that slavery is of itself right—that it is not a sin against God—that it is not an evil, moral or political. . . . In this way, and this way only, can we prepare our people to defend their own institutions." "If we contend in a cause which our understandings and conscience tell us to be wrong," added William Harper, "we are already prepared for defeat."[47]

The proslavery argument which Harper and others systematized in the 1830's was a short but significant step from the necessary-evil argument of the 1820's. In the prenullification decade, planters had chanted that slavery was evil because it violated natural rights but necessary because it fulfilled practical needs. In the years after nullification, Carolinians merely had to deny the existence of a priori natural law and proclaim the validity of a posteriori utilitarian judgments. Proslavery theorists declared "self-evident" laws in general and the Jeffersonian doctrines in particular nothing but a pack of pernicious abstractions. Men could obtain social truth only by examining societies as they exist, determining which of the various types of imperfect human institutions contributed the greatest happiness to the greatest number of individuals.

Given the shift from universal to utilitarian assumptions, the same arguments which made slavery a necessary evil in the 1820's made it a positive blessing in the 1830's. The best proslavery polemicists admitted that bondage, like all human institutions, had its defects. But no conceivable institution, argued Harper and

---

[47] *Winyaw Intelligencer*, Jan. 8, 1833; A. D. Sims, *A View of Slavery . . .* (Charleston, 1834), p. vi; *United States Telegraph*, Dec. 21, 1833, Sept. 16, 1835; Harper, *Anniversary Oration*, p. 8; *Columbia Telescope*, Apr. 23, 1833; *Pendleton Messenger*, Aug. 21, 1835. For an excellent discussion of the purposes of the proslavery argument, see Ralph Morrow, "The Pro-Slavery Argument Revisited," *Mississippi Valley Historical Review*, XLVIII (June 1961), 79–94.

similar theorists, could contribute more pleasure and less pain to the Negro slave, to the white southerner, and in more general terms to the lower class everywhere. The Negroes were too degraded to prosper as freedmen, and the South would be abandoned without black men to work the fields. Furthermore, some men labor for others in all societies. The chattel slave of the South, shielded by his benevolent master from the cares of sickness, unemployment, and old age, was better off than the wage slave of the North. Finally, proslavery theorists reassured those who preferred religious certitudes to pragmatic calculations that the Bible sanctions human bondage.

In order to convince the community that slavery was a blessing, proslavery theorists had to direct their polemics against the most pernicious abstraction of all, the notion that "all men are born free and equal and are endowed with certain unalienable rights." The Jeffersonian cant made for soaring Independence Day rhetoric, the defenders of slavery admitted, but it had little to do with societies as they exist. Children are born, not men; children are wholly dependent, not free; men are completely unequal in every important way—in strength, in intelligence, in character, in color. Men are not born with rights, but rather are given privileges by the society to which they belong.

Rejecting the equal-rights philosophy, which was one of the great legacies of the Age of Reason, southerners retreated to the medieval, Aristotelian concepts of hierarchy, rank, and order. The best society, they argued, gives all men power in proportion to their unequal natural endowment; "the basis of civilization is order, which implies distinctions and differences of condition." Slavery is right because the slaveholder has the endowment to command, the Negro only the discernment to obey. To upset the hierarchy—to allow the worst men equality with the best—is to overturn the natural condition of human society.[48]

The Carolinians' hierarchical social theory necessarily affected

[48] The South Carolina defense of slavery can best be followed in the essays by Harper, Hammond, and William Gilmore Simms in Harper *et al., The Pro-Slavery Argument.* For an unusually good statement of the hierarchical social theory, see "Reflections Elicited by Judge Harper's Anniversary Oration . . ." in *The Southern Literary Journal and Monthly Magazine,* II (July 1836), 375–92.

their conception of democracy. Universal manhood suffrage might overturn the primacy of the elite. South Carolinians had always tempered their democratic enthusiasm with aristocratic practices. But after the rise of the proslavery argument, fire-eaters explicitly repudiated all belief in "wild-eyed democracy." Northern visitors to South Carolina were astonished "to hear men of the better class express themselves openly against a republican government, and to listen to discussions of great ability, the object of which was to show that there can never be a good government if it is not administered by gentlemen."[49]

Carolina radicals disliked undiluted democracy primarily because it left property owners defenseless against the "mob." The "hungry multitude," infatuated with the notion of human equality, would not tolerate unequal economic conditions for long. Abolitionism was the first stage of a leveling crusade which would tear down the hierarchy in the North as well as in the South. Calhoun begged northerners to unite with southerners against the "agrarianism" of the "rabble"; McDuffie declared to Nicholas Biddle that "an unmixed democracy, without . . . a check to secure property against numbers, will prove I fear, to be a disastrous experiment." He considered slavery a blessing partly because it disenfranchised the lower class, thereby protecting those with "a stake in society" against the "despotism of the multitude." Considerations like these led McDuffie to tell the Carolina legislature in 1835 that "Domestic slavery . . . instead of being a political evil, is the cornerstone of our republican edifice."[50]

Calhounites feared not only the dictatorship of the proletariat but also the dictatorship of the politicians. The grave danger the rule of the "rabble" posed was that the "mob" would use political power to rob their betters and that demagogues would use the "mob" to feast on patronage. Spoilsmen, by seizing government control from the natural elite, could threaten the social hierarchy as thoroughly as the "rabble" they so easily deluded.

[49] Featherstonhaugh, *Excursions Through the Slave States,* p. 157.
[50] [Hammond], *Remarks . . . on . . . Abolition . . .* (Washington, D.C., 1836), pp. 14–16; [Pickens], *Speech . . . on . . . Abolition . . .* (Washington, D.C., 1836), p. 14; Hammond to Pickens, Sept. 6, 1836, Hammond Papers, DU; Calhoun to Samuel Ingham, Apr. 3, 1836, Calhoun Papers, SC; Richard Current, "John C. Calhoun, Philosopher of Reaction," *The Antioch Review,* III (Summer 1943), 223–34; McDuffie to Biddle, Jan. 25, 1835, Biddle Papers; *Camden Journal,* Nov. 28, 1835.

As Calhounites looked back over American history with this fear of spoilsmen in mind, they thought they saw (and to some extent, correctly saw) a portentous change in the nature of national political leadership. In the era of the Founding Fathers, the Carolinians believed, the President, for example, Jefferson, had been a philosopher-statesman, not altogether above party intrigue but primarily devoted to a reign of the enlightened. In the age of Jackson, the philosopher-statesman had given way to the political manager, as such men as Van Buren ascended to power. Calhounites had fought this trend from the beginning. They had opposed the caucus maneuvers of Crawford and the "corrupt bargain" of Adams, and their war against the tariff had been partly designed to cut down the spoils available to the new breed of politicos.

In the mid-1830's Jackson's exaltation of the spoils system seemed to Carolina radicals a climactic announcement of the debasement of American democracy. To Cooper it appeared that "the immense patronage, operating upon men ready to sell themselves . . . is irresistible"; Hayne believed that the President's control of "the vast patronage of a consolidated Government" was rapidly turning the Republic "into an irresponsible despotism"; Calhoun feared that "the immense corps of office holders and expectants, which live, or expect to live, by the government will continue to control public opinion . . . 'till it shall acquire a complete ascendancy over the Government and people." William J. Grayson, a leading nullifier and a famous proslavery poet, brilliantly summed up South Carolina's fear of demagogical spoilsmen when, writing in the 1860's, he pronounced this verdict on the causes of the Civil War:

According to the theory of Republics, the highest places in the Commonwealth are the rewards of the most distinguished virtue and ability. It was so at first in our practice. But now the most exalted station is the prize of the man who is most plastic in the hands of the political managers and demagogues. How could the government go on when its forms only were left, when cupidity took the place of public spirit, when greediness for office and emolument became the sole principle of action with politicians of all parties, when members of Congress hungered after petty appointments, consulships in obscure places, clerkships in Washington, the merest old clothes of executive patronage. The rabble had come to rule. The Republic was at an end. This has been the substantial cause of the Country's ruin. The reasons usually assigned were themselves effects not causes. If the right men had continued to govern there could have been no tariffs to promote monopolies and no improper interference with the institutions of the States.[51]

In the end, the proslavery argument was a mammoth reaction which carried its Carolina defenders beyond a repudiation of the Jeffersonian equal-rights philosophy to a rejection of America's "unmixed" democracy. Of course many southerners applauded slavery without questioning democracy. Furthermore, the most aristocratic defenders of bondage, as Louis Hartz has brilliantly demonstrated, retained enough of their enlightenment faith to defeat their medieval arguments; the proslavery theory of such racists as James Hammond ended up by being feudal for Negroes, democratic for whites.[52]

Yet if lingering Jeffersonianism often led proslavery theorists to develop an abortive reactionary philosophy, their hierarchical assumptions sometimes led to serious doubts about the style of democracy emerging in mid-nineteenth-century America. The proslavery theory is an important example of the fact that while Americans have almost always favored democracy in general, they have sometimes differed profoundly over the type of republic they desired. At the same time as the rise of romanticism was giving most Americans a boundless faith in the wisdom of the common man, the proslavery argument was leading South Carolinians to make explicit and theoretical their eighteenth-century passion for an aristocratic republic. To southerners who took the aristocratic cult seriously—and nowhere was it taken so

[51] Cooper to Hammond, Feb. 12, 1836, Hammond Papers, LC; Cooper to Biddle, May 1, 1834, Biddle Papers; *Pendleton Messenger,* Dec. 3, 1834; Calhoun to E. W. North *et al.,* March 24, 1835, *Charleston Mercury,* March 27, 1835; Grayson Autobiography, pp. 225–6. Calhoun's obsession with demagogical spoilsmen—his conviction that democracy by numerical majorities would be subverted by corrupt politicos as well as by selfish interests—is an important key to his mature political philosophy. William W. Freehling, "Spoilsmen and Interests in the Thought and Career of John C. Calhoun," *Journal of American History,* LII (June 1965), 25–42. After publication of the above, a different formulation of a similar proposition came to my attention. See Ralph W. Lerner, "Calhoun's New Science of Politics," *American Political Science Review,* LVII (Dec. 1963), 918–32.

[52] Hartz, *Liberal Tradition in America,* part 4.

seriously as in South Carolina—it seemed likely that hungry demagogues would capture the Republic by feeding the "rabble" antislavery nonsense. In the mid-1830's this profound political distrust was an important cause of South Carolina's increasing alienation from the federal Union.

9

The public discussion of slavery in South Carolina in the years after 1832 was a monologue rather than a debate. Carolinians who espoused the old necessary-evil argument were frowned on in 1834 and silenced by 1836. To go further—to hint at colonization, to criticize the Negro seamen law, to urge that slaves be allowed to read their Bibles—was cause for mob justice. The tribulations of the Reverend Pinney were a tame rehearsal of the vigilant justice which awaited many dissenters in the years after 1833. As Clement Eaton has pointed out, informal daily pressures were even more important than occasional lynch mobs in producing the Old South's massive orthodoxy. But whether carried on by overt violence or covert pressures, the Great Reaction achieved the most thoroughgoing repression of free thought, free speech, and a free press ever witnessed in an American community.[53]

The decision to discuss slavery openly intensified those dilemmas of discipline which often beset a scrupulous slavemaster. Never before had it seemed so hard to reconcile the need to treat one's people with familial affection with the need to maintain slave property with thoroughgoing punishment. Despite their attempts to glorify the institution, proslavery writers such as Hammond admitted that "in the face of discussions which aim at loosening all ties between master and slave, we have in some measure to abandon our efforts to attach them to us, and control them through their affections and pride. We have to rely more and more on the power of fear." It is dubious whether many planters drew "the rein tighter and tighter day by day," as Hammond claimed. But unquestionably masters imposed harsh controls during the periodic insurrection panics which swept over the Old South during the years before the Civil War. Given the "severe

[53] Eaton. *The Freedom-of-Thought Struggle in the Old South* (New York, 1964).

and jealous scrutiny" which the open discussion of slavery engendered, the relationship between master and slave was probably
marked by less "confidence and good will," more "distrust and
aversion." For planters whose qualms about slavery were never
quite removed by the proslavery argument, the "sterner control"
which sometimes seemed necessary may well have been "painful."[54]

In the 1830's the Carolina legislature augmented the stricter
discipline on individual plantations by enacting a more rigorous
slave code. Whitemarsh Seabrook and other planters remained
convinced that "the use of intoxicating liquors" was an important
cause "of every insurrectionary movement which has occurred in
the United States." The Georgetown Conspiracy of 1829 had
demonstrated that ardent spirits and Yankee peddlers were an inflammatory combination. From 1831 to 1834 the legislature passed
a series of laws prohibiting slaves from using a distillery or selling
whiskey under any circumstances and from buying spirits without
their owners' permission. The legislature also prohibited the purchase of cotton, rice, corn, and wheat from slaves. The law, when
properly enforced, kept bondsmen from buying their grog and
protected planters from costly depredations. Finally, in 1835, the
legislature imposed a prohibitive $1,000 tax on peddlers, ridding
the state of northerners who "were probably disposed, and had
great opportunities, to disturb our domestic institutions."[55]

The slave liquor laws, although violently opposed and stealthily
circumvented by Charleston retailers, provoked little debate in
the Carolina legislature. But the most important part of the new
slave code, the law prohibiting slaves from learning to read and
write, was passed only after the most vigorous—and revealing—
opposition. Indeed, the reluctance to prohibit slave literacy, like
Charleston's earlier decision to build a treadmill in order to relieve scrupulous masters of the task of punishing their people,

[54] I am paraphrasing the admissions of Hammond and Harper in the midst of their
mature proslavery argument; the quotes are from their essays. Harper *et al., The
Pro-Slavery Argument,* pp. 94, 126–7.
[55] Seabrook, *Essay on the Management of Slaves,* p. 7; Laurens, *Letter to Seabrook,*
p. 11; *Columbia Telescope,* Dec. 20, 1831; *Pendleton Messenger,* Dec. 25, 1835;
Statutes at Large, VI, 433–4, 516–17, 529, VII, 467–70.

betrays in the most illuminating fashion the problems confronting conscientious planters.

The bill, proposed in the House as early as 1827, was reintroduced by Rhett in December 1832. Despite the heightened fear of slave uprisings caused by the Turner Revolt and the Nullification Crisis, Rhett's bill was postponed after two readings. In 1833 the fire-eaters, led by Seabrook and Edward Laurens, tried again. Radicals urged that the new policy of open discussion made literate bondsmen more dangerous than ever; and Seabrook argued that anyone who wanted slaves to read the *entire* Bible was fit for a "room in the Lunatic Asylum." Other legislators, however, opposed "interfering with the spiritual well being of the slave." In the end this "sickly humanity" prevailed. The Senate rejected the bill.[56] The vote provides a portrait of the degree to which various Carolinians worried about servile insurrection. Nullifiers voted for the bill, sixty-four to twenty-nine; unionists opposed it, twenty-four to four. The tidewater parishes supported the bill, thirty-three to twelve; the rest of the state opposed it, forty-one to thirty-five.[57]

In 1834 radicals finally pushed the bill through the legislature. White persons convicted of teaching slaves to read and write were liable to a one-hundred-dollar fine and six months in jail; free Negroes convicted of the same offense could be given fifty lashes and fined fifty dollars. The legislators, however, refused to prohibit free Negroes from learning to read and write. Those whose thoughts continued to dwell on Denmark Vesey considered this lingering instance of "sickly humanity" foolhardy.[58]

Unfortunately there is no way of determining the precise effect of the slave literacy laws. Only a small minority of bondsmen learned to read before 1834, some learned to read thereafter; and the concern about slavery discussions would have led to a repression of slave education if the legislature had failed to act. Yet the

[56] *Southern Patriot*, Nov. 30, 1827; S. C. Jackson to Truc, Dec. 14, 1832, S. C. Jackson Papers; "Legislative Proceedings, 1832," in *Acts and Resolutions, 1832*, pp. 11, 24, 28, 41, 53; Seabrook, *Essay on the Management of Slaves*, pp. 15, 28–30; Laurens, *Letter to Seabrook*, pp. 7–8.

[57] The votes in the House and Senate have been combined. "Legislative Proceedings, 1833," in *Acts and Resolutions, 1833*, pp. 48, 52.

[58] *Statutes at Large*, VII, 468.

law may have had an effect on the many slaveholders who wavered between their desire to be paternal and their desire to safeguard slave property. Dissenters, among them Judge John B. O'Neall, would probably not have bothered writing courageous arguments for repeal (and the community would probably not have responded so angrily) if the law had been only a paper edict.

Still, the great importance of the new education laws lay not in their practical effect on the Negroes but rather in their psychological impact on the slaveholders. Outlawing slave education, like all the other aspects of the Great Reaction, only made the bondsmen's lot a bit harder. Raising slavery from a necessary evil to a positive good merely made explicit a long-standing determination to preserve the institution. In both cases, what had really changed was the white man's attempt to face and to justify a set of practices which had previously been glossed over by silence. And as the debate over slave education revealed, South Carolinians could not pass laws or proclaim doctrines on subjects which they had long sought to evade without showing signs of a lingering sense of doubt.

The new legal restrictions on slave education somewhat vitiated one of the few progressive results of the Great Reaction, the renaissance in slave religion. The most extreme proslavery writers had always favored the proper type of religious training. The community had shuddered at projects like the St. Luke's Missionary scheme in 1831 and Francis Goulding's African Sabbath School in 1833 because many southern ministers were covert abolitionists. But oral lessons taught by proslavery clergymen based on the proper Biblical passages could reduce Negro insubordination and ease a slaveholder's conscience. As the Great Reaction swept over the Old South, ministers, like everyone else, conformed to the massive orthodoxy, and a new era in slave religion commenced.

Before 1844 the religious revival proceeded with hesitation. In 1829 the gentry had been nervous when three Methodist missionaries came to the lowcountry. In 1845 Methodists still had only twenty-two exhorters in the field, but tidewater planters called for more. After the Methodist and Baptist churches split into northern and southern branches in 1844, most qualms vanished. By 1860 missionaries of all denominations traversed the lowcountry, and slaves throughout South Carolina poured into Christian churches. The argument that slavery had Christianized the heathen became one of the most effective means proslavery theorists used to assuage the conscience of their followers; this is why the Reverend Mr. Pinney had enjoyed his brief popularity in Columbia in 1833.[59]

Yet the slaves' religious experience was at best an abortive affair. Planters often refused to allow or failed to finance separate Negro congregations; and leading ministers continued to find that erudite sermons addressed to educated whites elicited little response from illiterate slaves. More important, Protestant sects believed that the Savior had enjoined all Christians to read His words, and planters kept slaves from reading the Scripture. Judge O'Neall could not see "*how we can justify it, that a slave is not permitted to read his Bible*"; an embittered minister, Robert A. Fair, admitted that "many" slaves were saved by oral instruction but suspected that "many more" would "be saved by means of the reading the Word." Fair protested against the "fearful responsibility" of standing "in the way of salvation of souls—yea of even *one* soul."[60]

But most Carolinians, recalling that a slave who could read the Bible could also read the *Liberator*, found Hammond's statement more to the point. "Allow our slaves to read your writings, stimulate them to cut our throats!" he exclaimed. "Can you believe us to be such unspeakable fools?"[61]

[59] Luther P. Jackson, "Religious Instruction of Negroes, 1830–1860, With Special Reference to South Carolina," *Journal of Negro History*, XV (Jan. 1930), 72–114; Nathaniel Bowen, *A Pastoral Letter on the Religious Instruction of the Slaves* . . . (Charleston, 1835) ; Rev. Rufus William Bailey, *The Issue* . . . (New York, 1837) ; *Proceedings of the Meeting in Charleston, S.C. May 13–15, 1845, on the Religious Instruction of the Negroes* . . . (Charleston, 1845) ; Charles Colcock Jones, *Suggestions on the Religious Instruction of the Negroes in the Southern States* . . . (Philadelphia, 1847). For an intriguing example of the lingering dilemmas about religious education for slaves, see Robert F. Durden, "The Establishment of Calvary Protestant Episcopal Church for Negroes in Charleston," *South Carolina Historical Magazine*, LXV (Apr. 1964), 63–84.
[60] John Witherspoon to Susan McDowell, Jan. 2, 1847, Witherspoon-McDowell Papers, NC; O'Neall, *The Negro Law in South Carolina* (Columbia, 1848), p. 23; Fair, *Our Slaves Should Have the Bible* . . . (Due West, S.C., 1854), esp. p. 14.
[61] Harper *et al.*, *The Pro-Slavery Argument*, p. 124.

Southerners often argued that the limitations on slave religion, like all the new shackles imposed on the bondsmen, had been caused by northern "fanatics." Instead of improving the lot of southern Negroes, "incendiaries" had made the slaves' plight worse than ever. "If the slave is not allowed to read his Bible," wrote Hammond, "the sin rests upon the abolitionists; for they stand prepared to furnish . . . a key to it, which would . . . convert the reader, not into a christian, but a demon."[62] This sort of argument had a potent effect on slaveholders. Abolitionists became hated scapegoats for all anxieties more repressive practices engendered on southern plantations. Yet when planters stopped to examine the radicals' logic, perhaps during those torrential storms which drove all southerners indoors to muse and to brood, they must have wondered whether an institution which could be preserved only at so heavy a price was worth saving at all. Such doubts, too disturbing to be entertained for long, must have been quickly repressed. Many planters probably emerged from these sporadic bouts of conscience with a renewed hatred of northern abolitionists and a more fervent dedication to the fire-eaters' crusade.

10

The abortive slave religion of the later ante bellum period was typical of the limited success of the postnullification reaction. Unionists remained as potentially "disloyal" as ever, the Carolina militia could not hope to withstand a determined national invasion, and few slaveholders showed interest in a southern convention.

But worst of all, the new attitude about slavery was replete with irony, and the irony was never more obvious or more painful than at the beginning of the Great Reaction. Over a period of years, and particularly when a new generation grows up, a society can teach citizens to reverse their values. By 1860 it is likely that many (although certainly never all, and perhaps never most) southerners honestly believed that slavery was a positive good. But a society cannot change its fundamental beliefs overnight; the at-

[62] *Ibid.*

tempt to do so is bound to strike many citizens as the worst hypocrisy. In 1835 many South Carolinians must have been made more uneasy by the attempt to call their curse a blessing.

Furthermore, at the moment that radicals asked their followers to believe that the necessary evil was a positive good, slavery was becoming a more repressive institution in which it was harder to believe. The fact that antislavery ideas were being bandied about led suspicious masters to punish more strictly, and the outlawing of slave education seemed to reduce the bondsmen's chance for eternal salvation. Meanwhile, the inception of open newspaper discussions made slaveholders more uneasy about servile insurrection. No wonder that Pierce Butler found that "there are men among us—(not union men) that are fanatical and crazy on this subject."[63]

By 1860 the proslavery argument and the tighter shackles imposed on the bondsmen had no doubt lightened the guilt and fear which afflicted many slaveholders. But in 1835 the Great Reaction may well have made both problems worse.

Three years after the Nullification Crisis, then, Carolina radicals had more reasons for dreading a direct encounter with the abolitionists. The antislavery movement had prevailed in England and seemed to be gaining in the North; the whole world seemed at war with the peculiar institution. Abolitionists appeared capable of provoking serious slave revolts and of "perverting" the scrupulous slaveholder's already uneasy conscience. A multibillion-dollar investment—indeed the future of southern white civilization—seemed at stake. Carolina radicals were certain to meet the abolitionists' first direct attack with a desperation which would match the nullification crusade. The attack was not long in coming.

---

[63] Butler to Hammond, July 10, 1835, Hammond Papers, LC. See also John Knox to Hammond, March 24, 1836, Hammond Papers.

10

The Dreaded Encounter

On July 29, 1835, the steamboat *Columbia*, sailing out of New York, arrived in Charleston and delivered its cargo. The mail from the North was dispatched to Charleston Postmaster Alfred Huger, who dutifully supervised the sorting of the letters and papers. Any semblance of routine, however, quickly vanished from the postmaster's activities. To his horror, Huger found that the mails were swollen with thousands of antislavery tracts addressed to leading members of the Charleston community, including, as the *Mercury* made a point of reporting, "the clergy of all denominations." The American Anti-Slavery Society had begun its intensive campaign to convince slaveholders that bondage should be abolished.

Huger quickly wrote an express letter to Amos Kendall, President Jackson's postmaster general, requesting instructions for dealing with the crisis. Pending Kendall's reply, Huger determined to keep the "incendiary" propaganda under lock and key. The more hotheaded Charlestonians were not disposed to await federal instructions. By evening an angry mob, three hundred strong, assembled to seize the mails. As the mob marched toward the post office it was met by the city guard and "persuaded" to disperse. Later in the night, a few incorrigible slaveholders broke into the post office and confiscated the heavy sacks of abolitionist tracts. The next evening the antislavery propaganda was burned at an enormous public bonfire on the Charleston parade grounds;

effigies of Garrison, the Tappans, and other northern "fanatics" fed the blaze. Hayne and other leading nullifiers considered the mob action precipitous. Yet radicals agreed that abolitionist propaganda could not be permitted to circulate in a community full of uneasy planters and restless slaves.[1]

This time Carolina fire-eaters did not stand alone. The abolitionists' assault was more effective in unifying South Carolina than a thousand test oaths would have been. The support of Carolina unionists paralleled the militancy of other southern states; postmasters censored the mails and mobs roamed the countryside throughout the South in the late summer of 1835. Still, the reaction of no other southern community matched Charleston's frenzy. Once again, tidewater South Carolina, with its peculiar type of plantation and its enormous concentration of slaves, was in the vanguard of the states' rights movement.[2]

Two days after Charleston's roaring bonfire, the excitement in the city threatened to disrupt all law and order. On August 1 the city council called an immediate public meeting and came close to abdicating in its favor. For the next week an extralegal committee of five, indirectly appointed by the public meeting and headed by Hayne, ruled the terrorized city. The committee met all steamboats, accompanied the mails to the post office, and made arrangements with Huger to suppress antislavery tracts. Schools for free Negroes and religious classes for slaves were suspended; suspicious bondsmen received more than their share of lashes; close watch was kept on all strangers entering the city; and lynch mobs roamed the streets, establishing their own kangaroo courts.[3]

In Washington Postmaster General Kendall conferred with Jackson and responded to Alfred Huger's cry for instructions. The President, deploring "this wicked plan of exciting the negroes to insurrection and to massacre," informed Kendall that "we can

[1] *Charleston Mercury,* July 30, 31, 1835; *Southern Patriot,* July 30, 1835; Schirmer Diary, entry for July 29, 1835; Frank Otto Gatell (ed.), "Postmaster Huger and the Incendiary Publications," *South Carolina Historical Magazine,* LXIV (Oct. 1963), 193–201.

[2] Eaton, *Freedom-of-Thought Struggle,* pp. 196–215.

[3] All Charleston newspapers, Aug. 1–15, 1835; Schirmer Diary, entry for Aug. 21, 1835.

do nothing more than direct that those inflammatory papers be delivered to none but who will demand them as subscribers." Kendall, despite graver doubts about the federal government's authority, issued instructions which in effect gave Huger sweeping power to suppress the tracts. After admitting that the post office had no authority to interfere with the delivery of mail, Kendall "did not hesitate to say" that "the circumstances of the case justified the detention of the papers." In other words, if Huger censored the mails, the Washington authorities would do nothing to enforce the laws.[4]

Kendall's instructions eased the crisis in Charleston. By mid-August Hayne's extralegal committee of five had turned the city government back to the elected officials. Thereafter a committee of the city council met every arriving steamboat and conveyed the mails to the post office. Vigilance committees were not so quick to "resign" as Hayne's committee of five. In late October "armed bands of volunteers" continued to help civil authorities quench "the torch of the incendiary."[5]

As the original hysteria subsided the lowcountry aristocracy laid plans for avoiding similar crises in the future. On August 10 the Charleston public meeting reconvened and passed a series of resolutions demanding that northern states enact penal laws to suppress abolitionist societies and that Congress forbid the delivery of mails outlawed by state edict. The rest of the state followed Charleston's lead. Almost every district in South Carolina called public meetings in the early fall of 1835; almost every meeting endorsed the Charleston resolves and formed vigilance committtes. In September alone, at least three lynchings took place in the upcountry and at least three tidewater counties urged South Carolina to secede immediately if northern states failed to suppress "incendiary" propaganda.

Carolinians left no doubt about what they considered "incendiary." A tract was "inflammatory and seditious" if it con-

[4] Jackson to Kendall, Aug. 9, 1835, Jackson, *Correspondence,* V, 360–1 ; *Congressional Globe,* 24 Cong., 1 sess., appendix, p. 9.
[5] *Southern Patriot,* Oct. 24, 1835.

tained provoking pictures or woodcuts, or if it was "calculated to shake or destroy the confidence of any, in relation to the tenure, by which our slave property is held, or to create an idea, that it is an evil in a civil, moral or political point of view." As South Carolinians saw it, *any* argument against slavery was an invitation to insurrection.[6]

Yet even amid the excitement of the Charleston post-office affair, planters ridiculed the notion that a slave revolt could succeed. An unsuccessful servile uprising would, of course, lead to gruesome scenes; and Alfred Huger, a confirmed unionist, warned leading northerners that he would not sit by indifferently while abolitionists inspired the Negroes to put "a torch to my own House" and subject "my family . . . to brutality and butchery." Still, an equally pressing danger, so the planters believed, was that continual insurrection panics would drain away the uneasy South's prosperity, morale, and will to resist. As Arthur P. Hayne confessed to Jackson, "there is in existence unfortunately a restless feeling now at the South . . . in relation to the Question of Property at the South, and unless this feeling be put at rest, who would desire to live in such a community?"[7]

Northerners were far from unsympathetic about South Carolina's predicament. Northern cities held numerous mass meetings in the fall of 1835, and each of the meetings expressed its loathing for the abolitionists' crusade. Sympathy, however, was one thing, action quite another. Whatever the wishes of northern public meetings, abolitionists remained free to fling "incendiary" pamphlets at the embattled South throughout September and October of 1835.

When the Carolina legislature convened in late November, Governor McDuffie urged his compatriots to demand that north-

[6] *Proceedings of the Citizens of Charleston, on the Incendiary Machinations, now in Progress against the Peace and Welfare of the Southern States* (Charleston, 1835); Prior, "History of the *Charleston Mercury*," p. 293; *Camden Journal*, Aug. 29, Sept. 19, 1835; *Charleston Mercury*, Sept. 5, 18, 1835; *Pendleton Messenger*, Sept. 11, 1835; Edmund Bellinger, Jr., *A Speech on the Subject of Slavery* . . . (Charleston, 1835).
[7] Huger to Samuel Gouverneur, Aug. 6, 1835, *South Carolina Historical Magazine*, LXIV (Oct. 1963), 196–7; Hayne to Jackson, Nov. 11, 1835, Jackson Papers.

ern state governments outlaw agitation of the issue. His message
was referred to a special Joint Committee on Federal Relations,
composed of leading members of both houses. The committee
proposed, and the legislature unanimously adopted, resolutions
"earnestly" requesting that the nonslaveholding states "promptly
and effectually suppress all those associations, within their respective limits, purporting to be Abolition Societies, and that they
will make it highly penal to print, publish and distribute newspapers, pamphlets, tracts and pictorial representations, calculated . . . to excite the slaves of the Southern States to insurrection
and revolt."[8]

Carolinians realized that so extreme a demand deserved a candid
explanation. The committee, in its preamble to the resolutions, explained why South Carolina could not tolerate the agitation of
northern "fanatics." The preamble deserves to be extensively
quoted and closely read. Never before and never again did the
gentry so honestly confess the intolerable anxieties which led it to
rage at any antislavery attack throughout the years when South
Carolina's loyalties were shifting from nation to section. "Let it be
admitted," declared the legislature,

that the three millions of free white inhabitants in the slave-holding
States are amply competent to hold in secure and pacific subjection the
two million of slaves. . . . Let it be admitted, that, by reason of an
efficient police and judicious internal legislation, we may render
abortive the designs of the fanatic and incendiary within our own
limits, and that the torrent of pamphlets and tracts which the Abolition
presses of the North are pouring forth with an inexhaustible complete-
ness, is arrested the moment it reaches our frontier. Are we to wait
until our enemies have built up, by the greatest misrepresentation and
falsehoods, a body of public opinion against us, which it would be
almost impossible to resist, without separating ourselves from the . . .
civilized world? Or are we to sit down content, because from our
own vigilance and courage the torch of the incendiary and the dagger
of the assassin may never be applied? This is impossible. No people
can live in a state of perpetual excitement and apprehension, although
real danger can be long deferred. Such a condition of the public mind
is destructive of all social happiness, and consequently must prove

[8] *Camden Journal and Southern Whig,* Nov. 28, 1835; *Charleston Mercury,* Dec.
19, 1835.

essentially injurious to the prosperity of a community that has the weakness to suffer under a perpetual panic.[9]

While the legislature was meeting in Columbia, South Carolina's representatives were journeying to Washington for the congressional session of 1835–6. The Carolina congressmen believed that the most formidable and important problems awaited them. The mails had to be secured and abolitionist petitions to Congress stopped. Since the days of Denmark Vesey, South Carolinians had fought to suppress congressional slavery debates. They were willing to provoke a debate in 1835–6, but only as a desperate attempt to escape the issue forever.

The importance of coming to terms with the antislavery movement was enough by itself to ensure the most militant, uncompromising stand by the Carolina representatives. But what gave South Carolina's latest crusade its edge of desperation was the fire-eaters' perception of the impossible odds against which they were contending. "I cannot say I have quite given up," Hammond wrote to Preston in the fall of 1835, but "I am so much overwhelmed by a sense of the difficulties by which we of the South are surrounded that I hate to dwell upon the subject, & never do unless forced to it." Henry J. Nott, long an eminent professor in Cooper's South Carolina College, expressed the apprehensions of many South Carolinians more systematically. "I have made up my mind fully on the matter, & believe all is lost," Nott wrote Hammond in early 1836.

Europe is against us & the North is against us. . . . How do we stand at home? Every town & village is full of northern people many of whom are *feebly* with us & many in secret decidedly against us—In many of the districts too, the great body of the poor people of some of the sects would on the ground of republicanism as well as religion either be inefficient friends or decided opponents. . . . With the property . . . not worth holding, when the Country is flooded with incendiary publication, when our slaves are encouraged to escape over the border, when eventually we fear open rebellion & secret poison? May not we be wearied out, if not forced? . . . We must battle every inch of ground in Congress and elsewhere, but I fear our only chance, is to profit as far as we can, by our present prosperity.

[9] *Ibid.*

Severe pessimism about so vital an issue could not help but drive most South Carolina nullifiers to sustain another great national campaign.[10]

2

The 1835–6 congressional debate on the circulation of abolitionist propaganda in the mails began as soon as Jackson presented his seventh annual message. In an important policy statement, understandably ignored by those historians who regard Old Hickory as an unsullied champion of the American liberal tradition, the President went so far as to declare antislavery tracts "unconstitutional and wicked." Jackson called on northern states to suppress the abolitionists and urged Congress to pass "such a law as will prohibit, under severe penalties, the circulation in the Southern States, through the mail, of incendiary publications intended to instigate the slaves to insurrection."[11]

Jackson's extreme position embarrassed Calhoun almost as much as it enraged northern abolitionists. Carolina radicals wanted the

[10] Hammond to Preston, Nov. 4, 1835, Hammond Papers, DU; Nott to Hammond, March 8, 1836, Hammond Papers, LC. Of course not all South Carolina radicals were afraid of the slavery issue. Thomas Cooper and a few others betrayed no qualms about the matter; they apparently used what they knew to be an explosive question to gain their own political objectives. Still, most South Carolina leaders, including James Hammond, a prominent Cooper lieutenant, were large slaveholders as well as aspiring politicians, and they revealed all the torment of the planter community in the way they raged at the abolitionists. Equally important, Carolina radicals, whatever their motives, could pursue their purposes with the full confidence that the state would stand behind almost any proslavery demand. It is this susceptibility of the community to agitation which explains why Hammond and Calhoun rather than Poinsett and Petigru held sway in South Carolina politics during the great campaigns of the thirties.

[11] Richardson (ed.), *Messages and Papers*, II, 1394–5. This is not to deny that Jackson took a "liberal" position on certain economic issues. For example, the Jacksonian crusade against governmental aid to privileged groups (whether waged in the interest of petty entrepreneurs or the nonpropertied classes) expressed one of the dominant themes of the American liberal tradition. But pre-Civil War statesmen must be classified on the basis of their stand on slavery as well as on economic issues. It is striking how often ante bellum statesmen who were "liberal" on economic issues were "conservative" on slavery. Andrew Jackson, Roger B. Taney, James K. Polk, Martin Van Buren in the early stage of his career, John Randolph of Roanoke, and Amos Kendall spring to mind. Conversely, the great antislavery politician often espoused neo-Federalist economic doctrines. One thinks of John Quincy Adams, Abraham Lincoln, Charles Sumner, William Seward, and even William Lloyd Garrison. Considerations like this make it difficult to establish a "liberal" tradition in ante bellum American politics. For a vigorous presentation of an opposite viewpoint, see Arthur M. Schlesinger, Jr., *The Age of Jackson* (Boston, 1950), esp. p. 433.

separate states, not the national government, to be given discretionary authority to censor the mails. If Congress had authority "to determine what papers are incendiary, and . . . to prohibit their circulation through the mails," Calhoun warned, Congress "necessarily" had "the right to determine what are not incendiary, and to enforce their circulation." Jackson's program for suppressing the abolitionists would "virtually . . . clothe Congress with the power to abolish slavery." A northern majority, by insisting on the delivery of the mails, could break down "all barriers which the slaveholding states have erected for the protection of their lives and property."[12]

Calhoun, knowing that northerners controlled the Senate Committee on Post Offices and Post Roads, moved that Jackson's proposal be referred to a special select committee. After protracted debate the motion passed, and the special committee, dominated by southerners, was selected. Calhoun chaired the committee and reported out a bill prohibiting federal postmasters from delivering any mails forbidden by the laws of a state. He defended his bill with the same constitutional logic which the South Carolina Association had used to defend the Negro seamen law in 1823. The power to deliver the mails, like the power to make treaties, was a specifically delegated power belonging exclusively to the federal government. But incendiary tracts, like Negro seamen, could provoke servile insurrections. The states remain sovereign under the Constitution; a sovereign which cannot protect itself against internal revolution is a contradiction in terms; hence any state action required to preserve "safety and security" takes precedence over any federal law.[13]

Calhoun's senatorial colleagues found the argument more clever than convincing; and the Senate voted, twenty-five to nineteen, to turn down the proposal.[14] Since Congress refused to authorize state interference with federal deliveries, the explosive problem

---

[12] Calhoun, *Works*, V, 196–7.

[13] *Ibid.*, II, 519ff.

[14] The vote was actually taken on a substitute bill, acceptable to Calhoun, proposed by Felix Grundy. The Senate's consideration of Calhoun's bill can be followed in *Register of Debates*, 24 Cong., 1 sess., pp. 1103–8, 1136–53, 1155–71, 1374, 1675, 1721–37.

was again thrust into the hands of the President. Jackson and his ante bellum successors proceeded to give informal sanction to Kendall's principles. The federal government did nothing to enforce the laws when southern states censored the mails. This extralegal arrangement was fully as effective as Calhoun's plan in preserving the South's vital cordon sanitaire. South Carolinians had failed to nullify the tariff. But they succeeded throughout the pre-Civil War years in defying all federal laws and treaties which protected Negro seamen and assured the delivery of the mails.

The extralegal settlement of the post-office issue, if as effective as the scheme devised by Calhoun, was also no less precarious than the plan Jackson proposed. South Carolinians had challenged the President's proposal because a Congress which could censor could also refuse to censor. But a President who permitted the mails to be stopped could also insist that the mails be delivered. As secessionists did not fail to remind their followers after Abraham Lincoln won the election of 1860, a hostile President who vigorously enforced the laws could permit abolitionist tracts to flood the South. Calhoun and his cohorts had successfully stopped the mails. But the patently illegal methods which they had been forced to use would cause the issue to smolder throughout the remainder of the ante bellum period.

3

By the end of December 1836 the controversy over the post office was closely connected with the dispute over abolitionist petitions. To most Carolina radicals, the prospect of incessant congressional debates on antislavery petitions was almost as intolerable as the circulation of antislavery propaganda in the South. As the Vesey Conspiracy had demonstrated, slaves were sometimes aware of what transpired in Congress. Moreover, congressional reception of antislavery petitions seemed to stimulate the abolitionist movement and appeared likely to undermine the morale of the more scrupulous slaveholders. Carolinians hoped to "gag" the abolitionists by establishing a permanent congressional policy of refusing to receive antislavery petitions.

Almost all the abolitionist petitions in the 1830's prayed for abolishing slavery and/or the slave trade in Washington, D.C., rather than for emancipating slaves in southern states. Many clauses of the federal Constitution gave at least implicit sanction to southern slavery, and middle-class Yankees regarded a frontal assault on the South's billion-dollar investment as far too radical. On the other hand, Congress had clear constitutional authority to govern in Washington, D.C., and most northerners regarded slavery in the country's capital as a national disgrace. By concentrating their initial attack on slavery in Washington, political abolitionists shrewdly appealed for the widest possible northern support.

To Carolina planters, the assault on slavery in Washington was almost as disturbing as an attack on bondage in the South. Both cases involved incessant discussion of slavery. Moreover, abolishing slavery in Washington would set the precedent for a later assault on the South itself.

Until the 1835–6 congressional session, antislavery petitions had usually been referred to the standing Committee on the District of Columbia and thereafter ignored. But on December 18, 1835, Hammond, rising to his feet when one of the first petitions of the session was presented, demanded that the House of Representatives "put a more decided seal of reprobation" on abolitionist activities. He denied that Congress had the slightest constitutional right to abolish slavery in Washington, D.C.; he moved that the House refuse to receive the petition altogether.[15]

The House debated Hammond's motion periodically for over six weeks; meanwhile Calhoun led a similar fight in the Senate. The old policy of receiving the antislavery petitions and then automatically rejecting their prayer, argued Calhoun, constituted a complete surrender to the abolitionists. By receiving the petition and acting on the prayer, Congress implied that it had constitutional authority over the subject; if the South yielded the constitutional question now, a simple majority could abolish slavery in Washington later. But by rejecting the petition altogether, Congress would proclaim its lack of authority to consider the question.

[15] *Ibid.*, pp. 1966ff.

Hammond's motion, if adopted, would establish the crucial constitutional principles—the vital outposts—which would give the minority South permanent protection against the northern "fanatics." This overwhelming congressional victory, concluded Calhoun, would permanently cripple the abolitionist movement.[16]

Calhoun's congressional strategy was also probably designed to force Van Buren to take a pro-southern position on the slavery issue. Van Buren, only months away from running for President on the Democratic party's ticket, could ill afford to lose his southern supporters. If the South united behind South Carolina's crusade to meet the question at the threshold, Van Buren and his party might be forced to court the slaveholders by suppressing the abolitionists.

The Little Magician had no intention of falling into Calhoun's trap. Refusing to receive antislavery petitions and denying that Congress could constitutionally interfere with slavery in Washington, D.C., would please the South but alienate the North; Van Buren sought a formula which would satisfy moderates in both sections of his party. The best available alternative seemed to be

---

[16] Calhoun, *Works*, II, 465ff. This is not to say that Hammond introduced the gag rule for Calhoun's reasons, but rather that most nullifiers shared Calhoun's objectives. Hammond's intentions remain enigmatic. Wiltse's argument that Hammond acted as Calhoun's agent is not convincing; it is based too much on the circumstantial evidence that they both lived in the same boarding house. Wiltse, *Calhoun: Nullifier*, p. 281. But Hammond later claimed that he had acted spontaneously, and his remarks in fact read like the impulsive explosion of a young Carolina Hotspur, stung by antislavery criticisms and alarmed by southern supineness. Moreover, it is clear from Hammond's correspondence in LC that he was allied with the tiny coterie of extremist Columbians led by Cooper and E. W. Johnston. It appears that Hammond and his allies disliked the way Calhoun was developing an issue they regarded as initially their own. "Your views about Calhoun," Johnston wrote Hammond on Feb. 28, 1836, ". . . are . . . stolen, I think, from myself. I have been, for the last 3 years, steadily cursing Calhoun in particular, for precisely this thing. We work on here, and make a doctrine popular. Of a sudden, he comes forward, seizes it, spoils it with some vast nonsensical supplement of his own, and ruins the impression which might have been made on the country, by stitching the whole affair to his own political kite-tail." Hammond Papers, LC.

Since the Cooper faction had long since given up on saving the Union, it is possible that Hammond's ultimate intentions were the reverse of Calhoun's—that he was at least unconsciously using the slavery issue to alarm the South and to push toward disunion. In the gag-rule fight, as in the Nullification Controversy and the campaign for a southern convention, South Carolina radicals were split between secessionists led by Cooper and McDuffie and "conservatives" led by Calhoun, and by 1836 Hammond was closer to Cooper. But I know of no other South Carolina congressman connected with the Cooperites. All the evidence I have seen indicates that most South Carolina radicals supported the gag rule in the spirit of Calhoun—to meet the question at the threshold, to save the Union by scotching the abolitionists.

a declaration that abolishing slavery in Washington was constitutional but inexpedient; thus Congress should receive the petitions but automatically table them. In other words, Van Buren favored resolutions which would institutionalize the old policy.

Having chosen his strategy, the Little Magician maneuvered with his usual skill. He selected (or agreed to allow) a leading South Carolina nullifier to present the proposition. Henry L. Pinckney, now Charleston's representative in the national House of Representatives, approved of the Van Burenites' proposal and agreed to sponsor it. Pinckney's motives are obscure. His Carolina contemporaries believed he was thirsting for patronage or seeking the limelight; Pinckney claimed he was acting out of disinterested conviction. Whatever his real reasons, Pinckney's rationale was persuasive. Calhoun's plan, argued the ex-editor of the *Charleston Mercury*, would never be passed by Congress; and the South would be left without any protection against the petitions. The wiser course was to support the strongest gag rule which had a chance of enactment.[17]

On February 4, 1836, Pinckney presented his plan to the House. The Pinckney Resolutions declared that Congress could not interfere with slavery in the South and should not free the slaves in Washington; thus all antislavery petitions should be referred to a specially elected select committee, and the select committee should be instructed to report back "that Congress ought not to interfere in any way with slavery in the District of Columbia." After the committee reported, the House could automatically table all antislavery petitions.[18]

Within the week, Pinckney forced a vote on his resolutions. The House overwhelmingly affirmed them all. The crucial resolution setting up the select committee was passed, 174–48. The slaveholding states opposed the resolution, 47–45; Carolinians could not persuade the South to maintain a united front even on the slavery issue. The select committee was promptly elected and Pinckney became its chairman.[19]

The committee delayed reporting back to the House for months,

[17] *Pendleton Messenger*, Feb. 26, 1836.
[18] *Register of Debates*, 24 Cong., 1 sess., pp. 2482–3.
[19] *Ibid.*, pp. 2498–2502.

partly because Pinckney wished to see how his constituents would react to his aberrant course. The response was far from encouraging. Most unionists rejoiced at the compromise resolutions, but most nullifiers condemned Pinckney; the *Charleston Mercury* viciously attacked its old editor. Pinckney had surrendered the crucial constitutional principle, the radicals argued. Worse still, by advocating compromise, he had prevented the final showdown. The slavery issue was so dangerous that the slightest temporizing would be disastrous; as one leading Carolina legislator put it, "every hours delay adds strength to the Fanatics, and at the same time weakens us at home." South Carolina would have to wage yet another crusade, and "at length after such protracted agitations, a spirit of insubordination may be found upon our slaves that may render even a separation from the confederacy an inadequate remedy for our evils."[20]

Calhoun himself, speaking to the nation from the floor of the United States Senate, gave more systematic expression to South Carolina's persuasions. If Congress refused to receive antislavery petitions and thereby declared it had no jurisdiction over the subject, Calhoun argued, the abolitionist crusade would be permanently crippled. But Pinckney's compromise, by implicitly affirming that Congress could discuss the subject, would give renewed hope to the northern "fanatics." The continued abolitionist onslaught "would compel the southern press to discuss the question in the very presence of the slaves." Inevitably "the ignorant slave population" would "believe that one half of the people of this Union were their friends, and that all they had to do was to organize a successful insurrection for those friends to come to their aid." The incessant barrage of moral condemnation would compel slaveholders "to sit in silence to witness the assaults on our character and institutions, or to engage in an endless contest in their defence. Such a contest," concluded Calhoun, "is beyond mortal endurance. We must in the end be humbled, degraded, broken down and worn out."[21]

[20] Thomas Harrison to Hammond, Feb. 16, 1836, James Davis to Hammond, Apr. 2, 1836, Hammond Papers, LC.
[21] *Congressional Globe,* 24 Cong., I sess., pp. 75, 81; Calhoun, *Works,* II, 483–90.

Undaunted by the storm his strategy had aroused among his old compatriots, Pinckney at last pressed on with the resolutions. On May 18, 1836, the select committee reported three resolutions to the House, affirming the principles which Pinckney had earlier espoused. Congress had no constitutional jurisdiction over slavery in the South; abolishing slavery in Washington would be inexpedient; antislavery petitions should be received but immediately tabled. The last proposition, the famous gag rule, provoked one of the angriest congressional debates in American history. Speaker of the House James Polk at times despaired of keeping order as northern and southern extremists tore into one another and the resolution. But moderates in both sections rejoiced at the compromise, and Van Burenites applauded the "final" resolution of the dangerous problem. In the end, all of Pinckney's resolutions passed by large majorities; the gag rule was adopted, 117–68. The Senate unofficially adopted procedural devices which had more or less the same effect as the gag rule passed by the House.[22]

Pinckney triumphantly informed his constituents that the abolitionists had been put down forever.[23] But there was no rejoicing among Carolina radicals. The vital outposts had been surrendered. Congress had indirectly affirmed that it could abolish slavery in Washington, D.C., and would receive the abolitionists' petitions. Northern state legislatures were doing nothing to suppress the abolitionists, and the Senate had refused to authorize southern censoring of the mails. The first direct encounter with the abolitionists had yielded a hollow victory, as had the nullification crusade. Once again, South Carolina had failed to escape from the tensions generated by an antislavery attack.

4

The fire-eaters proceeded to vent their frustration on Pinckney. The bulk of the Charleston radicals refused to support him for re-election and eventually backed the unionists' nominee, Hugh S. Legaré. Some unionists, pleased with Pinckney's stand on the

---

[22] *Register of Debates*, 24 Cong., 1 sess., pp. 3756–7, 4050–5, appendix, pp. 104–14.
[23] Pinckney, *Address to the Electors of Charleston District, South Carolina, on the Subject of the Abolition of Slavery* (Washington, D.C., 1836).

gag rule, deserted Legaré; the shifting alignments destroyed the old Charleston parties. Pinckney continued to command the loyalties of Charleston's lower class. But in the end nullifiers had their revenge when Legaré, supported by most of the planters, swept the election.[24]

Pinckney's defeat offered most radicals meager satisfaction. The real culprit, they believed, was not the Charleston traitor but rather the federal Union. By the end of 1836, in view of the repeated failures of Calhoun's campaigns to purify the Republic, Cooper's conceptions were rapidly gaining dominion over the South Carolina mind. A full twenty-five years before the Civil War, a large percentage—perhaps a majority—of the South Carolina planters agreed with Hammond in considering it "inevitable that this abolition question will produce a speedy dissolution of the Union." Like McDuffie, the fire-eaters were "only concerned that South Carolina, and every other Southern state should be prepared for the crisis that awaits them." One visitor to Columbia in the mid-1830's "could not help asking, in a good-natured way, if they called themselves Americans yet." He received a jolting response: "If you ask *me* if I am an American, my answer is, No Sir, I am a South Carolinian." Many chivalric Carolinians would have agreed. The bulk of the Carolina radicals, having learned the folly of single-state action in the nullification crisis, dedicated themselves to awakening the rest of the South throughout the remainder of the ante bellum period.[25]

On the issue of secession, Calhoun continued to drag behind his compatriots. Compared to the classic fire-eaters—Cooper, McDuffie, Rhett, and Yancey—Calhoun remained devoted to his country and was loath to break it up. In the years after 1836, Calhoun continued to hope that a militant southern crusade would

[24] Schirmer Diary, entry for Oct. 11, 1836; *Pendleton Messenger,* Oct. 21, 1836. The Pinckney-Legaré election signified the breakup of parties throughout the state; South Carolina returned to prenullification, personal, factional politics. See Player to Hammond, Dec. 12, 1836, Hammond Papers, LC.

[25] Hammond to B. Tucker, March 11, 1836, McDuffie to Hammond, Dec. 19, 1836, Butler to Hammond, July 10, 1835, Cooper to Hammond, Jan. 8, 1836, J. H. Adams to Hammond, March 29, 1836, Thomas Stark to Hammond, Apr. 14, 1836, Hammond Papers, LC; Seabrook to Crallé, Jan. 15, 1837, Jan. 10, 1838, Crallé Papers, Clemson College; Featherstonhaugh, *Excursion Through the Slave States,* p. 157.

save both slavery and the Union. But in the Nullification Crisis, the great Carolinian had been almost paralyzed by conflicting loyalties to nation and section. In the postnullification period, he more clearly recognized that his primary aim was to save the South, and he confessed a greater willingness to destroy the Union. "I . . . am not prepared to say, that the . . . Union can be preserved under the baneful influence of the abolition spirits at the North," he wrote Pickens. "I hold it rash to form a definitive opinion either way; and that the wise course is to act on the supposition that the . . . government may be . . . saved; but at the same time to adopt the most effectual constitutional means to arrest . . . abolitionism, even tho disunion should be the consequence. If possible, let us save the liberty of all, but if not, our own at all events." For the most dedicated nationalist among the Carolina radicals, the years of the Great Reaction had led to a fateful alienation from the federal Union.[26]

In retrospect, it is hard to see why Carolinians considered the gag rule a crushing setback. Pinckney's scheme was as effective as Calhoun's. In practical terms, it made little difference whether Congress refused to receive or automatically tabled the vexing petitions. In both cases, the constituents' prayer would have been refused without a hearing. Moreover, a simple majority could have repealed a resolution to refuse reception as easily as a resolution to table; indeed, if a simple majority could declare abolishing slavery in Washington unconstitutional, the same majority could later declare emancipation constitutional. Calhoun's exquisitely wrought distinctions made sense only in theoretical terms. That Calhounites should have insisted doggedly on these razor-thin abstractions indicates the tenacity of the belief that the South was lost if the slightest compromise was made. The fact that Calhounites considered Pinckney's gag rule a disastrous southern defeat betrays better than anything else the intense anxiety with which they waged their first congressional campaign against the abolitionists.

From the beginning of the nullification years, South Carolina's

---

[26] Calhoun to Pickens, Aug. 17, 1836, Calhoun Papers, LC. See also Calhoun to Anna Maria Calhoun, Jan. 25, 1838, Calhoun, *Correspondence*, pp. 390–2.

commitment to salvation by constitutional abstractions was always somewhat incongruous. The passion for airy logic was, after all, surely the wrong style of thinking for men addicted to the proslavery assumptions. The essence of the case for slavery was an urge for specifics, a taste for concrete experience, a sense that abolitionism was insane precisely because it was so ridiculously abstract. And in addition to the absurdity of using an abstraction to fight the idea of abstractions, the nullifiers' ideals were exactly the sort of rarefied concepts which had little to do with the world as it really exists. One could hardly hope to forestall a worldwide antislavery revolution with a rarefied version of constitutional law. Nor could one halt a worldwide upcountry cotton glut by waging war on a provincial tariff. The most perceptive nullifiers had always recognized the futility of their campaign. "We may nullify" the tariff, Preston had written Hammond in early 1832, "but we cannot nullify the climate & soil of Alabama and Mississippi."[27]

Yet the gag-rule abstractions were more than ironic, worse than irrelevant. They were perfectly calculated to aggravate the danger they sought to end. The real disaster for South Carolina was not that Calhoun's logic was rejected but rather that any gag rule was passed. The gag-rule strategy was self-evidently suicidal. In the mid-1830's the antislavery crusaders were a tiny minority scorned throughout the nation. But refusing a constituent's right to have his request duly considered by Congress—in addition to censoring the mails and demanding that the North repress the antislavery movement—was bound to alarm even northerners who detested the abolitionists. Southerners invited antislavery crusaders to switch the argument from the enslavement of southern Negroes to the civil liberties of northern whites. On that basis, abolitionism acquired a respectability it had never had before. The Carolinians' crusade of 1836, in short, was a desperate and foolhardy gamble which gave their opponents incalculable advantages. But this underscores again the fact that the prospect of incessant slavery debates was so alarming to South Carolinians that they were incapable of dispassionately analyzing their predicament.

[27] Preston to Hammond, n.d. [Jan. 18, 1832], Hammond Papers, LC.

5

The Nullification Controversy and the gag-rule fight are complementary events which clarify each other. The dread with which Carolinians approached their first direct encounter with the abolitionists, the suicidal program which they espoused, the unyielding standards by which they judged their own success, all help to explain why nullifiers had found the slavery issue so distressing four years earlier. The anxiety produced by the direct encounter in 1836 illuminates why South Carolina infinitely preferred to fight the abolitionists indirectly in 1832.

On the other hand, the Carolinians' apprehensions about the slavery issue during the decade preceding the Nullification Crisis is the necessary background for understanding the intensity of their gag-rule campaign. As South Carolinians saw it, the slavery controversy had not been suspended between 1820 and 1835. Rather, a disposition to discuss bondage had grown steadily in the North, and Carolina statesmen had opposed it every step of the way. In contending against the Ohio Resolutions of 1824, the Rufus King resolution of 1825, the Panama Conference of 1826, the colonization petition of 1827, the D'Auterive affair of 1828, and the Mercer bill of 1830, leading Carolinians had demonstrated again and again their irrevocable commitment to keeping the subject buried. The same concern had remained important throughout the nullification campaign against the tariff; and the defeat of nullification had led to the 1833–6 reaction. The gag-rule fight marked the climax of South Carolina's desperate attempt to escape the lash of an antislavery attack.

Viewed in the longer perspective of subsequent sectional controversy, the nagging slavery disputes of the 1820–36 period illuminate that pattern of interaction between North and South which forms so important a theme in the history of the American nation. During the last generation, historians have often argued that the proslavery campaign preceded, and therefore had no relation to, the antislavery onslaught. This history of the nullification era might seem to substantiate that contention. At least in Charleston and the tidewater parishes, slaveholders were defending their peculiar institution a decade before the rise of Garrison.

Still, even in the South Carolina lowcountry, the full thrust of the Great Reaction came only after the Garrisonian attack. Furthermore, the fact that the political defense of slavery preceded the *Liberator* does not mean that it preceded *any* antislavery efforts. South Carolina's outbursts on slavery in the twenties and thirties were, in fact, always a response to a *slight* external provocation. What is most revealing about the nullification years is not that proslavery campaigns predate antislavery crusades, but rather that South Carolina statesmen grossly overreacted to any northern critique. The South Carolina crusades of 1832 and 1836 indicate the enormous effect a few abolitionists could have on southern public opinion. And the gag-rule debacle illustrates the way these irrational southern explosions helped break through the North's massive indifference to the antislavery campaign.[28]

This pattern of interaction between the two sections would continue throughout the pre-Civil War years—indeed, still continues in our own time. Again and again, the North, disturbed by its own racial problems and anxious to conciliate white southerners, has remained conservative on the Negro issue and largely indifferent to the agitation of radicals. And again and again, the South, partly because of its fear of Negro uprisings, partly because of its troubled conscience, partly because of its fear of what the North might eventually do, has raged at "outside agitation" and forced racial issues to national consciousness. During the pre-Civil War years, the South's extreme demands on the territorial and fugitive-slave issues brought eminently conservative northerners into the Republican ranks. During the critical year of the Reconstruction episode, the South's black codes, its race riots, and its refusal to ratify the Fourteenth Amendment forced many moderate Republicans into the hands of Thaddeus Stevens and Charles Sumner. During the early 1960's, the police dogs in Birmingham and the police brutality in Selma helped awaken the North to the need for new desegregation and voting laws. South Carolina's

[28] See the excellent analysis by Russel B. Nye, *Fettered Freedom: Civil Liberties and the Slavery Controversy, 1830–1860* (East Lansing, 1963), esp. pp. 41–85.

capacity to overreact to the slavery issue in the era of nullification marked only the beginning of that process by which the South has been, throughout its history, its own worst enemy, its own executioner.

6

The South Carolina planters that came of age before the War of 1812 and lived on into the troubled 1830's had witnessed as monumental changes in their position in the Republic as ever beset the citizens of a state. In 1816 the planters had been confident, secure aristocrats, enjoying the fruits of bountiful prosperity, taking an accustomed position in the highest national councils, endorsing the mild nationalistic measures designed to ward off foreign aggression. Then, gradually, their world had fallen apart. For many planters, particularly in the upcountry, the 1820's brought severe financial distress; for others, especially in the lowcountry, the rise of antislavery agitators produced intolerable psychic tension; for most of them, throughout the state, the end of foreign crisis and the hegemony of Adams-Clay nationalism turned the republic from friend to foe. With their purses threadbare, their honor besmirched, their statesmen shoved aside, the proud gentlemen of Carolina, in their fear and in their rage, found irresistible attractions in extreme states' rights doctrines. By 1832 most of them were seeking to nullify laws. By 1836 many of them were trying to break up the Union. And so this history of the nullification era has turned necessarily into a case study of the most radical southern state's fateful transition from nationalism to extreme sectionalism in the two decades after the War of 1812.

In the quarter century remaining before the transaction at Fort Sumter, South Carolina's reaction to political issues would by no means remain the same. The tariff question, for example, would never again be so important as it had been in the four years after the Bill of Abominations. The mere discussion of the slavery issue would gradually lose its terror. By 1850 South Carolinians were trying to win the debate rather than seeking to suppress it. The fear of slave revolts became somewhat less acute than it had been in the decade which began with Denmark Vesey and ended with

Nat Turner. The apprehension that incessant antislavery agitation would undermine slave values, so important in the 1820's and 1830's, dissolved in the face of rising slave prices in the 1850's. Finally, the proslavery argument probably eased the guilty consciences of many slaveholders. The intense fear and guilt which seemed destined to destroy all hope of an effective southern defense of slavery in the early 1830's proved to be, in part, the products of the years of transition in southern history.

But ante bellum South Carolina never really escaped from the trauma of the early 1830's. Insurrection panics continued to distress the planters, and many slaveholders never quite repressed their misgivings about bondage; the Great Reaction could not let up as long as slavery survived. Furthermore, the Great Reaction, whatever its success in resolving the crisis in South Carolina, intensified the antislavery campaign in the North. As the 1840's and 1850's progressed, the political antislavery movement grew steadily more powerful. By 1860 the other states of the Deep South agreed with South Carolina that the slaveholders' multibillion-dollar investment in land and slaves—to say nothing of the future of southern white civilization—could be saved only outside the federal Union. As the sequel would demonstrate, the decision for disunion was as suicidal as the earlier commitments to nullification and to the gag rule had been. In the end, the crisis posed by the rise of a concentrated antislavery attack could be completely resolved only by an abolitionist victory, which, even in its economic results, would never quite fulfill the premonitions of the South Carolina nullifiers.

APPENDIX A

Statistics on the South Carolina Economy

TABLE 1 CAROLINA STAPLES AND COST-OF-LIVING FIGURES, 1800–1860[a]

Year	Sea-Island Cotton[b]	Santee and Mains Cotton[c]	Short-Staple Cotton[d]	Rice[e]	Cost-of-Living Index[f]
1800			24.9¢	3.85¢	
1801			25.4	4.93	
1802			17.4	3.89	
1803			16.5	5.31	
1804			16.4	3.97	
1805			21.6	4.56	
1806			19.9	3.61	
1807			19.5	3.60	
1808			12.8	2.15	
1809			12.6	2.19	
1810			14.0	2.50	
1811			11.5	3.10	
1812			8.7	3.85	
1813			9.7	3.32	
1814			14.2	1.99	
1815			20.7	3.09	
1816	47¢	36¢	27.2	4.12	
1817	50	38	28.7	5.94	
1818	50	40	30.8	6.38	167
1819	35	26	17.2	4.15	135
1820	32	24	16.8	3.03	87
1821	28	22	14.0	2.94	109
1822	26	22	13.5	2.91	109
1823	25	19	12.1	3.41	87
1824	24	21	13.1	3.11	84
1825	52	38	18.1	3.40	89

(Table 1 continued on next page)

Year	Sea-Island Cotton[b]	Santee and Mains Cotton[c]	Short-Staple Cotton[d]	Rice[e]	Cost-of-Living Index[f]
1826	25¢	20¢	9.9¢	3.12¢	97
1827	22	17	9.3	3.17	83
1828	25	21	9.7	3.36	93
1829	23	18	8.6	3.00	83
1830	25	20	9.9	2.75	86
1831	20	17	8.3	3.17	86
1832	24	18	9.5	3.25	97
1833	27	20.5	12.2	3.06	95
1834	26	22	12.6	3.00	92
1835	30	36	16.0	3.73	104
1836	32	38	16.8	3.61	140
1837			10.0	3.74	
1838			9.9	4.51	
1839			12.9	4.37	
1840			8.4	3.34	
1841			9.6	3.44	
1842			7.8	3.04	
1843			6.5	2.63	
1844			7.1	2.97	
1845			6.6	3.85	
1846			7.9	3.78	
1847			10.6	4.53	
1848			6.1	3.19	
1849			8.4	3.18	
1850			12.6	3.34	
1851			9.8	3.21	
1852			9.3	3.76	
1853			10.6	4.08	
1854			9.7	4.18	
1855			9.9	5.16	
1856			11.3	4.40	
1857			13.6	4.10	
1858			12.2	3.46	
1859			12.0	3.99	
1860			11.5	4.12	

[a] All figures quoted are yearly averages.
[b] Figures quoted are the price per pound of normal, unstained sea-island cotton. I could not locate reliable figures for the pre-1816 period. Superfine cotton, of course,

TABLE 2 A COMPARATIVE STATEMENT OF THE EFFECT OF THE VARIOUS STAGES OF DEPRESSION ON PRICES IN SOUTH CAROLINA*

1. The Currency Contraction of 1818–1822

Commodity	1818	1822	Percent Decline
Sea-island cotton	50¢	26¢	48%
Santee and mains cotton	40	22	45
Upland short-staple cotton	30.8	13.5	56
Rice	6.38	2.91	54
Cost-of-living index	167	109	35

2. The Overproduction Depression of 1822–1829

Commodity	1822	1829	Percent Decline
Sea-island cotton	26¢	23¢	12%
Santee and mains cotton	22	18	18
Upland short-staple cotton	13.5	8.6	36
Rice	2.91	3	0
Cost-of-living index	109	86	21

(Table 2 continued on next page)

sold for more, and badly stained sea-island cotton for less, than the price given here. The figures are derived from the Charleston newspapers, using the methods employed by George R. Taylor, "Wholesale Commodity Prices at Charleston, South Carolina, 1796–1861," *Journal of Economic and Business History*, IV (supplement to Aug. 1932 issue), 848–68.

[c] Figures quoted are the price per pound of mains and santee varieties. Stained mainland luxury cotton sold for around the same price as upland brands. Prices are derived from Charleston newspapers, using Taylor's methods.

[d] Figures quoted are the price per pound of middling short-staple brands. Derived from Taylor, *loc. cit.*, Table I, with a few minor corrections based on my own figures from the Charleston newspapers.

[e] Figures quoted are the price per pound of prime rice. Derived from *ibid.*, Table I, with a few minor corrections based on my own figures from Charleston newspapers.

[f] Figures quoted are an average yearly rate of selected commodities excluding Carolina staples. The figures are comparative, based on the base monthly average of these commodities, 1818–42. Average = 100. Figures over 100 denote higher than average living costs, and figures under 100 denote lower than average living costs. Derived from *ibid.*, Table VI.

3. The Overall Period, 1818–1829

Commodity	1818	1829	Percent Decline
Sea-island cotton	50¢	23¢	54%
Santee and mains cotton	40	18	55
Upland short-staple cotton	30.8	8.6	72
Rice	6.38	3	53
Cost-of-living index	167	86	49

* All figures in Table 2 are taken from Table 1 above.

APPENDIX B

Statistics on the Election of 1832

A Comparison, District by District, of the Relationship Between Percent of Negroes in Population and Percent of Votes for Nullification

For the purposes of analysis, I have divided the South Carolina districts into three groups on the basis of the proportion of Negroes in their population. Group 1 includes districts with over 42 percent Negroes; Group 2 includes districts with between 35 and 41 percent Negroes; Group 3 includes districts with 33 percent or less Negroes. All districts in Group 1 except Kershaw and Darlington voted for the nullifiers; all districts in Group 3 except Pendleton voted for the unionists. The districts in the middle range, represented by Group 2, had a mixed record, with four voting for the nullifiers and two voting for the unionists.

GROUP 1   DISTRICTS WITH 42 PERCENT OR MORE NEGROES IN POPULATION

District	Percent Negroes in Population[a]	Percent Vote for Nullifiers, 1832[b]
Abbeville	47%	64%
Barnwell	46	65
Beaufort	85	84
Charleston (rural)	90	61

(Group 1 continued on next page)

District	Percent Negroes in Population[a]	Percent Vote for Nullifiers, 1832[b]
Charleston (urban)	61%	52%
Chester	42	59
Colleton	80	67
Darlington	51	42
Edgefield	51	73
Fairfield	55	94
Georgetown	90	61
Kershaw	63	39
Lexington	42	100
Marlborough	51	100
Newberry	49	89
Orangeburg	59	90
Richland	65	75
Sumter	68	53
Williamsburg	69	50

GROUP 2   DISTRICTS HAVING BETWEEN 35 AND 41 PERCENT NEGROES IN POPULATION

District	Percent Negroes in Population[a]	Percent Vote for Nullifiers, 1832[b]
Chesterfield	37%	38%
Lancaster	41	41
Laurens	35	60
Marion	35	61
Union	41	71
York	37	51

Group 3 Districts with 33 Percent or Less Negroes in Population

District	Percent Negroes in Population[a]	Percent Vote for Nullifiers, 1832[b]
Greenville	30%	28%
Horry	33	14
Pendleton	23	67
Spartanburg	23	31

[a] Derived from *Ninth Census,* I, 60–1.
[b] Derived from the map in Chauncey Boucher, *The Nullification Controversy in South Carolina* (Chicago, 1916), p. 203.

Part II

Statistical Study of the Charleston Political Alignments, 1832

In the effort to get a more precise idea of voting alignments in 1832 than the gross district statistics in Part I can yield, I kept a close record, from the beginning of my research, of all individuals who could be identified as nullifiers or unionists. By use of private correspondence, toasts at public dinners, membership on party committees, etc., I eventually gathered a file of over 3,000 individuals. My intention was to determine, by use of manuscript state-tax returns, the property holdings, income, etc., of all individuals identified. I also hoped to ascertain, by employing the Charleston City Directory, the occupations of all Charlestonians identified.

The statistical study of rural districts failed. With the exception of a few lowcountry parishes, I was never able to gather an adequate sample of nullifiers or unionists. Furthermore, despite the much-appreciated efforts of Charles Lee, director of the South Carolina Archives, the manuscript state census returns could not be located.

The study of Charleston, on the other hand, proved worthwhile. I was able to identify the party allegiance of 584 Charlestonians. Through the Charleston City Directories collected at the South Caroliniana Library, I learned the occupation of 437, or 75 percent, of these men.

My sample seems to be reasonably representative in several ways. First of all, 437 men form a healthy 16 percent of the total number who voted in the Charleston 1832 election. Second, 57 percent of the men in my sample favored the nullifiers; this would seem to compare favorably with the 52 percent who voted for the nullifiers in the 1832 city election. Finally, with certain glaring exceptions, the occupational breakdown of the following sample is somewhat close to the breakdown in the 1831 City Directory:

Occupation	Percent in Sample	Percent in 1831 City Directory
Mechanics	15%	21%
Planters	18	10
Shopkeepers	12	30
White-collar workers	17	14
Lawyers	15	6
Merchants	18	16
Doctors	5	3

The sample clearly has too few shopkeepers and too many lawyers and planters. These discrepancies may not be altogether unfortunate; my impression is that planters and lawyers were the two most politically active groups in Charleston politics. At any rate, the discrepancies are not, I think, serious enough to destroy all value of the sample.

The following table summarizes the breakdown of the sample by party and by occupation:

Occupational Group	Number in Sample Who Favored the Nullifiers	Number in Sample Who Favored the Unionists	Percent of Occupational Group Favoring the Nullifiers
Mechanics	47	19	75%
Planters	53	24	69
Shopkeepers	35	19	65
White-collar workers	41	34	55
Lawyers	34	32	52
Merchants	29	47	40
Doctors	9	14	39

This statistical study indicates that the nullifiers drew heavy support from the mechanics, town-dwelling planters, and shopkeepers, with the unionists drawing heavy support from the mercantile community. It should be noted in addition that only three of the nullifier merchants in the sample were at all prominent in East Bay circles; the rest were obscure capitalists of whom I have heard nothing in any other context. On the other hand, the unionist merchants identified were usually leading magnates in the Charleston mercantile community.

Bibliographical Essay

Since my complete bibliography is of unwieldy dimensions, and since it is already available to scholars in the Ph.D. dissertation on which this book is based, it seems more worthwhile to append here a critical, highly selective essay on the most important sources. For the benefit of future historians of the Nullification Controversy, the dissertation has been microfilmed (William W. Freehling, "The Nullification Controversy in South Carolina" [Ann Arbor, Mich.: University Microfilms, 1965]), and I have deposited several copies at the South Caroliniana Library.

Manuscript Collections

In the fifty years since the last full-scale study of the Nullification Controversy was published, an immense amount of manuscript material on all aspects of life in ante bellum South Carolina has become available to scholars. My friends in other historical fields tell me that manuscript collections often merely fill out a story previously gleaned from other sources. I can only say that in a society like the ante bellum South, where public statements were by necessity so often a quasi-deliberate form of lie, the availability of private manuscripts is of the greatest historical importance.

The manuscript collections of leading South Carolina politicians can be located with the help of Phillip M. Hamer (ed.), *A Guide to Archives and Manuscripts in the United States* (New Haven, 1961). In addition, it pays to go through all the manuscripts for the period in the South Caroliniana Library and all the manuscripts bearing on ante bellum South Carolina in the Duke University Library; the Library of Congress; and the Southern Historical Collection, University of North Carolina Library. All these libraries have helpful cross-cataloging records, and the relevant letters of obscure common people can be located with a minimum of trouble.

By far the richest collection left by a leading nullifier is the James Hammond Papers, split between LC and SC. Some of the choicest items in the Hammond Papers, LC, have been printed in "Letters on the Nullification Movement in South Carolina, 1830–1834," *AHR*, VI (July 1901), 736–65, VII (Oct. 1901), 92–119.

For the purposes of preparing *The Papers of John C. Calhoun*, Robert L. Meriwether and W. Edwin Hemphill, eds. (15 vols. planned, 2 publ.; Columbia, 1959–), photocopies of all known letters to and from Calhoun have been gathered in the John C. Calhoun Coll., SC. Only a fraction of the letters in the Calhoun Coll. have been previously published; many of them were located in obscure manuscript collections and thus have never been used by Calhoun's most industrious biographers. The newly discovered materials, particularly the Calhoun letters in the L. W. Smith Coll., Morristown [N.J.] National Historical Park and in the Virginia Carrington Scrapbook, Preston Family Papers, LC, leave no doubt that Calhoun remained more attached to the Union than any other leading nullifier.

The manuscript collections of other Carolina radicals tend to be thin and disappointing. But there are still indispensable items in the George McDuffie and Edward Harden Papers, DU; in the Richard Crallé, Edward Frost, Duff Green, and Waddy Thompson, Jr., Papers, LC; in the James Hamilton, Jr., and Robert Barnwell Rhett Papers, NC; in the William Campbell Preston, Robert Y. Hayne, Beaufort Taylor Watts, and Townes Family Papers, SC; and in the Richard Crallé Papers, Clemson College Library.

The manuscript collections of leading unionists are scattered throughout the country, and, unfortunately, at the time of writing there were no pending plans to publish any of them. There is a mass of useful material in the Benjamin F. Perry Papers, Dept. of Arch. and History, Montgomery, Ala.; in the William Drayton and Joel Poinsett Papers, Historical Soc. of Pennsylvania; in the Elliott-Gonzales Papers, NC; in the Williams-Chestnut-Manning Papers, SC; and in the Chestnut-Manning-Miller Papers, SCHS. There are also helpful items in the Benjamin F. Perry Diary and Mitchell King Papers, NC; in the Randall Hunt Journal, SCHS; and in the David R. Williams Papers, SC. The Hugh Legaré Papers, SC, contain several crucial letters not printed in *The Writings of Hugh S. Legaré*, Mary S. Legaré, ed. (2 vols.; Charleston, 1846), but the important letters in the James L. Petigru Papers, LC, can all be found in James Petigru Carson, *Life, Letters and Speeches of James Louis Petigru, the Union Man of South Carolina* (Washington, D.C., 1920).

The manuscript collections of leading national figures often contain interesting letters from South Carolina politicians. See especially the

Nicholas Biddle, John McLean, Martin Van Buren, Levi Woodbury, and John Floyd Papers, LC. The Andrew Jackson Papers, LC, contain several important letters not in *The Correspondence of Andrew Jackson*, John S. Bassett and J. Franklin Jameson, eds. (7 vols.; Washington, D.C., 1926–35).

The most significant material on nullification at the National Arch. is in the Treasury Dept. Records. The most helpful papers in the South Carolina Arch. are the manuscript journals of the state legislature and the petitions to the legislature on banking, internal improvements, and slavery. In addition, the South Carolina Arch. has very revealing material on the Denmark Vesey Conspiracy, collected with Governor Thomas Bennett's Message #2, 1822.

Private manuscript collections also provide indispensable information on the socioeconomic structure of ante bellum South Carolina. The Hammond Plantation Journal, SC, and the Manigault Plantation Records, NC, are both fine records of plantation life. Only slightly less valuable plantation sources are the J. H. Furman and Henry L. Pinckney Plantation Books, Lucy Ruggles Diary, William Renwick Papers, DU; the John Ball and John B. Milliken Plantation Journals, Coffin Point Plantation Records, SCHS; the Moses Waddel Diary, Pinckney Family Papers, LC; the Keating, John S., and William Ball Plantation Books, John Ashmore Plantation Journal, James Edward Calhoun, David Gavin, and John H. Cornish Diaries, James Hamilton Couper and Sparkman Family Papers, NC; the Ball Family and Robert F. W. Allston Papers, Michael Gramling Plantation Journal and James Edward Calhoun Diary, SC. The tone of aristocratic life is particularly well revealed in the John Ball Papers, DU; the Singleton Family Papers, LC; the Manigault Family Papers, Jacob Schirmer Diary, SCHS; the John Berkeley Grimball Papers, NC; and the Mrs. William Preston Diary, Seibels Family Papers, William J. Grayson Autobiography, SC. The Witherspoon-McDowall Papers, NC, and the Richard Furman Papers, SC, are revealing on the conflicts over slave religion. The Langdon Cheves Papers, SCHS, and the Ernest Haywood Papers, NC, are helpful on the Vesey Conspiracy. The William Ogilby Papers, SC, provide an excellent portrait of the Charleston mercantile community. The S. C. Jackson Papers, SC, contain some vivid descriptions of Columbia during the nullification winter.

Newspapers

The surviving files of South Carolina newspapers in the 1820's and 1830's can be located with the help of Winifred Gregorie (ed.), *American Newspapers, 1821–1936: A Union List of Files Available in the United States and Canada* (New York, 1937). SC has over 50 percent of the files, either in the original or on microfilm.

Henry L. Pinckney's *Charleston Mercury* was probably the most valuable single source for this book. Pinckney's slashing style still makes for exciting reading, and the apprehensions about discussing slavery are particularly well revealed in his paper. Other nullifier newspapers which I found valuable include the [Charleston] *Evening Post, Winyaw Intelligencer, Pendleton Messenger,* [Columbia] *Southern Times, Columbia Telescope,* and *Camden and Lancaster Beacon.* Duff Green's *United States Telegraph* is indispensable for a study of the 1833–6 reaction, while John Hemphill's *Sumter Gazette* is especially revealing in early 1832, during Hemphill's controversy with Maynard Richardson's [Sumterville] *Southern Whig.*

On the unionist side, Jacob Cardoza's [Charleston] *Southern Patriot* was often more than a match for any nullifier sheet, especially on economic questions. For a time William Gilmore Simms, the famous novelist, edited the [Charleston] *City Gazette and Commercial Daily Advertiser,* but this excursion into journalism cannot be called Simms' happiest effort. More important for an analysis of the unionist impulse are the *Charleston Courier, Camden Journal,* and Benjamin F. Perry's *Greenville Mountaineer.*

Contemporary Periodicals

For my purposes, the *S Ag,* 1828–40, remains the most valuable periodical source; it is especially revealing on economic questions and also has excellent material on the dilemmas of plantation management. The *SR,* 1828–32, was primarily a literary journal, but it carried occasional important pieces on politics by, among others, Thomas Cooper and William Harper. The *Carolina Planter,* 1840, and the *Southern Literary Journal and Monthly Magazine,* 1835–8, also have some useful material.

Contemporary Pamphlets

The age of nullification, like the age of the American Revolution, was an era of the pamphleteer. I have seen at least 250 contemporary pamphlets, most of them devoted to political controversy, and all of them, taken together, supplying an excellent portrait of the South Carolina social order.

The pamphlets can be located with the aid of Robert John Turnbull, *Bibliography of South Carolina,* 1563–1950 (6 vols.; Charlottesville, Va., 1956–60). At least 90 percent of the surviving pamphlets can be found in the incomparable South Caroliniana Library.

The 1820's began with a pamphlet war between nationalists and Smithites, best exemplified by [George McDuffie], *National and*

States Rights, Considered by "One of the People," in Reply to the "Trio" (Charleston, 1821); and [Thomas Cooper], *Consolidation . . .* (Columbia, 1824). The Denmark Vesey Conspiracy and its shattering impact on South Carolina's nationalism can best be observed in Lionel H. Kennedy and Thomas Parker, *An Official Report of the Trials of Sundry Negroes Charged with an Attempt to Raise an Insurrection* (Charleston, 1822); [Nicholas Herbemont], *Observations Suggested by the Late Occurrences in Charleston . . .* (Columbia, 1822); [Edwin C. Holland], *A Refutation of the Calumnies Circulated Against the Southern . . . States . . .* (Charleston, 1822); [Isaac E. Holmes and Robert J. Turnbull], *Caroliniensis on the Arrest of a British Seaman* (Charleston, 1823); and Whitemarsh B. Seabrook, *A Concise View of the Critical Situation and Future Prospects of the Slaveholding States . . .* (Charleston, 1825). South Carolina's early case against the tariff is summed up well in Robert Y. Hayne, *Speech . . . Against the Tariff Bill . . . April 12, 1824* (Charleston, 1824), and Jacob Cardoza, *The Tariff: Its True Character and Effects Practically Illustrated* (Charleston, 1830). The best pamphlets penned by leading nullifiers include [Robert J. Turnbull], *The Crisis . . .* (Charleston, 1827); James Hamilton, Jr., *A Speech . . . at Walterborough . . . 21st October, 1828 . . .* (Charleston, 1828); George McDuffie, *Speech . . . at . . . Charleston, S.C., May 19, 1831* (Charleston, 1831); and William Harper, *. . . Speech April 1, 1832 . . .* (Charleston, 1832). The most revealing pamphlets on the unionist impulse are William Drayton, *An Oration Delivered . . . in Charleston . . . July 4, 1831* (Charleston, 1831); and [Langdon Cheves], *Occasional Reviews I-III* (Charleston, 1832). Important speeches during two phases of the nullification episode are recorded in *The Debate in the South Carolina Legislature in December, 1830 . . .* (Columbia, 1831); and in *Speeches Delivered in the Convention . . . March, 1833 . . .* (Charleston, 1833). The intensity of the Great Reaction and of the gag-rule campaign is evident in Whitemarsh Seabrook, *An Essay on the Management of Slaves . . .* (Charleston, 1834), Edward Laurens, *A Letter to the Hon. Whitemarsh B. Seabrook* (Charleston, 1835); [William Harper], *Anniversary Oration . . . December 9, 1835* (Charleston, 1836); and James H. Hammond, *Remarks . . . on the Question of Receiving Petitions for the Abolition of Slavery . . .* (Washington, D.C., 1836).

Contemporary Books

Robert J. Mills, *Statistics of South Carolina . . .* (Charleston, 1826); *The Proceedings of the Agricultural Convention and of the State Agricultural Society, From 1839 to 1845 . . .* (Columbia, 1846); *Supplement to the Proceedings of the State Agricultural Society . . .* (Columbia, 1847); and *A Compilation of Documents in Relation to the*

Bank of the State . . . (Columbia, 1848) are all useful on the socio-economic background. The most helpful travel accounts for my purposes were Frederick Law Olmsted, *A Journey in the Seaboard States* (New York, 1856); and George W. Featherstonhaugh, *Excursion Through the Slave States* . . . (New York, 1844). South Carolina local and state laws are easily available in Thomas Cooper and D. J. McCord (eds.), *Statutes at Large of South Carolina* (10 vols.; Columbia, 1836–1841); and George B. Eckhard (ed.), *A Digest of the Ordinances of* . . . *Charleston* . . . (Charleston, 1844). Biographical data can be found in Benjamin F. Perry, *Reminiscences of Public Men* (Philadelphia, 1883); Perry, *Reminiscences of Public Men with Speeches and Addresses* (Greenville, 1889); and John B. O'Neall, *Biographical Sketches of the Bench and Bar of South Carolina* (2 vols.; Charleston, 1859). Important documents on the theory and practice of nullification are gathered in *State Papers on Nullification* . . . (Boston, 1834); and *Book of Allegiance* . . . (Columbia, 1834). The proslavery argument can best be studied in William Harper *et al.*, *The Pro-Slavery Argument* . . . (Philadelphia, 1853).

Other Printed Sources

In addition to the printed sources listed in Manuscript Collections above, the most important volumes include John C. Calhoun, *Works* . . . , Richard Crallé, ed. (6 vols.; New York, 1854–7); Calhoun, *Correspondence* . . . , J. Franklin Jameson, ed., in *Annual Report of the American Historical Association* . . . *1899* (2 vols.; Washington, D.C., 1900), Vol. 2; David Kohn (ed.), *Internal Improvements in South Carolina, 1817–1828* (Washington, D.C., 1938); and J. H. Easterby (ed.), *The South Carolina Rice Plantation as Revealed in the Papers of Robert F. W. Allston* (Chicago, 1945). *The Annals of Congress, Register of Debates, Congressional Globe*, and John D. Richardson (ed.), *A Compilation of the Messages and Papers of the President* (11 vols.; Washington, D.C., 1897–1909), are all indispensable for a study of national politics. Herman V. Ames (ed.), *State Documents on Federal Relations* . . . (Philadelphia, 1906), has several important documents on South Carolina politics in the 1820's. It will soon be supplemented by William W. Freehling (ed.), "The Nullification Crisis: A Documentary Record," to be published by Harper & Row in early 1967.

Secondary Sources

Of the older studies of nullification, Chauncey Boucher, *The Nullification Controversy in South Carolina* (Chicago, 1916), is the fullest account, while David F. Houston, *A Critical Study of Nullifica-*

tion in South Carolina (Cambridge, Mass., 1896), is more analytical and insightful. Frederick Bancroft, *Calhoun and the South Carolina Nullification Movement* (Baltimore, 1928), is a good volume, but it has been superseded by Charles M. Wiltse, *John C. Calhoun* (3 vols.; Indianapolis, 1944–51). While I often disagree with Wiltse's value judgments about Calhoun, Jackson, and the South Carolina unionists, his volumes form by far the fullest modern account of the period, and I have found them extremely helpful. See also Wiltse's fine essay on nullification in his *The New Nation, 1800–1845* (New York, 1961), ch. 6.

For my approach to southern history, I owe most to Charles G. Sellers, Jr., "The Travail of Slavery" in Sellers (ed.), *The Southerner as American* (Chapel Hill, 1960), ch. 3. See also Sellers' recent reassertion of his position in George Harmon Knoles (ed.), *The Crisis of the Union, 1860–1861* (Baton Rouge, 1965), pp. 80–9. In my judgment, Sellers has slightly overstated the political importance of southern guilt about slavery and has underestimated the causal significance of the South's fear of slave revolts and its concern that abolition would *eventually* prevail in the North. But "The Travail of Slavery" has brilliantly placed the focus in the debate over the causes of the Civil War where I believe it belongs—on the psychological torment which led southerners to rage at the slavery issue and to precipitate almost every pre-Civil War sectional crisis. Other historians who have elucidated the same theme include Wilbur J. Cash, *The Mind of the South* (New York, 1941); Clement Eaton, *The Freedom-of-Thought Struggle in the Old South* (New York, 1964); and Kenneth M. Stampp, *The Peculiar Institution: Slavery in the Ante-bellum South* (New York, 1956).

In the past generation, many writers have clarified special aspects of the Nullification Controversy, and I have often depended on their work. William A. Schaper, *Sectionalism and Representation in South Carolina* in *Annual Report of the American Historical Association for the Year 1900* (2 vols.; Washington, D.C., 1901), I, 217–463, is excellent on the prenullification intrastate sectional controversy. The socioeconomic background of political events is clarified in Lawrence Fay Brewster, *Summer Migrations and Resorts of South Carolina Low-Country Planters* (Durham, 1947); Samuel M. Derrick, *Centennial History of South Carolina Railroad* (Columbia, 1930); Howell M. Henry, *Police Control of the Slave in South Carolina* (Emory, Va., 1914); Daniel Walker Hollis, *The University of South Carolina* (2 vols.; Columbia, 1951–3); Luther P. Jackson, "Religious Instruction of Negroes, 1830–1860, With Special Reference to South Carolina," *Journal of Negro History*, XV (Jan. 1930), 72–114; Guion G. Johnson, *A Social History of the Sea Islands* (Chapel Hill, 1930); Ernest M. Lander, Jr., "Manufacturing in Antebellum South Carolina" (unpubl.

diss., Univ. of N.C., 1950); Marjorie S. Mendenhall, "A History of Agriculture in South Carolina, 1790 to 1860" (unpubl. diss., Univ. of N.C., 1940); Alfred G. Smith, Jr., *Economic Readjustment of an Old Cotton State: South Carolina, 1820–1860* (Columbia, 1958); Rosser H. Taylor, *Antebellum South Carolina: A Social and Cultural History* (Chapel Hill, 1942); and John G. Van Deusen, *Economic Bases of Disunion in South Carolina* (New York and London, 1928).

There are several good biographies of leading South Carolina politicians, including Wiltse, *Calhoun;* Gerald M. Capers, *John C. Calhoun—Opportunist: A Reappraisal* (Gainesville, Fla., 1960); Donald Morgan, *Justice William Johnson: The First Dissenter* (Columbia, 1954); Dumas Malone, *The Public Life of Thomas Cooper, 1783–1839* (New Haven, 1926); and Laura A. White, *Robert Barnwell Rhett: Father of Secession* (New York, 1931). Among the more disappointing biographies are Harvey T. Cook, *The Life and Legacy of David Rogerson Williams* (New York, 1916); Edwin L. Green, *George McDuffie* (Columbia, 1936); Theodore D. Jervey, *Robert Y. Hayne and his Times* (New York, 1909); Lillian Kibler, *Benjamin F. Perry, South Carolina Unionist* (Durham, 1946); Elizabeth Merritt, *James Henry Hammond, 1807–1864* (Baltimore, 1923); and J. Fred Rippy, *Joel R. Poinsett, Versatile American* (Durham, 1935). It is a scandal of South Carolina historiography that there is no full-scale study of the fabulous James Hamilton, Jr.

Among the monographs on political and intellectual aspects of the nullification era, Norris W. Preyer, "Southern Support of the Tariff in 1816—A Reappraisal," *Journal of Southern History*, XXV (Aug. 1959), 306–22, is an important essay which deserves to be more widely known. The Negro Seamen Controversy is well treated in Phillip M. Hamer, "Great Britain, the United States, and the Negro Seamen's Acts, 1822–1848," *Journal of Southern History*, I (Feb. 1935), 3–28. Adrienne Koch and Harry Ammon, "The Virginia and Kentucky Resolutions: An Episode in Jefferson's and Madison's Defense of Civil Liberties," *William and Mary Quarterly*, 3rd Series, V (Apr. 1948), 148–76, is an important piece on the antecedents of Calhoun's theory. The doctrine of nullification is brilliantly analyzed in Louis Hartz, "South Carolina vs. the United States," Daniel Aaron (ed.), *America in Crisis* (New York, 1952), pp. 73–91. Although Charles Sydnor, *The Development of Southern Sectionalism, 1819–1848* (Baton Rouge, 1948), has a rather pedestrian chapter on nullification, it remains the best study of the broader transitions in southern life which led to the great confrontation between Andrew Jackson and the South Carolina nullifiers.

I cannot close this bibliographical essay without adding that three works on special aspects of the period appeared after these chapters were substantially completed, and all of them would have eased my way if they had been available earlier. John M. Lofton, *Insurrection in South Carolina: The Turbulent World of Denmark Vesey* (Yellow Springs, Ohio, 1964), has useful material on the political legacy of the Vesey affair. Daniel Boorstin, *The Americans: The National Experience* (New York, 1965), contains a fine analysis of the southern code of honor. Finally, Richard H. Brown, "The Missouri Crisis, Slavery, and the Politics of Jacksonianism," *South Atlantic Quarterly*, LXV (Winter 1966), 55–72, is a very suggestive essay which indicates that the anxiety about slavery, which reached its peak in South Carolina, was also important in other southern states and had much to do with establishing the contours of Jacksonian democracy in the 1820's.

Index

Revised January, 1970

harper ⚡ torchbooks

† The New American Nation Series, edited by Henry Steele Commager and Richard B. Morris.
‡ American Perspectives series, edited by Bernard Wishy and William E. Leuchtenburg.
a History of Europe series, edited by J. H. Plumb.
§ The Library of Religion and Culture, edited by Benjamin Nelson.
‖ Researches in the Social, Cultural, and Behavioral Sciences, edited by Benjamin Nelson.
Σ Harper Modern Science Series, edited by James A. Newman.
° Not for sale in Canada.
+ Documentary History of the United States series, edited by Richard B. Morris.
# Documentary History of Western Civilization series, edited by Eugene C. Black and Leonard W. Levy.
∧ The Economic History of the United States series, edited by Henry David et al.
¶ European Perspectives series, edited by Eugene C. Black.
** Contemporary Essays series, edited by Leonard W. Levy.
* The Stratum Series, edited by John Hale.

4

R. H. TAWNEY: The Agrarian Problem in the Sixteenth Century. *Intro. by Lawrence Stone* TB/1315

H. R. TREVOR-ROPER: The European Witch-craze of the Sixteenth and Seventeenth Centuries and Other Essays ° TB/1416

VESPASIANO: Rennaissance Princes, Popes, and XVth Century: *The Vespasiano Memoirs. Introduction by Myron P. Gilmore. Illus.* TB/1111

History: Modern European

RENE ALBRECHT-CARRIE, Ed.: The Concert of Europe # HR/1341

MAX BELOFF: The Age of Absolutism, 1660-1815 TB/1062

OTTO VON BISMARCK: Reflections and Reminiscences. *Ed. with Intro. by Theodore S. Hamerow* ¶ TB/1357

EUGENE C. BLACK, Ed.: British Politics in the Nineteenth Century # HR/1427

D. W. BROGAN: The Development of Modern France ° Vol. I: *From the Fall of the Empire to the Dreyfus Affair* TB/1184 Vol. II: *The Shadow of War, World War I, Between the Two Wars* TB/1185

ALAN BULLOCK: Hitler, A Study in Tyranny. ° *Revised Edition. Iuus.* TB/1123

GORDON A. CRAIG: From Bismarck to Adenauer: *Aspects of German Statecraft. Revised Edition* TB/1171

LESTER G. CROCKER, Ed.: The Age of Enlightenment # HR/1423

JACQUES DROZ: Europe between Revolutions, 1815-1848. ° *a Trans. by Robert Baldick* TB/1346

JOHANN GOTTLIEB FICHTE: Addresses to the German Nation. *Ed. with Intro. by George A. Kelly* ¶ TB/1366

ROBERT & ELBORG FORSTER, Eds.: European Society in the Eighteenth Century # HR/1404

C. C. GILLISPIE: Genesis and Geology: *The Decades before Darwin* § TB/51

ALBERT GOODWIN: The French Revolution TB/1064

JOHN B. HALSTED, Ed.: Romanticism # HR/1387

STANLEY HOFFMANN et al.: In Search of France: *The Economy, Society and Political System In the Twentieth Century* TB/1219

H. STUART HUGHES: The Obstructed Path: *French Social Thought in the Years of Desperation* TB/1451

JOHAN HUIZINGA: Dutch Civilisation in the 17th Century and Other Essays TB/1453

WALTER LAQUEUR & GEORGE L. MOSSE, Eds.: Education and Social Structure in the 20th Century. ° *Volume 6 of the* Journal of Contemporary History TB/1339

WALTER LAQUEUR & GEORGE L. MOSSE, Ed.: International Fascism, 1920-1945. ° *Volume 1 of the* Journal of Contemporary History TB/1276

WALTER LAQUEUR & GEORGE L. MOSSE, Eds.: Literature and Politics in the 20th Century. ° *Volume 5 of the* Journal of Contemporary History. TB/1328

WALTER LAQUEUR & GEORGE L. MOSSE, Eds.: The New History: *Trends in Historical Research and Writing Since World War II.* ° *Volume 4 of the* Journal of Contemporary History TB/1327

WALTER LAQUEUR & GEORGE L. MOSSE, Eds.: 1914: *The Coming of the First World War.* ° *Volume 3 of the* Journal of Contemporary History TB/1306

JOHN MCMANNERS: European History, 1789-1914: *Men, Machines and Freedom* TB/1419

PAUL MANTOUX: The Industrial Revolution in the Eighteenth Century: *An Outline of the Beginnings of the Modern Factory System in England* TB/1079

KINGSLEY MARTIN: French Liberal Thought in the Eighteenth Century: *A Study of Political Ideas from Bayle to Condorcet* TB/1114

NAPOLEON III: Napoleonic Ideas: *Des Idées Napoléoniennes, par le Prince Napoléon-Louis Bonaparte. Ed. by Brison D. Gooch* ¶ TB/1336

FRANZ NEUMANN: Behemoth: *The Structure and Practice of National Socialism, 1933-1944* TB/1289

DAVID OGG: Europe of the Ancien Régime, 1715-1783 ° *a* TB/1271

GEORGE RUDE: Revolutionary Europe, 1783-1815 ° *a* TB/1272

MASSIMO SALVADORI, Ed.: Modern Socialism # TB/1374

DENIS MACK SMITH, Ed.: The Making of Italy, 1796-1870 # HR/1356

ALBERT SOREL: Europe Under the Old Regime, *Translated by Francis H. Herrick* TB/1121

ROLAND N. STROMBERG, Ed.: Realsim, Naturalism, and Symbolism: *Modes of Thought and Expression in Europe, 1848-1914* # HR/1355

A. J. P. TAYLOR: From Napoleon to Lenin: *Historical Essays* ° TB/1268

A. J. P. TAYLOR: The Habsburg Monarchy, 1809-1918: *A History of the Austrian Empire and Austria-Hungary* ° TB/1187

J. M. THOMPSON: European History, 1494-1789 TB/1431

DAVID THOMSON, Ed.: France: Empire and Republic, 1850-1940 # HR/1387

H. R. TREVOR-ROPER: Historical Essays TB/1269

W. WARREN WAGAR, Ed.: Science, Faith, and MAN: *European Thought Since 1914* # HR/1362

MACK WALKER, Ed · Metternich's Europe, 1813 1848 # HR/1361

ELIZABETH WISKEMANN: Europe of the Dictators, 1919-1945 ° *a* TB/1273

JOHN B. WOLF: France: 1814-1919: *The Rise of a Liberal-Democratic Society* TB/3019

Literature & Literary Criticism

JACQUES BARZUN: The House of Intellect TB/1051

W. J. BATE: From Classic to Romantic: *Premises of Taste in Eighteenth Century England* TB/1036

VAN WYCK BROOKS: Van Wyck Brooks: The Early Years: *A Selection from his Works, 1908-1921 Ed. with Intro. by Claire Sprague* TB/3082

RICHMOND LATTIMORE, Translator: The Odyssey of Homer TB/1389

ROBERT PREYER, Ed.: Victorian Literature ** TB/1302

BASIL WILEY: Nineteenth Century Studies: *Coleridge to Matthew Arnold* ° TB/1261

RAYMOND WILLIAMS: Culture and Society, 1780-. 1950 ° TB/1252

Philosophy

HENRI BERGSON: Time and Free Will: *An Essay on the Immediate Data of Consciousness* ° TB/1021

LUDWIG BINSWANGER: Being-in-the-World: *Selected Papers. Trans. with Intro. by Jacob Needleman* TB/1365

H. J. BLACKHAM: Six Existentialist Thinkers: *Kierkegaard, Nietzsche, Jaspers, Marcel, Heidegger, Sartre* ° TB/1002

MARTIN HEIDEGGER: Discourse on Thinking. *Translated with a Preface by John M. Anderson and E. Hans Freund. Introduction by John M. Anderson* TB/1459
IMMANUEL KANT: Religion Within the Limits of Reason Alone. § *Introduction by Theodore M. Greene and John Silber* TB/FG
H. RICHARD NIERUHR: Christ and Culture TB/3
H. RICHARD NIEBUHR: The Kingdom of God in America TB/49
JOHN H. RANDALL, JR.: The Meaning of Religion for Man. *Revised with New Intro. by the Author* TB/1379

Science and Mathematics

W. E. LE GROS CLARK: The Antecedents of Man: *An Introduction to the Evolution of the Primates.* ° *Illus.* TB/559
ROBERT E. COKER: Streams, Lakes, Ponds. *Illus.* TB/586
ROBERT E. COKER: This Great and Wide Sea: *An Introduction to Oceanography and Marine Biology. Illus.* TB/551
F. K. HARE: The Restless Atmosphere TB/560
WILLARD VAN ORMAN QUINE: Mathematical Logic TB/558

Science: Philosophy

J. M. BOCHENSKI: The Methods of Contemporary Thought. *Tr. by Peter Caws* TB/1377
J. BRONOWSKI: Science and Human Values. *Revised and Enlarged. Illus.* TB/505
WERNER HEISENBERG: Physics and Philosophy: *The Revolution in Modern Science. Introduction by F. S. C. Northrop* TB/549
KARL R. POPPER: Conjectures and Refutations: *The Growth of Scientific Knowledge* TB/1376
KARL R. POPPER: The Logic of Scientific Discovery TB/576

Sociology and Anthropology

REINHARD BENDIX: Work and Authority in Industry: *Ideologies of Management in the Course of Industrialization* TB/3035
BERNARD BERELSON, Ed., The Behavioral Sciences Today TB/1127
KENNETH B. CLARK: Dark Ghetto: *Dilemmas of Social Power. Foreword by Gunnar Myrdal* TB/1317
KENNETH CLARK & JEANNETTE HOPKINS: A Relevant War Against Poverty: *A Study of Community Action Programs and Observable Social Change* TB/1480
LEWIS COSER, Ed.: Political Sociology TB/1293
ROSE L. COSER, Ed.: Life Cycle and Achievement in America ** TB/1434
ALLISON DAVIS & JOHN DOLLARD: Children of Bondage: *The Personality Development of Negro Youth in the Urban South* || TB/3049
ST. CLAIR DRAKE & HORACE R. CAYTON: Black Metropolis: *A Study of Negro Life in a Northern City. Introduction by Everett C. Hughes. Tables, maps, charts, and graphs* Vol. I TB/1086; Vol. II TB/1087

PETER F. DRUCKER: The New Society: *The Anatomy of Industrial Order* TB/1082
LEON FESTINGER, HENRY W. RIECKEN, STANLEY SCHACHTER: When Prophecy Fails: *A Social and Psychological Study of a Modern Group that Predicted the Destruction of the World* || TB/1132
CHARLES Y. GLOCK & RODNEY STARK: Christian Beliefs and Anti-Semitism. *Introduction by the Authors* TB/1454
L. S. B. LEAKEY: Adam's Ancestors: *The Evolution of Man and His Culture. Illus.* TB/1019
KURT LEWIN: Field Theory in Social Science: *Selected Theoretical Papers.* || *Edited by Dorwin Cartwright* TB/1135
RITCHIE P. LOWRY: Who's Running This Town? *Community Leadership and Social Change* TB/1383
R. M. MACIVER: Social Causation TB/1153
GARY T. MARX: Protest and Prejudice: *A Study of Belief in the Black Community* TB/1435
ROBERT K. MERTON, LEONARD BROOM, LEONARD S. COTTRELL, JR., Editors: Sociology Today: *Problems and Prospects* || Vol. I TB/1173; Vol. II TB/1174
GILBERT OSOFSKY, Ed.: The Burden of Race: *A Documentary History of Negro-White Relations in America* TB/1405
GILBERT OSOFSKY: Harlem: The Making of a Ghetto: *Negro New York 1890-1930* TB/1381
TALCOTT PARSONS & EDWARD A. SHILS, Editors: Toward a General Theory of Action: *Theoretical Foundations for the Social Sciences* TB/1083
PHILIP RIEFF: The Triumph of the Therapeutic: *Uses of Faith After Freud* TB/1360
JOHN H. ROHRER & MUNRO S. EDMONSON, Eds.: The Eighth Generation Grows Up: *Cultures and Personalities of New Orleans Negroes* || TB/3050
ARNOLD ROSE: The Negro in America: *The Condensed Version of Gunnar Myrdal's* An American Dilemma. *Second Edition* TB/3048
GEORGE ROSEN: Madness in Society: *Chapters in the Historical Sociology of Mental Illness.* || *Preface by Benjamin Nelson* TB/1337
PHILIP SELZNICK: TVA and the Grass Roots: *A Study in the Sociology of Formal Organization* TB/1230
PITIRIM A. SOROKIN: Contemporary Sociological Theories: *Through the First Quarter of the Twentieth Century* TB/3046
MAURICE R. STEIN: The Eclipse of Community: *An Interpretation of American Studies* TB/1128
FERDINAND TONNIES: Community and Society: *Gemeinschaft und Gesellschaft. Translated and Edited by Charles P. Loomis* TB/1116
SAMUEL E. WALLACE: Skid Row as a Way of Life TB/1367
W. LLOYD WARNER and Associates: Democracy in Jonesville: *A Study in Quality and Inequality* || TB/1129
W. LLOYD WARNER: Social Class in America: *The Evaluation of Status* TB/1013
FLORIAN ZNANIECKI: The Social Role of the Man of Knowledge. *Introduction by Lewis A. Coser* TB/1372